THE ADVAITA TRADITION IN INDIAN PHILOSOPHY

The Advaita Trādition in Indian Philosophy

A STUDY OF ADVAITA IN BUDDHISM, VEDĀNTA AND KĀSHMĪRA SHAIVISM

CHANDRADHAR SHARMA
M.A., D.PHIL., D.LITT., ĀCHĀRYA
Formerly Professor of Philosophy
University of Jabalpur

MOTILAL BANARSIDASS PUBLISHERS
PRIVATE LIMITED • DELHI

Revised Edition: Delhi, 2007
First Indian Edition: Delhi, 1983, 1996

ISBN: 978-81-208-1312-0

MOTILAL BANARSIDASS
41 U.A. Bungalow Road, Jawahar Nagar, Delhi 110 007
8 Mahalaxmi Chamber, 22 Bhulabhai Desai Road, Mumbai 400 026
203 Royapettah High Road, Mylapore, Chennai 600 004
236, 9th Main III Block, Jayanagar, Bangalore 560 011
Sanas Plaza, 1302 Baji Rao Road, Pune 411 002
8 Camac Street, Kolkata 700 017
Ashok Rajpath, Patna 800 004
Chowk, Varanasi 221 001

Printed in India
BY JAINENDRA PRAKASH JAIN AT SHRI JAINENDRA PRESS,
A-45 NARAINA, PHASE-I, NEW DELHI 110 028
AND PUBLISHED BY NARENDRA PRAKASH JAIN FOR
MOTILAL BANARSIDASS PUBLISHERS PRIVATE LIMITED,
BUNGALOW ROAD, DELHI 110 007

अनेन ज्ञानयज्ञेन त्वमिष्टः परमेश्वर ।
तव वस्तु तव प्रीत्यै तुभ्यमेव समर्पये ॥

अद्वैते परमार्थेऽपि व्यवहारे समर्पणम् ।
समर्पणेन देवः स्वां प्रीतो विवृणुते तनूम् ॥

This sacrificial fire of knowledge is enkindled for your worship, O Lord ! You are all and all is yours, so yours is dedicated to you for your joy, O Lord !

Though unity with the Lord is eternal and dedication to Him is temporal, yet the Lord, pleased with dedication, may reveal His Luminous Body of Bliss !

Preface

The present work undertakes a comparative and critical study of Shūnyavāda, Vijñānavāda, Advaita Vedānta and Kāshmīra Shaivism which are the four main systems of Advaitavāda or spiritual non-dualism or absolutism in Indian philosophy. It is based on my study of the original sources and on my lectures to the post-graduate classes in the Banaras Hindu University and in the University of Jabalpur for more than three decades. On almost all fundamental points, I have either quoted from the original texts or referred to them, to enable the interested reader to compare the interpretations with the texts. In the exposition and evaluation of these systems, I have tried to be fair and impartial to them and to present many difficult and obscure points in as clear and correct a manner as I could. During the course of the treatment here, specially of Vijñānavāda and of Gauḍapāda-kārikā, some of the interpretations are my own and there are some points of importance which may be called new. As my approach has been comparative and critical, I have discussed in detail the points of similarity and of difference among these systems. It is hoped that this book will be found useful not only by the post-graduate students of Indian philosophy but by all those who are interested in Buddhism, Vedānta and Kāshmīra Shaivism and who want a clear and accurate exposition of the development of the Advaita tradition in Indian philosophical thought.

In the chapters dealing with Mahāyāna Buddhism and Advaita Vedānta of my book *A Critical Survey of Indian Philosophy*, I have incorporated substantial material from my thesis on 'Dialectic in Buddhism and Vedānta' approved for the degree of Doctor of Philosophy by the University of Allahabad. A good amount of this material and some other relevant material from my thesis on 'The Reign of Dialectic in Philosophy—Indian and Western' approved for the degree of Doctor of Letters by the University of Allahabad have been incorporated in the present work.

It is a pleasure to acknowledge my obligations to the eminent scholars who or whose works have been a source of help and inspiration to me. I have derived much help from the works of Th. Stcherbatsky and Professors S.N. Dasgupta, S. Radhakrishnan, R.D. Ranade and Vidhushekhara Bhattacharya. I pay my respects to my teachers, the late Professors R.D. Ranade and A.C. Mukerji, who adorned the chair of philosophy in the University of Allahabad and who gave me their inspiring guidance and affectionate encouragement. Gurudeva R.D. Ranade also headed the *Gaddī* of a religious sect at Nimbāl and I pray that this revered God-realised mystic saint of Nimbāl may shower his blessings on me. I express my deep gratitude to the eminent scholar Professor H.D. Bhattachāryya for his kind help and affectionate encouragement. I pay my homage to my revered father and to the revered saint Shri Radha Baba who have ascended their Abode of Bliss. I pay my respects to Svāmī Rāmeshvarāshrama ji Maharaj for his inspiring kindness. It is due to their blessings that the present work is seeing the light of publication.

I thank M/s Motilal Banarsidass Publishers Private Limited, who are publishing this work.

Kota, Rajasthan, CHANDRADHAR SHARMA
Shrāvaṇī Pūrṇimā, 2051
21st August, 1994

A Note on Transliteration

I have made the following changes in the generally accepted method of transliteration:

श = sha

च = cha

छ = chha

Contents

Preface vii

Introduction 1

PART ONE

BUDDHISM

1. THE PHILOSOPHY OF BUDDHA 15
Introduction. Pratītyasamutpāda.
Buddha's Silence on the Avyākṛta.
Anātmavāda and Nirvāṇa.

2. SHŪNYAVĀDA OR THE MĀDHYAMIKA SCHOOL 37
The Rise of Mahāyāna. The Mahāyāna-Sūtras.
The Meaning of Shūnya or Shūnyatā. The Mādhyamika Dialectic. Application of the Dialectic—The Critique of Causation—Criticism of some other categories. Shūnyatā Explained and Objections Answered. Nairātmyavāda. Nirvāṇa.

3. VIJÑĀNAVĀDA OR THE YOGĀCHĀRA SCHOOL 73
The Rise of Vijñānavāda. Idealism of Laṅkāvatāra-Sūtra. Vijñaptimātratā-Siddhi. Is Vijñāna-pariṇāma Real or Apparent? The Triple Modification of Vijñāna. The Three Svabhāvas. Abhūta-Parikalpa and Shūnyatā. Saṅklesha and Vyavadāna. The Later Form of Vijñānavāda. Evaluation of Vijñānavāda.

PART TWO

VEDĀNTA

4. PRE-SHAṄKARA VEDĀNTA 119
The Source of Vedānta. Some Ancient Teachers of Vedānta. Āchārya Gauḍapāda: Māṇḍūkya-kārikā. Ajātivāda. Ātmavāda. Asparshayoga. Gauḍapāda and Mahāyāna; Gauḍapāda and Vijñānavāda.

5. SHAṄKARA VEDĀNTA 165
Introduction. Māyā, Avidyā or Adhyāsa. Vivartavāda. Ātmā or Brahma. Īshvara, Jīva and Sākṣī. Mokṣa; Jīvanmukti; Jñāna, Karma, Refutation of Mīmāmsā view, Upāsanā. Shruti, Tarka and Anubhava. Criticism of other Schools: Criticism of Vaisheṣika and Nyāya; of Sāṅkhya; of Sarvāstivāda Buddhism and its Theory of Momentariness; of Vijñānavāda; Buddhism; of Shūnyavāda Buddhism.

6. POST-SHAṄKARA VEDĀNTA 219
Maṇḍana-Sureshvara Equation. Māyā or Avidyā. Ātmā or Brahma. Īshvara, Jīva and Sākṣī. Objections against Māyā and Advaita Answered. Difference Refuted and Advaita Established. Further Dialectical Exposition of the Ultimate Unreality of the World.

PART THREE
KĀSHMĪRA SHAIVISM

7. KĀSHMĪRA SHAIVISM: AN EXPOSITION 249
Introduction. The Union of Shiva-Shakti; Prakāsha and Vimarsha; Chit and Kriyā. Kriyā Different from Karma. Five Aspects of Shakti. Creation is Līlā. The Thirty-six Tattvas. Ābhāsavāda. Bandha, Mokṣa and Pratyabhijñā.

8. KĀSHMĪRA SHAIVISM: A CRITICAL ESTIMATE 263
The Unity and Creativity of the Absolute. Meaning of Advaita. Kāshmīra Shaivism and Vijñānavāda. Evaluation of Ābhāsavāda. Evaluation of Pratyabhijñā.

Index 279

Introduction

Advaitavāda which means spiritual non-dualism or absolutism has been the most logical and the most celebrated tradition in Indian philosophy. The Upaniṣads which are the concluding portion of the Veda as well as the cream of the Vedic philosophy are rightly regarded as the source of all Indian philosophy. Advaitavāda is found well established in the Upaniṣads as their central teaching. Its seeds can be traced back in the early Vedic philosophy. For example, the Nāsadīya-sūkta of the Ṛgveda (X, 129) says:

> 'Then there was neither Aught nor Nought, no air nor sky beyond,
> What covered all? Where rested all? In watery gulf profound?
> Nor death was then, nor deathlessness, nor change of night and day,
> That One breathed calmly, self-sustained; not else beyond it lay.
> Who knows, who ever told, from whence this vast creation rose?
> No gods had then been born—who then can e'er the truth declare?
> Whence sprang this world, and whether framed by hand divine or no—
> Its Lord in heaven alone can tell, if even he can show?[1]

In this hymn, we find the essence of advaitavāda. Creation is here viewed as the spontaneous emanation of the ultimate Reality which is treated as the supra-sensible and non-dual Absolute (*Tad Ekam*—That One). All opposites like being and non-being, life and death, good and evil, light and darkness, gods and men, soul and nature are viewed as manifestations of the Absolute which is

---

1. Translation by J. Muir.

immanent in the universe and yet transcends it. The Puruṣa-sūkta of the Ṛgveda (X, 90) (found also in the Yajurveda) also emphasises the immanent and the transcendent nature of the Real, the Absolute Self (*Puruṣa*) by declaring that the Supreme Self is all that is, all that was and all that shall be, that it pervades the universe on all sides and yet it stands out beyond it.[1] There are many Vedic mantras which declare the ultimate Reality as one, non-dual, immortal, blissful and self-shining which is at once transcendent and immanent.[2]

It is in the Upaniṣads that we find advaitavāda well established. Āchārya Shaṅkara has logically proved that advaitavāda is the central teaching of the Upaniṣads. In spite of the attempts of non-advaita teachers of Vedānta, who came after Āchārya Shaṅkara, to foist their respective views on the Upaniṣads, advaitavāda shines forth as their fundamental teaching and is too strong to be missed or misinterpreted without the obvious straining of language. Advaita accommodates the other interpretations from the phenomenal standpoint, but those who deny advaita cannot reconcile the phenomenal with the transcendent and fail to realise the true nature of the Upaniṣadic philosophy. The Upaniṣads repeatedly emphasise advaita which reveals the transcendent non-dual nature of the Real, called Brahma and identified with *Ātmā*, insisting at the same time on its immanence in the phenomenal world of subject-object duality which is only its appearance through its indescribable power *avidyā* or *māyā*. The Upaniṣadic sage Yājñavalkya who explains the immanent and the transcendent nature of Brahma and says that these are the two poises of the same Brahma which is non-dual *Ātmā*—the self-shining and self-proved foundational Self, and who employs the negative dialectic (*neti neti*) shines forth as the first exponent of advaitavāda in the world.

Buddha knows and accepts this Upaniṣadic advaitavāda and preaches it in the light of his own experience. His anātmavāda is the denial only of the false notion of the 'I' and the 'mine' (*nirahaṅkāra-nirmama-vāda*) which Vedānta also accepts. Buddha does not expressly identify the Absolute with the pure Self, though this implication is clearly there, for if the non-self (*anātma*) is

1. Ṛgveda, X, 90, 1-3.
2. Ṛgveda, I, 22, 21; I, 164, 46; III, 55; I, 89, 10; X, 190, 1; X, 121, 1; X, 90, 18; Atharvaveda, X, 8, 44; XI, 9, 1.

perishable (*anitya*) and miserable (*duḥkha*) that which is eternal and supreme bliss must be the true Self. Buddha identifies the Absolute with *Nirvāṇa* and uses the same or similar epithets for it which the Upaniṣads use for Brahma or *Ātmā* which is identified with *Mokṣa* (*Brahmabhāvo hi Mokṣaḥ*). The Upaniṣadic seers and Buddha both believe that the Absolute is at once transcendent to thought and immanent in phenomena. Both take *Avidyā*, the beginningless cosmic Ignorance as the root-cause of phenomenal existence and suffering. Both believe that thought is fraught with inherent contradictions and cannot reveal the Real which can be realised only through immediate spiritual experience. Both prefer the negative dialectic for indirectly pointing to the inexpressible Real. For both silence is the language of the Real.

The Hīnayāna schools missed Buddha's advaitavāda and elaborated a metaphysics of radical pluralism. The inner contradictions in their metaphysics led to the rise of the Mahāyāna schools of Mādhyamika and Vijñānavāda. .

The Mādhyamika is the most faithful representative of Buddha. All the important aspects of Buddha's advaitavāda indicated above have been faithfully and systematically developed by the Mādhyamika in his philosophy. Like Buddha, he emphasises that the Absolute is transcendent to thought and can be realised only by immediate non-dual supra-relational experience called Bodhi or Prajñā-pāramitā and identified with *Nirvāṇa.* All views (*dṛṣṭi*) and theories (*anta*) are merely thought-constructions (*vikalpa, kalpanā*) which falsify the Real instead of revealing it. All categories (*koṭi*) of thought are beset with the inherent contradictions and give rise to the phenomenal, dependent, relative which turns out to be indescribable either as real or as unreal and therefore treated as false. The sharp negative dialectic of the Mādhyamika, like Nāgārjuna and Chandrakīrti, with its *reductio ad absurdum* method (prasaṅgāpādana) demolishes all the phenomena as self-contradictory, relative and false. The Mādhyamika, following the spirit of Buddha and consistent with his negative logic has refrained, even at the risk of being misunderstood as a nihilist, from indulging in constructive metaphysics which he regards as falsification of the Real. His aim is to show the futility of thought and thus direct the aspirant towards spiritual discipline which helps in the realisation of the Absolute.

Earlier Vijñānavāda school of Asaṅga, Vasubandu and Sthiramati represents another formulation of advaitavāda. It wishes to synthesise the Mādhyamika absolutism with Sautrāntika pluralism which is an impossible task. The total rejection of speculative metaphysics by the Mādhyamika appeared to it as an unwarranted extreme and it returned to constructive metaphysics with full acceptance of absolutism from the ultimate standpoint. 'Shūnyatā' is not 'absolute negation', but 'negation of subject-object-duality' in Vijñāna which is the only reality. But Vijñānavāda revives the Hīnayāna interpretation of pratītyasamutpāda as the theory of causation governing the momentary real, though its application is restricted to the flow of momentary vijñānas only, as vijñāna (whether pure or impure) is treated as the only reality. The 'object', which includes physical objects, mental states and individual subjects which constitute our entire empirical world, is rejected as utterly unreal like the 'sky-flower'. Vijñānavāda upholds not only ontological, but also epistemic idealism. It separates the 'content' from the 'form' of consciousness, rejecting the objective 'content' as absolutely unreal (*parikalpita*) and retaining the 'form' as relatively real (*paratantra*). It thus rejects all our normal worldly experience as utterly unreal. Āchārya Shaṅkara's refutation of the epistemic idealism of Vijñānavāda Buddhism and in the West Kant's refutation of subjective idealism have become classic.

In spite of these, the earlier Vijñānavāda firmly clings to advaitavāda from the ultimate standpoint. The Absolute Vijñāna (*Pariniṣpanna*) when it is infected with Transcendental Illusion (*Avidyā* or *Mūlā Vāsanā*) engendering subject-object duality, it appears as conditioned by causation (*paratantra*) or as creative will undergoing modification and then the causal wheel, in which vijñānas and vāsanās (which force vijñānas to assume various forms) go on determining one another, revolves in full swing. Thus the creativity of consciousness, the wheel of causation, momentary vijñānas, vasanās or karmic impressions and projection of 'forms' are all due to Avidyā or Transcendental Illusion. In itself the Absolute is Vijñaptimātratā or pure, eternal, non-dual consciousness which is beyond senses, thought and speech. It is indeterminate and transcendent knowledge (*nirvikalpam lokottaram jñānam*). It is ever-free from the subject-object duality (*grāha-dvaya-shūnyatā*). It is the reality (*dharmatā*) of the phenomena (*dharmas*). Hence it is called Dharma-dhātu, the ultimate reality of all phenomena. It is Tathatā, for it is eternal and always remains the same. It is self-shining (*svaprakāsha*) and self-proved (*svayamsiddha*). It is pure bliss (*sukha*), because it is eternal (*nitya*), for that which is momentary is the miserable (*yad anityam tad duḥkham*). It is absolute purity (*anāsrava*). It is absolute freedom (*vimukti* or *nirvāṇa*). This non-dual vijñāna is realised in the immediate spiritual experience. When in the indeterminate (*nirvikalpaka*) *samādhi,* the notion of objectivity is rooted out from consciousness, the subject glides away in it, and with the eradication of subject-object duality, Avidyā vanishes and the non-dual Vijñāna shines in its pristine purity.

The later Vijñānavāda school of Diṅnāga, Dharmakīrti and Shāntarakṣita, which we call Svatantra-Vijñānavāda, kicks out absolutism, universalises momentariness, treats causation as real and takes the fleeting momentary vijñānas as the only reality. The flow of vijñāna-moments defiled by *avidyā* is *samsāra* or bondage; the flow of pure vijñāna-moments freed from *avidyā* or subject-object-duality is *nirvāṇa.*

Āchārya Gauḍapāda's Kārikā on the Māṇḍūkya-Upaniṣad is the first systematic treatise on Advaita Vedānta which is available to us. He is the grand teacher of Shaṅkarāchārya. His Karikā is treated as the quintessence of the Upaniṣadic philosophy and firmly establishes advaitavāda on the authority of the Shruti or the scripture (the Upaniṣads) and also on the strength of rational arguments. His ajātivāda means ātmavāda as well as māyāvāda. The non-dual Self is eternal, unborn and unchanging. The empirical world too is not a real creation but an appearance. Worldly objects like objects in illusion and dream are false, because they are indescribable either as real or unreal, yet they stand on a higher level, because they are sublated only by the realisation of the Absolute. The Absolute through its beginningless and indescribable power called *māyā* or *avidyā* appears as the empirical world of individual subjects and objects. Just as 'space in a jar' is non-different from the universal space, similarly the individual self is non-different from the Supreme Self and its finitude, limitation and plurality are due to the adjuncts of *māyā.* The Absolute is also the reality of the objective world. The Absolute is the self-shining and self-proved Self, the foundation of all experience. The Real is transcendent to senses, thought and language and can be directly realised through immediate experience which shines in *nirvikalpa samādhi* which Āchārya Gauḍapāda calls *asparsha-yoga.* In the last fourth chapter of the Kārikā, the Āchārya compares his Advaita Vedānta with the Mādhyamika and the Vijñānavāda absolutism and proves the soundness of Vedānta on both.

The credit of establishing Advaita Vedānta as a full-fledged and sound philosophical system goes to Āchārya Shaṅkara with whose name it is associated and known as Shāṅkara Vedānta. He is the grand disciple of Āchārya Gauḍapāda and undoubtedly is one of the greatest philosophers of the world and a realised saint. His contribution to Indian philosophy and to Vedic religion and culture is unparalleled.

Āchārya Shaṅkara proves that the systems of pluralistic realism do not represent the philosophy of the Veda, although some pay homage to the Vedic authority. He reverses the Mīmāmsā interpretation of the Veda which says that action is the primary import of the Vedic texts by showing that the aim of the Veda is to reveal the Real and therefore those texts (mainly the Upaniṣads) which deal with knowledge of Reality are primary. He proves, beyond doubt, on the basis of copious quotations from the texts and also by arguments that advaita is the central philosophy of the Upaniṣads, that the creation-texts speak of empirical difference only, and that the views which accept ultimate difference are not only inconsistent with the Upaniṣadic texts but are also illogical and self-contradictory.

He begins his celebrated Brahma-sūtra-bhāṣya with an acute analysis of illusion (*adhyāsa*), empirical as well as transcendental. All empirical experience involves two factors, the subjective or the transcendental 'I' which is the pure consciousness and the objective which is the 'this', the 'non-I' given as an 'other' and known as an object by the subject, which are opposed like light and darkness. That power which appears to perform the logically impossible feat of relating these two incompatibles is called *adhyāsa*, *avidyā* or *māyā*, the beginningless transcendental Illusion which is the mother of this phenomenal world of subjects and objects, giving rise to the notion of the 'I' and the 'mine' leading to the cycle of birth and death, unless it is rooted out by the immediate realisation of the non-dual Self. Illusion is the misapprehension of something (e.g., rope or shell) as something else (e.g., snake or silver) and is due to the superimposition of the unreal (not-given) on the real (given). The illusory object cannot be characterised either as 'real', for it is cancelled by the right knowledge, or as 'unreal', for it appears as 'real' during the illusion, and so it is treated as false (*mithyā*). The utterly unreal (*tuchchha*) like the sky-flower cannot even appear. The illusory (*pratibhāsa*) is cancelled by the empirical (*vyavahāra*), but the latter can be cancelled only by the realisation of the transcendental real (*paramārtha*). Negation is always a cancellation of illusion as only the illusory can be negated. The real can never be negated. Negation is the conscious denial of the apparent reality of a thing mistaken as real. The Real can be realised only by negation of its imposed character. And negation of negation does not reinstate the object negated, but the ground on which negation rests.

The Absolute is Brahma or *Ātmā*, the foundational Self which is self-proved, self-shining and eternal bliss. As immanent it is the reality of the individual subjects and the objective world. As transcendent it cannot be known by thought as an 'object', but can be realised through immediate experience.

Avidyā works with *bheda* or difference, the basic difference being the subject-object duality. The trinity of knower, known and knowledge is the projection of relational thought. In fact, the 'knower' is not the individual *jīva*, but the non-dual Self, *sākṣī*, *Ātmā* or Brahma which appears as *jīva*; the 'known' is not the object, external or internal, but Brahma itself which is the reality of the objective world; and knowledge is not relational knowledge generated by thought-categories, but eternal non-dual consciousness. This empirical trinity is transcended in the Absolute which is at once pure Subject, pure Object and pure Knowledge. There is absolute identity between *jīva* and Brahma (*Tat tvam asi*; That thou art). When the verbal knowledge of this identity culminates in immediate experience (*aparokṣānubhūti*), *mokṣa* is realised here and now (*jīvan-mukti*). There is no temporal sequence involved in the removal of *avidyā* and the Brahma-realisation; *Avidyā-nivṛtti*, *Brahma-bhāva* and *Mokṣa* are one and the same.

Āchārya Shaṅkara has criticised the schools of realistic pluralism, Vaisheṣika, Nyāya, Sāṅkhya, Mīmāmsā and Jainism. His detailed criticism of the Buddhist theory of Universal Momentariness and of the epistemic idealism of Vijñānavāda is classic. He is also opposed to *Brahma-pariṇāma-vāda* (prevalent before him) for creation is only an appearance and there can be no modification of the Real. He makes it clear that he has criticised other views not for any interest in discussion and criticism, but for the sole purpose of helping the aspirants for *Mokṣa* to enable them to reject false views hindering the true path leading to Bliss. The self-awareness of thought of its own limitation should lead to a firm conviction in the truth of Advaita Vedānta and finally to its realisation through the spiritual discipline.

Maṇḍana Mishra, the author of *Brahma-siddhi* and a contemporary of Shaṅkarāchārya is a self-confident teacher of Advaita Vedānta, who does not refer to Shaṅkara as his teacher and who passes from Mīmāmsā to Vedānta. We cannot say with certainty whether he is identical with or different from Sureshvara, the disciple of Shaṅkara.

Among the most eminent post-Shaṅkara teachers of Advaita Vedānta are Padmapāda and Sureshvara, the two direct disciples of Shaṅkarāchārya, Vāchaspati Mishra, Sarvajñātma-muni, Vimuktātmā, Ānandabodha, Shrīharṣa, Prakāshātma-yati, Chitsukhāchārya, Vidyāraṇya-svāmī, Ānandagiri, Prakāshānanda, Madhusūdana Sarasvatī and Nṛsimhāshrama Sarasvatī.

These Advaitins have produced enormously rich and valuable philosophical literature in the form of commentaries, sub-commentaries and original treatises. They have elaborated in minute details the conception of *māyā* or *avidyā* and the falsity of the world meticulously; they have thrown ample light on the concepts of *Ātmā,* Brahma, *Sākṣī,* Īshvara and *jīva*; they have put forward different theories regarding the relation between Īshvara and *jīva;* and they have clarified the nature of *Mokṣa, jīvan-mukti,* means to *Mokṣa* and the spiritual discipline. They have successfully answered the charges against *māyā* and *advaita* levelled among others by Rāmānuja and his follower Veṅkaṭanātha, and by Jayatīrtha and Vyāsatīrtha of the Mādhva school. And with very great dialectic skill, they have attacked the position of the opponents by demolishing the notion of difference and the ultimate reality of the phenomenal world. Shrīharṣa, Chitsukha and Madhusūdana Sarasvatī are among the greatest dialecticians of the world. Shrīharṣa and Chitsukha show the utter dialectical hollowness of the categories and concepts of thought. They also refute the various definitions of *pramā* (right cognition) and pramāṇas given by Nyāya and Mīmāmsā. They also refute difference and the ultimate reality of the world. The controversy between Vyāsatīrtha, the follower of Madhva and the author of Nyāyāmṛta, and Madhusūdana Sarasvatī, the author of Advaita-siddhi has been classic. Madhusūdana has successfully defended the concept of the falsity of the world and advaita against the terrible attacks of Vyāsatīrtha and has counter-attacked and demolished the dvaita position by refuting the notion of difference.

Another important system of advaita is Kāshmīra Shaivism also known as Pratyabhijñā-darshana and Īshvarādvaita. It claims to be based on the Shaiva Āgamas or Tantra. Vasugupta, Somānanda, Utpaladeva, Abhinavagupta and Kṣemarāja are among the most eminent writers of this system which has a voluminous literature.

Kāshmīra Shaivism, like Advaita Vedānta, maintains that the Absolute Self (Īshvara or Shiva) is the only reality and is infinite, indeterminate and pure consciousness, which is self-shining and self-proved. As transcendent (*vishvottīrṇa*) he is beyond senses, thought and language, and as immanent (*vishvātmaka*) he is one with the universe manifested by him. But unlike Vedānta this system maintains that Shiva as the Absolute, projects the universe by himself, on himself and within himself. The universe is neither pariṇāma or modification nor vivarta or unreal appearance. It is his ābhāsa in the sense of real manifestation. The key-principle of this system is the perfect union (*sāmarasya*) of Shiva and Shakti, *prakāsha* (pure consciousness) and *vimarsha* (self-consciousness or will), *chit* (knowledge) and *kriyā* (spontaneous activity), and subject and object. For Kāshmīra Shaivism, 'advaita' is not 'denial of duality' but 'complete union of the two' (*sāmarasyam ubhayoḥ*) in which the two are distinguishable in thought, but indivisible in fact. It is strongly opposed to the Advaita Vedānta conception of the Absolute which it calls inactive and lifeless and to *māyāvāda* which reduces the world to an illusory show of unconscious *māyā*. For Kāshmīra Shaivism, *māyā* is the power of obscuration and generates externality, finitude, limitation and difference. It also believes in beginningless innate Ignorance which it calls 'pauruṣa-ajñāna' which conceals the nature of the self and leads to its supposed finitude and imperfection and is the cause of bondage, and its removal by *pauruṣa-jñāna* or immediate spiritual intuition leading to pratyabhijñā or recognition by the self of its own nature as Supreme Self (Shiva) is freedom or *Mokṣa,* which is obtained here and now (*jīvan-mukti*). On analysis pratyabhijñā turns out to be the immediate realisation (*aparokṣānubhūti*) in Vedānta.

We thus find that there are four main systems of advaitavādā in Indian philosophy, namely, the Mādhyamika, Vijñānavāda, Advaita Vedānta and Kāshmīra Shaivism. Of these, the Advaita

Vedānta in its initial form as the central philosophy of the Upaniṣads is the earliest. It has influenced Buddha and through him the Mādhyamika and Vijñānavāda absolutism. The development of the dialectic as criticism of relational thought and the elucidation of ajātivāda in the Mādhyamika system, and the trenchant criticism of realism in Vijñānavāda have, in turn, influenced Advaita Vedānta as developed by Āchārya Gauḍapāda and Shaṅkara. Kāshmīra Shaivism is influenced by Advaita Vedānta and Vijñānavāda.

Sometimes a distinction is made between 'advaya-vāda' and 'advaita-vāda'. Advaya literally means 'non-two' and advaita means 'non-dual'; the former approach is said to be epistemic and the latter ontological. May be; but there is no substantial difference between the two and both point to the same non-dual Real. The denial of the 'two', i.e., two extreme views and with it all views, or the two basic categories of thought, 'is' and 'is not', 'real' and 'unreal', or the subject and the object in subject-object duality however reveals reality as non-relational, non-dual and differenceless.

These four systems of advaitavāda share some common features which are essential for absolutism. But they also differ among themselves due to the mode of their approach, as in the Absolute itself, evidently, there can be no difference. Some of these differences are only a matter of emphasis. But some of the differences which pertain to the nature of the Absolute and of the manifested world are substantial and real. The essential features shared in common by these four advaita systems are:

1. Advaitavāda is always spiritual non-dualism or absolutism.
2. The Absolute is at once transcendent to and immanent in the manifested world.
3. As transcendent, the Absolute is indeterminate (*nirvisheṣa*). It is beyond senses (*atīndriya*), thought (*nirvikalpa*) and language (*anirvachanīya*). It is pure consciousness and bliss.
4. As immanent, the Absolute is the reality of the manifested world of individual subjects and objects. It is infinite, all-pervasive and all-inclusive.
5. The Absolute cannot be known as an 'object' by relational thought. But as the foundation of all empirical knowledge and experience, it shines forth as the eternal non-dual Self, self-proved and self-shining. It can be realised in non-rela-

tional immediate spiritual experience (called *bodhi, prajñāpāramitā, lokottara jñāna, vijñaptimātratā, aparokṣānubhūti, pauruṣa-jñāna, pratyabhijñā*).

6. Absolutism makes a distinction between reality (*paramārtha*) and appearance (*vyavahāra, samvṛti, ajñāna*).
7. The Absolute appears as or projects this world through its own power (*shakti*) which is beginningless, transcendental and inseparable from it.
8. *Avidyā* or transcendental Illusion generates the notions of externality, difference, limitation and finitude. It can be removed only by the immediate realisation of the Absolute.
9. The Absolute is not proved by positive arguments. The advaitins negate the illusion of duality and the Absolute shines as the ground-reality.
10. *Mokṣa* or *Nirvāṇa* is absolute freedom which is complete identity with the Absolute. It is the realisation of one's own true nature through supra-relational knowledge or immediate experience.
11. Intense spiritual discipline is prescribed as a help towards this realisation.

Some of the important differences among these four advaita systems may also be noted. These are:

1. The Mādhyamika and Advaita Vedānta believe that the Absolute appears as the phenomenal world through its own power *Avidyā* which is transcendental Illusion. Creation, therefore, is a false show of *Avidyā*. Vijñānavāda agrees in believing that the Absolute Vijñāna which is pure eternal consciousness, due to its false association with transcendental Ignorance (*Avidyā*) which consists in the transcendental Illusion of Objectivity, leading to subject-object duality appears as creative Will and projects the phenomenal world which consists of vijñānas and *vāsanās* which force vijñānas to assume the 'forms' of objects. Kāshmīra Shaivism, on the other hand, believes that the Absolute Self which is pure consciousness (*prakāsha*) is at once self-conscious Will (*vimarsha*) and this inseparable Consciousness-Force (*chit-shakti*) is the spontaneous activity (*kriyā*), the absolute freedom and joy of the Real through which the Absolute projects the world which is real manifestation (*ābhāsa*) and not an illusory show of

unconscious Avidyā on an inactive ground.

2. The Mādhyamika, Vijñānavāda and Advaita Vedānta believe that in the non-dual Absolute the subject-object duality is totally negated. Kāshmīra Shaivism, on the other hand, believes that the Absolute is the complete union of the subject and the object (*ekarasyamubhayoḥ*) and true '*advaita*' is not the utter denial of duality but denial only of the illusory sense of duality (*bheda-pratīti*) and the realisation of complete union with the Absolute.
3. The Mādhyamika and Advaita Vedānta believe that *Avidyā* works with subject-object duality and gives rise to the categorising function of thought which instead of revealing the Real distorts it. Both employ dialectic as the criticism of relational thought which reveals its inherent self-contradictory nature and its inability to grasp the unrelated Real. The distinction between Reality (*paramārtha*) and Appearance (*samvṛti, vyavahāra*) is maintained. Appearances are graded into empirical (*mithyā samvṛti, pratibhāsa*) and transcendental (*loka samvṛti, vyavahāra*). Vijñānavāda, however, makes the distinction between the Real as it is (*pariniṣpanna*) and as it appears conditioned through Avidyā (*paratantra*). It rejects the world of subject-object duality as utterly unreal like the sky-flower (*parikalpita*). It maintains ontological as well as epistemic idealism. The Mādhyamika and Advaita Vedānta maintain only ontological idealism and vehemently reject Vijñānavāda's epistemic idealism as unwarranted and illogical.
4. The Absolute is reached through negation. The Mādhyamika negates views (*dṛṣṭi*), theories (*anta*) and thought-constructions (*vikalpa, kalpanā*). Vijñānavāda negates objectivity (*viṣayatā*). Advaita Vedānta negates difference (*bheda*). Kāshmīra Shaivism negates the illusory sense of duality (*bheda-pratīti*).

The Mādhyamika, Vijñānavāda, Advaita Vedānta and Kāshmīra Shaivism, these four main systems of advaitavāda in Indian philosophy form the subject-matter of our study. We are presenting in this work a detailed and comparative exposition of these systems along with their evaluation.

PART ONE
BUDDHISM

CHAPTER ONE

The Philosophy of Buddha

I. INTRODUCTION

Gautama, the Buddha was born in Lumbinī forest in the 7th or 6th century B.C. According to tradition, he renounced the household life at the age of 29 and after six years of rigorous spiritual discipline found enlightenment, and then preached the truth he had discovered for about 45 years, wandering from place to place in the ancient kingdoms of Magadha (Bihar) and Kosala (Avadh) till he attained *Nirvāṇa* at the ripe old age of over 80 years in Kushīnagar (Kasaya, Dist. Devaria, U.P.) in 544 B.C., according to Buddhist tradition and near about 486 B.C. according to some scholars. He preached orally and has not left anything in writing.

Buddhism flourished in India for about fifteen centuries and was divided into many schools and sub-schools, sects and sub-sects. Realism, empiricism, pragmatism, idealism, subjectivism and absolutism are all found in Buddhism itself. Prof. M. Hiriyanna is right in saying that "we have, so to speak, philosophy repeated twice over in India—once in the several Hindu systems and again in the different schools of Buddhism."[1]

Buddhist historians like Bu-ston (1290-1364) and Tāranātha (1574-1608) speak of the 'Three Swingings of the Wheel of Dharma' (*dharma-chakra-pravartana*) which metaphor means that there were three main turning-points in the history of Buddhism[2]. These are:

1. The earlier phase of pluralistic realism comprising Theravāda,

---

1. *Outlines of Indian Philosophy,* p. 198
2. *Bu-ston's History of Buddhism* (Tr. by Dr. Obermiller) Vol. II, pp. 52-4. Also, Stcherbatsky : *Buddhist Logic,* Vol. I, pp. 3-14.

Sarvāstivāda (*Vaibhāṣika*) and Sautrāntika schools of Hīnayāna.
2. The middle phase of absolutism was represented by Shūnyavāda or Mādhyamika school of Nāgārjuna and Āryadeva.
3. The last phase of idealism comprising the Absolute idealism of Vijñānavāda or Yogāchāra school of Maitreya, Asaṅga, Vasubandhu and Sthiramati and the subjective idealism of the later Svatantra-Vijñānavāda or Sautrāntika-Yogāchāra school of Diṅnāga, Dharmakīrti, Shāntarakṣita and Kamalashīla.

Inspite of the fact that Buddha himself left nothing in writing and that Buddhism is divided into a bewildering number of schools and sub-schools, it is possible to glean the basic philosophical teachings of Buddha and to see their interpretation in the Buddhist systems. We list some points below which will be helpful in understanding the treatment of the subject presented here:

1. The Tipiṭaka canon of Theravāda was compiled by the Third Buddhist Council (*Saṅgīti*) under the presidentship of Tissa (*Tiṣya*), summoned by King Ashoka at Pātaliputra near about 249 B.C. It was taken to Simhala (Sri Lanka) by King Ashoka's son (or younger brother) Mahendra in the third century B.C. and was, later on, recorded in writing during the regime of the Simhala king Vaṭṭagāmaṇi Abhaya in the first century B.C. This Pāli canon is the oldest record of Buddha's teachings available to us.
2. The fundamental teachings of Buddha can be gleaned from the Vinaya and the Sutta Piṭakas and the Buddhist schools grow out of them.
3. The Abhidhamma treatises of the Pāli canon though called 'the word of Buddha' (Buddha-vachana) are really the Theravāda interpretation that misses the deeper truth in Buddha's teachings. The Abhidharma works of the Sarvāstivāda canon in Sanskrit though attributed to different authors, are no better.
4. Buddha is a non-dualist whose central teaching is spiritual absolutism taken from the Upaniṣads, which is not incompatible with epistemic realism. Buddha, like the Upaniṣads, insists on the direct realisation of the Absolute which he calls '*Nirvāṇa*' and prescribes an elaborate spiritual discipline for its realisation.
5. Buddha is inspired by and has great respect for the Vedic and

the Upaniṣadic seers whom he calls 'the true knowers of the Veda and the Vedānta (Vedagu; Skt. Vedajña and Vedantagu; Skt. Vedāntajña)'. He was opposed to the karma-kāṇḍa of the Veda. The Upaniṣads and the Gītā also voice this opposition.[1] Buddha calls himself 'a critical analyst' (vibhajja-vādī; vibhajya-vādī in Sanskrit) opposed to all dogmatism (*ekamsa-vādo*; Skt. *ekāmsha-vāda*)[2]. He admits that the Upaniṣadic seers had realised the non-dual Absolute which he himself has realised. But he emphasised his own realisation and preached to his disciples the spiritual path by which he had realised the Absolute, the *Nirvāṇa*. The Upaniṣadic seers identified the Absolute with the Pure Self (*Ātmā*) and realised it by universalisation of the ground-reality of the 'I'; Buddha took the word *ātmā* in the sense of the finite relational self, the projection of avidyā, and identified the Absolute with Nirvāṇa and realised it by annihilation of the finite 'I' (anātma). Inspite of the difference in the paths, the goal realised is the same, the non-dual Absolute. The Vedānta also condemns the finite jīva, the locus of the notion of 'I' and the 'mine', as projection of avidyā and Buddha admits the reality of the non-dual Absolute as *Nirvāṇa,* though he does not use the word *Ātmā* for it. Hence the view that Buddha founded a new metaphysics of *anātma-vāda* in direct opposition to the atma-vāda tradition of the Upaniṣads is extremely misleading. We shall discuss it in detail later on.[3]

6. The 'silence' of Buddha on the fourteen metaphysical questions does not indicate his ignorance of metaphysics or his agnosticism or his nihilism. It indicates his absolutism by revealing that contradictions are inherent in thought and can be solved only by rising to immediate spiritual experience[4]. Nothing can be farther from the truth than to jump from Buddha's 'silence' to the conclusion that he was innocent of metaphysics, had no reasoned conviction and taught only morality and yoga. He was a metaphysician of a very high order, though constructive metaphysics for him is fraught

1. *Chhāndogya Upaniṣad,* I-12-4,5; *Gītā,* II, 42-6.
2. *Majjhima Nikāya, Subha Sutta,* Vol. II p. 197 (PTS ed.) and Vol. II, p. 469 (Nalanda ed.).
3. See *infra,* pp. 25-36.
4. See *infra,* pp. 20-25.

with self-contradictions and has to be transcended in immediate spiritual experience. Morality and yoga constitute the necessary spiritual discipline for the realisation of the Real.

7. The basic philosophical doctrines of Buddha are found in all schools of Buddhism, though in varying degrees and with diverse interpretations.
8. The deeper truth in Buddha's teachings finds its development in the school of Shūnyavāda and to some extent in earlier Vijñānavāda.
9. The later school of Vijñānavāda which we have designated as Svatantra-Vijñānavāda and which is also called as Sautrāntika-Yogachāra is the logical school of Diṅnāga, Dharmakīrti and Shāntarakṣita. It dilutes the absolute idealism of the earlier school of Asaṅga and Vasubandhu with the critical realism of the Sautrāntika and has degenerated into subjectivism. It has, like Hīnayāna, deviated from the real teaching of Buddha.
10. The fundamental philosophical ideas in Mahāyāna can be traced in Hīnayāna and the former arose as a logical necessity to remove the inner contradictions of the latter.

II. PRATĪTYASAMUTPĀDA

Buddha summarises his teaching in the four noble truths (*ārya-satya*) which are suffering (*duḥkha*), its cause (*samudaya*), its cessation (*nirodha*) and the way leading to its cessation (*nirodha-pratipat* or *mārga*). Sometimes including the second in the first and the fourth in the third, he declared: Two things only do I teach—suffering and its cessation. Suffering is *samsāra* and its cessation is *nirvāṇa.* This central teaching of Buddha is called *pratītya-samutpāda.* From the relative standpoint of thought it is the twelve-linked wheel of relative causation and from the absolute standpoint it is the blissful *nirvāṇa* itself where all pain and plurality cease. Buddha identifies it with *bodhi* (enlightenment) and *dhamma,* Skt. *dharma* (the true doctrine). Nagārjuna salutes Buddha as the best of the teachers, the teacher of the blissful pratītya-samutpāda.[1] Shāntarakṣita also does the same.[2]

The twelve links of the causal wheel of pratītya-samutpāda are: (1) Beginningless and cosmic Ignorance (*avidyā*), (2) impressions

1. *Mādhyamika-Kārikā,* opening verses.
2. *Tattva-saṅgraha,* I, 6.

of karmic forces (*saṁskāra*), (3) individual consciousness (*vijñāna*) (4) psycho-physical organism (*nāma-rūpa*), (5) six sense- organs including manas (*ṣaḍāyatana*), (6) sense-object-contact (*sparsha*), (7) sensation (*vedanā*), (8) desire for sense-enjoyment (tṛṣṇā) (9) clinging to sense enjoyment (*upādāna*), (10) will to be born for experiencing sense-enjoyment (*bhava*), (11) birth including rebirth (*jāti*), and (12) disintegration and death (*jarā-maraṇa*). This viscious cycle of causation, in which each preceeding link is the cause of the succeeding one, does not end with death which is only the beginning of a new birth. In this way this beginningless cycle of birth-and-death (*saṁsāra*) goes on revolving till its root-cause *avidyā* is destroyed. As *avidyā* is transcendental Ignorance it can be removed only by transcendental knowledge or non-dual spiritual experience (*bodhi* or *prajñā*).

When the Absolute appears as tinged with avidyā the cycle of causation starts. Pure consciousness appears through avidyā as cosmic Will containing all potential forces (vāsanā) or impressions (*samskāra*) of karma which are the seeds of the phenomenal world. Through *avidyā* and *karma-samskāras* the process of individualisation and objectification starts and pure consciousness appears as individualised consciousness (*vijñāna*), which, then, gets clothed with a psycho-physical organism (*nāma-rūpa*). It, then, develops six sense-organs (*ṣaḍāyatana*), the five senses of smell, taste, sight, touch and sound and the sixth internal organ called manas, which are treated as powers (*shakti-rūpa*). The senses come into contact (*sparsha*) with their objects. The sense-object contact leads to sense experience (*vedanā*), which in turn produces a desire (*tṛṣṇā*) to experience pleasant sensations again and again. This desire leads to a firm clinging (upādāna) to sense-experience. This clinging engenders the will to be born again and again to undergo sense-experience. This will to be born (*bhava*) drags down the individual consciousness to take birth and rebirth (*jāti*). And when there is birth, decay and death (*jarā-maraṇa*) must follow. *Jarā* or old age here means decay or disintegration and jarā-maraṇa is a symbolic expression for the misery of phenomenal existence. And death is only the beginning of a new life. The cycle of birth and death goes on till its root-cause *avidyā* is destroyed. And transcendental *avidyā* can be removed only by non-dual spiritual experience (*bodhi*) which transcends the categories of thought. Of the four categories of thought, affirmation, negation, both and neither, the first two are primary in nature. Buddha teaches us to rise above these categories of affirmation and negation, existence and non-existence, eternalism and nihilism. All objects of thought are pratītya-samutpanna for they arise depending on their causes and conditions and have only relative existence, not real existence. They are neither real nor unreal. Relative causation rules out both eternalism (shāshvata-vāda) and nihilism (uchchheda-vāda). Pratītya-samutpāda is *madhyamā pratipat* (middle path). But as relativity itself is not final, for it is related to the Absolute, pratītya-samutpāda itself, viewed through vidyā, is the blissful Absolute where all misery and plurality is merged. Madhyamā pratipat, therefore, is not a middle view between two extreme views, but the denial of all views which itself is not a view; the wise person does not stop at the middle but transcends the middle also.[1] Everything in the world, the subject as well as the object, is relative (*pratītya-samutpanna*), perishable (*anitya*), miserable (*duḥkha*) and devoid of ultimate reality (*anātma* or *svabhāva-shūnya*). *Nirvāṇa* alone is the Absolute, the imperishable, the blissful, the supreme Real.

III. BUDDHA'S SILENCE ON THE AVYĀKṚTA

When metaphysical questions about matter, soul and God (Tathāgata or Perfect Being) were put to Buddha, he answered them by silence. These fourteen questions were declared unanswerable or inexpressible (*avyākata*, Skt. *avyākṛta*) by Buddha. His silence on these questions has been variously interpreted. Some say that Buddha kept silent because he did not know the answer. He was ignorant of or atleast uninterested in metaphysics. He was a practical person emphasising morality and yoga. Buddha compares a metaphysician to that foolish man whose heart is pierced by a poisonous arrow and who, instead of taking it out, whiles away his time on idle speculation about the origin, size, metal, maker and thrower of that arrow; the man would die before he got satisfactory answers to such questions.[2] He who searches after metaphysical entities like an eternal soul is compared by Buddha to that foolish lover who says he has fallen in love with the most beautiful damsel in the State whom he has never seen

1. maddhe'pi sthānaṃ na karoti paṇḍitaḥ. Samādhirājasūtra, p.30.
2. *Majjhima Nikāya*, I, 63 (Chūla Mālunkya Sutta)

and about whose existence, residence, caste, size, colour, age and beauty he knows nothing.[1] This interpretation of Buddha's silence is wrong, as Buddha was himself a metaphysician of a very high order. He has told at many places that he knows these metaphysical views under discussion and knows much more, but he does not advocate them because they are not conducive to spiritual life and do not lead to knowledge, illumination, peace, *nirvāṇa.*[2] His condemnation of metaphysics was from a higher standpoint of spiritual experience.

Another interpretation of Buddha's silence is that he was an agnostic and reality for him was unknown and unknowable, and that he had no 'reasoned conviction on the matter'. This is also wrong. There is no note of doubt, despair and agnosticism in his teachings. He claimed in absolutely clear and unambiguous terms to have realised the truth and engaged himself in guiding his disciples towards this realisation. Thought cannot know the Real, but the Real thereby does not become unknowable, for it can be realised through non-dual spiritual experience which transcends thought. This is absolutism and not agnosticism.

Still another interpretation of his silence is nihilistic. His silence is taken as the negation of all metaphysical entities like matter, soul and God. He did not believe in any positive reality and therefore kept quiet. This interpretation too is incorrect. Buddha was as much opposed to nihilism as he was to eternalism. He has declared in most emphatic and positive terms and at many places the reality of *Nirvāṇa,* the eternal and blissful Absolute. No Buddhist has ever taken the teachings of Buddha as nihilism, as the denial of *Nirvāṇa.* The world of plurality and all views of the Real may be negated in the Absolute as thought-constructions, but the Absolute itself shines as the self-proved transcendental background of all phenomena. This is absolutism and not nihilism.

The Hīnayāna interpretation of Buddha's silence on the *avyākṛta* questions is in accordance with its view of radical pluralism. According to Hīnayāna, Buddha advocated the theory of elements and denied the ultimate reality of matter, souls and God. He could not answer the questions about the reality of matter, souls and God in the affirmative, because he did not believe in their ultimate reality; and he did not answer them in the negative

1. *Dīgha Nikāya,* 9 (Poṭṭhapāda Sutta)
2. *Ibid.*

because that would be to deny even their empirical reality. To the simple objection as to why did not Buddha, then, answer these questions by saying that ultimately only the elements were real, and matter, souls, etc., enjoyed only empirical reality for the sake of spiritual discipline, the reply of Hīnayāna was that those who put these questions to him were too stupid to grasp the theory of elements. This interpretation too is incorrect. Buddha who preached throughout his life would not and could not keep quiet and refuse expression of his own view on vital metaphysical issues. It is also not possible to believe that those who put questions to Buddha were incapable of grasping his theory of elements. Hīnayāna forgets the fact that Buddha was as emphatic in rejecting the reality of elements as he was in rejecting the reality of primordial matter, eternal souls and personal God. For him all views of the Real, qua views, are self-contradictory and are transcended in the Real.

The correct interpretation of Buddha's silence lies in his absolutism as explained by Mahāyāna. Thought necessarily works in duality and its categories instead of revealing the Real, falsify it by distorting it. Buddha's silence on the *avyākṛta* questions means that thought cannot give satisfactory answers to the metaphysical problems concerning the supra-sensuous and the supra-relational Real. The Absolute is inexpressible, indeterminate, indefinable and ineffable. It is above thought-constructions and can be directly realised through spiritual experience.

Questions are said to be of four kinds:

(1) Those which can be directly answered (*ekāṃsha-vyākaraṇīya*), e.g., Is man mortal? Yes.
(2) Those which can be conditionally and analytically answered (*vibhajya-vyākaraṇīya*), e.g., Is man wise? Some are, some are not.
(3) Those which require a counter-question (*pratipṛchchhā-vyākaraṇīya*), e.g., Is man tall? In relation to whom?
(4) Those which cannot be answered (*sthāpanīya*), e.g., the metaphysical questions about the reality of the non-empirical matter, souls and God.

To this last class (*sthāpanīya*) belong the famous fourteen questions called *avyākṛta* or inexpressible. These are grouped under four sets, three of which have four alternatives each and the fourth only two. It is not clear why logically the fourth set too should not have four alternatives. The questions are[1]:

(1) Is the world (*loka*) eternal (*shāshvata*)? Or not? Or both? Or neither (1-4).
(2) Is the world finite (*antavān*) ? Or not? Or both? Or neither? (5-8).
(3) Does the Tathāgata exist after death (*param maraṇāt*)? Or not? Or both? Or neither? (9-12).
(4) Is the soul (*jīva*) identical with the body (*sharīra*)? Or not? (13-14).

The four alternatives are called *Chatuṣkoṭi* or the four views of thought. The division is exhaustive and further alternatives are ruled out. The first two alternatives are basic (*mūlā koṭi*). The first is a thesis and is opposed by the second which is its anti-thesis. The third is formed by a conjunctive affirmation of the first and the second, and the fourth by a disjunctive denial of the first and the second.

The above four sets of questions are about the ultimate reality or the transcendent ground of the object and of the subject and of the unity of the two, and not about their empirical nature, as their empirical reality is admitted.

The first set of questions is about the eternality of the world. Eternality means the beginninglessness and limitlessness of this world in time. The discussion is about the origin or beginning of this world in time (*pūrvā koṭi* or *pūrva anta*). The empirical world-objects are not the subject-matter of discussion. Nobody denies the origin and the changing character of empirical objects. The question is: Is there a transcendental substance, a primordial matter which may be treated as eternal and uncaused cause of all material objects? And, is the world as such beginningless or does it have an origin in time when it was first created? The thesis affirms such transcendent substance and also the beginninglessness of creation. The anti-thesis denies it. Here, Sāṅkhya view may be taken as the thesis and Chārvāka view as the anti-thesis.

The second set of questions is about the finitude of the transcendent cause of world-objects. Is this cause limited in space and

1. *Dīgha Nikāya*, 9 (Poṭṭhapāda Sutta); *Majjhima Nikāya* I, 63 (Chūla Mālunkya Sutta) and I, 72 (Aggivachchhagotta Sutta), etc.

so subject to destruction (*aparānta*)? Will the world as such come to an end for ever? The thesis asserts the limited spatial character of this cause, while the anti-thesis denies it. Here the order of the thesis and the anti-thesis is reversed. Here, Chārvāka view serves as the thesis and Sāṅkhya view as the anti-thesis.

The third set of questions is about the transcendental ground of the subject-object unity, i.e., the Perfect Being or God. Tathāgata (Buddha) is called the Perfect Person (*Puruṣottama* or *Parama Puruṣa* or *Dvipadām Vara*) and the phrase *param maraṇāt* means 'beyond death.' Here too, Sāṅkhya which most probably was theistic in the beginning and other theistic schools provided the thesis and Chārvāka the anti-thesis.

The fourth set of questions is about an eternal individual soul-substance and not about the empirical ego whose relative reality is not questioned. The word 'body' (*sharīra*) includes the psycho-physical organism and the mental states. The thesis identifies the soul with the body and the mental states. The anti-thesis denies it and treats the soul as an eternal substance, immortal and free. Here also, like in the second set, the order of the thesis and the anti-thesis is reversed. Charvāka provides the thesis and Sāṅkhya the anti-thesis.

There is a striking similarity between these *avyākṛta* questions and the antinomies of Kant. The threefold nature of the questions about matter, soul and God corresponds to the problems raised by Kant in Rational Cosmology, Rational Psychology and Rational Theology. The antinomies have a thesis and an anti-thesis each which are declared to be insoluble by thought. The antinomies are:

1.	Thesis	:	The world has a beginning in time and is limited in space.
	Anti-thesis	:	The world has no beginning in time and is not limited in space.
2.	Thesis	:	Every compound substance is made up of simple parts.
	Anti-thesis	:	No compound substance is made up of simple parts.
3.	Thesis	:	There is free causation.
	Anti-thesis	:	There is mechanical causation.
4.	Thesis	:	An absolutely necessary Being exists.
	Anti-thesis	:	No such Being exists.

The first antinomy includes the first and the second sets of the *avyākṛta.* The third antinomy corresponds to the fourth set of the *avyākṛta,* for, if the soul is different from the body causation will be free and if the soul is identical with the body causation will be mechanical. The fourth antinomy corresponds to the third set of the *avyākṛta.* The second antinomy is implied in the second set of the *avyākṛta.* Kant also declares that these antinomies are insoluble by thought. But there are vital differences also between Kant and Buddha. Kant is an agnostic, while Buddha has the certitude of realisation. Kant's philosophy is vitiated by dualism and pluralism, while Buddha believes in spiritual absolutism. Kant has pinned reality to sense-experience, while Buddha believes in non-dual spiritual realisation which is supra-sensible and supra-relational.

IV. ANĀTMAVĀDA AND NIRVĀṆA

It is said that there are two traditions in Indian philosophy—one is the ātmavāda tradition of the Upaniṣads accepted by the orthodox systems and the other is the anātmavāda tradition initiated and established by Buddha and accepted by all schools of Buddhism. It is believed that Buddha starts with a distinct spirit of opposition to the ātmavāda of the Upaniṣads. The notion of self or soul or substance, eternal and unchanging is a primordial false notion (*avidyā*) which is the root-cause of all misery and pain and which renders spiritual life meaningless and must be annihilated in order to realise *nirvāṇa.* The Upaniṣads, on the other hand, sing the glory of the Self and identify it with the Real; *Ātmā* is Brahma. It is the not-self (*anātma*) which is the root-cause of all misery and pain. All the schools of Buddhism belonging to Hīnayāna or Mahāyāna are unanimous in denying the self. And the non-Buddhist Vedic and Jain systems also characterise Buddhism as anātmavāda. Now, all this has to be properly understood. Most of the philosophical quarrels are usually based on misunderstanding of the meaning of the terms employed. The fight between ātmavāda and anātmavāda in Indian philosophy is a classical example of such misunderstanding.

The word *ātmā* is used in Indian philosophy in three different senses, namely, (1) in the sense of an empirical ego (*vyāvahārika jīvātmā*) which, due to its involvement in *avidyā* and *karma,* is transmigrating in the cycle of birth and death *(saṁsāra)*, which is the finite centre of egoity *(ahaṁkāra-mamakāra)*, which is the finite knower *(pramātā* or *jñātā)*, agent (*kartā*) and enjoyer (*bhoktā*) and which is the object of introspection; (2) in the sense of a real individual self (*tātvika jīvātmā*) which is an eternal spiritual substance and is the centre, not of egoity, but of individuality (*ahantā*) and which maintains its unchanging identity either inspite of or in and through its changing modes; and (3) in the sense of the pure subject (*sākṣī*), the non-dual universal Self (*paramātmā*) which is the eternal, self-shining and undeniable transcendent ground of all empirical phenomena.

No great philosopher has denied the empirical validity of the ego. Even the schools of Hīnayāna which are most vocal in rejecting the reality of the *ātmā* have accepted its validity as an empirical ego by calling it 'empirically real' (*prajñapti sat*) and denying it as an ultimate real (*vastu sat*). Those who believe in the reality of the self take it either in the sense of an eternal spiritual substance or in the sense of the pure transcendent subject. The pluralistic realists take it in the sense of an eternal substance. Some of them like the Sāṅkhyas, the Jainas and the theistic Vedāntins, treat consciousness as its inseparable essence (*svarūpa*), while others like the Vaisheṣikas, the Naiyāyikas and the Mīmāmsakas like Prabhākara, take consciousness as its quality which arises in it by its contact with the object. Some, like the Sāṅkhyas, the Vaisheṣikas, the Naiyāyikas and the Mīmāmsakas believe that it is all-pervading (*vibhu*), while others like the theistic Vedāntins believe that it is atomic (*aṇu*). All the realists believe that the souls are many in number. As the realists do not accept the distinction between the empirical and the Absolute, for them the 'empirical ego' is also real as it is the individual self itself in real bondage, though it realises its real nature when liberated. The Upaniṣadic seers and the Advaita Vedāntins use the word *ātmā* in the sense of the pure transcendent subject, which is at once pure consciousness and bliss. Buddha and the Buddhists, on the other hand, use the word *ātmā* in the sense of an empirical ego or in the sense of an eternal individual substance and reject its ultimate reality, while accepting its empirical validity. Hīnayāna reduces the self to a series of fleeting mental states which are taken as real. Buddha has repeatedly rejected the views of eternalism (shāshvata-vāda) and nihilism (uchchheda-vāda). Hīnayana rejects only the eternal ego, but glorifies the uchchheda-dṛṣṭi (the nihilistic view) by accepting the reality of the mental states. Mahāyāna, following Buddha, takes both the ego and the mental states as relative and therefore only empirically real and identifies the Real with the Absolute. In Buddha and Mahāyāna, the denial of the self is its denial as an eternal substance; it is not the denial of the absolute Self. Anātmavāda or nairātmyavāda is really the nirahaṅkāra-nirmama-vāda of Vedānta. It denies neither the empirical validity of the ego nor the ultimate reality of the Absolute Self. It is the denial only of the false notion which mistakes the empirical ego as an eternal spiritual substance and attempts to objectify the subject and realise it through thought-categories. To take the self as an eternal substance is to cling to it eternally and this is *avidyā* which is the root-cause of all attachment, desire, misery and bondage. It leads to the four kinds of suffering (*klesha*)—which are self-notion (*ātma-dṛṣṭi*), self-delusion (*ātma-moha*), self-pride (*ātma-māna*) and self-love (*ātma-sneha*). Ātma-dṛṣṭi is called pudgala or satkāya dṛṣṭi. Pudgala is that which is subject to decay and death (*pūrayati galati cha*). Satkāya is identification of the Self with the living body. This is *avidyā* for it confuses the Self with the body and the mental states and mistakes that which is subject to birth and death as an eternal Self. It is this false notion which is condemned by Buddha as 'the doctrine of the fools' (*kevalo bāladhammo*).

Buddha says: "If I, Ānanda, when the wandering monk Vachchhagotta asked me: 'Is there the ego?' had answered: 'The ego is' then that Ānanda would have confirmed the doctrine of the Shramaṇas and Brāhmaṇas who believe in permanence (of the ego). If I, Ānanda, had answered: 'The ego is not', then that Ānanda would have confirmed the doctrine of the Shramaṇas and Brāhmaṇas, who believe in annihilation (of the ego)."[1] For Buddha the individual self is neither an eternal substance nor a non-entity. It is neither real nor unreal; it is relative and phenomenal. Buddha compares him who clings to the self without knowing it to that foolish lover who says he has fallen in love with the most beautiful damsel in the State (*jana-pada-kalyāṇī*) whom he has never seen and about whose residence, caste, size, colour, age and beauty he knows nothing.[2] Buddha is condemning those who

1. *Samyutta Nikāya,* 44, 10.
2. *Dīgha Nikāya,* 9.

without realising the Self, mistake the not-Self as the Self and cling to it. This is *avidyā*; this is running after phantoms. Nowhere has Buddha categorically denied the true Self. He has always preached like this: the body (*kāya*) is not the Self, the mind (*chitta*) is not the Self; sensation, perception, volition or idea is not the Self; nor do the five skandhas together constitute the Self.[1] According to Buddha the real Self is transcendent and cannot be bound in thought-constructions. It is, therefore, futile to spin theories about it. To hold any view or theory about the Inexpressible is illegitimate. Such attempts land one 'in the wilderness of views (*diṭṭhi-gahana*, Skt. *dṛṣṭi-gahana*), in the jungle of theories (*diṭṭhi-kantāra*, Skt. *dṛṣṭī-kāntāra)*, in the net of thought-constructions, in the bondage of the categories.'[2] When Vachchha-gotta asks: 'But has Gotama any theory of his own?' Buddha answers: 'The Tathāgata, O Vachchha, is free from all theories. . . . Therefore the Tathāgata has attained deliverance and is free from attachment and all false notions of the 'I' and the 'mine' (*sabba-ahaṅkāra-mamaṅkāra-mānānusayānam khayā vimutto*).[3] Buddha has repeatedly declared all objects of thought (*samskṛta dharma*) as relative and ultimately unreal. They are perishable, miserable and devoid of ultimate reality. That which is perishable (*anichcha*, Skt. *anitya*) is miserable (*duḥkha*) and that which is '*duḥkha*' is '*anattā*' (Skt. *anātma*), i.e., unreal, not-Self, and that which is '*anattā*' is not mine, I am not that, that is not my Self'.[4] This does not mean that there is no real Self. Sāṅkhya which admits the reality of Self as pure consciousness says that the contemplation on 'I am not the not-Self, the not-Self is not mine, that I am absolutely different from the not-Self' generates pure knowledge.[5] For Buddha, the real Self is the transcendent Absolute which is also immanent in the phenomena. He calls the Absolute as *Nirvāṇa.* He does not expressly identify the Absolute with the Self, but the implication is clearly there, for, if the *anātma* or the not-Self is perishable and miserable, that which is eternal (*nitya*) and blissful (*sukha*) must

1. *Dīgha N.* 15; Majjhima Nikāya 72; Samyutta N. 44, 8.
2. *Majjhima N.* 72; Dīgha Nikāya 1.
3. *Majj. N.* 72.
4. Sabbe saṅkhārā anichchā. Yad anichcham tam dukkham, yam dukkham tad anattā, yad anattā tam netam mama, nesohamasmi, na me so attāti. Samyutta Nikāya 22, 15.
5. Sāṅkhya-Kārikā, 64, nāsmi na me nāham iti kevalam utpadyate jñānam.

be the true Self (*ātmā*). *Nirvāṇa,* like the Upaniṣadic *Ātmā,* is repeated described by Buddha as calm (*shānta*), immortal (*amṛta*), unproduced (*akṛta*), uncaused (*asamskṛta*), unborn (*ajāta*), undecaying (*ajara*), undying (*amara*), eternal (*nitya*), abiding (*dhruva*), unchanging (*shāshvata*), highest joy (*parama sukha*), blissful (*Shiva*), desireless (*tṛṣṇā-kṣaya*), cessation of plurality (*bhava-nirodha; prapanchopashama*) and the fearless goal (*abhaya pada*).[1] All the epithets (or their synonyms) which the Upaniṣadic seers use for the *Ātmā,* Buddha uses for *Nirvāṇa. Ātmā* and *Nirvāṇa* stand for the Inexpressible and the Ineffable Absolute which is transcendent to thought and is realised through immediate spiritual experience (*bodhi* or *prajñā*). The fact that all phenomena are subject to birth, becoming, decay and death logically implies that there is the Absolute, unborn, unchanging and imperishable. If there were no such Absolute, there would be no escape from bondage.[2] As *Nirvāṇa* is beyond thought, it cannot be described by the categories of *nitya* or *anitya* and of empirical *sukha* or *duḥkha.* Buddha was emphatic in denying that *Nirvāṇa* is annihilation or momentary. True to his negative dialectic, Buddha uses negative terms for *Nirvāṇa,* but due to the nature of thought and language, positive terms also are sometimes used. As the Upaniṣadic 'neti neti' negates all descriptions of *Ātmā,* not the *Ātmā* itself, so the negative method of Buddha denies the descriptions and characteristics of *Nirvāṇa* as being final, but do not deny *Nirvāṇa* itself. Silence is the highest philosophy for both. The Bliss of *Nirvāṇa* is beyond the empirical pleasure and pain.

Even Hīnayāna which ignored the absolutism of Buddha and elaborated a system of radical pluralism and which was emphatic in denying the self, admitted *Nirvāṇa* as an eternal positive reality, calm and blissful. But it degraded *Nirvāṇa* to the level of an eternal substance (*asamskṛta dharma*) set over and above the worldly objects (*samskṛta dharmas*) in which there was cessation of misery. It was corrected by Mahāyāna which revived the absolutism of Buddha and treated *Nirvāṇa* as the transcendent Absolute at once immanent in the phenomena, the 'dharmatā' of all dharmas.

In a celebrated passage in the *Mahāparinibbāna Sutta,* the ailing Buddha says to Ānanda: 'O Ānanda! I have taught the Dhamma

1. Udāna, 73; Suttanipāta, Ratan Sutta; Itivuttaka, 112; Dhammapada, 18, etc.
2. Udāna, 73.

(Dharma) without any reservation and have not kept anything secret like a tight-fisted teacher (āchārya-muṣṭi). Now I am eighty years old and am somehow pulling on (the body) like an old tattered cart bound with ropes. I am going to leave the world soon. But there is no cause for grief as the light of Dharma is there. Ānanda! my message for all of you is this: Let the Self be your light (*attadīpa*, Skt. *ātma-dīpa*), let the Self be your shelter (*attasaraṇa*, Skt. *ātma-sharaṇa*); let the Dharma (the real) be your light (*dhamma-dīpa,* Skt. *dharma-dipa*), let the Dharma be your shelter (*dhamma-saraṇa,* Skt. *dharma-sharaṇa*); do not seek light and shelter outside.'[1] Even if, as some scholars do, the word *attā* (*ātmā*) in *attadīpa* is interpreted as meaning just 'oneself' without any reference to an ontological reality called 'Self' and the phrase 'attadīpa' is taken to mean 'you yourself are your light', it has to be admitted that Buddha is asking his disciples to seek light within and not outside. Now, if there is no true 'Self', then who is to seek the light and where? And if all objects as Buddha says are perishable and miserable and the light is to be sought only in the subject, then the reality of the transcendent subject is clearly implied in this passage. Again, if the word *dhamma* in *dhammadīpa* and *dhamma-saraṇa* is taken to mean 'the doctrine taught by Buddha', where light and shelter are to be sought, even then the importance is to be given to *Dharmatā* of all the dharmas which is *nirvāṇa* itself, embodied in his teaching. *Nirvāṇa* or the Absolute Self is the light of all lights, the ultimate shelter and the goal of life; its teaching is only a means to guide us to the goal. Buddha himself has explained how a *Bhikṣu* becomes Ātmadīpa and Dharmadīpa. He says: He who realises the real nature of the body and the various dharmas, he who realises that the five *skandhas* and all objects of thought are subject to origination and destruction, are perishable (*anitya*), miserable (*duḥkha*) and devoid of Self (anātma), he who gives up the notion of the 'I' and the 'mine' (*ahaṅkāra-mamakārā-nirodha*), who rises above attachment, aversion and delusion (*vīta-rāga-dveṣa-moha*), who is desireless (*vīta-tṛṣṇa*) and who enjoys the highest samādhi, he, indeed, enjoys the light of 'Self' and the light of '*Nirvāṇa*' or 'Dharma' (in the sense of

1. Dīgha Nikāya, 16: attadīpā viharatha attasaraṇā anañña saraṇā dhammadīpā dhammasaraṇā anaññasaraṇā.

Dharmatā).[1] When Buddha was about to leave his body and was bidding good-bye to his disciples, it is but natural that in his last speech he should be giving them the essence of his life-long teaching. His last speech as recorded in the *Mahāparinibbāna Sutta* runs thus: "Now, my disciples, I take leave of you. All produced objects (samskāras; samskṛta dharmas) are perishable (vyayadharma); realise (the Imperishable *Nirvāṇa*) with diligence.' This is the last speech of the Tathāgata."[2] All worldly objects including the empirical ego are relative (*samskṛta, pratītya-samutpanna*) and therefore ultimately unreal (*anātma*). *Nirvāṇa* alone is the Real, the Absolute which is transcendent to thought and immanent in phenomena. It can be realised in immediate spiritual experience which dawns through undergoing spiritual discipline. Buddha, in his last speech asks his disciples to realise this *Nirvāṇa,* this Real Self, so that they may enjoy eternal Bliss and may say like Buddha: 'The cycle of birth and death has ended, the spiritual life is fulfilled, what had to be done has been accomplished and nothing remains now to be done, there is no further birth now.'[3]

Thus we find that it is incorrect to hold that Buddha starts with a spirit of opposition to the Upaniṣads and initiates a new tradition of anātmavāda against the Upaniṣadic tradition of atmavāda. The anātmavāda is nirahankāra-nirmamavāda, the removal of the false notion of the 'I' and the 'mine', which the Upaniṣadic seers themselves unmistakably voice and which all systems of Indian philosophy believing in spiritual discipline accept. The Upaniṣadic seers and Buddha both are opposed to the view of realistic pluralism that the self is an ultimate individual substance and that there is a plurality of such eternal selves. Buddha carries on the tradition of absolutism so clearly set forth in the Upaniṣads. For both, the Real is the Absolute which is at once transcendent to thought and immanent in phenomena. Both take *avidyā,* the

1. Kāye kāyānupassī dhammesu dhammānupassī. . . . rūpam vedanā saññā sankhārā viññaṇam anichcham dukkham anattā'ti yathābhūtam pajānāti . . . ahankāra-mamankāra-nirodhā taṇhā-khayā vimutto hoti . . . samādhim upasampajja viharati. . . evam kho attadīpo dhammadīpo viharati.—Dīgha Nikāya 16, Samyutta 18,22; 22, 12-15, 43.
2. Vayadhammā sankhārā appamādena sampādethā' ti. ayam Tathāgatassa pachchhimā vāchā.—*Dīgha Nikāya* 16.
3. Khīṇā jāti, vusitam Brahmacharyam, katam karaṇīyam, nāparam itthatāyā'ti. (*Dīgha Nikāya,* 10). This is found in many dialogues.

beginningless and cosmic Ignorance as the root-cause of phenomenal existence and suffering. Both believe that thought is inherently fraught with contradictions and thought-categories, *instead of* revealing the Real distort it, and therefore, one should rise above all views, all theories, all determinations, all thought-constructions in order to realise the Real. For both, the Real is realised in immediate spiritual experience. Both prescribe moral conduct and spiritual discipline as means to realise the Real, the fearless goal, the abode of Bliss. There is, however, difference in the method used by them. The Upaniṣadic seers reach the Absolute by the universalisation of the 'I', while Buddha reaches it by the annihilation of the 'I'. But much should not be made of this difference. The 'I' is the 'co-mingling' of the Real and the unreal, the True and the false, the Pure *Ātmā* and *avidyā.* As the 'I' in the sense of the empirical ego is annihilated, the 'I' in the sense of the foundational Self shines at once. The end realised is the same, the non-dual Absolute. Both believe in the established canon of logic that it is the unreal alone which can be negated. For both, that which is negated in *avidyā,* the imposed empirical character of the 'I', and that which is retained is the Absolute. Both use the negative dialectic, the '*neti neti*' (not this, not this) for indirectly pointing to the nature of the Inexpressible. All the epithets which the Upaniṣadic seers use for *Ātmā* or Brahma (or their synonyms) Buddha uses for *Nirvāṇa.*[1] *Ātmā* and *Nirvāṇa* both stand for the ineffable non-dual Absolute. It must, however, be admitted that while the Upaniṣadic seers openly identify the Absolute with the Pure Self which is at once pure consciousness and bliss, Buddha, true to his negative logic, does not expressly identify the Absolute with the Pure Self, though the implication is clearly there. He identifies the Absolute with *Nirvāṇa.* Buddha's omission to identify the Absolute with the Transcendent Self has led to the misunderstanding of his ānātmavāda. But though Buddha does not expressly identify the Absolute with the Pure Self, nowhere has he expressly denied it. His descriptions of *Nirvāṇa* are similar to the descriptions of the Upaniṣadic *Ātmā* and leave no doubt that he is carrying on the tradition of the Upaniṣadic absolutism. Mrs. Rhys Davids is right in believing that Buddha did not deny the

1. See supra, pp. 28-9.

true self and that he carried on the Upaniṣadic tradition. The words 'body is not the self', 'mind is not the self' cannot rationally be said to imply that there is no self or soul.[1] 'The Śakyan mission was out "not to destroy, but to fulfill", to enlarge and enhance the accepted faith-in-God of their day, not by asseverating, but by making it more vital.'[2] It is significant to note, as Dr. E. J. Thomas points out, that among the views mentioned and rejected in the *Brahmajāla Sutta* (Dīgha Nikāya, 1), the Upaniṣadic view of the *Ātmā* is not included.[3]

Buddha, according to the Mahāyāna Buddhists, is a skillful teacher (*upāya-kushala*) who teaches in keeping with the intellectual ability of the disciples. To the beginners, he preaches the existence of the empirical ego so that they may not be frightened by *nairātmyavāda* and may not give up cultivation of moral virtues; to those who are a little advanced he preaches that critical analysis reveals that there is no self as an eternal spiritual substance and that what we experience is only an imposed ego on the stream of mental states; lastly, to those who are highly advanced he preaches that ultimately neither the empirical ego nor the mental states are real, that both these views, like all views of thought, should be transcended in immediate experience of the Absolute.[4] Just as a tigress takes her cub to a safe place, holding it in her mouth with the grip neither too tight to hurt the cub with her sharp teeth nor too loose to let it fall, similarly Buddha takes his disciples to the safe place of *nirvāṇa* in such a way that neither they fall from moral virtues and spiritual discipline nor do they get lost in the dense forest of views entangled in the piercing categories of thought.[5]

The word *anātma* or *nairātmya* was rightly interpreted by Mahāyāna as 'devoid of ultimate reality, i.e., as relative existence', and whereas Hīnayāna was content only with the denial of individual self (*pudgala-nairātmya*) Mahāyāna, following Buddha, extended its application to all objects of thought (*dharma-nairātmya*).

1. *Outlines of Buddhism*, p. 46.
2. *A Manual of Buddhism*, p. 194
3. *The Life of Buddha*, p. 201.
4. ātmetyapi prajñapitam anātmetyapi deshitam. Buddhair nātmā na chānātmā kashchidityapi deshitam. *Mādhyamika Kārikā*, 18, 6.
5. dṛṣṭi-damṣṭrāvaghātam cha bhramsham chāvekṣya karmaṇām. deshayanti jinā dharmam vyāghrī-potāpahāravat.

Not merely the individual self, but all objects of thought are devoid of ultimate reality (*anātma*). And at the same time Mahāyāna reaffirmed the ultimate reality of the true Self, the Absolute. The names used for the Absolute are Tathatā, Shūnyatā, Vijñaptimātratā, Dharmadhātu, etc. Asanga calls it pure Self (*shuddhātmā*), universal Self (*mahātmā*) and highest Self (*paramātmā*).[1]

Many Vedic schools of Indian philosophy have noticed the similarities between Mahāyāna Buddhism and Advaita Vedānta. Eminent Advaitins like Gauḍapāda, Shrīharṣa and Chitsukha have pointed out the similarities between Mahāyāna and Vedānta. Gauḍapāda approves of the doctrine of ajātivāda and the critique of causation in Shūnyavāda and the arguments of Vijñānavāda against realism.[2] Shrīharṣa says that the onslaught of the dialectic of Shūnyavāda and Advaita Vedānta is valid against all views and cannot be set aside.[3] Chitsuka admits the similarity of the Mādhyamika distinction between *samvṛti* and *paramārtha* with the Vedāntic distinction between *vyavahāra* and *paramārtha* and defends the former against the attacks of Kumārila Bhatta.[4] Even Kumārila, who is an arch-opponent of Buddhism, admits that anātmavāda is helpful for purification of mind and detachment. The theistic Vedāntins, Bhāskara, Rāmānuja, Madhva, etc., are unanimous in condemning the Advaitin as a crypto-Buddhist (prachchhanna-Bauddha) which shows that they admit the similarities between Mahāyāna and Advaita Vedānta.

The fact that Buddha carried on, according to his own realisation, the Upaniṣadic tradition of Absolutism and that Mahāyāna Buddhists developed it in the light of the teaching of their Founder, is undeniable. Can anyone say that Buddha who accepts the Absolutism of the Upaniṣads and Mahāyāna Buddhists who follow him and develop it are opposed to the Upaniṣadic tradition, because they reject the ultimate reality of the individual self, while the schools of Vaisheṣika and Nyāya which pay allegiance to the Vedas, but which have reduced the self to an eternal substance devoid of consciousness and bliss like a stone-slab have

1. Buddhāḥ shuddhātmalābhatvād gatā ātma-mahātmatām. Mahāyānasūtrālaṅkāra, IX, 23. anena Buddhānām anāsrave dhātau paramātmā vyavasthāpyate. *Ibid.*, pp. 37-8.
2. *Gauḍapāda-kārikā* IV, 5, 19, 22, 28, 72.
3. *Khanḍana-khanḍa-khādya*, p. 61.
4. *Tattva-pradīpikā*, pp. 42-3.

continued the Upaniṣadic tradition?

Thus we see that Buddha's teachings of pratītyasamutpāda, anātmavāda, *Nirvāṇa,* spiritual discipline and his silence on the *avyākṛta* reveal him as a great teacher of absolutism who carried on the tradition of the Upaniṣadic seers. We find these teachings scattered in the Suttapiṭaka. Hīnayāna schools of Theravāda, Sarvāstivāda (Vaibhāṣika) and Sautrāntika, due to an imperfect understanding of these teachings, forgot his absolutism and created a metaphysics of radical pluralism in the form of the theory of momentary elements in their Abhidharma treatises and commentaries thereon. They substituted the dogmatism of the eternalists by an equally strong dogmatism of momentary elements which culminates in nihilism. But even in their Abhidharma works absolutism of the Founder raises its head here and there. Buddha's teaching of *Nirvāṇa,* the unconditioned and Inexpressible Real beyond all categories of thought and his repeated advice to rise above all views and theories through moral and spiritual discipline was too strong to be missed even by Hīnayāna. These Abhidharma works are, what Mrs. Rhys Davids rightly calls, 'the verbal superstructures'[1], 'the monk-dressed utterances[2] and 'monkish gibberish, often put forth as the word of Buddha. You may find that genuine Śākya more in what the Piṭakas betray and have suffered to survive than in what they affirm as chief and fundamental.'[3] The contradictions in Hīnayāna philosophy were pointed out by Mahāyāna schools of Mādhyamika and early Vijñānavāda who correctly interpreted the absolutism of the Founder. The germs of all the important doctrines of Mahāyāna are scattered in the Piṭakas themselves, especially in the Suttapiṭaka, where there are many passages containing the spiritual absolutism of Buddha.

Buddha has repeatedly declared all phenomena as ultimately unreal (*shūnya*), as relative (*pratītyasamutpanna*), as finally false (*mṛṣā*). The world is accustomed to rely on duality (*dvaya-nishrita*), on existence and non-existence, on 'is' and 'is not', on eternalism and nihilism. But these, says Buddha, are the categories of thought and the Tathāgatha has risen above all duality and all categories

1. *A Manual of Buddhism,* Preface, ix.
2. *Śākya* or *Buddhist Origins,* p. 200.
3. *Ibid.*, pp. 5, 339.

of thought. *Nirvāṇa* is the only Real, the non-dual Absolute to be realised by immediate spiritual experience. The teaching of Dharma is only a means to realise the Real, to 'express' the Inexpressible, and finally it too has to be transcended. Buddha compares his teaching to a raft (*kullūpama*) which has to be left aside after crossing the stream and not to be carried on the shoulders as a burden.

CHAPTER TWO

Shūnyavāda or the Mādhyamika School

I. THE RISE OF MAHĀYĀNA

The seeds of Mahāyāna can be traced back to the second Buddhist Council held about a century after Buddha's *nirvāṇa.* The Mahāsaṅghikas, who branched off from Theravāda in this Council were the forerunners of Mahāyāna. The Mahāvastu which is the Vinaya of the Lokottaravādins belonging to the Mahāsaṅghikas; the Avadāna literature glorifying the Bodhisattva ideal; and the epics of Ashvaghoṣa represent a distinct transition towards Mahāyāna. The nine Mahāyāna-sūtras are held in great veneration by all schools of Mahāyāna. Of these Aṣṭasāhasrikā Prajñāpāramitā, Saddḥarma-puṇḍarīka and Samadhirāja Sūtras are the oldest and are prior to Nāgārjuna and even to Ashvaghoṣa. The main doctrines of Mādhyamika and Vijñānavāda were developing from the time of the Sūtras, but as a full-fledged system the Mādhyamika school was established first in the second century A.D. by Nāgārjuna and Āryadeva. The Mūla-Vijñānavāda or Yogāchāra school as a system was established in the fourth century A.D. by Maitreya, Asaṅga and Vasubandhu.

In Mahāyāna, Buddha is transformed into God or the Absolute. Devotion to Buddha is extolled. The Bodhisattva ideal is glorified. The Bodhisattva is he who attains perfect wisdom, ever dwells in it, and inspired by the love of all beings, ceaselessly works for their salvation. He differs his own nirvāṇa and is ready to suffer gladly so that he may liberate others. He is guided by the spirit of Buddha who said: 'Let all the sins and miseries of the world fall upon my shoulders so that all the beings may be liberated from them.'[1]

---

1. Kalikaluṣa-kṛtāni yāni loke mayi tāni patantu vimuchyatām hi lokaḥ.

We have said above that Mahāyāna arose as a logical necessity to remove the inner contradictions of Hīnayāna. The radical pluralistic realism of Hīnayāna is replaced in Mahāyāna by an equally radical absolutism which is the real teaching of Buddha. For Hīnayāna pratītyasamutpāda is real causation; for the Mādhyamika and the Mūla-Vijñanavāda it is relative and therefore ultimately unreal causation. For the former it is the causal law governing the emergence and annihilation of the momentary dharmas; for the latter it is the theory of relativity grounded in the Absolute. For the former the momentary is the efficient and the real; for the latter the momentary is the miserable and the unreal. For Hīnayāna Buddha's silence on the *avyākṛta* is the result of his denial of God, souls and matter, and his acceptance of the reality of momentary dharmas; for Mahāyāna schools of Mādhyamika and Mūla-Vijñānavāda it is the result of his absolutism which denies both eternalism and nihilism. For Hīnayāna anātmavāda is only pudgala-nairātmya or denial of self; for Mahāyāna it is also dharma-nairātmya or denial of momentary elements. For Hīnayāna *Nirvāṇa* is an eternal uncaused or asamskṛta *dharma;* for Mādhyamika and Mūla-Vijñānavāda it is the *dharmatā* of all dharmas (*dharmāṇām dharmatā*), the ground reality of all phenomena, the Absolute itself which is at once immanent in phenomena and transcendent to all phenomena and thought-constructions.

II. THE MĀHĀYĀNA SŪTRAS

The basic concepts of Shūnyavāda or the Mādhyamika school of Nāgārjuna which is one of the most important schools of Buddhism are found scattered in the Mahāyāna Sūtras, specially in the Prajñāpāramitā Sūtras. The destructive as well as the constructive side of the Mādhyamika dialectic is also found scattered in these Sūtras. The Mahāyāna Sūtras repeatedly declare all objects of thought to be mere appearance. Thought implies subject-object duality and is infected with relativity and contradiction. All objects of thought are *shūnya,* i.e., *svabhāva-shūnya* (devoid of self-existence) or *niḥsvabhāva* (without self-reality or inner essence); they are *pratītyasamutpanna* (dependent or relative). Not only the individual souls but all objects of thought without exception are appearance. Along with *pudgala-nairātmya, dharma-nairātmya* is also emphasised. There is no origination, no decay, no cessation, no change. The real is neither one nor many, neither permanent nor momentary, neither substance nor quality nor relation; it is free from all the constructions of thought-categories and can be realised in non-dual knowledge. In their zeal to deny reality to all objects of thought, the Mahāyāna Sūtras very often and repeatedly condemn them to be like dream, echo, reflection, image, illusion, mirage, magic, magical city of Gandharvas, hair-like objects seen floating in the space through defective vision, illusion of the double moon, illusory circle presented by a moving fire-brand and even like hare's horn, barren woman's son and sky-flower.[1] These similes may suggest that phenomena are utterly unreal, but the intention of the Sūtras is not to deny their empirical reality[2]; on the other hand they maintain that even an illusion is not baseless. The distinction between relative and absolute truth is emphasised. The Real is at once transcendent and immanent and is to be realised in immediate spiritual experience.[3] The importance of four dhyānas, three samadhis, six pāramitās and ten Bodhisattva-bhūmis as spiritual discipline is emphasised and these are explained in detail.

The *Saddharma-puṇḍarīka-Sūtra* says: He who knows that all empirical dharmas are shūnya or devoid of self-reality, knows the supreme wisdom of the Buddhas.[4] He who knows that all worldly objects are like illusion and dream, essenceless like a plantain trunk, only echoes of Reality, that there is neither bondage nor release, that all dharmas are essentially the same, that in fact difference does not exist, knows the truth and attains the immortal blissful Nirvāṇa.[5] As long as we are entangled in thought-categories we are like blind-born men completely in the dark; when we reach the point where finite thought confesses its limitation and indirectly points towards Reality our blindness is cured but our vision is still blurred; it is only when we embrace non-

---

1. For example, *Saddharma-puṇḍarīka*, pp. 142-3; *Aṣṭasāhasrikā*, pp. 25, 39-40, 196-200, 205, 279, 403-4; *Shatasāhasrikā*, pp. 119-20, 185, 262; *Laṅkāvatāra*, pp. 22, 51, 62, 84-5, 90, 105; *Samādhirāja*, pp. 27 and 29; *Lalitavistara*, pp. 176-81; *Suvarṇaprabhāsa*, pp. 31-4.
2. For example, *Aṣṭa*, pp. 23, 181, 236, 287; Lankā, pp. 146-7.
3. For example, *Saddharma*, pp. 29, 39, 116, 134; Aṣṭa, pp. 47, 290-1, 386-7; *Lankā*, pp. 142-3, 516, 190, 194.
4. *Saddharma*, p. 138.
5. *Ibid.*, pp. 142-3.

dual pure knowledge (*uttama agra bodhi*) we clearly see the Real and become one with it.[1]

The *Aṣṭasāhasrikā Prajñāpāramitā* says: There is no substance, no quality, no matter, no mental state, no soul, no element. Every object of thought without exception, from the lowest matter to the highest *nirvāṇa* (conceived as an object of thought) is an illusion or a dream.[2] There are two standpoints—the empirical and the absolute. The former deals with the categories of intellect (*koṭi*), with name and form (*nāma-rūpa*), with thought-construction (*vikalpa*), with dependence and relativity (*nimitta*), with appearances (*samvṛti* or *vyavahāra*); the latter transcends the former and deals with perfect knowledge (*prajñā pāramitā*), which is non-dual (*advaya*), independent (*animitta*) and the real, the Absolute (*paramārtha*).[3] But the Real is also immanent in the phenomenal world. There is no object in which the Real is not present.[4] To transcend the phenomenal, we have to take the help of the fully mature intellect itself, just as to have clean water we have to use a fully baked pot, because if we fetch water in an unbaked earthen pot the pot will became a lump of mud and the water will became muddy.[5] The *Shatasāhasrikā Prajñāpāramitā* also condemns all dharmas as illusory. They are neither eternal nor momentary, neither existent nor non-existent, neither *shūnya* nor *ashūnya*. They are mere names and forms and are therefore, *māyā*. And *māyā* has no nature of its own; it is neither real nor unreal.[6] Dependent origination is not real causation. That which is conditional and conventional has neither origination nor cessation; it is a mere name, a convention, a usage, a practical compromise.[7]

The *Laṅkāvatāra-Sūtra* tells us that thought gives us a world which is its own construction (*vikalpa*). It functions in subject-object duality (*dvaita*) and therefore cannot reveal the non-dual

1. *Ibid.*, pp. 134, 29, 39, 116.
2. *Aṣṭa*, p. 40, nirvāṇamapi māyopamam svapnopamam.
3. *Ibid.*, pp. 177, 191-2, 274, 356, 444.
4. na Subhūte! Tathatāvinirmukto'nyaḥ kashchid dharma upalabhyate.—*Ibid.*, p. 453.
5. *Ibid.*, pp. 287-8.
6. nāma-rūpameva māyā māyaiva nāma-rūpam—*Shatasāhasrikā*, p. 898; māyāyāḥ padam na vidyate.—*Ibid.*, p. 1209.
7. yachcha prajñaptidharmam tasya notpādo na nirodho'nyatra samjñā-saṅketa-mātreṇa vyavahṛiyate. *Ibid.*, p. 325.

(*advaya*) Real. This entire empirical world depends on the four categories of thought.[1] Just as elephants get stuck in deep mud, so do the worldly persons get entangled in thought-constructions, in language, in letters, words and names.[2] Reality is silence. From that night when Buddha became Enlightened up to that night when he attained *nirvāṇa,* not a single word was uttered by him. The teaching of Buddha is truly beyond language. He who teaches with words merely babbles for reality is beyond language and thought.[3] Yet thought points to the Real and ultimately merges in immediate experience; and it is the language itself which tries to express the Inexpressible through its imposed or symbolic use. The Laṅkāvatāra makes it clear that all objects of thought, when critically analysed are found to be without inner essence, without self-reality and therefore they are said to be relative and indescribable either as real or as unreal.[4] Yet their validity cannot be denied. They are not 'mere nothing'. Shūnyatā is relativity and not mere negation. It is far better to entertain, from the empirical standpoint, an idea of existence or affirmation of a substance, as big in magnitude as the Sumeru mountain than to take shūnyatā as a 'mere nothing'. One who understands shūnyatā as mere negation is a self-condemned nihilist.[5] Shūnyatā is also said to be the 'Middle Path' (*madhyamā pratipat*), because it avoids the two extremes of eternalism and nihilism, existence and non-existence, purity and impurity, etc. But, as the *Samadhirāja-Sūtra* says, it transcends the extremes as well as the middle; it is not the 'middle view' but a denial of all views.[6] Shūnyatā is the non-dual blissful Nirvāṇa where all plurality and suffering cease.

The spiritual discipline by which the intellect may be trans-

1. Chātuṣkoṭikam cha Mahāmate! lokavyavahāraḥ.—*Laṅkāvatāra,* p. 88.
2. *Ibid.*, p. 113.
3. avachanam Buddhavachanaṃ . . . . yo' kṣarapatitam dharmam deshayati sa pralapati nirakṣaratvād dharmasya. *Ibid.*, pp. 142-3, 194.
4. buddhyā vivichyamānānām svabhāvo nāvadhāryate I tasmādanabhilapyāste niḥsvabhāvāshcha deshitāḥ II *Ibid.*, p. 116.
5. varam khalu sumerumātrā pudgaladṛṣṭiḥ na tu nāstyastitvābhimānikasya shūnyatādṛṣṭiḥ . . . (sa) hi vaināshiko bhavati. *Ibid.*, p. 146.
6. tasmādubhe anta vivarjayitvā madhye'pi sthānam na karoti paṇḍitaḥ II *Samadhirāja,* p. 30.

formed into non-dual spiritual experience consists of four meditations (*dhyāna*), four meditative joys (*Brahma-vihāra*), three higher meditations or deep concentrations (*samādhi*), six excellences (*pāramitā*) and ten stages of spiritual advancement (*bhūmi*). In the first *dhyāna,* there is working of intellect (*savitarka, savichāra*) and there is pleasure (*prīti, sukha*). In the second, intellect is in the process of giving place to intuitional vision (*avitarka, avichāra*) and pleasure to higher happiness (*samādhijaprīti–sukha, ātma-samprasāda*). In the third, intellect ceases (*avichāra*) and pleasure ends (*niṣprītika*) and there is only higher happiness (*sukhavihāra*). In the fourth, intellect becomes one with immediate experience, pain and pleasure are transcended (*aduḥkhāsukha*) and this leads to unique bliss (*vihāra*).[1] The four Brahma–vihāras are—*maitrī* (love), *karuṇā* (compassion, grace), *muditā* (meditative higher happiness) and *upekṣā* (non-dual spiritual insight). The three *samādhis* are: (1) *shūnyatā samādhi* in which the phenomenal is realised as *svabhava-shūnya* or devoid of self-reality and the Absolute is realised as *prapañcha-shūnya* or devoid of plurality; (2) *ānimitta samādhi* in which the real cause of everything is known, the real is known as immanent in the phenomena; (3) *apraṇihita samādhi* in which the meditator directly embraces the Real through immediate spiritual experience.[2] The six *pāramitā* (excellences or perfections) are—*dāna* (charity), *shīla* (moral virtues), *kṣānti* (forbearance), *vīrya* (spiritual strength), *dhyāna* (meditation) and *prajñā* (non-dual spiritual experience). The ten stages (*bhūmi*) of Bodhisattvahood are—*pramuditā, vimalā, prabhākarī, archiṣmatī, sudurjayā, abhimukhī, dūraṅgamā, achalā, sādhumatī* and *dharmameghā.* In the first *bhūmi,* a Bodhisattva, realising the limitations of intellect, begins with great pleasure, his quest for true knowledge and gradually going through the eight intermediary stages reaches ultimately the tenth *bhūmi,* where he becomes one with the Real, the Buddha or the Absolute and like an heir-apparent is consecrated with 'Pure Non-dual Knowledge.'[3] He then defers his *Nirvāṇa* in order to liberate others.

---

1. *Shatasāhasrikā,* p. 1443; *Lalitavistara,* pp. 129 and 343.
2. *Shata,* pp. 1439-40.
3. *Dashabhūmika,* pp. 25-86.

III. THE MEANING OF SHŪNYA OR SHŪNYATĀ

The basic text of Shūnyavāda is Nāgārjuna's epoch-making work *Mādhyamika-kārikā,* which is commented upon by Chandrakīrti in his monumental commentary entitled *Prasannapadā Vṛtti.* The ideas of the *Mahāyāna-sūtras,* especially the doctrine of shūnyatā found in the *Prajñāpāramitā-sūtras,* were systematised and developed by Nāgārjuna and elaborately explained by his gifted commentator Chandrakīrti, who correctly interpreted Buddha's teaching as absolutism. The literal meaning of the word *shūnya* is void or negation or 'nothing'. But it is used in this system in an entirely different philosophical sense. Forgetting this fact, the Vedic and the Jaina schools of Indian philosophy have wrongly condemned Shūnyavāda as nihilism. The Mādhyamikas strongly protest against this and explain that their philosophy is not nihilism, but absolutism.

Nāgārjuna identifies shūnyatā with pratītyasamutpāda and says that it is phenomenal existence governed by causes and conditions (*upādāya prajñaptiḥ*) and it is also *madhyamā pratipat* or the 'middle path.'[1] Nāgārjuna has clearly and emphatically explained that *pratītya-samutpāda* is only dependent or relative causation and therefore no real causation. That which arises depending on causes and conditions (*pratitya yat samutpannam*) does not in fact arise (*notpannam paramārthataḥ*). Viewed from the empirical standpoint of relational thought, *pratītyasamutpāda* is the wheel of dependent origination beginning with *avidyā,* it is the cycle of birth-and-death (*saṁsāra*), it is phenomenal existence governed by causes and conditions (*pratītya*), it is the empirical world of suffering due to ignorance, volition, desire and attachment (*upādāya*). And this very *pratītyasamutpāda,* viewed from the absolute standpoint of non-dual spiritual insight (*prajñā*), as totally freed from the dependence on causes and conditions (*apratītya*), freed from *avidyā, karma,* desire and attachment (*anupādāya*) is *Nirvāṇa* itself which is pure bliss (*Shiva*) and is free from any trace of plurality and suffering (*prapañchopashama*).[2] Hence, viewed from the empirical

1. yaḥ pratītyasamutpādaḥ shūnyatām tām prachakṣmahe | sā prajñaptirupādāya pratipat saiva madhyamā || *Mādhyamika–kārikā,* XXIV, 18.
2. yaḥ pratītyasamutpādam prapañchopashamam shivam. *Ibid.,* Mangalācharaṇa; and XXV, 9, 19, 20. ya ājavañjavībhāva upādāya pratītya vā | so'pratītyānupādāya nirvāṇam upadishyate || XXV, 9.

standpoint of thought, of causation and mutual dependence, *shūnya* means *svabhāva-shūnya* or *niḥsvabhāva*, i.e., devoid of self-reality, devoid of independent existence, without any inner essence, conditional, relative; and viewed from the transcendental standpoint of spiritual insight (*prajñā*), *shūnya* means *prapañcha-shūnya* or devoid of plurality and thought-determinations, the non-dual Absolute (*Nirvāṇa*) which is transcendent to all the four categories of thought (*chatuṣkoṭi-vinirmukta tattva*). Shūnya in this sense is the symbol of fullness and round perfection (*pūrṇa*). *Niḥsvabhāva* in this sense means the Absolute, the indeterminate. Thus *shūnya* is used in a double sense. It means relativity as well as reality, *saṁsāra* as well as *Nirvāṇa*, phenomena as well as the Absolute. That which is phenomenal, that which is conditional and dependent and therefore relative cannot be called ultimately real, even as borrowed wealth cannot be called real capital. All appearances (*dharmas*) being relative and dependent (*pratītyasamutpanna*) have no real origination (*paramārthato' nutpanna*) and are therefore devoid of ultimate reality (*svabhāva-shūnya, niḥsvabhāva, anātma*). But they are not absolutely unreal (*asat*). They are indescribable (*avāchya, anabhilāpya*) either as real or as unreal. The Real is the Absolute which is non-dual and transcendent to all plurality, suffering and thought-determinations (*prapañcha-shūnya, niṣprapañcha, chatuṣkoṭi-vinirmukta, advaya tattva*). Shūnya therefore does not mean 'void', it means, on the other hand, 'devoid', so far as appearances are concerned, 'of self-reality', and so far as Reality is concerned 'of plurality and determinations'. *Shūnyatā* literally means 'the attribute or the essence of *shūnya*', but both these terms, *shūnya* and *shūnyatā* are freely used as synonyms. *Shūnya* or *shūnyatā* is called *madhyamā pratipat* or the middle path discovered by Buddha and the Shūnyavādin calls himself Mādhyamika or the follower of the middle path, which avoids the two extremes of existence and non-existence, eternalism and nihilism, purity and impurity, one and many, etc. But the middle path is not a middle view between the two extreme views. The Mādhyamika makes it clear that the wise person who denies the two extremes does not stop at the middle, but transcends the middle also.[1] The middle is a denial of the two primary categories

1. *Samadhirāja*, p. 30.

of *sat* and *asat,* which denial implies the denial of the two secondary categories of 'both' and 'neither'. The middle path, therefore, is a denial of all the four categories (*koṭi*) of thought. It is a denial of all views (*dṛṣṭi-shūnyatā*) and is itself not a view. Nāgārjuna warns us that those who mistake *madhyamā-pratipat* or shūnyatā as a category or a view of thought (*dṛṣṭi*) are incorregible and destined to doom.[1] The Mādhyamika is as opposed to nihilism (*nāstitva-dṛṣṭi* or *uchchheda-dṛṣṭi*) as he is to eternalism (*shāshvata-dṛṣṭi*). Shūnyatā is *Nirvāṇa,* the transcendent Real. But the Real is also immanent in phenomena and hence *shūnyatā* is the *dharmatā* (the immanent reality) of the *dharmas* or phenomena and is also called Dharmadhātu. *Shūnyatā* is also identified with Buddha, the Tathāgata, the *Ens perfectissimum,* the Absolute which is 'always the same'. It is *Bhūtakoṭi* (Reality) which is Tathatā (Always the Same).

Thus we see that shūnya or shūnyatā is *pratītyasamutpāda, upādāya prajñaptiḥ, madhyamā pratipat, saṁsāra* and *nirvāṇa*; and is identified with the Real which is *prapañchopashama, shiva, niḥsvabhāva, bhūtakoṭi, paramārtha, tathatā, dharmatā, dharma-dhātu* and *Tathāgata.*[2]

IV. THE MĀDHYAMIKA DIALECTIC

The Mādhyamika dialectic is a critique of all speculative metaphysics. Each metaphysical system claims to offer a complete and a true picture of reality. It wants to drag down the Real into the cobweb of theories which it spins around it. Each system has its generating insight in, what has been called in Buddhism and Vedānta, 'Transcendental Illusion' (*avidyā)* which supplies it with a basic unconscious bias for a particular concept which it universalises and accepts as a norm for evaluating all things and theories. This universalised concept which has no direct bearing on sensible facts, is called *dṛṣṭi* or *anta* by the Mādhyamika, *koṭi* by Vedānta, and 'Idea of Reason' by Kant. These concepts give rise to warring schools of speculative metaphysics and their conflicts are interminable as they cannot be settled by an appeal to sense-experience. Errors of common-sense can be corrected by scientific knowledge and conflicting hypotheses in science can be

---

1. *Ibid.*, XIII, 8; XXIV, 11.
2. *Laṅkāvatāra,* p. 325; Also, tathatā bhūtakoṭishcha nirvāṇam paramārthatā I dharmadhātushcha paryāyāḥ shūnyatāyāḥ samāsataḥ II

verified or rejected by an appeal to sensible facts. When the categories of understanding transform the scattered raw-material supplied by the senses into empirical knowledge, it is objectively valid. Scientific knowledge belongs to this sphere. But when reason tries to enter the suprasensible sphere and pretends to give true knowledge of this reality, it miserably fails and gives us only 'Ideas of Reason'. Philosophic knowledge belongs to this sphere of the suprasensible. Disputes in philosophy can neither be proved nor disproved by any appeal to sense-experience. These disputes result in interminable conflicts. Thought has to work within subject-object duality and is necessarily relational and therefore is beset with inherent contradictions. Thought works with its concepts and categories, but the Transcendent Real cannot be bound within them. All attempts of thought to categorise the Supreme, to describe the Indescribable, to determine the Indeterminate, to bind the Boundless, to catch the Transcendent within the network of its concepts and categories are doomed to fail. The Real is transcendent to thought and can be realised by non-dual spiritual experience. All views and theories are merely thought-constructions. They are ascriptions which thought flings on the Real and are therefore bound to be false. Dialectic is criticism from a higher level of self-consciousness which exposes the pretensions of thought to reveal the Real and shows that thought, instead of revealing the Real, distorts and falsifies it.

The Mādhyamika criticises all views and theories. He turns them inside out and shows their hollowness. He does not advocate any view or theory of his own; he has no thesis of his own to prove. Kant in his 'Antinomies of Reason' declares them insoluble by reason, because the arguments to prove the thesis as well as the antithesis are of equal strength and we are not in a position to take any decision in favour either of thesis or of antithesis. For him, a thesis is rejected because it is counter-balanced by an anti-thesis. For the Mādhyamika, on the other hand, a thesis is rejected because it is self-contradictory and not because it is counter-balanced by an anti-thesis. Every thesis or anti-thesis is self-convicted because of its inherent contradictions. Also, rejection of a thesis does not logically entail acceptance of its anti-thesis or of any other thesis. According to him, it is not necessary that each participant to a philosophic dispute must have a view of his own; what is necessary is that both the participants, during discussion, must accept common rules of logic. The Mādhyamika during discussion, provisionally accepts the logic of the opponent, and by using *reductio ad absurdum* arguments (*prasaṅgāpādana*) he reveals the inner contradictions in the thesis of the opponent and shows its absurdity with the help of the logic and with rules and procedure which the opponent himself accepts as valid. The logical function of the dialectic is, therefore, purely negative, analytic and critical. But the Mādhyamika is not a self-condemned nihilist whose aim is to destroy everything and who relishes in shouting that he does not exist. He is not even a positivist who pins his faith to sense-experience and condemns metaphysics as sheer nonsense. He is not an agnostic or even a sceptic because for him the Real is not unknowable and he has the certitude of Buddha's spiritual experience. He is a spiritual absolutist who accepts the Absolute, the non-dual blissful Real, transcendent to sense, thought and speech and realisable by non-conceptual spiritual insight for which a rigorous spiritual discipline, including morality and *yoga,* is prescribed. His denial of speculative metaphysics shows that the Real is inaccessible to thought, but realisable by non-dual spiritual experience (*prajñā* or *bodhi*).

Though the logical function of the dialectic is purely negative and destructive, yet it reveals its positive side also. The Mādhyamika accepts that significant negation presupposes affirmation and relativity itself is related to the Absolute and that, therefore, the denial of relative phenomena can be meaningful only with reference to the acceptance of an absolute reality transcendent to thought. The dialectic necessarily presupposes the distinction between the empirical and the transcendent truth and reality. This distinction, epistemically, is between two aspects of truth and, ontologically, between two levels of reality. Nāgārjuna says that Buddha has preached his Dharma by accepting two truths, empirical (*samvṛti* or 'covering') and absolute (*paramārtha*) and those who do not understand this distinction cannot understand the reality of the deep teachings of Buddha.[1] But the dialectic also makes it clear

1. dve satye samupāshritya Buddhānām dharma-deshanā I
lokasamvṛti satyam cha satyam cha paramārthataḥ II
ye'nayor na vijānanti vibhāgam satyayor dvayoḥ I
te tattvam na vijānanti gambhīram Buddha-shāsane II
—*Mādhyamika-kārikā,* XXIV, 8-9.

that this distinction is made by relational thought and is therefore valid only empirically and not finally. There are not *two* different truths or *two* different sets of reality. The absolute truth is the only truth, while empirical 'truth' is 'truth so-called'; in fact it is falsity mistaken as 'truth' as long as the non-dual Real is not realised. But its authority in the phenomenal world which is the sphere of thought is unquestionable, for thought cannot condemn itself from its own standpoint.

Samvṛti literally means 'covering'. It 'covers' the Real and also makes it appear as something else. It is *avidyā* or *ajñāna* with its two aspects of 'covering' and 'projection'[1]. Chandrakīrti says that *samvṛti* is *ajñāna* which thoroughly veils the real;[2] it is *moha* (delusion) which covers the Real and makes the false appear as true[3]. *Samvṛti* is relative causation[4]. It is a symbolic device (*saṅketa*) or a practical reality (*lokavyavahāra*)[5]. Chandrakīrti divides *samvṛti* into *loka-samvṛti* and *mithyā-samvṛti*;[6] the former corresponds with vyavahāra and the latter with *pratibhāsa* in Vedānta. *Samvṛti* is Ignorance or Illusion, which is non-apprehension as well as misapprehension of the Real.[7] *Samvṛti* works with thought-constructions and hence thought itself is called *samvṛti* (*buddhiḥ samvṛtiruchyate—Bodhicharyāvatāra,* IX, 2). The *a priori* thought-categories are of the nature of transcendental Ignorance.[8] The importance of *samvṛti* lies in its being the 'means' (*upāya*) to realise the 'end' (*upeya*) of *Nirvāṇa.*[9] As a vessel is needed for fetching water so *samvṛti* is necessary for understanding the teachings of *Nirvāṇa* and for following spiritual discipline to realise the end.[10]

The empirical 'truth' (*samvṛti*) guarantees the empirical valid-

1. abhūtam khyāpayatyartham bhūtamāvṛtya vartate.—Quotated in *Bodhicharyāvatāra-panjikā,* p. 352.
2. samantād āvarąṇam samvṛtir ajñānam. *Mādhyamika Kārikā Vṛtti,* p. 492.
3. mohaḥ svabhāvāvaraṇāddhi samvṛtiḥ satyam tayā khyāti yadeva kṛtrimam. *Madhyamakāvatāra,* VI, 29.
4. *Mādhyamika Kārikā Vṛtti,* p. 492.
5. *Ibid.*
6. *Madhyamakāvatāra,* VI, 25.
7. Tattvāpratipattiḥ mithyāpratipattirajñānam avidyeti. Quoted in *Bodhicharyāvatāra-pañjikā,* p. 352.
8. Vikalpaḥ svayamevāyam avidyārūpatām gataḥ. *Ibid.,* p. 366.
9. upāyabhūtam vyavahārasatyam upeyabhūtam paramārtha-satyam *Madhyamakāvatāra,* VI, 80.
10. nirvāṇādhigamopāyatvād avashyameva samvṛtirabhyupeyā bhājanamiva salilārthineti—Mādhyamika Kārikā Vṛtti, p. 482.

ity of the phenomenal world and prevents it on the level of thought from collapsing into an empty void or absolute unreality. Similarly, the transcendent Absolute is the only Reality and the phenomenal world is mistaken as real by thought till the realisation of the Absolute by non-dual *prajñā* or *bodhi.* Hence, for the Mādhyamika, there is no distinction, ultimately, between the world of phenomena (*samsāra*) and the Absolute (*Nirvāṇa*).[1] *Pratītyasamutpada* viewed from the dependent and deluding standpoint of thought is the wheel of relative causation, the cycle of birth-and-death; but the same, realised by spiritual insight is the non-dual blissful *Nirvāṇa* itself.[2] It is the Real itself which appears. Phenomena and the Absolute are not *two* realities set apart from each other; the Absolute is the *reality* of phenomena. The dialectic which reveals the Absolute as transcendent to thought, at the same time, reveals it also as immanent in phenomena, as their inner reality or *dharmatā.* Dialectic is the critical awareness of thought at a higher level of self-consciousness, which is analytical and reflective of its own nature as essentially relational, determinate, chained to subject-object duality and beset with inherent self-contradictions. It is also the awareness by thought of its limitation and its inability to grasp the Real, which awareness logically implies the reality of a higher non-dual spiritual knowledge or immediate experience which alone can realise the transcendent and blissful Absolute by being one with it. The positive side of the dialectic consists is emphasising the immanence of the Real in phenomena; the Absolute itself is the immanent inner reality of phenomena. Though the dialectic shatters the ultimate reality of phenomena, it does not condemn them as absolutely unreal or as mere 'nothing'. They are declared as relative, dependent, 'neither real nor unreal' appearances and their empirical validity is not questioned. The dialectic as self-conscious thought does not and cannot claim to reveal the Real, yet nothing can prevent it from realising its own limitation and from pointing to the Real as the undeniable transcendent and immanent ground of all phenomena and to the non-dual spiritual insight in which it culminates and which is also the fruition of theoretical, practical and religious consciousness. The dialectic is not a speculative

1. *Ibid.*, XXV, 19.
2. *Ibid.*, opening verse 2; XXV, 9.

jugglery. It has a spiritual purpose which shows that the Real is transcendent to thought and is to be realised by non-dual spiritual insight which is identical with the blissful Absolute or *Nirvāṇa.* If this purpose is missed, the Mādhyamika dialectic would be misunderstood as intellectual acrobatics or at best as the logic of abstract identity.

It has been shown above that dialectic is a critique of thought itself. Thought works with its categories (*dṛṣṭi, vikalpa*) but the Real cannot be categorised. As there are four categories of thought, four and only four views are possible on any subject. The first two categories are primary and the other two are secondary. The first category (*sat*) gives us the view of Being, affirmation, permanence, substance, *identity*. The second category (*asat*) gives us the view of Non-Being, negation, change, modes, *difference.* The third category (*sadasat* or *ubhaya*) affirms both the first and the second and gives us the view either of syncretism or of synthesis of both *identity and difference.* The fourth category (*anubhaya*) denies both the first and the second and gives us the view of *neither identity nor difference* which is the view of scepticism and agnosticism, of doubt and despair, of extreme non-committal (sandehavāda, ajñānavāda and ajñeyavāda). This category should not be confused with the 'inexpressibility' (*anirvachanīyatā*) of the dialectic, though both are expressed in the same verbal form of 'neither real nor unreal'. The fourth category leads to doubt, despair, ignorance and unreflectively denies every view just for the sake of denial, while the dialectic questions the ability of thought to grasp the Real and reveals the inherent contradictions in every view of thought from a higher critical level of self-consciousness and declares it as an appearance, not reality. Nāgārjuna and Chandrakīrti take Sāṅkhya as the representative of the first category, early Buddhism as an example of the second, Jainism as an advocate of the third and Chārvāka and the ajñānavāda of Sañjaya Velaṭṭhiputta (or Belaṭṭhaputta)[1] as examples of the fourth. These four categories serve as the schema to classify the various systems of philosophy and the dialectic reveals their contradictory nature. Like Kant, the Mādhyamika believes that the categories of thought are empirically real and transcendentally ideal. The conflict in thought is interminable and can be got rid of only by rising to a higher plane of non-dual immediate spiritual experience.

1. *Dīgha Nikāya,* 2.

V. APPLICATION OF THE DIALECTIC

(1) THE CRITIQUE OF CAUSATION

Dialectic is criticism of thought at a higher reflective level of self-consciousness. Its application, therefore, is unrestricted within phenomena in the sense that it applies to all speculative views or theories or systems woven by thought to catch the Real within their network. Dialectic is the critique of all philosophy. Causality has been the central problem of philosophy. All the systems which believe in the efficiency of thought believe in real causation. The central teaching of Buddha is *Pratītyasamutpāda* or the Wheel of Dependent Causation. The Hīnayāna schools interpreted it as real causation and developed the theory of momentariness and a philosophy of radical pluralism based on it. The Mādhyamika enters into a detailed and vehement criticism of this radical pluralism and correctly interprets *Pratītyasamutpāda* as relative, and therefore ultimately unreal, causation and revives Buddha's absolutism. The Mādhyamika dialectic, therefore, begins with the critique of causation.

Nāgārjuna opens his great work, *Mūla-Madhyamaka-kārikā,* by boldly proclaiming the doctrine of No-origination (*ajātivāda*). In the very first benedictory verse he gives his famous eight 'negations' and in the second salutes Buddha, 'the greatest of all teachers who has taught *Pratītyasamutpāda*', which is interpreted by the Mādhyamika as *shūnyata.* The eight 'negations' are: no origination, no cessation; no permanence, no momentariness; no identity, no difference; no bondage, no liberation. This means that these eight characteristics belong only to phenomena and are denied to Noumenon. In the second verse two significant adjectives are used for Pratītyasamutpāda, of which one is negative and the other positive. The negative adjective is *prapañchopashamam* or cessation of *prapañcha.* The word *prapañcha* means the empirical existence of plurality, thought-categories and suffering; it is the beginningless cycle of *samsāra*—the wheel of birth-and-death, which is symbolically expressed by the word *duḥkha* (suffering) and which is due to beginningless *avidyā* the transcendental illusion which covers the Real and projects through its innate thought-forms the world of phenomena. *Pratītyasamutpāda* is this wheel of causation or suffering. But as this causation is relative and ultimately unreal, *Pratītyasamutpāda* itself, viewed without causation and attachment, is also the cessation of this suffering or *prapañcha.* It is the Absolute or *Nirvāṇa* itself. Lest this non-dual Absolute be mistaken only as a negative state free from suffering, Nāgārjuna is cautious enough to add the second positive adjective immediately after the negative one. This positive adjective is '*shivam*' which means pure bliss. So the Absolute or *Nirvāṇa* is not only the cessation of all suffering, but is also pure, unalloyed, limitless bliss[1]. It may be noted here that the Upaniṣads repeatedly declare Brahma or *Ātmā* to be *Prapañchopashamam* and *Shivam,* to be shāntam, shivam and advaitam.[2]

After the benedictory verses, Nāgārjuna begins his work with a devastating criticism of causality. The very first verse of the *Kārikā* declares: Never and nowhere can anything have an origination, either out of itself or out of something else or out of both or out of neither (i.e., out of sheer chance).[3] The Absolute can have no origination because it is always and everywhere, transcendent to origination, decay and destruction. The phenomenal world too can have no real origination for, being the appearance of the Real, it is non-different from it. Causation operates only within phenomena which are mutually dependent and casually related. Its empirical validity is guaranteed, but ultimately, it is an appearance, not reality.

On the problem of causation, as on any other problem of thought, only four views are possible. The relation between cause and effect may be conceived as that of identity or of difference or of both or of neither.

The first view advocates identity between cause and effect. The effect is taken as the self-expression of the cause. The effect is implicitly contained in the cause (sat-karyavāda). This is the theory of self-becoming or self-production (*svataḥ utpāda*). The effect is not a new creation. The cause continues in and is identical with the effect. There is substantial identity between the two. The effect is a real transformation or modification (*pariṇāma*) of the cause. This view

1. anirodham-anutpādam-anuchchhedam-ashāshvatam I
anekārtham-anānārtham-anāgamam-anirgamam II
yaḥ pratītyasamutpādam prapañchopashamam shivam I
deshayāmāsa sambuddhas tam vande vadatām varam II

—*Mādhyamika-kārika,* opening verses.

2. For example, Māndūkya, 7; Taittarīya, II, 1; Bṛhadāraṇyaka, III-9-28, IV-3-23.
3. na svato nāpi parato na dvābhyām nāpyahetutaḥ I utpannā jātu vidyante bhāvāḥ kvachana kechana II M.K., I, 1

is advocated by Sāṅkhya, older Vedānta and the later schools of theistic Vedānta. The Mādhyamika criticises this view by saying that identity militates against causation. Pure identity is impossible; without difference it cannot even be expressed. If the effect is contained in the cause, it is already an existent fact and its further production is useless. There is no point in unnecessary reduplication (*utpāda-vaiyarthya*). Besides, there will be no end to this useless process of self-duplication (*anavastha-doṣa*). Moreover, creation should be simultaneous and not successive, for it would be logical for the cause to manifest at once everything contained in it in order to save the trouble of infinite duplication. Again, there should be no novelty and variety in this universe, because the cause would go on duplicating itself *ad nauseum* without giving rise to the variety of effects. Further, if the distinction between cause and effect is denied, there would be no causation; and if the distinction between the two is maintained, there would be no self-causation. The advocate of self-causation replies that he denies only the substantial difference between cause and effect and not the modal difference between the states of the same substance. But even this admission that cause and effect are identical as substance and different as modes does not solve the difficulty, for, it gives up the theory of pure identity. Again, his reply that the effect is only potentially contained in the cause and that when it is actualised, its manifestation (*abhivyakti*) is certainly new, does not remove the difficulty. In this case, the manifestation itself would be real causation and the cause being treated as self-contained nothing should prevent it from actualising its potentiality at once. And then, such creation should be simultaneous and not successive. Moreover, the cause and the effect cannot be identical regarding the manifest form, otherwise clay would serve the same purpose as a pot does.

The second view advocates difference between cause and effect. The effect is not implicitly present in the cause (*asat-kāryavāda*). It is a new creation and its existence begins with its production (*ārambhavāda*). Causation is emergent, not continuous. The effect is produced not out of itself but out of the cause which is different from it (*parataḥ utpāda*). This view is advocated by Nyāya-Vaisheṣika and in its extreme form by early Buddhism. The Mādhyamika criticises this view by showing that pure difference, like pure identity, is impossible. Without identity, it cannot even be expressed. There can be no negation without affirmation. If the cause and the effect are totally different, then they are not relevant to each other. Then, nothing would produce anything or anything would produce everything (*sarvasambhava-prasanga*). The cause would always be an 'other' to the effect. Then, light should produce darkness, water should change into curd, and sand, when crushed, should yield oil, as 'otherness' is common to both cause and non-cause. If it is replied that the cause is not one, but a series of several factors (*pratyaya*) which cooperate in producing an effect, the difficulties would be increased. What turns these several disconnected factors into a cause or causes? What accounts for their cooperation? If some other factor is brought in to explain this coordination, it would lead to the fallacy of infinite regress (*anavasthā-doṣa*). Hence, either difference or causation is to be given up.

The third view combines the above two views by insisting on identity as well as difference between cause and effect. Causation is continuous as well as emergent (*svataḥ parataḥ utpāda*). The combination may be only a syncretism, as in Jainism, if both identity and difference are separately and equally emphasised. Or, it may be a synthesis, as, later on, in Rāmānuja, if identity and difference are fused into one with substantial emphasis on identity, difference being treated as a mode or attribute of identity. The former combination represents the view of identity-and-difference, the latter that of identity-in-difference. The Mādhyamika criticises this view by showing that identity and difference, being opposed to each other, cannot be put together or synthesised. If the cause and the effect are neither identical nor different, how can they be both? This view contains the contradictions found in both the views which it tries to combine. The other alternative of identity-in-difference, though valid for thought, cannot be taken to be ultimate. If identity and difference are treated as contradictories, their synthesis is out of question; and even if they are taken as contraries, their synthesis cannot be real, for, one of them would be treated as principal and the other dependent and the dependent, in the last analysis, would be found to be dispensible and would melt into the other. This view, then, would reduce itself either to the first or to the second.

The fourth view believes that things are produced by sheer chance (*ahetutaḥ utpāda*) and there is no invariable relation between cause and effect; there is mere succession but no causation (*svabhāva-vāda*). This is the view of the materialist Chārvāka, of the sceptics, who are extreme empiricists and of the ajñānavādins like Sañjaya mentioned in the Dīgha Nikāya (2). The Mādhyamika shows that this view degenerates into self-condemned nihilism.

Thus the Mādhyamika finds all views of causation inconsistent and self-contradictory. He, therefore, concludes that causation is an appearance, not reality.[1] It is valid within the empirical world, but cannot be extended to the Absolute.

(2) CRITICISM OF SOME OTHER CATEGORIES

Like the category of causality, every category of thought is found to be self-contradictory when analysed by dialectic. Every object of thought, every phenomenon is relative, dependent and therefore only an appearance, not reality. Origination and cessation, permanence and change, motion and rest, substance and quality, time and space, identity and difference, agent and action, mind and matter, terms and relations, self and the mental states, bondage and liberation, all these are thought-constructs which melt into appearances when their inner contradictions are exposed by the heat of the dialectic. Dependence and relativity are marks of the empirical which is 'neither real nor unreal'.

Before the mighty strokes of the destructive dialectic of Nāgārjuna and Chandrakīrti, the entire structure of phenomena crumbles down like a house of cards or a palace on sand; though its empirical validity is admitted. Ultimately, all objects of thought turn out to be thought-constructions foisted on the Real by *avidyā* or transcendental illusion; they are mutually dependent, relational and, therefore, false in the sense of 'neither real nor unreal'.

Motion and rest are mutually dependent and so ultimately are unreal. We cannot travel a path which has already been travelled, nor can we travel a path which is not yet travelled. And a path which has neither been travelled nor yet to be travelled is also not being travelled. The mover does not move; the non-mover of course does not move. What is that third, then, which is neither a mover nor a non-mover, which can move? Hence motion, mover and destination are all unreal.[2] Similarly, the seer, the seen and the sight are also unreal.[3]

1. *Mādhyamika Kārika,* I, 1-14 (with Chandrakīrti's Vṛtti)
2. *Ibid.*, Chapter II
3. *Ibid.*, Chapter III.

The five skandhas are also unreal. For example, matter (*rūpa*) does not exist. If it exists it has no cause because it already exists, and if it does not exist then too it has no cause, as it is a non-entity like a hare's horn; and uncaused matter is impossible. Similarly, feeling (*vedanā*), conception (*samjñā*), forces (*samskāra*) and individual consciousness (*vijñāna*) are all unreal.[1] The elements of earth, water, fire and air, and space are also unreal.[2]

We know only the attributes or qualities, we do not know the substance. Without attributes we cannot perceive a substance and without a substance attributes cannot exist. Substance and attributes are neither the same nor different. Both are relative and so unreal.[3]

The Mādhyamika refutes the doctrine of momentary elements of Hīnayāna. It is a false and unwarranted superstructure built on Buddha's teaching. It is wrong to interpret *Pratītyasamutpada* as the temporal sequence of origin and cessation of momentary elements. Causation is relative and not real. This doctrine of universal momentariness collapses into nihilism. Buddha was even more opposed to it than he was to the opposite view of eternalism. Origination, duration and cessation can characterise a compositive substance, neither singly nor jointly. The existent needs no origination and the non-existent cannot originate. If there is no origination, how can there be duration and cessation?[4] These characteristics apply to a thing neither successively nor simultaneously. If these are taken to apply to a thing successively (*kramashaḥ*), we shall have a thing which has either origination only or duration only or cessation only, without the other two. And if these are taken to apply to a thing simultaneously (*yugapat*), it would be absurd, for these mutually opposed characteristics cannot belong to a thing at the same time.[5] Again, origination also, being a thing, should be subject to origination, duration and cessation and this would lead to the fallacy of infinite regress[6]. There can, therefore, be no momentary entities flashing into

1. *Ibid.*, Ch. IV.
2. *Ibid.*, Ch. V.
3. *Ibid.*, Ch. VII.
4. *Ibid.*
5. utpāda-sthiti-bhaṅgānām yugapannāsti sambhavaḥ I kramashaḥ sambhavo nāsti sambhavo vidyate kutaḥ? II *Chatuḥshataka*, 361; Also *Mādhyamika Kārikā*, VII, 2.
6. *Mādhyamika Kārikā*, VII, 3, and vṛtti on it.

existence for a moment and then ceasing to exist. Neither the momentary nor the permanent can be causally efficient. Causation is relative and this alone can vindicate the empirical validity of the world. To imagine permanent entities or momentary elements as constituting the essence of this world is to make it eternal or to reduce it to zero and in either case we have a flagrant contradiction of experience.

Buddha said that the universe is beginningless and endless. And it is an accepted canon of logic, urges Nāgārjuna, that if a thing does not exist in the beginning and in the end, it cannot exist in the middle also[1]. Hence, beginning, middle and end; birth, duration and death are all unreal.

Change too is unreal. If the changeless does not exist, then what is it that changes? And if a thing is changeless, how can it change?[2] If the Real does not exist, what is that which appears? And if it is Real, how can it be an appearance? Again, if action is real, it will be eternal and actionless. Then all empirical life will collapse. Action, agent and result are all unreal.[3] The individual self is neither identical with nor different from the mental states. If the self is identical with the mental states, then it too, like the states, will be subject to change, to birth, decay and death; and if it is different from them, it cannot be known[4]. Neither they who uphold the identity of the self and the mental states, nor they who advocate their difference know the real teaching of Buddha.[5] Bondage and liberation, *samsāra* and Nirvāṇa, are also ultimately unreal. If bondage is unreal, how can liberation be real? Ultimately even the consciousness of attainment of Nirvāṇa is an appearance. Time, space, substance, attribute, relation, causation, self, object, identity, difference, etc., are the constructions of the categories of thought which are due to *avidyā*. When *avidyā*, alongwith the 'I' and the 'mine', is removed by Prajñā, the cycle of birth and death comes to a stand-still.[6]

1. naivāgram nāvaram yasya tasya madhyam kuto bhavet? *Ibid.*, XI, 2.
2. kasya syād anyathābhāvaḥ svabhāvash chen na vidyate I kasya syād anyathābhāvaḥ svabhāvo yadi vidyate II *Ibid.*, XIII, 4.
3. *Ibid.*, XVII, 30.
4. *Ibid.*, XXVII, 6-7.
5. *Ibid.*, X, 16.
6. *Ibid.*, XVIII, 4.

VI. SHŪNYATĀ EXPLAINED AND OBJECTIONS ANSWERED

The meaning and significance of shūnyatā have already been explained before.[1] People, says Nāgārjuna, not understanding the meaning of shūnyatā, wrongly accuse us of nihilism. Mistaking shūnyatā in the sense of mere negation they urge that we have negated all phenomena, that we have utterly denied bondage and liberation, the four Noble Truths, the Order, the Religion and even the Buddha, and that we have logically no room even for practical compromises.[2] We reply: These people do not understand even the meaning of *shūnyatā* much less its significance. Misunderstanding *shūnyatā* in the sense of mere negation, they wrongly criticise us and charge us with defects which *shūnyatā* does not possess.[3]

If everything is *ashūnya* (non-relative or absolute), then it must exist independently and must be absolutely real. Then there should be no dependent origination and hence no production, no destruction, no birth, no death, no bondage, no liberation, no Noble Truths, no Order, No Religion and no Buddha. Everything being real should be eternal, unchanging (*kūṭastha*) and motionless. Then there should be no change, no variety, no world.[4] Thus, those who maintain the absolute reality of world-objects undermine the distinction between the relative and the absolute with the result that in their zeal to preserve the reality of the world they lose even the phenomenal. By denying *shūnyatā* in the sense of relativity and dependent origination, they negate all phenomena and all worldly practices.[5] They are unmindful of the absurdities in their own view and forgetting the defects in their own view, like a rider who forgets the very horse he is riding on, they wantonly fling their own defects on us.[6] On the other hand, if everything is *shūnya* in the sense of absolute negation, then the world cannot be called even an appearance. Verily the hare's

1. *Supra*, pp. 43-45.
2. *Mādhyamika kārika*, XXIV, 1-6.
3. *Ibid.*, XXIV, 7 and 13.
4. *Ibid.*, XXIV, 20-38.
5. sarvasamvyavahārānshcha laukikān pratibādhase I
   yat pratītyasamutpādashūnyatām pratibādhase II *Ibid.*, XXIV, 36.
6. sa tvam doṣān ātmanīnān asmāsu paripātayan I
   ashvamevābhirūḍhaḥ san ashvamevāsi vismṛtaḥ II *Ibid.*, XXIV, 15.

horn does not even appear. Thus, we who accept shūnyatā as relativity can explain everything in the world as empirically real, while those who deny shūnyatā negate everything.[1]

In his Vigraha-Vyāvarttanī with his own commentary, Nāgārjuna gives the anticipated objections of the opponents against *shūnyatā* and refutes all of them. The main arguments of the opponents are:

(1) *Shūnyatā* which denies the existence of all *dharmas* is not true:
(a) Because the arguments used for the *existence* of *shūnyatā* are also unreal.
(b) And if they are not unreal, they undermine the Shūnyavādin's premises for then he at least maintains the *reality* of his arguments.
(c) And there is no *pramāṇa* to establish *shūnyatā*.
(d) And shūnyavāda which negates everything is a self-condemned nihilism.

Nāgārjuna replies:

(1) *Shūnyatā* which denies the ultimate reality of all *dharmas* is true:
(a) Because the ultimate unreality of arguments does not render *shūnyatā* as unreal; it reveals its relativity only.
(b) Our arguments do not undermine our premises. We do not say: This particular argument of ours is true, while all others are false. We say: All arguments are ultimately unreal.[2] We have no thesis of our own to prove and hence no words and no arguments. How can we be charged with defects then?[3] But from the empirical stand-point we admit the reality of the arguments because the empirical cannot be condemned by its own logic.[4]
(c) The validity of pramāṇas themselves cannot be established.

1. sarvam cha yujyate tasya shūnyatā yasya yujyate I
sarvam na yujyate tasya shūnyam yasya na yujyate II *Ibid.*, XXIV, 14.
2. Vigraha-vyāvarttanī, Kārikā 22, 67 and Vṛtti. yadi hi vayam brūmaḥ idam vachanam ashūnyam sheṣāḥ sarvabhāvāḥ shūnyāḥ iti tato vaiṣamikatvam syāt, na chaitadevam. *Ibid.*, p. 12.
3. nāsti cha mama pratijñā tasman naivāsti me doṣaḥ I —*Ibid.*, K.29.
4. *Ibid.*, p. 14.

A *pramāṇa* like fire cannot prove itself. If fire can enkindle itself, it will also burn itself. A *pramāṇa* cannot be established by another pramāṇa for this will lead to infinite regress. A *pramāṇa* cannot be proved by a *prameya*, for a *prameya* itself is to be proved by a *pramāṇa*. And a *pramāṇa* of course cannot be proved at random by accident.[1]

(d) We are not nihilists. We believe in the relativity of the phenomena and the non-duality of the Absolute. We do not negate anything; there is nothing to be negated except illusion. Hence the charge that we negate everything is falsely made by our opponents.[2]

Chandrakīrti fully supports and explains Nāgārjuna. He upholds the Prāsaṅgikā-Mādhyamika school of Buddhapālita which condemns independent reasoning against the Svatantra-Mādhyamika school of Bhāvaviveka which wants to support Shūnyavāda by independent reasoning. Chandrakīrti says that for him who accepts the ultimate validity of logic the Mādhyamika system is a hindrance rather than a help.[3] Logic has only a negative value for us. We only refute the view of our opponent without however, accepting the opposite view or any other view. Our words are not policemen. They cannot arrest us. They simply enable us to express something.[4] Ultimately every argument is either unreal (*asiddha*) or self-contradictory (*viruddha*). But then, urges the opponent, is not this very argument, being an argument, ultimately unreal or self-contradictory? Chandrakīrti replies: This objection is valid only against those who give an independent status to reasoning. We simply repudiate the arguments of our opponents. We have no thesis of our own to prove. We are not positively proving that every argument is either unreal or self-contradictory for the simple reason that we cannot do so. We accept the empirical reality of logic, but it is a reality which ultimately undermines itself. We point out to our opponent that his thesis cannot be proved even by his own logic. We have no thesis of our own and no logic of our own to prove it. We only

1. *Ibid.*, K. 32-52.
2. pratiṣedhayāmi nāham kiñchit pratiṣedhyamasti na cha kiñchit. *Ibid.*, K. 64.
3. *Mādhyamika-Vṛtti*, pp. 24-5.
4. na hi shabdā dāṇḍapāshikā iva vaktāram asvatantrayanti—*Ibid.*, p. 24.

demonstrate negatively and by the logic accepted by the opponents that every argument or view is self-contradictory and ultimately unreal.[1] Criticism of all views is itself not a view; rejection of all theories is itself not a theory.

Chandrakīrti also makes it clear that the objections of the opponents are based on a confusion between the two standpoints, the relative and the Real. The Real is beyond all duality, all assertions and denials, all belief and doubt, all the categories of thought. The saints who have realised *Nirvāṇa* remain merged in its bliss. They have risen above thought and language. This highest state is silence.[2] But when the saints want to impart instruction about the Real, they do so from the standpoint of *samvṛti* by employing thought and language. But even from this standpoint of empirical truth, they have no thesis or argument of their own to put forward. They resort to thought and language as a practical necessity and make others understand by commonly accepted arguments and logical methods that the Real is beyond the categories of thought and beyond language and can be realised by non-dual spiritual experience.[3] Even the teachings of Buddha are from the empirical standpoint.[4]

Shūnyatā is the transcendence of all views (*dṛṣṭi-shūnyatā*). Those who mistake it as a view (*shūnyatā-dṛṣṭi*) are declared as hopelessly incurable.[5] We are warned that *shūnyatā*, if wrongly understood in the sense of a category of thought, will lead to the philosophical doom of the person who misunderstands it, just as a snake, if carelessly caught at the wrong end, will bite the person who catches it and will kill him by its poison or just as wrong knowledge may prove dangerous or *tantra*, if wrongly practised, will

1. svatantramanumānam bruvatām ayam doṣo jāyate. na vayam svatantram anumānam prayañjmahe, parapratijñāniṣedhaphalatvād asmad anumānānām—*Ibid.*, p. 34.
2. paramārtho hi āryāṇām tūṣṇīmbhāvaḥ—*Ibid.*, p. 57.
3. na khalu āryā lokasamvyavahāreṇopapattim varṇayanti, kintu lokata eva yā prasiddhopapattis tām parāvabodhārtham abhyupetya tayaiva lokam bodhayanti—*Ibid.*, p. 57.
4. laukika eva darshane sthitvā Buddhānām bhagavatām dharmadeshanā.—*Ibid.*, p. 75.
5. shūnyatā sarvadṛṣṭīnām proktā niḥsaraṇam Jinaiḥ I
yeṣām tu shūnyatā-dṛṣṭis tānasādhyān babhāṣire II —*Mādhyamika Kārika*, XIII, 8.

destroy the person who practises it.[1] Chandrakīrti quotes *Ratnakūṭa Sūtra* to the effect: A doctor administers a drug to cure a patient. Now this drug after throwing all impurities out of the stomach, does not itself come out, but remains in the stomach to disturb it, do you think, O Kāshyapa, that the patient is cured ?[2] In the same Sūtra we find: Shūnyatā is the giving up of all views; he, O Kāshyapa, who mistakes it as a view is incurable.[3] If a person says to another: 'I shall give you nothing', and the latter replies: 'Please give me this "nothing"', how can he be made to understand the meaning of 'nothing'?[4]

Chandrakīrti distinguishes the Mādhyamika from the nihilist (*nāstika*) by saying that the Mādhyamika is an absolutist who goes beyond both affirmation and negation, while the nihilist clings to absolute negation which is a self-condemned view; the Mādhyamika does not deny empirical reality to phenomena, while the nihilist does deny it; the Mādhyamika shūnyatā is not negation but relativity, while the nihilist, in a self-contradictory manner, negates everything. Though ultimately the world is unreal for both, yet the vital difference between them lies in the fact that the Mādhyamika, by making a distinction between the relative and the absolute, preserves everything from the relative standpoint of thought, while the nihilist who does not believe in this distinction loses even the phenomenal and lands in self-condemned void. Chandrakīrti illustrates the difference between the two by this example: Suppose a person has committed theft. Now a man, not knowing this gives evidence, simply prompted by the enemies of the thief that that person is the thief. Another man who caught the thief *flagrante delicto* also gives evidence to the same effect. The evidence in both cases is the same. But the former man is a liar even though he has unintentionally spoken the truth, while the latter man is truthful because he knows and has intentionally told the truth. The difference between the nihilist and the Mādhyamika is the difference between the former and the latter.[5]

---

1. vināshayati durdṛṣṭā shūnyatā mandamedhasam |
sarpo yathā durgṛhīto vidyā vā duṣprasādhitā ||—*Ibid.*, XXIV, II.
2. *Mādhyamika Vṛtti*, p. 248.
3. *Ibid.*, (See supra, p. 41)
4. *Ibid.*, pp. 247-8.
5. *Ibid.*, p. 368.

Nāgārjuna says that *shūnyatā,* viewed through *avidya,* through the glasses of dependent causation and relativity, viewed *sub specie temporis,* is the phenomenal world of plurality and suffering or the cycle of birth-and-death constituting bondage. And the same *shūnyatā,* viewed through *prajñā* or non-dual experience, without relativity and attachment, viewed *sub specie aeternitatis,* is liberation or *nirvāṇa,* the blissful Absolute.[1] Buddha has repeatedly asked us to rise above all categories of thought, to transcend the duality of thesis and antithesis, to go beyond affirmation and negation, beyond existence and non-existence. Buddha has declared this phenomenal world constructed by *a priori* thought-categories as an appearance; it is 'neither real nor unreal', 'neither existent nor non-existent' and has asked us to realise *nirvāṇa* by transcending the thought-forms and attaining non-dual spiritual experience. Nāgārjuna says: Please ask the Sāṅkhyas, the Vaisheṣikas, the Jainas, the Soul-upholders (*pudgalavādins*) and the Skandhavādins whether they declare the world as 'neither existent nor non-existent'. The Real transcends all thought-forms and the phenomenal is the relative as it is an appearance which is neither existent nor non-existent, neither real nor unreal—this is the noble present or gift of our Religion, the deep truth, the nectar of the teaching of Buddha.[2]

VII. NAIRĀTMYAVĀDA

Nairātmyavāda or anātmavāda has been discussed in detail above.[3] Nairātmyavāda has been interpreted by Hīnayāna as the denial of the reality of the individual self (*pudgala-nairātmya*). This is partial. Mahāyāna declares not only the individual self as unreal but also all objects of thought as equally unreal (*dharma-nairātmya*). Buddha has repeatedly rejected both the views of eternalism and nihilism. Hīnayāna rejects only the eternal ego and the eternal objects, but glorifies the nihilistic view by accepting the reality of

1. *Mādhyamika Kārikā,* XXV, 9; See *supra,* pp. 43 and 49.
2. sasānkhyaulūkya-nirgrantha-pudgalaskandhavādinam I
   pṛchchha lokam yadi vadatyasti-nāstivyatikramam II
   dharmayautakamityasmān nāstyastitvavyatikramam I viddhi gambhīramityuktam
   Buddhānām shāsanāmṛtam II —*Ratnāvalī,* I, 61-2.
3. See *supra,* pp. 25-36.

the fleeting mental states and of the momentary dharmas. In Buddha and Mahāyāna, the denial of the self is not the denial of the empirical validity of the ego, but only the denial of the false notion which mistakes the empirical ego as an eternal spiritual substance and objectifies it. To take the self as an eternal substance is to cling to it eternally and this is *avidyā par excellence,* which is the root cause of all attachment, desire, misery and bondage. It gives rise to the four kinds of suffering (*klesha*) which are self-notion (*ātma-dṛṣṭi*), self-delusion (*ātma-moha*), self-pride (*ātma-māna*) and self-love (*ātma-sneha*). *Ātma-dṛṣṭi* is pudgala or *satkāya dṛṣṭi,* which mistakes the empirical ego as an eternal substance.

Avidyā or transcendental Ignorance with the help of its *a priori* categories throws as it were a two–fold veil on the subject as well as on the object. The first veil, which covers the real nature of the subject and makes it appear as the individual self is called 'the veil of suffering' (*kleshāvaraṇa*), because it gives rise to all kinds of suffering. The second veil which covers the real nature of the object and makes it appear as a real physical or mental object is called 'the veil on object' (*jñeyāvaraṇa*), because it gives rise to false knowledge of the object. The subject and the object are mutually dependent and related. Both of them are appearances of the Absolute. The intuitive realisation that the individual self which is the source of the false notions of the 'I' and the 'mine' and the root cause of suffering is ultimately unreal (*pudgala-nairātmya*) and is, in fact, the blissful Absolute itself, removes the 'veil on the subject' which constitutes suffering (*kleshāvaraṇa*). And the intuitive realisation that the object which appears as the 'thing-in-itself' is, infact, an *a priori* thought-construct, which is ultimately unreal (*dharma-nairātmya*) and is not different from the Absolute which is its immanent reality, removes the 'veil on the object' (*jñeyāvaraṇa*) and cancels the distorting function of thought-categories, leaving the non-dual Real to shine in its pristine purity. This immediate realisation in its two-fold aspects is called *nairātmyavāda* and is equated with *shūnyatā.* The word *nairātmya* or *anātma* means 'devoid of self (i.e., ultimate reality)' or 'devoid of self-reality or independent existence'; it stands for the mutually dependent or relative, for that which is an appearance of the real. Thus nairātmya-vāda is a synonym of pratitya-samutpāda and is identified with *shūnyatā.* Shāntideva says that *shūnyatā* is *nairātmya* of *pudgala* and *dharma*, which at once cancels kleshāvaraṇa and jneyavaraṇa.[1]

Nāgārjuna declares that Buddha has preached *nairātmya* in order to make us realise that the entire phenomenal world of subjects and objects is an appearance and that therefore we should try to realise the Real, the *nirvāṇa,* through immediate spiritual experience. The individual self cannot be reduced to the changing mental states that arise and perish; how can the subject of experience be identical with the experienced content?[2] Nor can the self be treated as an immutable substance different from the mental states, for we do not find any self without the mental states[3]. Hence, neither those who advocate the identity of the self and the mental states nor those who advocate their difference, know the real meaning of the teaching of Buddha.[4] The self and the mental states are relative and ultimately unreal. Like the selves, all objects of thought, whether they are the momentary elements (*dharma*) of Hīnayāna or the permanent entities like primordial Matter (*prakṛti*) or atoms (*paramāṇu*) of the non-Buddhists, are relative and ultimately unreal. Nāgārjuna says that to the beginners, Buddha has preached the existence of the empirical self, so that they may not give up cultivation of moral virtues, to those who are a little advanced he has preached that there is no self as an eternal substance, and to those who are highly advanced he has preached that both the self and the mental states are mutually dependent and ultimately unreal.[5] Āryadeva says that *nairātmya* is the non-dual blissful experience of the Buddhas, the Enlightened, which transcends thought and language and which frightens those who are entangled in the meshes of the categories of thought![6]

VIII. NIRVĀṆA

It is sometimes believed that in Hīnayāna, *nirvāṇa* is a negative state of the cessation of all desires and suffering like the extinc-

1. kleshajñeyavṛtitamaḥ-pratipakṣo hi shūnyatā.—*Bodhicharyāvatāra,* IX, 55.
2. *Mādhyamika Kārikā,* XXVII, 6.
3. *Ibid.*, XXVII, 7.
4. ātmanashcha satattvam ye bhāvānām cha pṛthak pṛthak I
nirdishanti na tān manye shāsanasyārthakovidān II *Ibid.*, X, 16.
5. See *supra*, p. 33.
6. advitīyam shivadvāram kudṛṭīnām bhayaṅkaram I
viṣayaḥ sarvabuddhānām iti nairātmyam uchyate II—*Chatuḥshataka*, 288.
Also, advitīyam shivadvāram ato nairātmyadarshanam.—*Tattvasaṅgraha,* 3492.

tion of the flame of a lamp when its oil is exhausted, and the saint who obtains *nirvāṇa* is literally 'blown out of existence'. But there are many passages and verses even in the Pāli canon, which describe *nirvāṇa* as an eternal and blissful positive state. Buddha's teaching regarding *Nirvāṇa* was too repeated and too emphatic to be missed. There can be no Buddha without *Nirvāṇa* and no Buddhism without Buddha. No school of Buddhism has taken *nirvāṇa* in the sense of a purely negative state. Theravāda and Sarvāstivāda take *nirvāṇa* as an *asamskṛta dharma,* an eternal uncaused positive entity in which there is complete cessation of sufferings. Sautrāntika criticises this and says that *nirvāṇa* cannot be a positive *dharma;* this does not mean that *nirvāṇa* is taken by him as *abhāvamātra* or mere negation. The negative expressions about *nirvāṇa* merely show that there is complete annihilation of suffering in it and not that *nirvāṇa* itself is annihilation.

The Mādhyamika points out that the Hīnayāna schools have failed to understand the real teachings of Buddha about *nirvāṇa.* Theravāda and Sarvastivāda mistake *nirvāṇa* as an eternal uncaused element (*asamskṛta dharma*) in which there is cessation of sufferings. *Nirvāṇa* is certainly eternal and uncaused and beyond suffering, but it is not an element or *dharma,* not even an uncaused element or *asamskṛta dharma.* It is the inner essence (*svabhāva*), the immanent reality (*dharmatā*) of all dharmas. There is no element, entity, thing or object, says Nāgārjuna, which is not dependent and relational. Any uncaused object (*asamskṛta dharma*) or absolute non-relational object (*ashūnya dharma*) is a contradiction in terms. This does not mean that there is no Absolute; it only means that the Absolute cannot be an object, it cannot be objectified.

The Absolute or *Nirvāṇa* is beyond sense, thought and language. It is supra-sensuous (*atīndriya*), indeterminate (*vikalpa-shūnya*) and inexpressible (*anirvachanīya*). It is non-dual (*advaya*) and beyond plurality (*prapañcha-shūnya*). It is called *chatuṣkotivinirmukta* or beyond the four categories of thought. It is beyond affirmation, negation, both or neither. It cannot be determined by any or all of these predicates. It is free from all empirical predicates, all determinations, all relations, all thought-forms or categories. It cannot be categorised, determined, objectified or phenomenalised. If it is viewed as 'existent', as an '*ens*', as a positive element (*bhāva*), then like other empirical elements (*dharmas*) or entities, it would be subject to dependent causation (*samskṛta*), to origination, decay and death, for no entity or object can be uncaused and independent.[1] And *nirvāṇa* is admitted as uncaused and independent. Nor can *nirvāṇa* be treated as 'non-existent', as a '*non-ens*', as mere negation (*abhāva*), for it would then be neither real nor independent[2]. Nor can it be both existent and non-existent, for, these, like light and darkness, are opposed to each other. And to say that it is neither is to give up thinking and embrace nihilism.[3] *Nirvāṇa* is the transcendence of all thought-categories. It is neither abandoned nor acquired, neither momentary nor eternal, neither destroyed nor produced.[4] *Nirvāṇa* is the giving up of all views of thought, of existence and non-existence, etc.[5] *Nirvāṇa* is the cancellation of all categorisations, of all thought-constructions of transcendental Ignorance by non-dual spiritual experience.[6] Shūnyatā itself which is the non-dual Real where all plurality is removed is called *Nirvāṇa*.[7] Nāgārjuna defines the Real thus: The Real is the self-existent Absolute which is realised through immediate spiritual experience (*apara-pratyayam*), which is blissfully calm (*shāntam*), which transcends the plurality and suffering of phenomenal life (*prapañchairaprapañchitam*), which is beyond all determinations of thought (*nirvikalpam*) and which is supra-relational and non-dual (*anānārtham*)—this is the definition (*lakṣaṇam*) of the Real (*tattva*).[8] It is identified with Prajñāpāramitā, Bodhi or Advayajñāna which is the highest intuitional knowledge, the non-dual realisation, the immediate spiritual experience. The trinity of empirical knowledge, knower, known and knowledge or subject, object and their relation, is transcended here. The Real cannot be determined in any way by thought-categories. Even existence, unity, eternality, joy, goodness, consciousness, etc., cannot be affirmed or denied of it. True, the Absolute exists; nay,

1. *Mādhyamika Kārikā,* XXV, 5-6.
2. *Ibid.*, XXV, 7-8.
3. *Ibid.*, XXV, 14, 16.
4. aprahīṇam asamprāptam anuchchhinnam ashāshvatam I
   aniruddham anutpannam etan nirvāṇam uchyate II *Ibid.*, XXV, 3.
5. bhāvābhāvaparamarshakṣayo nirvāṇamuchyate I *Ratnāvalī*, I, 42. Also, *Mādhyamika Kārikā*, XXV, 10.
6. niravasheṣa kalpanakṣayerūpameva nirvāṇam—*Mādhyamika Vṛtti*, p. 522.
7. shūnyataiva sarvaprapañchanivṛttilakṣaṇattvān nirvāṇamityuchyate—*Ibid.*, p. 351.
8. aparapratyayam shāntam prapañchairaprapañchitam I
   nirvikalpam-anānārthametat tattvasya lakṣaṇam II —*M. Kārika*, XVIII, 9.

it is the only self-existent Real, yet it does not exist in the way in which any object exists. As the transcendent source of all categories, it cannot be categorised. We cannot logically apply even the category of existence to it, for that would be to drag it down to the level of phenomenon. Its foundational unity (non-duality) is not abstract unity known through the category of 'unity'. It is pure consciousness or immediate spiritual experience, but we can have no idea of this 'experience' by our relational thought. It is Supreme Bliss, but worldly pleasure cannot give us even a shadow of this Bliss. It is the highest good, but its goodness is not empirical. All categories are relational and work within phenomena; they cannot be applied to the Absolute. To the objection that if the Absolute is utterly indeterminate and inexpressible, it becomes an abstraction empty of all content and is reduced to a mere nothing and we cannot even know that there is such Absolute, the Mādhyamika replies that though the Absolute is unapproachable by thought, it is not inaccessible to immediate spiritual experience; that though it is transcendent to sense, thought and language, and to all phenomena, yet it is also immanent in all phenomena as their indubitable inner reality. As the reality of the appearances it is there always and everywhere. Shāntideva says: Thought, of course, cannot positively know the Absolute but thought which is *samvṛti* can negatively point to it as the undeniable ground-reality of all phenomena realisable in non-dual spiritual experience[1]. And such spiritual experience of Buddha and Bodhisattvas is a positive proof of such realisation, at least for the believers. Thought cannot be condemned from its own standpoint and hence, as long as the Real is not realised, all the phenomenal things and practices are taken as practically real; they are *samvṛti* or conventional truth. Though ultimately false, *samvṛti* or thought can still indirectly indicate the Real and this constitutes its value.[2] Only the illusory, the 'neither real nor unreal' can be negated; the Real can never be negated. The Absolute is not a contentless void, for what is negated is the superimposed character and not the essential nature of the Ab-

1. buddheragocharastattvam buddhiḥ samvṛtiruchyate—*Bodhicharyāvatara*, IX, 2.
2. tiṣṭatu tāvadeṣā. . . . samvṛtir. . . mokṣāvāhakakushalamūlopachayahetur yāvan na tattvādhigamaḥ. *Mādhyamika Kārika Vṛtti*, p. 68.

solute. *Samvṛti* or thought-forms cover the Real and distort it by misrepresenting it as this world of plurality of subjects and objects; but *samvṛti* or thought itself can use words as symbols (*saṅketa*) or ascribed marks and these can serve to indicate the Real indirectly as the ground on which phenomena are superimposed. This is known as the method of removal of superimposition (*adhyāropāpavādanyāya*). There can be no other method of expressing the Inexpressible.[1] It is said that from the time Buddha became Enlightened till the time he obtained *parinirvāṇa* he, from the ultimate standpoint, did not utter a single word because the Real is beyond words.[2] Yet, from the standpoint of *samvṛti,* Buddha did preach and guide his disciples towards the realisation of *Nirvāṇa.* Hence the importance of *samvṛti* cannot be set aside. Thought and language, however defective these may ultimately be, are the only means available to us to attain to the Real. Just as a person who desires to fetch water must have some vessel, similarly he who wants to attain *Nirvāṇa* (*upeya*) must accept *samvṛti* as the means (*upāya*).[3] *Samvṛti* is dispelled only when *Nirvāṇa* or *Paramārtha* is realised, not before. Chandrakīrti compares phenomena to the steps in a staircase leading to the Real in which each step is higher because it is nearer the goal.[4] The Absolute (*Paramārtha*) cannot be preached without thought and language (*vyavahāra*) and Nirvāṇa cannot be attained without the realisation of the Absolute.[5] Ultimately samvṛti, however, dissolves itself without residue in *paramārtha. Samvṛti* and *paramārtha,* as has been explained before[6] are not *two* truths; *paramārtha* is the only truth and *samvṛti* is falsity mistaken as truth in empirical life. This sets

---

1. anakṣarasya dharmasya shrutiḥ kā deshanā cha kā? shrūyate deshyate chāpi samāropādanakṣaraḥ ||—Quoted in *Mādhyamika Vṛtti,* p. 264.
2. avachanam Buddhavachanam.—*Lankāvatāra,* pp. 142-3, 194. na kvachit kasyachit kashchid dharmo Buddhena deshitaḥ. MK XXV, 24.
3. nirvāṇādhigamopāyatvādavashyam eva samvṛtir abhyupeyā bhājanamiva salilārthineti. *Mādhyamika Vṛtti.* p. 494.
4. tattvāvatārasopānabhūtattvāt—*Chatuḥshataka Vṛtti,* p. 8.
5. vyavahāramanāshritya paramārtho na deshyate |
paramārthamanāgamya nirvāṇam nādhigamyate || *Mādhyamika Karika,* XXIV, 10.
6. See *supra,* pp. 47-8.

aside the objection raised by Kumārila Bhatta that if samvṛti is truth how can it be conventional and if it is false, how can it be a kind of truth?[1]

Ultimately the world of phenomena and the Absolute are one and the same. It is the Absolute itself which appears and is the reality of appearances. This cycle of birth-and-death (*samsāra*), this phenomenal world governed by causes and conditions and appearing through transcendental Ignorance, volitional forces, desire and attachment is really the Absolute (*nirvāṇa*) itself viewed through *avidyā* or thought and this very world, viewed through prajñā or immediate spiritual experience is *nirvāṇa* or *shūnyatā* or the Absolute itself shining in its blissful purity.[2] Hence there is not the minutest difference between *samsāra* and *nirvāṇa*.[3] When the attachment (*upādāna*) to the individual self (*pudgala*) which is the root cause of suffering and the source of the false notions of the 'I' and the 'mine' as well as the attachment to the worldly objects (*dharma*) due to transcendental ignorance is cancelled by immediate realisation of the Real, the false notions of the 'I' and the 'mine' are totally wiped out and the cycle of birth-and-death collapses.[4] This is *nirvāṇa* or *shūnyatā* which cancels the two-fold 'covering' (*āvaraṇa*) on the subject and the object.[5] If even the slightest trace of attachment persists, *nirvāṇa* is not attained. He who thinks thus: I shall obtain *nirvāṇa* by removing all attachment and *my nirvāṇa* will happen is still entangled in the terrible clutches of attachment to the 'I' and the 'mine'.[6] *Nirvāṇa* or *shūnyatā* is the transcendence of all thought-constructions, all views, all theories, all categories of thought engendered by transcendental Ignorance (*shūnyatā* of all *dṛṣṭi, anta,* vikalpa, kalpanā,

1. satyā chet samvṛtiḥ keyam mṛṣā chet satyatā katham? —*Shlokavārtika*, VI, 7.
2. ya ājavañjavībhāva upādāya pratītya vā I
   so' pratītyā'nupādāya nirvāṇamupadishyate II—*Mādhyamika Kārikā*, XXV, 9. See *supra*, pp. 43, 49.
3. nirvāṇasya cha yā koṭiḥ koṭiḥ samsaraṇasya cha I
   na tayorantaram kiñchit susūkṣmamapi vidyate II —M.K., XXV, 20.
4. mametyahamiti kṣīṇe bahirdhādhyātmameva cha I
   nirudhyata upādānam tat kṣayājjanmanaḥ kṣayaḥ II—*Mādhyamika Kārikā*, XVIII, 4.
5. See *supra*, pp. 64-5.
6. nirvāsyāmyanupādāno nirvāṇam me bhaviṣyati I
   iti yeṣām grahasteṣām upādānamahāgrahaḥ II—*Mādhyamika Kārika*, XVI, 9.

prapañcha).[1] It is the blissful Absolute itself (*shiva*) where all plurality (*prapañcha*) and suffering (*duḥkha*) of the worldly existence cease. *Nirvāṇa* is identified with *shūnyatā, dharmatā, dharmadhātu, dharmakāya, tathatā,* Tathāgata and Buddha. As the Absolute is the only reality and the world has only an epistemic status, there can be no relation between the two. Relation belongs to determinate thought. Ultimately, bondage and liberation both are due to *avidyā.* Neither the Absolute nor the individual self is ever bound and so the question of their liberation does not arise. The Absolute only appears as the world; it never really involves itself in the world. There could be no initial fall or degradation of the Absolute into the world and hence there is no need for its restoration or re-transformation into its original purity. The individual self also is really neither bound nor liberated. The world is neither lost nor retained in the Absolute. Just as a rope-snake, which really never is, is not 'lost' when the rope is known, so this empirical world, which really never exists, is not 'lost' when the Absolute is realised.[2] What is lost is only illusion and for this loss there should be no regrets. Nirvāṇa is Pure non-dual Experience, Pure Freedom, and Pure ineffable and infinite Bliss, transcendent to sense, thought and language.[3]

---

1. shūnyatā sarvadṛṣṭīnām proktā niḥsaraṇam Jinaiḥ, *Ibid.*, XIII, 8.
   sarvadṛṣṭiprahāṇāya yaḥ saddharmamadeshayat. *Ibid.*, XXVII, 30.
   sarvadṛṣṭi-prahāṇāya shūnyatā'mṛtadeshanā.
   niravasheṣakalpanākṣayarūpameva nirvāṇaṃ—*M. Vṛtti*, p. 522
   prapañchopashamam shivam. *M. Kārikā*, Maṅgalācharaṇa
   prapañchairaprapañchitam. *Ibid.*, XVIII, 9.
2. vastukachintāyām tu samsāra eve nāsti;tat kuto'sya parikṣayaḥ pradīpāvasthāyām rajjūragaparikṣayavat. *M. Vṛtti*, p. 220.
3. sarvopalambhopashamaḥ prapañchopashamaḥ shivaḥ.
   —*M. Kārikā*, XXV, 24.

CHAPTER THREE

Vijñānavāda or the Yogāchāra School

I. THE RISE OF VIJÑĀNAVĀDA

Just as Shūnyavāda is called Mādhyamika because it advocates the 'middle path' discovered by Buddha which avoids the two extremes of thesis and anti-thesis, so Vijñānavāda is also known as Yogāchāra because if emphasises the practice of yoga in spiritual discipline. Both these schools developed side by side, but as a full-fledged system Vijñānavāda came into existence after Shūnyavāda. Vijñānavāda is generally, though erroneously, treated as one school, but the earlier school should be distinguished from its later development. The earlier school of Vijñānavāda, which we call Mūla-Vijñanavāda or simply Vijñānavāda, found in *Laṅkāvatāra-sūtra* and advocated by Maitreyanātha, Asaṅga, Vasubandhu and Sthiramati is absolution or absolute idealism, while its later modification, which we call Svatantra-Vijñānavāda and which is also known as Sautrāntika-yogāchāra and the Logical school of Buddhism, founded by Diṅnāga and developed by Dharmakīrti, Shāntarakṣita and Kamalashīla is subjective idealism.

The Sautrāntika is the most critical school of Hīnayāna. It led, on the one hand, to the rise of the Mādhyamika absolutism, and on the other hand, to the Vijñānavāda idealism. The Sautrāntika recognises two elements in the constitution of empirical knowledge, (i) *pure sensation* which comes from the thing-in-itself (*svalakṣaṇa*) or the unique momentary particular which is the unrelated real (*dharma*), and (ii) *relations* which are imposed on it by the constructive ideation (*kalpanā*) of the *a priori* categories of thought. Thus the Kantian analysis of knowledge, many centuries before Kant, was formulated and developed in the Sautrāntika school.

The Mādhyamika completes the dialectical movement of criticism left in the middle by the Sautrāntika. The Mādhyamika says that if the unifying categories of unity, universality, substantiality and permanence are unreal thought-constructions, then the distinguishing categories of difference, particularity, modal change and momentariness are equally unreal thought-constructions. If the *pudgala* is an appearance, so are the *dharmas.* If the substance view of identity leads to dogmatism and eternalism, the modal view of difference leads to empiricism and nihilism.

The Sautrāntika is also responsible for giving rise to the Vijñānavāda idealism. If all our empirical knowledge is conditioned by the *a priori* thought-forms, then the supposed objective reality may also be the result of thought-construction; if the number of the *dharmas* can be reduced from seventy-five to forty-three by pronouncing some of them as thought-constructions, then by the same logic all the *dharmas* can be discarded as merely thought-constructions. If the objectively given is the categorised content itself, it is illogical to believe in an unknown substance. If this 'substance' is believed in as the cause to give rise to sensations, it would be more logical to find this cause within consciousness itself, rather than in this supposed external substance.[1] Thus we see that Vijñānavāda has developed its idealism by the criticism of critical realism of the Sautrāntika.

Vijñānavāda has been greatly influenced by the Mādhyamika absolutism. It has arisen to complement and supplement Shūnyavāda, and not to oppose or contradict it. The negative dialectic of the Mādhyamika and his total rejection of speculative metaphysics appeared as an unwarranted extreme to Vijñānavāda which returned to constructive metaphysics with full acceptance of absolutism from the ultimate standpoint. Vijñānavāda believes that in order to avoid possible misconceptions of shūnyatā, it is necessary to indulge in positive descriptions of the Absolute and to explain its immanence in phenomena. To the extent to which Vijñānavāda has remained faithful to the Mādhyamika absolutism,

---

1. In Western philosophy also, the 'unknowable substance' of Locke was dismissed by Berkeley as a 'stupid thoughtless somewhat' and the 'thing-in-itself' of Kant, along with its dualism between sense and thought was rejected by Fichte and Hegel, on the same ground.

the differences between the two have remained only of degree or emphasis or at most of approach, but when Vijñānavāda in its zeal for constructive metaphysics has overshot the mark, the differences have become real.

Vijñānavāda from the beginning has been a house divided against itself. Its rise and growth are due to two factors which are mutually incompatible. It has tried to synthesise the Mādhyamika absolutism with the Sautrāntika pluralism which is an impossible task. Earlier Vijñānavāda had to suppress its Sautrāntika leanings, while the later Vijñānavāda had to give up absolutism.

II. IDEALISM OF LAṄKĀVATĀRA-SŪTRA

Almost all tenets of Vijñānavāda are found scattered in *Laṅkāvatāra-Sūtra.* In this Sutra *tathatā, bodhi, prajñā, shūnyatā, bhūtakoṭi, nirvāṇa, dharmakāya, dharmadhātu, tathāgatagarbha* and *chittamātra* are used for *paramārtha* or ultimate reality.[1] The words *chitta, manas* and *vijñāna* are used as synonyms. The word *chitta* is generally used for Ālaya-vijñāna and the word *chitta-mātra* is used for pure absolute consciousness. Sometimes the words Vijñāna-mātra and Vijñapti-mātra[2] are also used for this pure consciousness. According to Laṅkāvatāra *chitta-mātra* or pure vijñāna is the ultimate reality. Consciousness-only, pure and absolute, is the established truth preached by Buddha. All dharmas or objects are unreal. All the three worlds (*kāma, rūpa* and *arūpa loka,* i.e. the world of matter, form and no-form) are the result of thought-construction (*vikalpa*). The so-called external object does not exist. *Chitta-mātra* or pure absolute consciousness is the non-dual prajñā of Tathāgata or Buddha[3]. It is beyond subject-object duality (*grāhya-grāhaka-vāsanā-rahita*) and beyond origination, existence and destruction (*utpāda-sthiti-bhaṅga-varjya*). It is to be realised by non-dual spiritual experience (*nirābhāsa-prajñā-gochara*).[4] When this *chittamātra* or pure Vijñāna appears to be tinged by beginningless *avidyā* or *vāsanā* of the subject-object duality, it manifests itself as *chitta* or *Ālaya*-Vijñāna. *Ālaya* is the store-house of all seeds (*bīja*), i.e., of

1. tathatā shūnyatā koṭir nirvāṇam dharmadhātukam. p. 325.
2. *Laṅkāvatāra-sūtra,* p. 169.
3. vikalpamātram tribhavam bāhyamartham na vidyate I chittamātrāvatāreṇa prajñā Tāthāgatī matā II *Ibid.*, p. 186.
4. *Ibid.*, pp. 42-6.

all impressions (*vāsanās*) and ideas (vijñānas) of all individuals. It is universal and ever-changing stream of consciousness. It manifests itself into seven vijñānas which include the six vijñānas of Sarvāstivāda (*chakṣu, ghrāṇa, shrotra, jivhā* and *kāya* vijñanas representing the five sense-cognitions and *mano*vijñāna or normal consciousness) and a seventh named *manas* representing continuous consciousness of the individual. This is a sort of intermediary between the six pravṛtti-vijñānas and the *Ālaya.* Vasubandhu calls it *kliṣṭa*-manovijñāna. *Ālaya* is called '*paratantra*' because it is fouled by transcendental Ignorance which engenders the subject-object duality and is conditioned by the causal law of pratītya-samūtpāda. Though the word '*paratantra*' (dependent or causally conditioned) is mainly used for Ālayavijñāna, it is also applied to its seven manifestations, the *manas* and the six pravṛtti-vijñānas and all these eight vijñānas are called *paratantra. Chitta-mātra* or pure vijñāna (undefiled by subject-object duality) is called 'parinispanna' or the ultimate reality. It is identified in this Sūtra with Tathāgatagarbha. The individual subjects (*pudgala*) and the so-called external objects (*dharma*) are declared to be '*parikalpita*' or absolutely non-existent like a hare's horn or a sky-castle. *Laṅkāvatāra* makes it very clear that the manifestation of *Chittamātra* as *Ālaya* and the manifestation of *Ālaya* as the *manas* and the six pravṛtti-vijñānas is only an appearance and the law of dependent causation is only empirically valid and is not ultimately real.

Pure *Chitta-mātra* appears as *chitta* or Ālayavijñāna due to transcendental Ignorance *avidyā* or *vāsanā.* This *vāsanā* is *a priori* construction of subject-object duality (*grāhya-grāhaka-vāsanā* or *grāhadvaya-vāsanā*). It consists in the transcendental idea of objectivity, which imagines the non-existent object (*abhūta-parikalpa-vāsanā*). It is the beginningless *vāsanā* which imagines this world of plurality (*anādi-prapañcha-dauṣṭhulya-vāsanā*). *Ālaya* or universal Vijñāna itself, which in fact is *chittamātra,* is called the locus (*āshraya*) and the object (*ālambana* or *viṣaya*) of this beginningless *vāsanā. Ālaya* itself appears as the subject and the object, the perceiver and the perceived, as the *manas* and the six pravṛtti-vijñānas which constitute this entire world of subject-object duality. The individual subjects and the external objects are absolutely unreal; it is the vijñānas themselves which appear in the 'form' (*ākāra*) of subjects and objects. *Manas* maintains continuity in the stream of individual pravṛtti-vijñānas; this power is derived by *manas* from

Ālaya. An infinite number of streams of momentary individual pravṛtti-vijñānas, each stream being determined by its *manas,* are continuously flowing within *Ālaya.* When *manas* temporarily merges in *Ālaya* during states like deep sleep, unconscious states and trance states, *Ālaya* by its continuous flow makes the continuity of the individual stream possible and when the above states are over, *manas* comes out of *Ālaya* to function by itself. *Vāsanā* is the force (*shakti*) of will-consciousness; it is the karma-samskāra in vijñāna defiled by *avidyā* and *karma.* In *Ālaya* individual *vāsanās* mature and produce vijñānas and vijñānas in turn leave their *vāsanās* in *Ālaya* and thus continuously replenish it.[1] Just as the waves stirred by the wind dance on the ocean, similarly the waves of individual vijñānas stirred by the wind of objects dance on the ocean of *Ālaya* and *Ālaya* itself appears to be dancing with them.[2] As the waves are neither identical with nor different from the ocean, similarly the seven vijñānas are neither identical with nor different from *Ālaya.*[3] The defilement of vijñānas is ultimately an appearance.[4] *Ālaya* or universal vijñāna is the seat (*āshraya*) of all *vikalpa* or volitional activity which constructs subject-object duality. It is the original (mūla) *vikalpaka* vijñāna. *Laṅkāvatāra* treats *manas* as 'vikalpaka manovijñāna' and says that when it rises above *vāsanā* or subject-object duality its flow dries up and alongwith it *Ālaya* also dries up for it and it merges with pure non-dual Vijñāna.

This merging of *manas* or *vikalpaka* manovijñāna in Pure Vijñāna by transcending subject-object duality is Nirvāṇa itself.[5] When the idea of objectivity is rooted out there is no object to be perceived and in the absence of an object, the subject also glides away, and consciousness shines as pure non-dual Absolute Vijñāna, the Vijñāpti-mātra, which it always is.[6]

Noticing that Chitta-mātra or Tathāgata-garbha comes very near *Ātmā* of the Upaniṣads, Laṅkāvatāra itself takes pain to distinguish it from *Ātmā* of the Non-Buddhists (Tīrthika). Mahāmati asks

1. *Laṅkāvatāra,* pp. 126-7.
2. ālayaughastathā nityam viṣayapavaneritaḥ I chitraistarangavijñānair nṛtyamānaḥ pravartate II p. 46.
3. *Ibid.*, p. 46.
4. *Ibid.*, pariṇāmo na labhyate.
5. vikalpakasya manovijñānasya vyāvṛttir nirvāṇam *Ibid.*, p. 126.
6. yadā tu ālambyam artham nopalabhate jñānam tadā vijñaptimātra-vyavasthānam bhavati, *Ibid.*, p. 169.

Bhagavān: Tathāgatagarbha is declared by you, O Lord, to be self-luminous (*prakṛti-prabhāsvara*), to be eternally pure (*ādi-vishuddha*), to be immanent in all beings (*sarva-sattva-dehāntara-gata*), to be immortal (*nitya*), eternal (*dhruva*), unchanging (*shāshvata*) and blissful (*shiva*). Then, how, O Lord, is it not similar to *Ātmā* of the Non-Buddhists? ...... Bhagavān replies: No Mahāmati, Tathāgatagarbha is not similar to *Ātmā* because it transcends all categories of thought (*nirvikalpa*), because it is neither affirmation nor negation nor both nor neither, and because it is to be directly realised by non-dual spiritual experience (*nirābhāsa-prajñā-gochara*), while *Ātmā* clings to affirmation and leads to eternalism.[1]

It must be remarked that this attempt to distinguish Tathāgatagarbha from *Ātmā* may be applicable to *Ātmā* of those schools which take it as an eternal spiritual substance and objectify it, but this attempt proves utterly futile in respect of the Upaniṣadic *Ātmā* which is transcendent to thought-categories, including the categories of affirmation and negation and which is realisable by non-dual spiritual experience and which has inspired Buddha's conception of *Nirvāṇa*.

Thus we find that almost all the important doctrines of Vijñānavāda are found scattered in *Laṅkāvatāra-sūtra*. Maitreyanātha, the author of Madhyānta-vibhāga-kārikā recited by Asaṅga on which Vasubandhu has written his Bhāṣya which has been commented upon by Sthiramati in his *Ṭīkā*; Maitreya's illustrious disciple Asaṅga, the author of *Mahāyāna-sūtrālaṅkāra* and of a voluminous work *Yogāchāra-bhūmi-shāstra* (of which some Bhūmis have been published); and Asaṅga's younger brother Vasubandhu, the author of *Vijñaptimātratāsiddhi*: Vimshatikā (with auto-commentary) and Trimshikā with Sthiramati's Bhāṣya; and the gifted commentator Sthiramati have established and developed Vijñānavāda as a full-fledged system.

III. CONSCIOUSNESS PROVED TO BE THE ONLY REALITY AND REALISM REFUTED

In his Vijñaptimātratāsiddhi: Vimshatikā, with his own commentary on it, Vasubandhu proves that consciousness is the only reality

1. *Ibid.*, pp. 77-9.

and that the so-called empirical subjects and the so-called external objects are purely imaginary and absolutely unreal like the hair-like objects seen floating in the atmosphere or like the perception of two moons by persons of defective vision.[1] In Mahāyāna all the three worlds (*kāma, rūpa* and *arūpa*) are declared to be *chitta-mātra* or consciousness-only. The words *chitta, manas,* vijñāna and Vijñāpti are synonyms. *Chitta* or consciousness, as used here, includes its modifications or the mental states also. The word '*mātra*' (in *chitta-mātra*) is used in order to negate the object.[2] The false notion of objectivity generates the subject-object duality but this duality is within consciousness itself. The entire empirical world of individual subjects and external objects is rejected as utterly unreal (*parikalpita*); it does not enjoy even empirical reality. The individual ego is an illusory superimposition on the stream of momentary mental states and the so-called external object is an illusory superimposition on its 'form' assumed by consciousness and projected as objective. Hence, even empirical reality is accorded to the stream of momentary vijñānas which, infected with the transcendental and beginningless *vāsanā* of subject-object duality which is the projective power of *avidyā* or transcendental Illusion, flows on, creating its content and projecting it as objective. Vijñāna or consciousness, whether ultimate or phenomenal, is the only reality. The Absolute Vijñāna, called Vijñāptimātra, is pure, non-dual, eternal, indeterminate and blissful consciousness which is free from subject-object duality and can be realised through immediate spiritual experience. As it is beyond senses, thought and language, it is the transcendental Real and is called *Parinispanna* or *Paramārtha.* As the immanent reality of phenomena, it is called *Dharmadhātu* or *Dharmakāya.* It is ever-free from transcendental Illusion, relativity, causation and modification. When this Absolute Vijñāna appears to be tinged with transcendental *Vāsanā* or *Avidyā,* it becomes *paratantra* (conditioned by *Avidyā* and *karma*). The Absolute becomes the relative; the Pure gets defiled; the Transcendent becomes phenomenalised; the Unconditioned becomes conditioned by causation; the Eternal becomes the momentary and Pure Consciousness becomes the self-conscious cre-

1. vijñaptimātramevaitadasadarthāvabhāsanāt | yatha taimirikasyāsatkesha-chandrādidarshanam || *Vimshatika, Kārikā 1.*
2. *Vṛtti* on K. 1.

ative will. The motivating force of this evolutionary process is the projective power of *Avidyā* known as *mulā vāsanā* or *grāhadvaya-vāsanā* which gives rise to the transcendental Idea of objectivity and confronts consciousness with an 'other' generating subject-object duality. The Vijñāna-moments are conditioned by the causal law of pratītyasamutpāda and their flow goes on. Karma leaves its impressions (*samskāra* or *vāsanā*) in vijñānas and these *vāsanās* when matured give rise to further vijñānas assuming 'forms' (of objects) which in turn lead to further *vāsanās* and thus the cycle of *vāsanās* and vijñānas goes on in full swing.

In Hīnayāna, *pratītyasamutpāda* is taken as real causation governing the temporal sequence of the momentary reals (*dharmas*). The real is momentary and *pratītyasamutpāda* is the mark of the real. The Mādhyamika showed the hollowness of this view by his classic criticism of causality. Pratītyasamutpāda is not the temporal sequence of the momentary *dharmas,* but relativity which infects all things and reveals their essential dependence on causes and conditions and therefore their ultimate unreality. Causation is relative and not real. Vijñānavāda revives the Hīnayana interpretation of *pratītyasamutpāda* as the theory of causation governing the momentary real. It also revives the *dharma* theory, though radically transforming it. Dharmanairātmya, for Vijñānavāda, only means that there are no *dharmas* as objective reals. But these *dharmas* are transformed into consciousness (*chitta*) and its modes (*chaitta*) and their elaborate classification is indulged in and their number increased to one hundred, though to save absolutism from being hurt by this pluralism, only phenomenal reality is granted to them. When consciousness is infected with subject-object duality, it appears as particular, discrete and momentary; it breaks up, as it were, into an infinite number of momentary ideas. These ideas appear in various 'forms' and these 'forms' are the *dharmas,* which qualify consciousness and make distinctions among the momentary ideas possible. These dharmas belong to consciousness only in its infected state and like the momentary ideas enjoy only empirical reality. The causal law of pratītyasamutpāda operates only within the realm of vijñānas which emerge into existence and pass out of it strictly according to the law of causation. The momentary vijñānas alone, and not the imaginary subjects (*pudgala*) and objects (*dharma*) are governed by *pratītyasamutpāda.* In Hīnayāna, *pratītyasamutpāda* governs all the momentary *dharmas,* the elements of existence, which include the subjective vijñānas as well as the objective reals. In Vijñānavāda, there are no objective dharmas and so *pratītyasamutpāda* operates only in the realm of the momentary vijñānas. The Absolute Vijñāna is beyond causation and the imaginary subjects and objects cannot be subject to causation. These are called parikalpita or purely imaginary or utterly unreal like barren woman's son or hare's horn or sky-flower. These may be valid for common sense (*loka-vyavahāra*) but these are not valid for genuine philosophy (*shuddha-laukika-vyavahara*). What is real, even empirically, is the 'form' (*ākāra* or *ābhāsa*) of the subject or of the object assumed by consciousness and not the imaginary subject or the object supposed to be existing independently and outside of consciousness. *Pratītyasamutpāda* is the mark of the creative Will-Consciousness which is not ultimately real.

Thus Vijñānavāda establishes its position. It is idealism *par excellence,* both ontologically as well as epistemologically. It knows that in order to prove its idealism it has to refute realism and answer the objections raised against it. This it undertakes to do in detail.

Vijñānavāda says that the notion of an object is purely imaginary. An object may be conceived either as a substance with its qualities or a whole made of parts.[1] What we perceive are its qualities and not a substance over and above them and these qualities are evidently mental. It is illogical to imagine the so-called material substance, unknown and unknowable, as the cause to produce what is mental.[2] Our empirical life is accounted for by our *karma-samskāras* (which are in the mind) which are the seeds which fructify as our empirical experience. If the seeds (*karma-samskāra* or *vāsanā*) are in consciousness, how can their fruits be imagined to be outside consciousness?[3] If creation is due to *karma-samskāra* or *vāsanā,* as it must be, then it is nothing but a modification of consciousness which contains the seeds of creation.[4] Again, if this supposed substance is treated as the modification of Primordial Matter (*Prakṛti*) it is not possible, for the

1. *Pramāṇa-vārtika,* II, 360 and *Tattvasaṅgraha-Pañjikā,* pp. 550-1.
2. Such arguments are also advanced by Berkeley against Locke's substance and by Hegal against Kant's 'thing-in-itself'.
3. karmaṇo vāsanā' nyatra phalam anyatra kalpyate I tatraiva neṣyate yatra vāsanā kinnu kāraṇam II *Vimshatikā,* Kārika 7.
4. *Vimshatikā,* Kārikā 6.

dependence of *Prakṛti* on Consciousness (*Puruṣa*) in some way or the other has to be accepted to explain evolution and the supposed independence of *Prakṛti* vanishes. Consciousness alone can be creative when it is Will-Consciousness. Nor can the object be supposed to be a whole made up of parts. The relation between a whole and its parts can be neither internal nor external. And if these wholes are reduced to their ultimate constituents which are called the indivisible atoms the position becomes worse. An atom is supposed to have magnitude and yet it is treated as partless! It has no extension and yet it occupies space! How can these atoms combine? If an atom is indivisible it cannot be conjoined with another, for contact is always between its parts. And if it is composed of parts, it is not an atom at all. And if an atom occupies space, it is simultaneously related to the six directions[1] and so it must have at least six parts and is no more an atom. The atomic theory cannot be logically proved[2]. Hence the notion of an object is self-contradictory.

Realism believes that the perceived content is entirely independent of the act of perception. Knowledge is like light, it merely reveals the given without affecting its nature.[3] It cannot make or unmake things; it merely discovers them and makes them known. There can be no knowledge without an object, for knowledge depends on the object which it reveals.[4] Knowledge is a subject-object relation; it arises in the subject, but it is produced by the object when the subject comes into contact with it. Realism believes, firstly, that the object exists independently and outside of consciousness; and secondly, that it is the object which produces knowledge which is merely representative and corresponds with the object[5]. Vijñānavāda rejects both these contentions. It points out that the object is the creation or projection of consciousness and therefore cannot exist independently and outside of consciousness.[6] And it also points out that knowledge is not representative but constructive; that it creates its content, projects it as objective and knows it as such.[7] Hence it is impossible for an

1. East, West, North, South, Up and Down.
2. *Vimshatika-Vṛtti*, pp. 6-8, on Kārikās, 11-15.
3. arthaprakāsho buddhiḥ.
4. na chā'viṣayā kāchid upalabdhiḥ.
5. yathārtham sarvavijñānam.
6. samvedanabāhyatvam ato'rthasya na sidhyati.—Prāmāṇa-vārtika, p. 32.
7. yadantar jñeyarūpam tad bahirvadavabhāsate.—*Ālambana-parīkṣā*, 6.

unreal object to produce knowledge; on the other hand, it is consciousness itself which assumes the 'form' of an object and projects it and knows it as objective.

Vijñānavāda first advances the argument of *sahopalambha-niyama* or *esse est percipi* in order to refute realism. The argument says that as the object and its perception are always found together, the being of the object consists in its being perceived. The blue (object) and the consciousness of the blue are identical (*abhedo nīlataddhiyoḥ*). Consciousness having the form of the blue appears as if it were an external blue object. How can the realist assert that the object is unaffected by knowledge when he cannot know what the object is before being perceived? The realist retorts that *sahopalambha-niyama* or the fact that the object is invariably perceived along with the knowledge of it has only epistemic validity and cannot be given an ontological status. Ontologically it can prove or disprove nothing, neither realism nor idealism. It is, what Perry calls, "the ego-centric predicament". It simply says: 'We cannot know without knowing'. This cannot prove that knowledge creates objects or that objects generate knowledge. This *niyama* positively proves nothing.

Realising this difficulty, Vijñānavāda undertakes the analysis of illusion, hallucination and dream in order to give a *positive proof* for the creativity of consciousness to supplement the argument from sahopalambha-niyama. *Illusion* has been the solid rock against which many well-built ships of different forms of realism have helplessly crashed. No form of realism, Indian or Western, has been able to satisfactorily explain the fact of illusion. If knowledge truly reveals the object, how can there be error or illusion at all? If there is no subjective element in knowledge to distort or falsify the real, the possibility of illusion is ruled out. There are two main forms of realism, naive and critical. Naive realism believes in the presentation theory of perception which is a two-term theory of direct perception, while critical realism believes in the representative theory of perception which is a three-term theory according to which the object is not directly presented in knowledge but represented indirectly through its image in knowledge which is called an 'idea'. Naive realism breaks down when we consider the subjective factor involved in perception. No two persons perceive an object in an identical way. Moreover, what we directly perceive is not the object but qualities which are subjective. Critical realism also breaks down. If consciousness perceives only its ideas or representations and not the objects, then the existence of the objects cannot be maintained. The correspondence theory of truth, to which this representative theory of perception leads, is also unsatisfactory. When we cannot know the original objects, how can we compare the images with the originals and say whether they correspond with them or not?

Some realists have made bold, but unconvincing, attempts to explain away illusion. Prabhākara denies the possibility of error by explaining it away as partial truth. There is no subjective element in knowledge which always represents its objects truly. Error is non-apprehension of the distinction between the two cognitions and their distinct objects. But this bold attempt to explain illusion away is entirely unconvincing. Error consists in misapprehension. The rope is misperceived as snake. The subjective element in error cannot be denied. The Naiyāyika goes to the length of saying that the illusory snake is perceived as an objective reality through extra-ordinary perception called *jñāna-lakṣaṇa-pratyakṣa.* This is, evidently, an arbitrary assumption to save the face of realism. When pressed, the Naiyāyika has to admit that error is misapprehension and that a subjective element is involved in it. But the application of the subjective is restricted only to a false relation. Error lies in the false relation between two unrelated reals (rope and snake in the above example). But in illusion the rope is not 'presented' in knowledge, otherwise there would be no illusion at all, and the real snake is also not there (it may be elsewhere), then what accounts for the false relation between the two? The relation of the rope with the illusory snake is false because the illusory snake is unreal in itself and there can be no relation between the real and the unreal. What is perceived in illusion is neither the real rope (which is there, but not perceived) nor the real snake (which is not there), but the illusory snake created and projected by consciousness as objective.

By an analysis of illusion Vijñānavāda shows that illusion takes away the very basis of realism that knowledge merely represents and does not construct its object which exists independently and outside of knowledge. In illusion consciousness creates its own content by assuming the form of the object and projecting it as objective. But in illusory perceptions in normal waking life an objective counterpart remains which serves as the ground on which the illusory object is superimposed, for example, rope in the 'rope-snake' and shell in the 'shell-silver' illusion. Vijñānavāda is not directly concerned with this ground, firstly, because the ground is not involved in any way in illusion; secondly, because it is interested in proving that consciousness creates its own content and projects it as objective, and thirdly, because the so-called objective ground (rope or shell, etc.) is nothing but a projection of universal consciousness (ālaya-vijñāna). Vijñānavāda, then, cites the examples of *hallucinations* and apparitions, where the creativity of consciousness is more manifest and there is no objective counterpart. But such examples are abnormal and rare. *Vijñānavāda*, therefore, takes as the *norm* that class of illusion which is normal and where the creativity of consciousness is fully manifest without any objective counterpart, namely, *dreams.* Dreams are illusory because they are cancelled on waking. But as long as the dream-world lasts it is complete in itself, is regulated by its own psychological laws of association, creates its own objects, projects them as objective and experiences them as such and is solely due to the creative activity of consciousness.

If consciousness can create its content and project it as objective in illusion, hallucination and dream, then it is logical to conclude that it can do the same in our waking experience of the so-called objective world. The realist strongly objects to this. He says that illusion or dream should not be universalised. Our real world is not an illusion or a dream. The realist distinguishes our world from illusory or dream world on four points. First and second, the real world which is regulated by physical laws is subject to spatial and temporal determination (*desha-kāla-niyama*); third, it is public and not private like illusion or dream, it is the world of intra-subjective experience (*santānāniyama*) and fourth, it leads to successful activity (*kṛtya-kriyā*).[1] Vijñānavāda replies: If the empirical world is determined by space and time, similar determinations obtain, even in the dream-world. Even in a dream things like a city, a garden, a woman or a man etc., are seen in a particular place and a particular time and not in all places and at all times. If the empirical world is governed by its physical laws,

1. yadi vijñaptiranarthā niyamo desha-kālayoḥ I santānasyāniyamashcha yuktā kṛtya-kriyā na cha II *Vimshatikā,* K. 2.

the dream-world is also governed by its own psychological laws of association. If we cannot project anything we like at our sweet will in the empirical world, we cannot cause any event to happen in our dreams. Our conscious mind has no control over the dream-experience. Again, if the knowledge of the empirical objects leads to fruitful activity, the dream-objects too are pragmatic in nature and lead to successful activity. The dream-food and dream-water quench the hunger and thirst in dream. The roaring of a dream-tiger causes real fear in the dreamer and affects his psycho-physical organism. The horror of a nightmare troubles the dreamer. An erotic dream is followed by real ejaculation.[1] The rope-snake affects a person in illusion in the same way in which a real snake would affect him in normal perception under those conditions. Hence the illusory and dream objects also lead to successful activity. Again, as to the distinction that experience in illusion and dream is essentially private while world-experience is public, Vijñānavāda replies that though this distinction is obvious, it is only one of degree and not of kind. The illusory and dream objects are the projection of individual consciousness (*kliṣṭa manas*) which is less powerful as it is crippled by Ignorance, while the world-objects are the projection of universal consciousness (ālaya-vijñāna) which is all-powerful. It would be utterly wrong to imagine that this distinction is due to the fact that world-objects are real and illusory and dream objects are false[2]. Both are unreal because both are *equally* 'forms' of consciousness. Moreover, it would be wrong to call the empirical world as *the* world. Experience is essentially personal and no two percipients could perceive the same object in an identical way. Each subject is a stream of consciousness (*chitta-santāna*). There is a harmony, in a general sense, among the experiences of such different streams because they flow within the *Ālaya* which is the universal stream of consciousness and because the empirical objects are projections of this universal stream. And some harmony may be found even in the experiences of similar illusion, dream or hallucination by different persons under similar conditions. It is not impossible that some persons may see a similar dream at the same time. Moreover, the departed persons (*preta*) who go to hell (*naraka*) experience the torture

1. *Vimshatika*, Karikā 3-4 with Vṛtti.
2. middhenopahatam chittam svapne tenā' samam phalam. *Ibid.*, K. 18 with *Vṛtti.*

and see the same river of pus, etc., and the same infernal guards who torture them who are not objective realities (as they do not experience the hellish torture) but mere creations of the *karma-saṁskāras* or *vāsanās* of these departed persons.[1] Vijñānavāda thus concludes that spatio-temporal determination, successful activity and harmony of intra-subjective experiences cannot prove the objective reality of the empirical world; on the other hand, these things, which are found in our experience of hallucination, illusion and dream also, prove that like the illusory and the dream-objects, the world-objects too are projections of consciousness, though of universal consciousness. The validity of illusion or dream cannot be questioned as long as it lasts for during its endurance it is treated as real; its unreality is realised only when illusion is dispelled by empirical knowledge or dream is sublated by waking state. Similarly, the world-objects are taken as real on the empirical level; their unreality is realised only when pure non-dual consciousness dawns[2].

The realist further objects that if there are no external objects, how can consciousness assume the form of objects and project them as objective ? Even illusion is rooted in reality. A person who has never seen or known a snake cannot mistake a rope for a snake. The content of dream-experience is supplied by the experience of the real world. Strange 'objects' which are not found in the real world may be seen in a dream, e.g., gold-mountain, man-lion, ten-headed person, sphinx, mermaid, unicorn, etc., but these are made by combination of different objects found and experienced in the real world. Had there been no external object, even the idea could not appear as if it were an external object. There can be no hypothetical without a categorical basis. And without the experience of a real object, even the idea of objectivity itself would be impossible. Vijñānavāda accepts that illusion is not possible without a real ground[3]. The illusion of subject-object duality is rooted in Vijñāna which is its supporting ground. This only proves that had there been no consciousness, there could have been no illusion of objectivity. The illusion of objectivity does not presuppose the existence of an external object. The question whether without a snake there could or could not

1. *Vimshatika,* K. 3-6 with Vṛtti.
2. svapne dṛgviṣayābhāvam nā'prabuddho' vāgachchhati, *Ibid.*, K. 17.
3. upachārasya nirādhārasyā'sambhavāt.—*Trimshikā-Bhāṣya,* p. 16.

be an illusory snake and without the empirical world there could or could not be a dream-world is a different question not relevant here because it has to be admitted, even by the realist, that it is the *idea* and not the object which directly works in illusion or dream. An analysis of the rope- snake illusion reveals the following points which are to be admitted: (1) that it is the *idea* of the snake, and not the snake itself, which directly gives rise to the illusory snake; (2) that consciousness assumes the *form* of the snake; and (3) that consciousness *projects* it as *objective* and perceives it as such because the projection of a content implies its perception as an object. Even granting that the idea of a snake is not possible without the experience of a real snake, this so-called real snake turns out to be not a real object but merely an idea projected by universal consciousness (ālaya vijñāna). And if an idea projected by individual consciousness (*kliṣṭa* manes) presupposes an idea projected by universal consciousness, it only means that an idea presupposes another idea, and not that an idea presupposes an object. An idea can be generated only by another idea and not by an unreal object. Creativity of consciousness does not mean that it actually produces external objects; it means that the idea itself appears as an external object. Universal consciousness projects the empirical world when it appears to be tinged with subject-object duality. This duality presupposes the idea of objectivity which is due to transcendental illusion. To the objection as to how consciousness can suffer from the idea of objectivity when there is no real object, the reply is that the idea of objectivity is a transcendental Illusion and is not empirical in nature. Objectivity is not an abstraction from empirical experience; on the other hand, it is an *a priori* category and as such it is the necessary pre-supposition of all empirical experience. It is not an empty form as the Kantian categories are. It is a form which creates its content and projects it as objective. As it is transcendental Illusion it works even without there being real external objects and real empirical subjects. The superimposition of the unreal subjects (*ātmā*) and objects (*dharma*) on the modification of consciousness (*vijñāna-pariṇāma*) is secondary (*gauṇa*), not primary (*mukhya*); the superimposition (*upachāra*) is said to be secondary when the superimposed content is unreal.[1] It is a false superimposition on

1. gauṇo hi nāma yo yatra avidyamānena rūpeṇa pravartate.—*Ibid.*, p. 17; also *Madhyāntaṭīkā* on K. I, 4.

the Real. As it is transcendental, it can be removed only by the realisation of pure, non-dual, absolute Vijñāna. As the imposed subjects and objects are utterly unreal and the transcendental Illusion which compels Vijñāna to undergo modification in diverse forms is also ultimately unreal, it is proved that Vijñaptimātra or the pure, non-dual, absolute consciousness is the only reality. It is beyond relational thought and can be realised only by the immediate spiritual experience of the Buddhas.[1]

IV. IS VIJÑĀNA-PARIṆĀMA OR THE MODIFICATION OF CONSCIOUSNESS REAL OR APPARENT?

Sthiramati in his Bhāṣya (commentary) on Vasubandhu's Trimshikā tells us that the aim of this treatise is to reveal the real meaning of *pudgala-nairātmya* (unreality of the ego) and *dharma-nairātmya* (unreality of the objects). The former removes the 'covering of suffering' (*kleshāvaraṇa*) and the latter the 'covering of ignorance of the Real' (*Jñeyāvaraṇa*). All suffering (*klesha*) flows from the false notion of the 'I' and the 'mine', which notion is due to the illusion of objectivity. Ignorance of the Real also owes its origin to this illusion of objectivity which forces the Real to assume the forms of the subject and the object and project and perceive them as objective. The primary *vāsanā* of objectivity is transcendental Illusion or *avidyā* which leads to *karma* (volitional activity) and its *samskāras* or *vāsanās* and *kleshas* which constitute bondage or empirical life (*samsāra*). When through intense discipline of yoga the illusion of objectivity is completely rooted out from the stream of consciousness, the subject also glides away alongwith it and the stream itself dries up, the cycle of dependent causation and the modification of consciousness collapse leaving consciousness to shine in its original non-dual absolute purity (Vijñaptimātratā). This is immediate spiritual Experience which is Freedom (*Nirvāṇa* or *Mokṣa*) and Omniscience (*sarvajñatā*).[2] It is also the aim of this treatise, Sthiramati continues, to show the genuine 'middle path' (*madhyamā pratipat*) by avoiding the two extreme views. Some believe that vijñeya or the object (i.e., the empirical subjects and objects which are projections of conscious-

1. sarvathā sā tu na chintyā Buddhagocharaḥ. *Vimshatikā*, pp. 10-11.
2. *Trimshikā-Bhāṣya*, p. 15; aviparītapudgala-dharma-nairātmyapratipādanārtham *Trimshikā-Vijñapti-prakaraṇārambhaḥ*.

ness and are perceived by it as 'objects') is also substantially real (*dravyataḥ eva*) like vijñāna; while others believe that vijñāna too, like vijñeya, is empirically real (*samvṛtitaḥ eva*) and not ultimately real (*na paramārthataḥ*). These are the two extreme views (*ekāntavāda*) of realism and nihilism which are to be avoided by the 'middle path'.[1] Sthiramati further observes: The empirical subjects and objects (*vijñeya*) are purely imaginary (*parikalpita*) as they are superimposed on the forms (*ākāra*) assumed by vijñāna and therefore they do not really exist (*vijñeyam vastuto na vidyate*). Hence, the extreme view that vijñeya too, like vijñāna, is substantially real should be discarded. Empirical subjects and objects, as superimposition, are unreal, but the basis of this superimposition, the modification of vijñāna, must be accepted as real because superimposition cannot be baseless. Hence the extreme view that vijñāna too, like vijñeya, is empirically real and not ultimately real should be rejected. Hence it must be admitted that all vijñeya (the individual subjects and objects) is purely imaginary (*parikalpita*) and really does not exist, while vijñāna, being conditioned by causation (*pratītyasamutpannatvāt*) substantially exists (*dravyato'sti*)[2].

An important question arises here. Is *vijñāna-pariṇāma* or modification of consciousness real or unreal? That is, is it absolutely real or relatively real? Is *pratītyasamutāpāda* which governs the flow of these momentary vijñānas real causation or relative and therefore ultimately unreal causation? Vijñānavāda, it seems, does not face this question squarely. As has been pointed out before, Vijñānavāda is influenced by the pluralism of the Sautrāntika and the absolutism of the Mādhyamika and these two cannot go together. It has revived the dharma-theory of the Sautrāntika, though after radically transforming the dharmas from momentary objective reals into momentary vijñānas and mental states. It has also revived the interpretation of pratītyasamutpāda as the causal

---

1. *Ibid*; asya dviprakārasyāpi ekāntavādasya pratiṣedhārtham prakaraṇārambhaḥ.
2. parikalpita evātmā dharmāshcha natu paramārthataḥ santīti vijñānavad vijñeyamapi dravyata eva ityam ekāntavādo nābhypeyaḥ. upachārasya cha nirādhārasyā'sambhavād avashyam vijñānapariṇāmo vastutostītyupagantavyo yatrātmadharmopachāraḥ pravartate. atashchāyamupagamo na yuktīkṣamo vijñānamapi vijñeyavat samvṛtita eva na paramārthata iti..... evam cha sarvam vijñeyam parikalpitasvabhāvatvād vastuto na vidyate, vijñānam punaḥ pratītyasamutpannatvād dravyatostītyabhyupeyam—*Ibid*., p. 16.

law governing the flow of momentary vijñānas. And it also accepts the absolutism of the Mādhyamika, though it openly identifies the Absolute with pure non-dual Vijñāna and indulges in speculative metaphysics. This background is mostly responsible for contradictions we find in Vijñānavāda. Vijñānavāda emphatically maintains that Vijñāna, whether pure or defiled, is the only reality; that objectivity is due to beginningless *vāsanā* which is transcendental Illusion (*Avidyā*); and that the individual subjects and objects, which constitute our world, are utterly unreal (*parikalpita*). It is keen to emphasise the creativity of consciousness, its defilement with beginningless *grāhadvayavāsanā* and its consequent purification by rooting out this *vāsanā* through intense yogic discipline from which it derives its name Yogāchāra. Let us now see how Vijñānavāda faces the question raised above. Vijñānavāda, on the one hand, declares that Vijñāna is creative, that its *pariṇāma* or modification is real and that the momentary vijñānas are really governed by the causal law of *pratītyasamutpāda.* And, on the other hand, it emphatically maintains that the creativity or modification of vijñāna is due to its defilement with the beginningless *Vāsanā* of subject-object duality which is transcendental Illusion or *Avidyā,* that it is this Illusion which makes Vijñāna conditioned by the causal law of *pratītyasmutpāda* and forces it to undergo modification and assume various forms of subjects and objects and project them as objective, and that vijñāna in its own nature is non-dual, pure and absolute Vijñaptimātra which is utterly untouched by this Illusion. Considering these two views expressed by Vijñānavāda and specially the passage from *Trimshikā-Bhāṣya* cited above (on page 90) in which Sthiramati has clearly stated that vijñāna-pariṇāma (modification of consciousness) is real and that vijñāna, which is conditioned by the causal law of *pratītyasamutpāda* should be treated as substantially real, some scholars have opined that according to Vijñanāvāda, pariṇāma is real, though not ultimate; and that as it believes in the creativity of consciousness it cannot accept vivartavāda. Now, the statement that *pariṇāma* is real, though not ultimate, is a case of clear self-contradiction, because metaphysically the real is always the ultimate. And as the motive power which forces Vijñāna to undergo modification is not treated as its real power or will, but declared to be transcendental Illusion (*mūlā vāsanā* or *Avidyā*), Vijñānavāda cannot logically accept the ultimate reality of modification or causation and in order to avoid self-contradiction has to accept vivartavāda. We have already pointed out above that two contradictory currents are found in Vijñānavāda due to the influence of the Sautrāntika pluralism and the Mādhyamika absolutism which cannot be harmonised. Vijñānavāda accepts absolutism and suppresses pluralism by according only phenomenal reality to the modification of Vijñāna, to causation, to plurality and momentariness of vijñānas. The later school of Svatantra-Vijñānavāda, however, kicked out absolutism and maintained the reality of the stream of momentary vijñānas only.

The 'reality' of the modification of consciousness can be reconciled with the ultimate reality of the Absolute Vijñāna by treating this 'reality' as phenomenal reality only. This is what Vijñānavāda has done and the passage from Sthiramati's commentary cited above has to be properly understood. Sthiramati in this passage brings out the absolute reality of vijñāna, the relative reality of *pariṇāma* and the utter unreality of the individual subjects and objects. What he means is that vijñāna-pariṇāma must be treated as substantially real (*dravyataḥ*) because it serves as the substance (*dravya*) or the basis (*āshraya*) on which the imaginary (*parikalpita*) is superimposed, as even an illusion cannot be baseless. But the vijñāna which undergoes *pariṇāma* is conditioned by *pratītyasamutpāda* and is *paratantra* (dependent, conditioned, relative). In reality, it is not different from the Unconditioned Vijñāna (*parinispanna*) which appears as *paratantra* due to transcendental Illusion. It is the Absolute which is the transcendental ground (*adhiṣṭhāna*) indirectly supporting the Illusion, but directly uninvolved in it. The *paratantra* vijñāna, which undergoes *pariṇāma* and projects its forms on which the imaginary subjects and objects are superimposed, acts as the immanent basis (*āshraya*) of this superimposition and is relatively real. The statement of Sthiramati that 'vijñāna is substantially real because it is conditioned by causation' means that vijñāna alone is real and that causation can obtain only in vijñānas and not in the imaginary subjects and objects; it does not mean that the conditioning of vijñāna by causation is real. That which is conditioned is relative and not ultimate. It is not the inherent nature of Vijñāna to change and put upon different forms. The motive power governing the process of evolution is not the real power or the free will of the Absolute, but transcendental Illusion of objectivity which does not affect the Absolute at all. The process is real phenomenally and is carried only upto the *Ālaya*-vijñāna, the *paratantra,* and not beyond. Sthiramati himself, in his *Ṭīkā* on the *Madhyānta-vibhāgasūtra-bhāṣya* of Vasubandhu, clearly observes: Paratantra is real, but not ultimately. It is real because it is the basis (*āshraya*) of the superimposition of the imaginary subject-object duality. Its modification in assuming the forms of the subject and the object is not ultimately real because it is due to transcendental Illusion.[1] Paratantra is clearly declared to be *samvṛti satya* or phenomenal truth.[2] The Parinispanna is the only absolute reality.[3]

Vijñānavāda repeatedly declares that *pariṇāma* of vijñāna is not ultimately real because it is due to transcendental Illusion. There is no real 'becoming' in the Absolute. The process is valid as long as we suffer from this transcendental Illusion. The words *pariṇāma* and *vivarta* acquired their fixed philosophical meaning only after Shaṅkarāchārya. Before him, the words *pariṇāma, vikāra* and *vivarta* were used as synonyms in the general sense of change (*anyathātva*) and it was to be found out from the context, whether this change was real or unreal. For example, *Laṅkāvatārasūtra*[4] uses the word pariṇāma in the sense of *vivarta,* when the waves are said to be the *pariṇāma* of the ocean. In *Trimshikā,* Vasubandhu names the relation between *Ālaya* and phenomena as '*pariṇāma*' by giving the simile of water and waves.[5] Even *Shāntarakṣitā* (8th century) uses *pariṇāma* and *vivarta* as synonyms.[6] Sthiramati also defines *pariṇāma* as 'change' (*anyathātva)* and not as real change.[7] The word *pariṇama* is used in Vijñānavāda clearly in the sense of vivarta or appearance. Vijñānavāda is absolutism and a self-consistent absolutism cannot believe in real transformation of the Absolute. Though ultimately bondage and liberation, defilement and purification both are appearance, yet the phenomenal reality of defilement of vijñāna and its consequent purification by intense yogic and spiritual discipline is fully emphasised.

1: paratantralakṣaṇaṃ sat, na tu tattvata iti. grāhya-grāhakādi-kalpita-vyavahārāshrayattvat sattvam.... yathā khyāti grāhya-grāhakākāreṇa naitadevam ato bhrāntiriti. *MVSBT,* p. 113. (on K., III, 3)

2. paratantraḥ samvṛtisatyam. *Ibid.*, p. 124.

3. ekameva mūlatattvam yaduta pariniṣpannaḥ svabhāvaḥ. *Ibid.*, p. 135.

4. p. 46; see *supra,* p. 77.

5. *Trimshikā, K.* 15.

6. *Tattvasaṅgraha, K.* 328-9.

7. koyam pariṇāmo nāma? anyathātvam. *Trimshikā-Bhāṣya,* p. 16.

V. THE TRIPLE MODIFICATION OF VIJÑĀNA

When the pure, absolute, non-dual Vijñānamātra somehow gets associated with the beginningless (*anādi*), transcendental (*mūlā*), *vāsanā* of subject-object duality, which is the projecting power (*shakti*) of transcendental Illusion (*Avidyā*), it appears as creative Will and the process of evolution of Vijñāna which diversifies itself into an infinite plurality of vijñānas creating their contents and projecting them as objective starts in full swing. *Mūlā Vāsanā* is the creative power of Vijñāna and though itself a transcendental Illusion is non-different from it and forces it to undergo modification by assuming different forms.[1] It gives rise to volitional activity (*karma*) which leaves its impressions called *vāsanā* or *samskāra* in vijñāna and their actualisation leads to further vijñānas which in turn give rise to further *vāsanās* and this cycle goes on constituting our world-experience.

Though Vijñāna diversifies itself into an infinite plurality of evolutes giving rise to world-experience, there are three main stages of this evolution. These are *Ālayavijñāna, kliṣṭa manas* and the six *viṣaya-vijñānas*[2] which are five sense-cognitions and mental states.

(1) *Ālaya-vijñāna:* This is the first stage in evolution. The pure non-dual Vijñaptimātra, through transcendental Illusion of objectivity becomes *Ālaya*-vijñāna. Pure Consciousness becomes self-consciousness. Pure knowledge becomes creative will. The Unconditioned Absolute (*Pariniṣpanna*) becomes conditioned and relative (*paratantra*). The *Ālaya,* though conditioned by *Vāsanā* or *Avidyā,* still stands on a transcendental level and is not empirical. It is the basis of all empirical experience generated by *a priori* categories implicitly contained in it. *Avidyā* does not cover the *Ālaya* and so it is entirely free from suffering (*klesha*). Only the projecting side of *avidyā,* the *mūlā grāhadvayavāsanā,* i.e., the transcendental Illusion of subject-object duality is present in the *Ālaya*

1. shaktirūpā hi vāsanā. *Pramāṇavārtika,* p. 22 jñānasyaiva shaktimātram vāsanā; asmākam tu vitathābhiniveshavāsanaiva avidyā. *Tattvasaṁgrahapañjikā,* p. 75. vāsanābhuto'sti kashchid visheṣaḥ...
yadādhipatyena parasparabhinnābhasam vijñānam prajāyate. *Madhyāntavibhāgatīkā,* p. 15, 19.
2. pariṇāmaḥ sa cḥa tridhā. vipako mananākhyashcha vijñaptir viṣayasya cha. *Trimshika,* K. 1-2.

in an undifferentiated (*idantayā asamvidita*) and indeterminate (*aparichchhinna*) state. The indeterminate content gets split up into an infinite plurality of empirical determinations the seeds of which are already present in the *Ālaya*. The subject-aspect flows into a variety of individual streams of consciousness called the *kliṣṭa manas* and the object-aspect flows into six kinds of *viṣaya*-vijñānas of empirical consciousness. The *Ālaya* is universal consciousness but it flows like a vast stream, including infinite individual streams within it, always changing and therefore momentary.[1]

The *Ālaya* is the Absolute itself appearing as fouled by the transcendental Illusion of subject-object duality implicitly present in it. It is the immanent basis (*āshraya*) of all phenomena which are implicitly contained in it. The word '*Ālaya*' means store-house. The *Ālaya*-vijñāna is so called because it is the store-house or the receptum of the seeds (*bīja*) or impressions (*vāsanā*) of all vijñānas (*tatrālayākhyam vijñānam vipākaḥ sarvabījakam*). It is 'the nurse and receptacle of all generation.' It is the immanent cause of all phenomena which are contained in it as its potential effects and which become explicit when actualised.[2] It is known as *vipāka* because it leads to the fructification of the seeds of all good or bad *karmas* contained in it by developing and maturing them.[3] It contains the impressions (*vāsanā*) of past vijñānas and by maturing these gives rise to present vijñānas which again leave their *vāsanās* or impressions in it. And thus this cycle goes on. The *Ālaya* is being continually replenished by further *vāsanās* so that the question of its getting exhausted is ruled out. The accumulation and maturity (*paripuṣṭi*) of *vāsanās* is called *hetu-pariṇāma*, while their actualisation (*abhinirvṛtti*) as effects is called *phala-pariṇāma*. *Vāsanā* is of two kinds—*vipākā-vāsanā*, which maintains the continuity of the stream of consciousness through successive births, and *niḥṣyanda-vāsanā* which supplies the content of each birth by actualising the impressions and gives rise to *kliṣṭa manas* and *viṣaya*-vijñānas.

---

1. tachcha vartate srotasaughavat. *Ibid.*, K.4. na hi tadekam abhinnam āsamsāram anuvartate, kṣaṇikatvāt. *Trimshikā-Bhāṣya*, p. 21.
2. ālīyante upanibadhyante asmin sarvadharmāḥ kāryabhāvena, ālīyate upanibadhyate asau kāraṇa-bhāvena sarvadharmeṣu iti ālayaḥ. *Ibid.*, p.18. Also *Madhyāntavibhāgaṭīkā*, p. 33-4 (K., I, 9).
3. sarvadhātugatiyonijātiṣu kushalākushalakarmavipākatvād vipākaḥ. *Trimshikā-Bhāṣya*, pp. 18-9.

In the *Ālaya* only the five mentals (*chaitta dharma*) called universal (*sarvatraga*) are present. These are: *sparsha, manaskāra, vedanā, samjñā* and *chetanā*.[1] *Sparsha* or contact is defined as *trika-sannipāta* which is the simultaneous flashing into existence of three factors of knowledge which are (i) the object or content cognised (*viṣaya*), (ii) the instrument of cognition or the sense-organ (*indriya*) and (iii) the cognising consciousness (vijñāna or *chitta*). Manaskāra is defined as attention or directing of the mind again and again to the same object (*chetasa ābhogaḥ*).[2] *Vedanā* is feeling, which may be pleasant, painful or indifferent. In the *Ālaya* there is only indifferent feeling (*upekṣā vedanā tatra*). Samjñā is apperception or conceptualising function leading to a determinate judgment like 'this is blue, not yellow'. It is defining the object by its characteristic mark.[3] *Chetanā* is volitional activity of the mind by which it flows as it were towards the object like iron getting attracted towards magnet.[4] These five mentals are present in the *Ālaya* in their pure and indeterminate form. As *avidyā* does not 'cover' the nature of the *Ālaya* it is called *anivṛta* or unobscured by suffering.[5] And as subject-object duality is present in it in its undifferentiated and indeterminate form it is called '*avyākṛta*' as it cannot be categorised as good or bad.[6] The *Ālaya* is not non-dual eternal consciousness; it is ever-changing and momentary. It flows like a universal stream of consciousness containing within it an infinite plurality of streams of individual consciousness (*chitta-santati*).[7] In *Nirvāṇa,* the stream of *Ālaya*-vijñāna dries up. When Buddhahood is attained, the *Ālaya* is transcended; the transcendental Illusion of objectivity is eradicated and consequently the operation of the *Ālaya* comes to a stop.[8]

Although the *Ālaya*vijñāna is not ultimate, its phenomenal reality must be accepted to account for bondage and liberation. There can be no bondage without *avidyā* and *samskāra* and *Ālaya* is the

1. sadā sparsha-manaskāra-vit-samjñā-chetanānvitam. *Trimshikā,* K. 3.
2. ābhogaḥ......ālambane punaḥ punaḥ chittasya āvarjanam. *Trimshikā-Bhāṣya,* p. 20.
3. viṣayanimittodgrahaṇam, viṣayavisheṣatvanirūpaṇam. *Ibid.*, p. 21.
4. chetanā chittābhisamskāro manashcheṣṭā. *Ibid.*
5. kleshairanāvṛtatvād anivṛtam. *Ibid.*
6. kushalākushalatvena avyākaraṇād avyākṛtam. *Ibid.*
7. tachcha vartate srotasaughavat. *Trimshikā,* K. 4.
8. tasya vyāvṛttirarhatve. *Ibid.*, K. 5.
   āshrayasya parāvṛttir dvidhā dauṣṭhulyahānitaḥ. *Ibid.*, K. 29.

receptum of these. Without a repository in which seeds of phenomena are stored, the flow of empirical life would come to an end. And there can be no *Nirvāṇa* unless this Illusion of objectivity and the *vāsanās*, alongwith the twofold coverings (*āvaraṇa*) of *klesha* and *jñeya*, are completely destroyed. The unbroken flow of the *Ālāya* also accounts for the continuity of individual existence during successive births and during deep sleep, unconscious states and trance states where empirical consciousness does not exist. Hence, to account for bondage, continuity of individual existence and liberation *Ālaya*vijñāna must be accepted over and above *pravṛtti*-vijñānas.[1]

Ālayavijñāna bears some points of resemblance to *Prakṛti* in Sāṅkhya, to *Adṛṣṭa* in Nyāya-Vaisheṣika and to *Īshvara* and *Sākṣī* in Advaita Vedānta. *Prakṛti*, like *Ālaya*, is *sarva-bījaka* as it implicitly contains the seeds of all phenomena. It also, like *Ālaya*, is an undifferentiated and indeterminate whole. Further, like *Ālaya*, it is changing every moment and is dynamic in nature. The inherent unstability forces *Ālaya* to evolve the determinate content; in *Prakṛti* too the lack of harmony among the *guṇas* (*guṇa-vaiṣamya*) leads to evolution. But there are fundamental differences also between the two. *Prakṛti* is ultimate, independent and unconditioned, while *Ālaya* is dependent on the Absolute and is conditioned by *avidyā* and *karma*. *Prakṛti* as ultimate cannot be annihilated; *Ālaya*-stream dries up in *Nirvāṇa*. *Prakṛti*, as objectivity itself, is given an ontologically independent status; *Ālaya* as primal subject is creative Will. In both Sāṅkhya and Vijñānavāda pure consciousness is treated as changeless and is not subjected to evolution and yet the involvement of pure consciousness somehow in objectivity is said to be the necessary condition of evolution. But the bias in favour of realistic pluralism leads Sāṅkhya to an irreconcilable dualism of *Puruṣa* and *Prakṛti*, to the degeneration of *Puruṣa* into an infinite plurality of empirical selves, to the independence of *Prakṛti*, the objective, and to treat its evolution as real. Vijñānavāda, on the other hand, is absolutism and idealism and refuses to accord an ontological status to objectivity and to the evolution engendered by it. Sāṅkhya makes *Prakṛti* independent and cre-

1. ālayavijñāne sati samsāra-pravṛttir nivṛttishcha nānyathā ityavashyam chakṣurādivijñānavyatiriktam ālayavijñanam abhyupagantavyam.
—*Trimshikā-Bhāṣya*, pp. 37-39.

ative, but fails to explain the association of *Prakṛti* with Puruṣa which supplies the motive force of evolution and in the end this association turns out to be only a semblance. Vijñānavāda maintains that consciousness alone can be creative and can evolve this world out of it, and that objectivity is a transcendental Illusion. In Sānkhya *Prakṛti* or Objectivity evolves this world due to its association with *Puruṣa* or Consciousness; in Vijñānavāda, Consciousness evolves this world due to its association with objectivity, the transcendental Illusion.

Again, *Ālaya* may be compared to *Adṛṣṭa* in Nyāya-Vaisheṣika. *Adṛṣṭa,* like *Ālaya,* is a store-house where the seeds of all karmas are implicitly contained and which matures them and thus supplies the motive force leading to evolution. Though each soul has its own *adṛṣṭa,* yet an universal *Adṛṣṭa* as the main reservoir is maintained by Nyāya-Vaisheṣika which like *Ālaya* is being replenished by fresh *karmas.* But this *Adṛṣṭa,* like *Prakṛti,* is treated as unconscious and has to function under the guidance of God. *Ālaya,* on the other hand, is universal consciousness appearing as defiled with *avidyā* and *karma* and needs no supervision.

Ālaya may be compared to Īshvāra or God in Advaita Vedānta. Both are absolute consciousness appearing tinged with *avidyā.* Both project and sustain this world. Both are unobscured by the covering side of *avidyā* and are completely free from suffering. Both are self-conscious creative Will. Both stand on a transcendental level. Both are transcended in liberation. Evolution is an appearance in both. But there are important differences also between the two. In Vijñānavāda *avidyā* is the transcendental Illusion of subject-object duality; in Advaita Vedānta *avidyā* or *māyā* is the power of the Absolute which is material (*jaḍa*) and indescribable either as real or as unreal (*sadasadanirvachanīya*). Vijñānavāda is idealism both ontologically and epistemologically; Advaita Vedānta is ontological idealism and epistemic realism. *Ālaya* is momentary and has no personality; Īshvara is a personal God in whose supreme personality knowledge, will and emotion are fully integrated. *Ālaya* is fouled by *avidyā* or transcendental Illusion of objectivity; Īshvarā is the Lord of *avidyā* or *māyā.* God's function as the creator, preserver and destroyer of this universe; His bestowing Grace on the devotees; His intimate relation with the individual selves and such other conceptions are lacking in Vijñānavāda.

Ālaya can also be compared to *Sākṣī* in Advaita Vedānta. *Sākṣī* is the unchanging (*kūṭastha*) and unaffected witness of the *jīva* and its actions and it is pure consciousness appearing as associated with *avidyā* or *antaḥkaraṇa* and is distinguished from the empirical and individualised consciousness of the *jīva* or *pramātā* which is limited (*avachchhinna*) by the internal organ (*antaḥkaraṇa*). Sākṣī is associated with (but not limited by) indeterminate and undifferentiated Ignorance (*avidyopahita*) and is not individualised. The objectivity confronting *Ālaya* is also indeterminate and undifferentiated. Both stand on the transcendental level and are not empirical. In both, *avidyā* stands on an epistemic level while consciousness stands on an ontological level. *Sākṣī* and *Ālaya* both account for the continuity of empirical life during deep sleep, unconscious states and trance.

(2) *Kliṣṭa Manas or Manovijñāna:* The second manifestation of Vijñāna is called *kliṣṭa manovijñāna*. It is a link between the *Ālaya*-vijñāna, the universal consciousness and the *pravṛtti*-vijñānas, the individual consciousness. It should be distinguished from the sixth *pravṛtti*-vijñāna called manovijñāna or empirical consciousness. The individualisation of the universal is possible only through categorisation or thought-construction. Hence the essence of the *kliṣṭa manas* is said to consist in categorisation or intellection (*manana*)[1]. The *kliṣṭa manas* through its inherent thought-forms differentiates the indeterminate content of the *Ālaya* into the determinate categories of empirical knowledge. It actualises the seeds implicit in the *Ālaya*. The subject-aspect of the *Ālaya* manifests itself into an infinite plurality of individual streams of *kliṣṭa manas* and the object-aspect into the various pravṛtti-vijñānas called *viṣaya*-vijñapti. Each *kliṣṭa manas* represents the unity of an individual stream of consciousness, while the *Ālaya* is the coordination of all such streams. The main function of the *kliṣṭa manas* consists in the projection of the ego. The *Ālaya* is the transcendental Ego, which is the presupposition of all knowledge and which gives unity to the manifold moments of consciousness. The *kliṣṭa manas* is the empirical ego which is the object of introspection. It derives its power of categorisation from the transcendental synthetic unity of the *Ālaya*. The *Ālaya* is called the locus (*āshraya*) as well as the

1. mano nāma vijñānam mananātmakam. *Trimshikā*, K. 5.

object (*ālambana*) of the *kliṣṭa manas.*[1]

The *kliṣṭa manas* is so called because it is always defiled by four kinds of suffering (*klesha*) which are called defiled (*nivṛta*) and indeterminate in themselves (*avyākṛta*). These four *kleshas* are: (1) notion of the ego (*ātma-dṛṣṭi*), (2) ignorance about the nature of the ego (*ātma-moha*), (3) vanity of the ego (*ātma-māna*), and (4) attachment to the ego (*ātma-sneha*).[2] The notion of the ego is the knowledge aspect, the vanity of the ego the volitional aspect and the attachment to the ego the emotional aspect in the personality of the ego. It is also accompanied by the five universal mentals, which are present in the *Ālaya* also, namely, contact, attention, affection, cognition and *conation.* The ignorance about the nature of the ego consists in the ignorance of the fact that the ego is only a superimposition on the five momentary mental states (*skandha*).

The *kliṣṭa manas* does not exist in liberation or Arhat-hood where all suffering is destroyed and the *Ālaya* itself is transcended. Its function is stopped in certain trance-states, though after the trance it arises again out of the *Ālaya.*[3] In the empirical life it always exists as it is the presupposition of empirical experience.

The *kliṣṭa manas* can be compared with the *jīva* or *pramātā* in Advaita Vedānta. Both stand for the empirical subject or ego-consciousness and are accredited with the function of categorisation. Both derive their power from the transcendental source, the *kliṣṭa manas* from the *Ālaya* and the *jīva* from the *Sākṣī.* Both give unity to our empirical experience and own it. Both are dissolved in liberation. Both are merged in universal consciousness (*Ālaya* or *Sākṣī*) in the trance-state of nirvikalpa samādhi (*nirodha-samāpatti*) out of which they arise again when the trance is over.

(3) *Viṣaya-Vijñapti:* This is the third manifestation of Vijñāna. It is the individual consciousness at the empirical level. It consists in the determinate awareness of the object. It is of six kinds and is divided into external and internal. The five sense-cognitions of

1. tadāshritya pravartate tadālambam mano nāma vijñānam. *Ibid.*
2. kleshaishchaturbhiḥ sahitam nivṛtāvyākṛtaiḥ sadā |
ātmadṛṣṭyātmamohātmamānātmasnehasañjñitaiḥ || *Ibid.*, K. 6.
3. Arhato na tat. na nirodha-samāpattau mārge lokottare na cha. *Ibid.*, K. 7.

colour, taste, touch, smell and sound obtained through the five sense-organs are called 'external' because they constitute our knowledge of the so-called 'external' world, while the sixth, the normal mental states (*manovijñāna*) comprising ideas, feelings and volitions, is called internal. These mental states, like the five sense-cognitions, are also *objects* for the *kliṣṭa manas.* The five kinds of sense-data and the resultant consciousness over which our normal mind or will has no control are the projections of the *Ālaya* and not of the *kliṣṭa manas,* which merely receives them and unifies them into knowledge. These are our world-objects. The objects in dream, illusion and hallucination and the objects of pure imagination are the projections of the *kliṣṭa manas.* These are less vivid and last for a short time because the power of the individual *kliṣṭa manas* is very much limited in comparison to the *Ālaya* and its consciousness is covered and defiled by ignorance and dullness.[1]

The six kinds of *viṣaya*-vijñāna are accompanied by fifty-one mentals (*chaitta dharma*) which comprise the five universal mentals (*sarvatraga*), five determinate mentals (*viniyata*), eleven meritorious mentals (*kushala*), six sufferings (*klesha*), twenty sub-sufferings (*upaklesha*) and four indeterminate mentals (*aniyata*). The feeling (*vedanā*), which is one of the five universal mentals, in viṣaya-vijñāna may be pleasant, unpleasant or indifferent. The four indeterminate mentals may be defiled (*kliṣṭa*) or undefiled (*akliṣṭa*). When these are defiled, they are treated as four more sub-sufferings.[2]

The five sensory vijñānas arise out of the *Ālaya* due to their respective *vāsanās* and before perishing lay their seeds or *vāsanās* in the *Ālaya,* which *vāsanās* give rise to further vijñānas and this cyclic order goes on. The sensory vijñānas are always followed by mental states (*manovijñāna*) which are said to be attendants on them (*anuchara*). A sensory vijñāna always gives rise to a manovijñāna though the latter may arise even without the former. Thus these six kinds of *viṣaya*-vijñāna which make up our phenomenal world arise out of the *Ālaya* which is their source (*mūla*-vijñāna). They may arise successively or simultaneously, singly or

1. *Vimshatikā,* K. 18.
2. These 51 mentals are explained by Sthiramati in his *Trimshikā-Bhāṣya* (pp. 25-33) on Kārikās 9-14.

jointly. One *ālambana-pratyaya* (object-consciousness) can produce many vijñānas simultaneously. Their number is not fixed. Their rising from the *Ālaya* is compared to the emergence of waves in an ocean (*taraṅgāṇām yathā jale*).[1] *Manovijñāna* or moments of empirical consciousness always arise and flow, with or without sensory cognitions, in an individual stream of consciousness except in five states which are, (1) liberation, (2) trance-states, (3) deep sleep, (4) swoon and (5) death.[2] The unbroken sequence of the *Ālaya* accounts for the continuity of empirical existence inspite of these gaps.

The modification of Vijñāna in these three main phases is not ultimate. It is engendered by transcendental Illusion of objectivity. The evolution of consciousness is merely logical and should not be mistaken as a historical process. There is a way from the world to the Absolute, but no way from the Absolute to the world. The Absolute is beyond time and causation. There is no real defilement of Vijñāna and so the consequent purification is not ultimately true. Still its phenomenal reality cannot be denied. The need for spiritual discipline is fully emphasised. Just as the unreality of dream-objects can be realised when the dreamer gets awake, similarly the unreality of the world can be realised only when a person slumbering in transcendental Illusion of subject-object duality awakes in the Absolute through immediate non-dual spiritual experience.[3] The pure non-dual Vijñaptimātratā can be realised not through thought, but only by the pure spiritual experience of the Buddhas.[4]

VI. THE THREE SVABHĀVAS

Vijñānavāda analyses the nature of empirical illusion and analogically extends it to transcendental illusion. The analysis of an empirical illusion reveals that it consists in the false idea of objectivity, is projected and sustained by the creativity of consciousness and has its ground finally in pure undisturbed consciousness. For

1. *Trimshikā*, K.15 with Bhāṣya.
2. *Ibid.*, K.16 with Bhāṣya.
3. *Vimshatikā*, K.17 and Vṛtti on it. evam vitathābhyāsavāsanānidrayā prasupto lokaḥ svapna ivābhūtam artham pashyan....lokottara-nirvikalpa-jñānalābhāt prabuddho bhavati tāda viṣayābhāvam yathāvadavagachchhati.
4. vijñaptimātratā Buddhānam gocaraḥ...tarkāviṣayatvāt. *Ibid.*, pp. 10-11.

example, in the rope-snake illusion instead of the objective snake we have merely its form in consciousness. The snake is illusory because it is mistaken as an external object.

Thus the analysis of illusion reveals three things which belong to three different levels of existence (*svabhāva*), namely, (1) the object which is superimposed (*adhyasta* or *āropita* or *upacharita artha*) and is utterly unreal; (2) the creative consciousness which assumes the form of the object (*arthākāra vijñāna*) and serves as the immanent basis (*āshraya* or *ādhāra*) of superimposition; and (3) the pure non-dual Consciousness (Vijñānamātra) which is the transcendent ground (*adhiṣṭhāna*) uninvolved in illusion. These three *svabhāvas* are respectively called the *parikalpita* (imaginary), the *paratantra* (relative or conditioned) and the *pariniṣpanna* (Absolute). The imaginary is cancelled by the mere knowing of it (*parijñāna*); the relative is to be purified by the removal of impurity of the transcendental Illusion of subject-object duality by intense yogic samādhi (*prahāṇa*); and the Absolute is to be directly realised by non-dual spiritual experience (*prāpti* or *sākṣātkāra*).[1]

(1) *The Parikalpita Svabhāva:* The *parikalpita* is the 'object' which is said to be pure imagination (*kalpanā-mātra*). The entire phenomenal world which we normally experience comes under this category. Whatever is perceived as an 'object' is a super-imposition on its 'form' assumed by creative consciousness and is therefore illusory. The sting of the illusory lies in the idea of objectivity. Hence the subject-object duality (*grāhya-grāhaka-vāsanā*) is very often expressed in this system only by the word 'object' (*artha*) and the illusory (*parikalpita*) is identified with the object.[2] The word 'object' in Vijñānavāda means that which confronts consciousness as an 'other' and includes external objects as well as individual subjects, sense-organs and mental states comprising ideas, emotions and volitions.[3] The word 'object' includes the entire phenomenal world of individual subjects (*ātmā* or *pudgala*) and all internal and external objects (*dharma*) from the lowest to

1. parijñānam prahāṇañcha sākṣātkaraṇameve cha I *Madhyānta-Vibhāga*, K., III, 9 Also, *Trisvabhāvanirdesha*, K. 31-32.
2. arthaḥ parikalpitasvabhāvaḥ. *Madhyānta-ṭīkā*, p. 18, 19, 22-3 (on K. I, 6)
3. arthāḥ rūpādayaḥ chakṣurādayaḥ ātma-vijñaptayashcha. *Ibid.*

the highest including even the attributes of Buddha and is declared to be illusory (*parikalpita*).[1] It is the result of imagination (*kalpanā*), super-imposition (*adhyāropa*) or projection (*upachāra*). It is called *parikalpita* because, though non-existent, it is imagined to exist; and it is called *svabhāva* because, though absolutely unreal, it is mistaken as 'real' by the ignorant common folks.[2]

(2) *The Paratantra Svabhāva:* It is called *paratantra* because it is governed by the causal law of dependent origination (*pratītya-samutpāda*).[3] Paratantra is creative consciousness which has lost its original purity and non-dual nature due to its association with transcendental illusion of objectivity, which subjects it to the operation of the causal law and compels it to undergo modification and assume various forms.[4] The word *paratantra* primarily stands for *Ālaya*-vijñāna and also denotes its seven satellites—the *kliṣṭa* manas and the six *viṣaya*-vijñānas. All these eight vijñānas are called *paratantra* because they have no independent existence and arise depending on their causes and conditions.[5] This Creative Consciousness as the universal reservoir of all *vasanās* is called *Ālaya*; as the immanent basis which projects the phenomenal world of subject-object duality and sustains its super-imposition on its modification it is called *āshraya*; and as the source of creative imagination (*parikalpa*) projecting the unreal object (*abhūta*) it is called *abhūta-parikalpa*.[6] This process, as explained before[7], is due to transcendental Illusion and is not ultimately real. The process of the phenomenalisation of the Real and the nature of the eight vijñānas have already been explained in detail.[8] The *paratantra*, in fact, is the parinișpanna itself appearing as fouled by the sub-

---

1. yena yena vikalpena yad yad vastu vikalpyate ādhyātmikam bāhyam vāntasho yāvad Buddha-dharmā api parikalpita evāsau svabhāvaḥ
—*Trimshikā-Bhāṣya*, p. 39.
2. abhūtamapi astīti parikalpyate. *Madhyānta-Tīka*, p. 19, 22 (K.I, 6).
3. paratantra-svabhāvastu vikalpaḥ pratyayodbhavaḥ. —*Trimshikā*, K. 21.
4. vasanādhipatyena bhinnābhāsam vijñānam prajāyate. *Madhyānta-Ṭīkā*, p. 15.
5. parair hetu-pratyayais tantryate janyate, na tu svayam bhavatīti paratantraḥ. *Ibid*, p. 19, 23 (K. I, 6)
Also *Trimshikā-Bhāṣya*, p. 39; aṣṭavijñānavastukaḥ paratantraḥ *M. Ṭīkā*, p. 15.
6. abhutaparikalpa eva paratantraḥ. —*Madhyānta-Ṭīkā*, p. 19.
7. See supra, pp. 92-3
8. See supra, pp. 93-102.

ject-object duality. When this duality due to transcendental illusion is eradicated, it shines as non-dual pure Consciousness which in fact it always is.

(3) *The Parinișpanna Svabhāva:* The *parinișpanna* is the Absolute eternally free from the subject-object duality.[1] It is the *paratantra* free from the *parikalpita.*[2] It is called *parinișpanna* because it is absolutely unchanging, ever the same, never touched by any process, change or modification.[3] It is pure, eternal and non-dual consciousness which is ever the same like space.[4] It is pure, non-dual and transcendental consciousness which is beyond empirical thought.[5] It is beyond senses, thought and language. It cannot be conceptualised, categorised or described. It is totally indeterminate and free from the subject-object duality. To drag it down and involve it in thought-relations would be its phenomenalisation. It is eternal for it is beyond time and space. It is *shūnyatā* because it is eternally free from the subject-object duality *(grāhadvaya-shūnyatā)*. It is the *dharmatā* (reality) of the *dharmas* (phenomena). It is the ultimate reality (*paramārtha*) of the phenomena (*dharmas*). It is *tathatā,* for it is eternal and always the same (*sarvakālam tathābhāvāt*). It is Vijñaptimātratā for it is pure non-dual consciousness.[6] As free from subject-object duality, it is called 'pure That' (*tan-mātra*) or 'Pure Being' (*vastumātra*).[7] It is 'pure Bliss' (*sukha*) for it is eternal, and that which is momentary is miserable.[8] It is absolute purity (*anāsrava*) and freedom (*vimukti*). It is *nirvāṇa* itself. It is pure consciousness, which is non-relational and transcendent to thought-determinations. Here, there is neither self-consciousness (*achitta*) nor object-consciousness

---

1. grāhya-grāhakābhāvaḥ parinișpannaḥ svabhāvaḥ. *Madhyānta-Ṭīkā,* p. 19, 22.
2. paratantrasya parikalpitena atyantarahitatā parinișpanna-svabhāvaḥ. *Trimshikā-Bhāṣya,* p. 40.
3. avikāraparinișpattyā parinișpannaḥ. *Ibid.*
4. ākāshavad ekarasam jñānam. *Ibid.*
5. nirvikalpam lokottaram jñānam. *Trimshikā Bhāṣya,* p. 43.
6. dharmāṇām paramārthashcha sa yatastathatā pi saḥ I
   sarvakālam tathābhāvāt saiva vijñapti-mātratā II *Trimshikā, Kārikā* 25.
7. *Trimshikā, Kārikā* 27; grāhya-grāhaka-rahitam vastumātram. Madhyānta-tīkā, p. 10.
8. sukho nityatvāt. yadanityam tadduḥkham, ayam cha nityaḥ ityasmāt sukhah. *Trimshika-Bhāṣya,* p. 44.

(*anupalambha*).[1] It is transcendental non-dual spiritual experience, which is *Nirvāṇa* itself, pure and eternal Bliss. At the same time, it is also the immanent reality of all the *dharmas*; no appearance is without it. It is *dharma-dhātu* or *dharma-kāya* of the Buddha.[2]

These three svabhāvas are neither three 'reals' nor three 'truths' nor even three 'degrees of reality'. The Absolute is the only reality and the only truth. The *parikalpita* is utterly unreal and the *paratantra* belongs to *samvṛti*. They are called 'svabhāva' only by courtesy.

It should be noted that the distinction among *pariniṣpanna, paratantra* and *parikalpita* in Vijñanavāda differs from the distinction among *paramārtha, vyavahāra* and *pratibhāsa* in Vedānta. The basis of this distinction is different in both these systems. Vijñānavāda distinguishes between two grades of Reality, Reality in itself as it is in its inherent purity (*pariniṣpanna*) and Reality as it appears defiled or conditioned by transcendental *avidyā* or vāsanā (*paratantra*). Vijñāna, whether pure or defiled, is the only reality. The third, the *parikalpita* is the imaginary 'object' (which includes our entire empirical world) which is declared as utterly unreal like the sky-flower and left ungraded. It places all illusion, empirical and world-illusion, on the same level. It distinguishes between two factors found in every illusion which are, *parikalpita* or the superimposed object (e.g. the 'snake' in rope-snake illusion and the 'rope' as an object in world-illusion) and *paratantra* or the 'form' of the object assumed by consciousness (e.g. the 'form of the snake' assumed by individual consciousness in rope-snake illusion and the 'form of the rope' assumed by the universal consciousness or Ālaya-vijñāna in world-illusion when we see a rope as an 'external object'). Vedānta, on the other hand, believes that the *paramārtha* is not subject to degrees, and grades appearances into transcendental or *vyavahāra* and empirical or *pratibhāsa.* These illusions belong to two different *orders* and cannot be placed on the same level. The two factors in illusion, for

1. achitto'nupalambho'sau jñānam lokottaram cha tat I *Trimshikā, Kārikā* 29.
2. sa eva'nāsravo dhāturachintyaḥ kushalo dhruvaḥ I
sukho vimuktikāyo' sau dharmākhyo'yam Mahāmuneḥ II *Trimshikā, Kārikā* 30.
dharmadhātur vinirmukto yasmād dharmo na vidyate I
Madhyānta-Vibhāga K., V, 19.

Vedānta, are the superimposed object (*adhyasta*) and the ground of superimposition (*adhiṣṭhāna*).

VII. ABHŪTA-PARIKALPA AND SHŪNYATĀ

Just as shūnyatā in the sense of the Absolute means *prapañcha-shūnyatā* or freedom from plurality of thought-constructions and when applied to phenomena means *svabhāva-shūnyatā* or the phenomenal world devoid of independent existence, similarly abhūta-parikalpa in the sense of the Absolute means the pure transcendent consciousness or the *pariniṣpanna* Vijñaptimātratā which is *grāha-dvaya-shūnyatā* or freedom from subject-object duality and when applied to phenomena means the constructive consciousness (*paratantra*) which undergoes modification and projects the world of subject-object duality (*parikalpita*) on its own forms. The *pariniṣpanna* is called *abhūta-parikalpa* in the sense of being the transcendent ground (*adhiṣṭhāna*) of phenomena absolutely free from all duality which indirectly allows itself to be superimposed upon without any involvement in superimposition (*abhūtasya parikalpo yasmin saḥ*). The *paratantra* is called abhūta-parikalpa in the sense of creative consciousness which, through its constructive ideation (*vikalpa*), projects and sustains the illusion of the world of subject-object duality as its immanent basis (*abhūtasya parikalpo yasmāt saḥ*). The *parikalpita* is called abhūta-parikalpa in the sense of the unreal (*abhūta*) world of subject-object duality which is superimposed (*parikalpita*) on the modification of consciousness (*abhūtashchā'sau parikalpitashcha*).[1]

Though all the three svabhāvas are called *abhūta-parikalpa* in three different senses, this word is usually applied to the *paratantra* or the eightfold vijñānās[2], i.e., the *Ālaya,* the *kliṣṭa manas* and the six viṣaya-vijñānas, and includes all the minds and mentals in all the three worlds.[3] Primarily, it stands for the Ālaya-vijñana, the first modification of the Vijñaptimātra, which partakes of both the

1. abhutamasmin dvayam parikalpyate iti....abhūtaparikalpo grāhya-grāhaka-rahitatayā pariniṣpannaḥ. abhūtamanena dvayam parikalpyate iti... sa eva hetupratyayapāratantryāt paratantraḥ. abhūtamapi dvayam astīti parikalpyate iti... sa eva grāhya-grahaka-rūpeṇa prakhyānāt parikalpitaḥ. *Madhyānta-Ṭīkā,* pp. 12 & 18-9 (on K. I, 2 & 6).
2. aṣṭavijñānavastukaḥ paratantro'bhūtaparikalpaḥ. *Ibid.,* p. 15.
3. abhūtaparikalpastu chitta-chaittāstridhātukāḥ. *Madhyānta,* K. I, 9

parinişpanna and the *parikalpita* and projects this world. Though both the *parikalpita* and the *paratantra* are negated, yet both do not enjoy equal status. The *parikalpita* is totally negated because it is utterly unreal; but the *paratantra* is negated only to the extent of its imputed character of subject-object duality. Negation in both cases is total because the imputed duality in the *paratantra* is totally negated and the real nature of the *paratantra* as the *parinişpanna* is reaffirmed.

Negation is always the cancellation of an illusion and is significant only as the denial of the false ascribed character of the Real (*adhyāropāpavāda*). *Shūnyatā* is not universal negation, but negation *of* subject-object duality *in abhūta-parikalpa.* That which is devoid is real; that of which it is devoid is unreal. Vijñāna or *abhūtaparikalpa* which projects the subject-object duality is real; the projected subject-object duality is unreal.[1] Negation of this duality reaffirms the non-dual nature of Vijñāna.[2] The parikalpita exists only as a superimposed object during illusion (*bhrāntimātraika-gochara*). The *paratantra* exists as a phenomenal reality from the standpoint of thought (*shuddha-laukika-gochara*). The parinişpanna is pure non-dual consciousness which can be realised through immediate spiritual experience (*avikalpa-jñāna-gochara*).[3]

VIII. SAṄKLESHA AND VYAVADĀNA

Saṅklesha means suffering, defilement, bondage; vyavadāna means end of suffering, purification, liberation. It has been explained before[4] that the pure non-dual Vijñaptimātra, through its beginningless and transcendental *vāsanā* or *Avidyā* appears as creative will and gives rise to our world of subject-object duality which is our suffering and our bondage. When this *vāsanā* is rooted out vijñāna shines in its absolute non-dual purity.

Vijñānavāda, as true absolutism, emphasises the fact that the

1. aviparītam shūnyatā-lakṣaṇam udbhāsitam. yachchhūnyam tasya sadbhāvād yena shūnyam tasya tatrābhāvāt.—*Madhyānta-ṭikā,* p. 12, 14.
abhūtaparikalpo'sti dvayam tatra na vidyate I
shūnyatā vidyate tatra tasyāmapi sa vidyate II *Madhyānta,* K. I, 2.
2. iyameva shūnyatā yā grāhya-grāhaka-rahitatā abhūtaparikalpe....na shūnyatā nāstitvam. *Madhyānta-Ṭikā,* p. 10, 11.
3. *Ibid.*, p. 19.
4. *Ibid.*, p. 15; see supra, pp. 94-102.

Absolute is at once both transcendent and immanent. If the Absolute were only transcendent, it would not constitute the reality of the world; and if it were only immanent, it would itself be a phenomenon.[1] If the Absolute were identical with the world, it would itself be defiled and would not serve as the basis of purification, or the world itself would be pure like the Absolute and there would be no suffering. And if it were different from the world, it would not be the reality of the world and the possibility of purification by negation of duality would be denied, or the world itself would be real and suffering would be eternal.[2] In both cases the spiritual discipline would be in vain and *Nirvāṇa* would not be attained. If the Absolute did not appear as defiled, there could be no suffering and all beings would be liberated without any effort; and if the Absolute were in itself not ever-pure and undefiled, all spiritual effort would go in vain and *Nirvāṇa* could not be attained.[3] Hence the Absolute is neither identical with nor different from the *paratantra*.[4] The importance of the phenomenal lies in the fact that the Absolute can be realised only through it by negating its ascribed character of subject-object duality.[5]

The defilement and purification of Consciousness are due to transcendental Illusion of objectivity. They do not belong to *parikalpita,* for the unreal can be neither defiled nor purified.[6] They do not pertain to *paratantra* even, for that too is due to transcendental Illusion.[7] So they must belong to the *parinișpanna* itself. But as the Absolute is eternally pure, they cannot really belong to it. Hence it must be admitted that both of these are due to transcendental Illusion.[8] Just as water, gold and space are in themselves pure but may appear as fouled by mud, alloy and

1. *Trimshikā-Bhāșya.* p. 40.
2. *Madhyānta-țīkā,* p. 40. na cha dharmāntaram dharmāntarasya dharmatā bhavitum arhati.
3. saṅkliṣṭā ched bhaven nāsau muktāḥ syuḥ sarva-dehinaḥ I vishuddhā ched bhaven nasau vyāyāmo niṣphalo bhavet II *Madhyānta-Kārika,* I. 22.
4. ata eva sa naivānyo nānanyaḥ paratantrataḥ. --*Trimshikā, Kārikā* 22.
5. saṅkleshapakṣādeva vyavadānapakṣo mārgayitavyaḥ —*Madhyānta-țīkā,* p. 12.
6. *Ibid.*, p. 223 (on K. V, 22).
7. *Ibid.*
8. kasya punaḥ te syātām? Dharmadhātoḥ tasyāpi vikalpanād eva, tayorāgaṇtukatvād Dharmadhātoshcha ākāshavad avikāratvāt. *Ibid.*, p. 224. (on K. V. 21)

dirt, and when these adventitious properties are removed they regain their own pure nature. Similarly, the Absolute appears defiled due to *avidyā* or *mūlāvāsanā* and when it is removed the Absolute regains its original purity.[1] It should be noted that the examples of water and gold do not indicate *real* defilement; they are cited merely for emphasising the importance of spiritual discipline from the phenomenal standpoint and lest these may be mistaken as indicating real defilement, the example of space is immediately added. Shaṅkarāchārya also gives this example.[2] Space is never really defiled; it merely appears to be so. Vijñānavāda repeatedly emphasises that this whole process is phenomenal only and is not ultimately real[3], that liberation is only the cancellation of transcendental Illusion.[4] But, unless the Absolute is realised, the subject-object duality cannot be transcended.[5] As the falsity of the dream-objects can be realised only when the dreamer gets awake, similarly the falsity of the phenomenal world can be realised only when pure non-dual consciousness is realised.[6] Though ultimately defilement and purification, bondage and liberation, both are unreal and even the consciousness of attainment of liberation is transcended, yet their phenomenal reality must be accepted. Vijñānavāda prescribes and stresses the paramount importance of an elaborate spiritual discipline (yoga) culminating in the highest meditation or *samadhi* for the cancellation of transcendental Illusion and the realisation of pure non-dual Vijñaptimātra.

IX. THE LATER FORM OF VIJÑĀNAVĀDA

The later form of Vijñānavāda which has kicked out absolutism and universalised momentariness should be treated as a separate school which we have designated as Svatantra-Vijñānavāda. This

1. abdhātu-kanakākāsha-shuddhivachachhuddhiriṣyate. *Madhyānta-Kārikā,* I, 17. yasyākāsha-suvarṇa-vārisadṛshī kleshād vishuddhir matā. –*Mahayānasūtrālaṅkāra,* p. 58.
2. bālāḥ ākāshe talamalinatvādi adhyasyanti. —*Shāṅkara-Bhāṣya,* Introduction.
3. malam tasya prahāṇañcha dvayamāgantukam matam I Dharmadhātor vishuddhatvāt prakṛtyā vyomavat punaḥ II —*Madhyānta-Vibhāga, Kārikā,* V, 21. na kliṣṭā nāpi chākliṣṭā shuddhāshuddhāpi naiva sā I –*Ibid, Kārikā* I, 23.
4. tatashcha mokṣo bhramamātrasaṅkṣayaḥ. —*Mahāyānasūtrālaṅkāra,* p. 22.
5. yāvad vijñaptimātratve vijñānam nāvatiṣṭhati I grāhadvayasyānushayastāvan na vinivartate II *Trimshikā, Kārikā* 26.
6. *Trimshikā-Bhāṣya,* p. 9.

school is also known as Sautrāntika-Yogāchāra and is founded by Diṅnāga and developed by Dharmakīrti and Shāntarakṣita who rank among the greatest dialecticians of India. They have vigorously attacked the other systems especially Nyāya and Mīmāṁsā, the schools of staunch realism which were the major opponents of Buddhism in those times. The Naiyāyikas and the Mīmāṁsakas in their turn not only defended their position, but also repaid the Buddhists in the form of ruthless counter-attacks. These attacks and counter-attacks resulted in the production of an enormously rich, valuable and voluminous philosophical literature. With the end of Svatantra-Vijñānavāda virtually ended Buddhist philosophy in India. As this school degenerated into pluralistic subjectivism, it has been vehemently criticised by the absolutists, within its own fold by the later Mādhyamikas like Chandrakīrti and Shāntideva and outside its fold by the great Shaṅkarāchārya. It is not our purpose to discuss this school in this work.[1] We may remark here that some scholars include Shāntarakṣita, the famous author of the great polemical work *Tattva-saṅgraha*, under the Mādhyamika or the Mādhyamika-Yogāchāra school. In our view this is incorrect. In his *Tattvasaṅgraha* he employs the negative dialectic to criticise other schools, but the entire work is written from the Svatantra-Vijñānavāda standpoint that consciousness is the only reality and that it is momentary. He himself admits that so far as ultimate reality is concerned he follows the foot-steps of the learned Āchāryas (i.e., Vasubandhu and Diṅnāga) who have proved and clarified Vijñaptimātratā.[2] This settles the issue. Poussin and Winternitz include him under Svātantrika-Yogāchāra school, according to Tibetan tradition.[3] His authorship of *Mādhyamikālaṅkāra*, even if proved, may not make him a Mādhyamika, even as the authorship of *Abhidharmakosha* does not make Vasubandhu a Sarvāstivādī. It may be an open question whether in his later years he inclined towards the Mādhyamika school. In any case, Shāntarakṣita's monumental work,

---

1. The interested reader may read the 8th Chapter of my book *A Critical Survey of Indian Philosophy*.
2. Vijñaptimātratāsiddhir dhīmadbhir vimalīkṛtā I asmābhistad dishā yātam paramārtha-vinishchaye II —*Tattva-saṅgraha*, Kārikā 2084.
   The reference here is clearly to Vasubandhu and Diṅnāga.
3. MCB, ii, p. 67 and *History of Indian Literature*, Vol. II. p. 374.

Tattvasaṅgraha reveals him as a Svatantra-Vijñānavādī and not as a Mādhyamika or Mādhyamika-Yogāchāra.

We shall briefly mention here the main points of difference between these two schools. This school has given up absolutism. The word 'Vijñaptimātra' or 'Vijñānamātra' is used in this school in the literal sense of 'Consciousness-only' which is declared to be momentary, i.e., in the sense of a Vijñāna-moment, and not in the sense of eternal and absolute Consciousness in which it is used in the earlier school of original Vijñānavāda. All the epithets which original Vijñānavāda uses for the Absolute Vijñāna are used by this school for a pure Vijñana-moment *except* the epithets of eternality and absoluteness. A pure Vijñāña-moment is non-dual (advaya), free from subject-object duality (*grāhya-grāhaka-rahita*), free from the defilement of *vāsanā* or *avidyā,* is formless (*nirākāra* or *nirābhāsa*) and self-luminous (*svaprakāsha*). Secondly, this school universalises the theory of momentariness. In original Vijñānavāda, momentariness is restricted to phenomena and the Absolute is declared to be eternal, because the momentary is the miserable; in this school momentariness applies even to reality, because the momentary is the real. A Vijñāna-moment, defiled by *vāsanā* on *avidyā,* constitutes misery and the same, freed from *vāsanā* or *avidyā,* regains its original purity and joy. Thirdly, this school treats *pratītyasamutpāda* as real causation which operates even in reality. In original Vijñānavāda causation is restricted within phenomena and the Absolute is declared to be beyond causation and change; in this school causation is real and operates within momentary ideas. Causation is efficiency and the momentary alone is the efficient. Momentariness and efficiency are equated and both are identified with reality. This school, therefore, is pluralistic and subjective idealism. Like original Vijñānavāda, it is idealism *par excellence,* both ontologically and epistemologically; but, unlike it, it has degenerated into pluralistic subjectivism. Ideas are moments and always flow in a series of causes and effects. The flow of Vijñāna-moments defiled by *vāsanā* or *avidyā* constitutes *samsāra* or bondage. When this beginningless *vāsanā* or *avidyā* is completely removed from the flow of Vijñāna-moments by eradicating objectivity through yoga, the Vijñāna-moments are restored to their original purity and the flow of these pure Vijñāna-moments through *vidyā* as pure, undefiled and self-luminous moments of consciousness is called *Nirvāṇa.*

X. EVALUATION OF VIJÑĀNAVĀDA

Vijñānavāda is idealism *par excellence*, ontological as well as epistemic. Absolutism advocates only transcendental or ontological idealism. Not only absolutism but any true idealism has to be ontological only. Empirical realism has to be admitted and it goes very well with ontological idealism. Advaita Vedānta and Kant both believe in transcendental idealism and empirical realism. Āchārya Shaṅkara's refutation of epistemic idealism of Vijñānavāda is fair, detailed and classic. Kant's refutation of subjective idealism is also treated as classic. To maintain idealism even epistemically, as Vijñānavāda and Svatantra-Vijñānavāda do, is absurd for it throws away common sense and all normal worldly experience without any gain. The 'object' in Vijñānavāda includes all external objects, all mental states (as mental objects) and all individual subjects which constitute our normal worldly experience. And all this is declared as utterly unreal like a sky-flower or a barren woman's son. Subjects and objects are treated as mere superimpositions on their 'forms' assumed by consciousness and are denied even empirical reality which is reserved only for their 'forms' in consciousness. Vijñānavāda says that every illusion, whether empirical or transcendental, contains two factors—the superimposed object which is *parikalpita* and its form in consciousness which is *paratantra*. In this way, Vijñānavāda separates the 'content' from its 'form', condemning the former as utterly unreal and retaining the latter as relatively real.

Now, this arbitrary separation of the content from its form is illogical, impossible and absurd. It blows up our entire empirical life into a non-entity. The superimposed object and its form in consciousness are inseparable; both appear together and both vanish together. The illusory snake is perceived, during illusion, as an 'object' out there in which content and form are inseparably united; and when the illusion is dispelled what is perceived is not the snake-form in consciousness but the rope. After the removal of illusion, we may, by an analysis of illusion, *infer* that what we perceived during illusion was not the objective snake, but only its 'form' in consciousness; but this is only inference and not perception. In fact, the snake-form is never perceived, neither during illusion nor after it. This also rejects the Vijñānavāda contention that the 'form' is of a higher order as it enjoys relative reality, while the 'content' is utterly unreal. The content and the form are of the same order and enjoy equal status, because both appear and vanish together. During illusion both appear together and both are relatively real; after the removal of illusion both vanish together and are equally unreal. When the illusion is dispelled, the snake-form is not re-instated for it is not perceived. In fact what enjoys reality is not the 'form of the snake' but consciousness which assumes this form and projects it as objective during illusion.

Again, the Vijñānavāda contention that empirical illusion and world-illusion are of equal status for both are 'illusion' in which consciousness assumes the form of an object and projects it as objective is untenable. Empirical illusion is rejected by our normal phenomenal experience, but world-illusion cannot be so negated. It stands on a higher level and its falsity can be realised only from the non-dual experience of pure Consciousness. Even Vijñānavāda has to admit that empirical illusion is the projection of individual consciousness which is limited and blurred, while world-illusion is the projection of universal consciousness or *Ālaya*-vijñāna which is all-powerful. Hence to put both types of illusion on the same level and condemn worldly experience of individual subjects and objects as utterly unreal like a barren woman's son or a sky-flower is not only illogical but highly absurd. Vijñānavāda has to admit that even an illusion cannot be baseless and finds this basis in the 'form of consciousness' which projects the illusory object. It also admits that to project such illusory object is always to project as objective and to perceive as objective. How can the 'object' then be utterly unreal like a sky-flower? A sky-flower can never be projected or perceived as objective. It can never appear as 'real', while the illusory object (empirical or transcendental) does appear as 'real' during illusion. Instead of grading Reality into absolute and phenomenal, it is more logical and convenient to grade appearance into empirical and transcendental. Again, the difference among 'forms of consciousness' or ideas must be due to the difference among 'objects', and not due to the difference among *vāsanās* or impressions. If the external objects do not exist, then impressions themselves cannot arise. And even if these impressions are held to be beginningless, the position is like a series of the blind, leading to the fallacy of infinite regress. If in the beginningless samsāra, impressions and ideas succeed each other, like seeds and sprouts, as causes and effects, these impressions must be traced to the beginningless transcendental *vāsanā* which Vijñānavāda accepts and calls 'Transcendental *vāsanā* of subject-object-duality', then this *vāsanā* would not be different from the Transcendental Ignorance or *avidyā* in Advaita Vedānta. From the phenomenal standpoint, empirical realism has to be accepted. If objects and ideas are presented together, it does not mean they are identical. To be perceived by the mind is not to be a portion of the mind. This proves that ideas and objects are distinct and that the plurality of ideas is due to the plurality of objects. To maintain idealism even epistemologically, as Vijñānavāda and Svatantra-Vijñānavāda do, is absurd for it explodes common sense and all normal worldly experience without any corresponding advantage.

The above criticism of Vijñānavāda applies with even greater force to Svatantra-Vijñānavāda. It maintains that the momentary alone is real for it alone is causally efficient, that the causal law of *Pratītyasamutpāda* governs the flow of these unique *vijñāna*-moments which flash into existence and immediately pass out of it after giving rise to the subsequent vijñāna in the second moment. And that this flow continues even in *Nirvāṇa* with this difference that in empirical life the vijñāna-moments are defiled with *avidyā* and its subject-object duality, but in *Nirvāṇa,* the flow is of pure non-dual Vijñāna-moments from which the *vāsanā* of subject-object duality is completely eradicated. Now, the plurality of defiled vijñanas may be explained by the plurality of vāsanās, but there is nothing to account for the plurality of the non-dual self-luminous vijñāna. What is the sense in imagining an infinite reduplication of the same pure vijñāna? Instead of maintaining the eternal light of the pure self-luminous Vijñāna-Sun in *Nirvāṇa,* this school reduces *Nirvāṇa* to mere flash of a candle-light of a momentary vijñāna. What a wonderful description of *Nirvāṇa*! In the words of Nāgārjuna (in the context of *Shūnyatā*), we may say that Buddha has declared such persons to be incorrigible.[1] Incorrigible in the sense that they admit *Nirvāṇa* to be beyond all categories and yet bind it with the categories of momentariness, causality, plurality, etc.!

If empirical life, bondage and liberation cannot be explained

---

1. tān asādhyān babhāṣire. *Mādhyamika Kārikā,* XIII, 8. teṣām kṣaṇabhaṅgo mahāgrahaḥ.

satisfactorily on the basis of an eternal entity, the theory of momentariness at once blows up all empirical life, knowledge, memory, recognition, law of *karma*, bondage, liberation and spiritual discipline. Reality is beyond all categories of thought, beyond permanence as well as momentariness, beyond eternalism and nihilism. But in our normal empirical life permanence and change both are to be accepted. There is no sense in unnecessarily and arbitrarily exploding all empirical life, common sense and accepted rules of logic. Svatantra-Vijñānavāda admits that the Real is the non-dual, pure and self-luminous Vijñāna beyond all categories of thought and yet clings to the theory of universal momentariness and flings the categories of momentariness, causality, plurality and particularity on the Real making it subject to the flow of arising and vanishing. A vijñāna-moment, as Shaṅkarāchārya says, cannot be non-dual and self-luminous; only the Eternal Self, the Transcendental Seer can be non-dual and self-luminous for whom the vijñāna-moments are 'objects' to be illuminated and perceived.

PART TWO

VEDĀNTA

CHAPTER FOUR

Pre-Shaṅkara Vedānta

I. THE SOURCE OF VEDĀNTA

Vedānta literally means 'the end or essence of the Veda' and denotes primarily the Upaniṣads which are the concluding portion of the Veda and also the essence of the Vedic philosophy. The meaning of this word has been extended to include all the vast literature written by way of commentary or gloss on the basic texts or any independent treatise or any system of philosophy claiming to be based on the Upaniṣads. The Upaniṣads, the *Brahma-sūtra* or Vedānta-sūtra of Bādarāyaṇa and the Bhagavad-gītā constitute the three basic texts *(prasthānatrayī)* of Vedānta, of which the Upaniṣads are the original texts or the *mūla-prasthāna.* The *Brahma-sūtra* of Bādarāyaṇa is treated as an aphoristic summary of the Upaniṣadic philosophy. The sūtras are cryptic statements and afford full freedom of interpretation to the commentators. It is for this reason that the Āchāryas of Vedānta have chosen the *Brahma-sūtra* to comment upon in their major work and their so-called commentaries are really their independent works on their respective systems. Shaṅkarāchārya's commentary on the *Brahma-sūtra* accords fully with the Upaniṣads. The Bhagavad-gītā is treated as the essence of the Upaniṣadic philosophy. It is said to be the immortal milk milked by the cowherd Lord Kṛṣṇa out of the Upaniṣad-cows, making Arjuna the calf, for the benefit of the learned.[1]

The Upaniṣads are not only the source of Vedānta but the source of all Indian philosophy, orthodox or heterodox. Tradition puts their number at one hundred and eight, but only eleven on which Shaṅkara has commented are to be taken as ancient,

1. sarvopaniṣado gāvo dogdhā Gopālanandanaḥ I Pārtho vatsaḥ sudhīr bhoktā dugdham Gītāmṛtam mahat II

authentic and principal.[1] The earlier Upaniṣads are pre-Buddhistic and are the earliest philosophical works of the world.

As part of the Veda, the Upaniṣads are venerated as shruti or revealed text. They are the utterances of the mystic sages who speak with authority of direct personal realisation of Reality According to tradition, the shruti or revealed text is said to be authorless (*apauruṣeya*), eternal (*nitya*) and beginningless (*sanātana*). The word shruti primarily refers to the Truth or Reality which is revealed and secondarily to the text in which this revelation is recorded. In the primary sense shruti is identical with the Real and as the Real is impersonal and eternal, so is shruti. The person who realises the Real becomes the Real. In the secondary sense, of course, the text which records this spiritual experience is conditioned by time and space and personality. The sages (*ṛṣayaḥ*) are called 'seers of Reality' (*mantra-draṣṭāraḥ*) or 'persons who have directly realised the Real' (*sākṣātkṛtadharmāṇah*). It is the intuitive experience which is valued; the text is a mere vehicle of expressing it in language. Revelation is of the Real and not of the text. It is spiritual illumination. The Upaniṣads teach knowledge of Brahma (*Brahma-vidyā*) which cannot be acquired through sense-perception, inference or introspection. The word 'revelation' in Vedānta is used in a different sense than that in which it is used in Christianity or other religions. The criterion of Reality is not imposed *ex cathedra*, but revealed through immediate spiritual experience (*svānubhava*).

As the Upaniṣads are the source and the final authority for Vedānta, every school of Vedānta tries to interpret them so as to suit its doctrines even through straining of the text. Inspite of the fact that the rich and varied spiritual content of the Upaniṣads permits a certain amount of flexibility in matters of choice and emphasis, and inspite of the fact that to a superficial reader certain seeming conflicts may appear here and there, the fundamental teaching of the Upaniṣads is too strong to be missed or misinterpreted without obvious straining of language. Among the teachers of the different schools of Vedānta, it is Āchārya Shaṅkara alone who has commented on all the principal eleven Upaniṣads and he also happens to be the earliest of them all. He has given

1. These are Īsha, Kena, Kaṭha, Prashna, Muṇḍaka, Māṇḍūkya, Taittirīya, Aitareya, Chhāndogya, Bṛhadāraṇyaka and Shvetāshvatara.

a coherent and systematic philosophy of the Upaniṣads in his Advaita Vedānta. One may or may not agree with the Upaniṣadic philosophy, but one cannot logically deny that Shaṅkara's account is true to the spirit of the Upaniṣads. Even George Thibaut who believes that Rāmānuja is a more faithful interpreter of the *Brahma-sūtra* than Shaṅkara, has to admit that Shaṅkara's teaching is in agreement with the Upaniṣads.

The advaita of Shaṅkara emphasises the transcendent non-dual nature of Reality, insisting at the same time on its immanence in the phenomenal world of plurality which is only its appearance. The vishiṣṭādvaita of Rāmānuja emphasises identity-in-difference. The world is different from, but not independent of, God who is the unity running through it and binding it together in an organic whole. The dvaita of Madhva insists on the difference between world and God. The dvaitādvaita of Nimbārka gives equal status to identity and difference. The shuddhādvaita of Vallabha believes that the world, though in essence identical with God, is yet different from Him as His real manifestation. The achintya-bhedābheda-vāda of Chaitanya and his followers stresses the incomprehensibility of the synthesis of identity and difference. Shaṅkara and Rāmānuja stand out as the two most important philosophers of Vedānta, the former emphasising the acosmic, transcendent and non-dual nature of Reality and the latter its cosmic, immanent and organic nature. But Shaṅkara has the merit of accommodating the immanent and cosmic character of Reality from the phenomenal standpoint, while those who deny advaita fail to realise the essential nature of the Real.

The central teaching of the Upaniṣads is undoubtedly absolutism or non-dual spiritualism as explained and elaborated by Āchārya Shaṅkara. The Absolute is called *Brahma* or *Ātmā*, the transcendental unity underlying the subject and the object. The word *Ātmā* here does not mean the individual self (*jīvātmā*) which is an appearance, but the true foundational Self, the self-luminous and the self-proved Real which is the inmost being of our individual self as well as of the objective phenomenal world. 'That thou art' (*tat tvam asi*) and 'This self is really the Absolute' (*ayam ātmā brahma*) and 'All this is Brahma' (*sarvam khalu idam brahma*) are the great sayings (*mahāvākya*) of the Upaniṣads. As the all-inclusive immanent ground Brahma is defined as 'Being, Consciousness and Infinitude' (*satyam jñānam anantam brahma*), as 'Consciousness and Bliss' (*vijñānam ānandam brahma*), or as simply 'Bliss' (*ānandam brahma*) which includes Being and Consciousness within it. This Absolute (*brahma*) appears as God (Īshvara), the creative Consciousness or Knowledge-Will, manifesting Himself as the Creator, Protector and Destroyer of this universe. In itself the Absolute or *para-brahma* is the transcendent non-dual super-cosmic (*niṣprapañcha* or *nirguṇa*) ground of which the world is an appearance. It is beyond senses, thought and speech and can be indirectly indicated through negative predicates (*neti neti*). But as the foundational Self, self-luminous and self-proved, it can be realised through immediate spiritual experience. The three states of empirical Consciousness—waking, dream and deep sleep are analysed with respect to their individual and cosmic reference and the Absolute is declared to be the Fourth (*turīya*), the Measureless (*amātra*), the ineffable foundational Self, which is immanent in all the three states and yet transcends them all.

The Upaniṣadic sage Yājñavalkya shines forth as the first exponent of Absolutism in the world. In the philosophical contest held at the court of King Janaka, Yājñavalkya in a series of answers to the questions of Uddālaka Āruṇi,[1] explains the immanent poise of Brahma, and in another series of answers to the questions of the learned lady Gārgī[2], explains the transcendent poise of Brahma, and then shows that these two poises are not of two different reals but of the same Supreme, whose essential nature as non-dual spiritual experience is not at all affected by the apparent change and multiplicity of the world. Yājñavalkya tells Uddālaka that Brahma is the thread-self (*sūtrātmā*), which runs through, binds and controls all from within, is the immanent innermost Self of all (*antaryāmī*). All things form his body; he is the immanent inner controller of all things, the Self, the immortal.[3] In itself it is the transcendent Real beyond senses, thought and language, which is described negatively (*neti neti*). *Neti neti* negates only the description of Brahma, not Brahma itself. Yājñavalkya, therefore, explains thus: 'Verily, the Imperishable, O Gārgī, is unseen but is the seer, is unheard but is the hearer, is unthought but is the thinker, is unknown but is the knower. There is no other seer,

1. Bṛhadāraṇyaka, III, 7.
2. *Ibid.*, III, 8.
3. yaḥ sarvāṇi bhūtāni antaro yamayati eṣa te ātmā antaryāmī amṛtaḥ.
—Bṛh. III, 7, 15.

hearer, thinker and knower, but this.'[1] In another context, Yājñavalkya at the time of his renouncing the household life teaches his wife Maitreyī, who is convinced that immortality cannot be obtained through wealth or worldly gains, thus: 'The Self, O Maitreyī, is all this and yet beyond it . . . Where there is duality as it were, there one can see the other . . . but where everything is realised as the Self, by what and whom should one see? How can the knower by whom all this is known himself be known?[2] The Self is 'not this, not this' . . . yet the sight of the immortal seer is never destroyed,[3] the knowledge of the knower never fades out.'

It is contended by some that the doctrine of *māyā* or *avidyā* is not found in the Upaniṣads and it is borrowed by Shaṅkara from Buddhism. This contention can be made only by those who are un-informed or ill-informed about the Upaniṣadic philosophy. The term '*māyā*' can be traced to the Ṛgveda (VI, 47, 18) where the one Supreme is said to appear in many forms through his power of *māyā*. The Shvetāshvatara (IV, 9-10) describes God as '*māyī*', Lord of *māyā*, and his wonder-working power of creation as *māyā*. The term '*avidyā*' is often used in the Upaniṣads in the sense of ignorance and appearance. The Muṇḍaka (II, 1, 10) compares ignorance to a knot which is to be untied by the realisation of the Self. The Kaṭha (I, 2, 4-5) says that worldly people live in ignorance and thinking themselves wise move about like blind men led by the blind. The same Upaniṣad (II,1,2) warns us not to find reality and immortality in things of this unreal and changing world. The Chhāndogya (VI, 1, 4) makes it clear that *Ātmā* is the only reality and that everything else is a mere word, a mode and a name. The same Upaniṣad (VIII,3,3) says that worldly people are covered with the veil of falsity. It also says (VII, 1, 3) that he who realises the Self goes beyond sorrow. The Īsha (7) assures us that delusion and suffering are gone for him who realises the unity of the Self. It also says (15) that the face of the Truth is covered by a golden veil and that the aspirant prays to God for its removal. It also compares ignorance with blind darkness (9). The Prashna (I, 16) tells us that Brahma can be realised by those who have neither crookedness nor falsehood nor illusion. The Kaṭha

1. *Ibid.*, III, 8, 11
2. vijñātāram are kena vijānīyāt –Bṛh. II, 4, 14 and IV, 5, 15.
3. nahi draṣṭur dṛṣṭeḥ viparilopo vidyate.... avināshitvāt.–*Ibid.*, IV, 3, 23 and 31.

(II, 1,10) makes it clear that he who sees as if there is plurality here goes on revolving in the cycle of birth and death. The Bṛhadāraṇyaka (II, 4, 14 and IV, 5, 15) says 'as if there were duality' implying that duality is a semblance, an appearance, an as it were. The same Upaniṣad (I, 3, 28) has the famous prayer which runs: Lead me from unreality to Reality, from darkness to Light, from death to Immortality. This implies the distinction between appearance and reality, between ignorance and knowledge and between change and eternity. Quotations from the Upaniṣads can be multiplied where the phenomenal world of plurality and change is declared to be mere appearance due to *māyā* or *avidyā* and *Brahma* is said to be the only Reality, the eternal, undeniable and non-dual Self. Prof. R.D. Ranade rightly points out the origin of the doctrine of *māyā* or *avidyā* in the Upaniṣads and concludes that "we do find in the Upaniṣads all the material that may have easily led Shaṅkara to elaborate a theory of Māyā out of it. . . . let no man stand up and say that we do not find the traces of the doctrine of *Māyā* in the Upaniṣads!"[1]

II. SOME ANCIENT TEACHERS OF VEDĀNTA

References to some ancient teachers of Vedānta are found in the Vedānta literature, but their works, if they composed any, are not extant. Bādarāyaṇa in his *Brahma-sūtra* names some teachers of old citing their views. They are: Jaimini, Āshmarathya, Bādari, Auḍulomi, Kāshakṛtsna, Kārṣṇājini and Ātreya. Of these Jaimini is the famous author of *Pūrva-Mīmāmsā-Sūtra*. Kāshkṛtsna probably was an Advaitin, because Shaṅkara refers to his view as agreeing with the Shruti. Āshmarathya and Auḍulomi probably taught identity and difference. Shaṅkara refers to Bhartṛprapañcha as a bhedābhedavādin. Dravidāchārya and Ṭanka are claimed by both advaita and vishiṣṭādvata as belonging to their tradition. Shaṅkara refers to Upavarṣa and Rāmānuja to Bodhāyana as 'vṛtttikāra.' Brahmadatta and Sundara Pāṇḍya were also leading teachers of their time and from the references to their views it is very probable that they were inclined towards Advaita. Bhartṛhari, whose Vākyapadīya, the famous work on the philosophy of grammar and language, is available was a renowned Shabdādvaitavādin. Though

1. A *Constructive Survey of Upaniṣadic Philosophy*, 2nd ed; pp. 163-5.

he was an uncompromising Advaitin and a supporter of vivartavāda, he is primarily a philosopher of grammar and language and his advaita is different from that of Shaṅkara.

There are two works on Vedānta, the *Paramārtha-sāra* attributed to Ādi-Sheṣa (later on adapted and expanded under the same name by Abhinavagupta into a handbook of *Pratyabhijñā-darshana*) and the Yogavāsiṣṭha attributed to the sage Vasiṣṭha, which bear some doctrinal and terminological similarities with Gauḍapāda's Kārikā. In the opinion of some these two works are earlier than the Kārikā, but the reasons assigned for this are unconvincing. On the other hand, there are strong reasons to believe that the Kārikā of Gauḍapāda is earlier than these two works.[1]

III. ĀCHĀRYA GAUḌAPĀDA: MĀṆḌŪKYA-KĀRIKĀ

Āchārya Gauḍapāda's Kārikā on the Māṇḍūkya Upaniṣad known as Gauḍapāda-Kārikā or Māṇḍūkya-Kārikā or the Āgama-shāstra is the first systematic treatise on Advaita Vedānta which is available to us. This work is highly respected in the advaita tradition. It is treated as the quintessence of the Upaniṣadic philosophy and is valued as a treasure by the sannyāsins and the aspirants for mokṣa. In Gauḍapāda we find a happy combination of mysticism and metaphysics, spiritual intuition and reason. He speaks, like the Upaniṣadic sages, with a voice of authority, which can come only from a realised saint.

It is usually accepted that Gauḍapāda flourished in the sixth century. Tradition says that he was the teacher of Govindapāda who was the teacher of Shaṅkarāchārya. Shaṅkara himself, in his commentary on the Kārikā[2], most respectfully salutes Gauḍapāda as his 'grand teacher' (*parama-guru*), who is the respected (teacher) of his respected (teacher), and in his commentary on the *Brahmasūtra*[3], quotes from and refers to him as 'the teacher who knows the tradition of Vedānta'. Shaṅkara's disciple Sureshvara also refers to him as 'the revered Gauḍa'.[4]

The long-accepted traditional view that the Kārikā is a free commentary (*prakaraṇa-grantha*) on the Māṇḍūkya Upaniṣad is

1. See Dr. S.L. Pandey's *Pre-Shaṅkara Advaita Philosophy*, chapter 6.
2. Last but one verse.
3. II, 1, 9 and I, 4, 14.
4. *Naiṣkarmyasiddhi*, IV, 44.

challenged by Mm. Professor Vidhushekhara Bhattacharya in his scholarly work, *The Āgamashāstra of Gauḍapāda.* Prof. Bhattacharya opines that the Māṇḍūkya Upaniṣad is based on the Kārikā and not *vice versa*;[1] and that the four chapters of the Kārikā are four independent treatises put together, later on, in a volume under the title of *Agamashāstra.*[2] The reasons assigned in support of his views by the learned Professor do not appear convincing to us. Also, there is sufficient unity among the four chapters to prove them chapters of the same treatise. The chief merit of Prof. Bhattacharya's work is to point out in detail the similarities between Gauḍapāda and Mahāyāna Buddhism. We shall discuss these in detail in the last section of this chapter.

Gauḍapāda-Kārikā is a free Commentary on the Māṇḍūkya Upaniṣad and is divided into four chapters. In the First chapter, the Āgama-prakaraṇa, the 12 *mantras* of the Māṇḍūkya have been explained in 29 Kārikās. *Brahma* or *Ātmā* is identified with *Praṇava* or *Omkāra.* The states of waking, dream and deep sleep are analysed both in microcosm and in macrocosm. Ātmā is immanent in all these and yet, in itself, it transcends these. It is the Fourth, the *Turīya,* the Measureless or the *Amātra,* the non-dual Pure Consciousness-Bliss. In the Second chapter, the Vaitathya-prakaraṇa, the Āchārya in 38 Kārikās has proved by rational arguments that this phenomenal world is *ajāti* or unreal creation as it is false and appears, like dream and illusion, due to *Māyā.* In the Third chapter, the Advaita Prakaraṇa, the Āchārya in 48 Kārikās has proved, by shruti and by reason, that the Supreme is the non-dual foundational Self which can be realised in immediate experience. In this chapter the Āchārya has further explained his famous Ajātivāda and has expounded A*sparsha*yoga. In the Fourth chapter, the Alātashānti-prakaraṇa which contains 100 Kārikās, the Āchārya according to us has elaborated and compared his Advaita Vedānta with the Mādhyamika and the Vijñānavāda schools of Mahāyana Buddhism, pointing out similarities and differences and proving the superiority of the Vedānta. We shall discuss this in detail later on in the last section of this chapter. This is necessary because the fourth chapter of the Kārikā has generated many misunderstandings and has not been properly evaluated.

---

1. *The Āgamashāstra of Gauḍapāda,* Introduction, p. XLVI.
2. *Ibid.,* p. LVII.

IV. AJĀTIVĀDA

The fundamental philosophical doctrine expounded by Āchārya Gauḍapāda is known as *ajātivāda* or the Doctrine of No-origination. It means ātmavāda as well as *māyāvāda*. According to it, there is no *jāti* or creation; nothing is created or produced or born and hence nothing is subject to origination, change or annihilation. The Absolute, the eternal non-dual Self is not subject to birth, change and death. It is *aja*, the unborn eternal, the unchanging Real. The empirical world too, constituted by conscious individual selves with their mental states and physical and biological objects, is not a real creation, but an appearance. Ajātivāda, therefore, is a denial of *jāti* or real creation; the world of plurality is an appearance and the Real is eternal. Negatively, it is a denial of difference; of origination, change and annihilation and positively, it is a re-affirmation of the non-dual Self, the supreme Real. Through its beginningless and indescribable power called *māyā* or *avidyā*, the Absolute appears as many. The empirical world of individual subjects and objects is false, because it is neither real nor unreal. 'Indescribability as either real or unreal' (*sadasadanirvachanīyatā*) is the mark of illusion (*bhrama*), appearance (*pratīti*) or falsity (*mithyātva* or *vaitathya*). The world of plurality, like a dream or an illusion, cannot be called 'real' because it is not eternal nor can it be called 'unreal' because, during perception, it appears as real. Hence it is 'neither real nor unreal' (*sadasadachintya*) which means that it is a projection of *māyā*, a mere appearance and so is false. As there can be no real creation, ajātivāda is proved.

Āchārya Gauḍapāda refers to various theories of creation and rejects them all: Some say that creation is the expansion (*vibhūti*) of God. Others say that it is like a dream (*svapna*) or an illusion (*māyā*). Some believe that it is the will (*ichchhā*) of God. Those who think about Time maintain that creation proceeds from Time (*kāla*). Still others declare that it is for enjoyment (*bhoga*). And some maintain that it is the sport (*krīḍā*) of God. All these views, *qua* views regarding creation, are unsatisfactory. Gauḍapāda means to say that there can be no expansion of God because He is Full; there is no addition to or substraction from or multiplication and division of the Full. Time cannot be the cause of creation, for, though creation is bound by space and time, its cause must be beyond space and time. Creation cannot be for enjoyment too; the enjoyment of the *jīva* who is subject to creation is apparent like him and God does not need an 'other' for enjoyment. It cannot be the 'sport' of God; for, why should God indulge in sport? Again, it cannot be the 'will' of God, for will presupposes imperfection and God is perfect; how can there be any desire or will in God who has realised all desires? Creation may be like a dream or an illusion, but dream or illusion is no real creation. After examining the various theories, Gauḍapāda concludes that creation may be said to be the 'nature' (*svabhāva*) of the self-shining Lord in the sense that it emanates or flows from Him, provided we remember that this 'flow' is an appearance only, like desert sand (due to sun-rays falling on it) appearing as water. It is not the 'nature' of the Lord to involve Himself in creation; it is the 'nature' of *avidyā* or *māya,* the inexpressible power of the Lord, to project the illusion of creation and the 'nature' of the Lord is to be the uninvolved ground on which creation is superimposed.[1]

Māyā or *avidyā,* in later Advaita Vedānta, is described as a power (*shakti*), which is beginningless (*anādi*), positive (*bhāvarūpa*), indeterminable either as real or as unreal (*sadasadanirvachanīya*) and of the nature of Cosmic Ignorance (*mūlāvidyā*) which can be removed by non-dual immediate experience of the Real (*jñāna-nirasya*). Gauḍapāda is fully aware of all these implications. *Māyā* is the own power of the Lord. It is beginningless (*anādi*).[2] Time itself is a product of *māyā* and so *māyā* can have no beginning in time. It has an end in as much as it can be destroyed by right knowledge (*jñāte dvaitam na vidyate*).[3] *Māyā* is negative, positive and neither negative nor positive. It is negative or absence of knowledge, as it acts as a veil or covering on the Real (*āvaraṇa, nidrā, agrahaṇa*).[4] It is positive or wrong knowledge as it projects the unreal on the Real (*vikṣepa, svapna, anyathā-grahaṇa*).[5] In itself it is unthinkable either as real (positive) or as unreal (negative); it is *sadasadachintya.*[6] Its product, the world of plurality, is also

1. Devasyaiṣa svabhāvo'yam āptakāmasya kā spṛhā? —*Gauḍapāda-Kārikā,* I, 7-9.
2. *Ibid.,* I, 16.
3. *Ibid.,* I, 18.
4. *Ibid.,* I, 15.
5. *Ibid.*
6. *Ibid.,* IV, 41 & 52.

achintya, for it is neither real nor unreal nor both. The Supreme Self imagines itself as many through its own *māyā.*[1] The Unborn (*Self*) appears as variously born through *māyā.*[2] Causation can be attributed to the Real only through *māyā,* and not in reality.[3] The unconditioned Brahma appearing as conditioned by *māyā* is called the lower Brahma (*aparam Brahma*)[4] or the Lord (*Īshvara*)[5] who is the creator, protector and destroyer of this world. The whole world is a product of His *māyā* by which He appears infatuated as it were.[6] The Supreme Brahma (*param Brahma*) is the Fourth (*turya* or *turīya*) or the non-dual (*advaita*) self-shining Self, beyond creation (*aja*), beyond measure (amātra), beyond sleep (*nidrā* or *āvaraṇa*) and dream (*svapna* or *vikṣepa*).[7]

Āchārya Gauḍapāda in the Second chapter of his Kārikā proves the falsity of the pluralistic universe of individual subjects and objects on the analogy of the dream-objects[8] and the illusory objects like the rope-snake.[9] Some other examples given by him are: the fire-circle (*alāta-chakra*)[10] which appears when a fire-brand is moved around and disappears when it is not moved; the magical elephant (*māyā-hastī*)[11] projected by the power of the magician, and the sky-city (*gandharva-nagara*).[12] Āchārya Gauḍapāda compares the world-objects with dream-objects and illusory objects and declares that both are ultimately false and in this sense can be placed on a par.[13] The objects seen in a dream are known to be false on waking. But the world-objects experienced in waking life are also false when the non-dual spiritual experience is attained. The empirical world which is 'too much with us' really consists of 'such stuff as dreams are made of'. When a rope is mistaken as a snake in waking life it appears as a real snake during illusion; its illusory character is realised only when the rope is perceived and the illusion is dispelled. Objects in dream and in illusion

---

1. *Ibid.*, II, 12.
2. *Ibid.*, III, 24.
3. *Ibid.*, III, 27.
4. *Ibid.*, I, 26.
5. *Ibid.*, I, 28.
6. *Ibid.*, II, 19.
7. *Ibid.*, I, 15, 16.
8. *Ibid.*, II, 5, 31
9. *Ibid.*, II, 17-18.
10. *Ibid.*, IV, 47-50.
11. *Ibid.*, IV, 44.
12. *Ibid.*, II, 31.
13. *Ibid.*, II, 5.

resemble the world-objects in many respects. Both are perceived as 'objects'. Though in dream the sense-organs do not function and therefore we have perception without sensation, yet it cannot be denied that the dreamer perceives the dream-contents as 'objects'. Again, both are determined in time and space. The dream-objects appear to the dreamer as 'external' and as 'occupying space' and are subject to temporal sequence, though the space-time determination of dream-objects is different from the spatio-temporal determination of world-objects. Strange 'objects' like 'man-lion', 'gold-mountain', 'ten-headed creature,' etc., which are not found in our world may appear in dream, but to the dreamer these objects appear quite normal in dream and their abnormality is realised only on waking. Again, it cannot be argued that dream-objects (and also illusory objects) lack pragmatic utility which the world-objects possess. The dream-water has the power to quench thirst in dream. If dream-water cannot quench thirst in waking life, water of waking life too cannot quench dream-thirst. The roaring of a dream-tiger or the vision of a nightmare causes real fear and the other psycho-physical reactions in the dreamer which may persist for some time even when the dreamer gets awake. The 'rope-snake' generates the same reactions like fear etc., in the person under illusion which a real snake generates in him when he perceives it. Hence, the objects perceived in dream and illusion and the world-objects perceived in normal empirical life are essentially similar. Both are real in their own sphere and are unreal from a higher standpoint. Both are indescribable and unthinkable either as real or as unreal or as both and therefore are due to *māyā* or *avidyā* and are false (*vitatha* or *mithyā*). In fact all these are unreal in all the three tenses, in past, present and future, like a hare's horn or a sky-flower, yet there is a vital difference between these objects and the non-entities like a sky-flower. Non-entities like a hare's horn or a sky-flower cannot even appear and are therefore called utterly unreal, while the objects in dream, illusion or empirical world do appear as 'real' in their respective sphere and are realised as 'unreal' when sublated by a higher experience. Hence these are declared as false, because these are neither real nor unreal nor both. The Āchārya says that the entire universe of plurality or difference which is presented as 'object' is false. This includes objects of dream, illusion and empirical world, and the world-objects include external material objects, internal mental states and the individual selves. These are not real in the beginning (*ādi*) before they appear or are produced, these are not real in the end (*anta*) when they are cancelled as unreal or are destroyed, so these are not real even in the middle when they appear to be so. Though unreal they appear as real and hence they are declared as false (*mithyā*).[1] As this world too is ultimately false like dream, illusion or magic, the learned persons in Vedānta (who have realised the non-dual Self) see it as such.[2]

It should be noted that though Āchārya Gauḍapāda places the objects in dream and illusion at par with the world-objects on the ground that both are ultimately false, yet he does assert the empirical difference between them. The difference between them, no doubt, is one of degree and is relative (*saṁvṛti*), but it is important for us. The Āchārya himself points out the difference between them thus: Dream-objects are mental (*antaḥ-sthāna*), while world-objects are external (*bahiḥ-sthāna*). In dream the sense-organs do not function and we have perception without sensation, while the sense-organs actively function in waking (*indriyāntara*) and perception is always preceded by sensation. Again, dream-objects and illusory objects also like rope-snake are *chitta-kāla*[3], i.e., they 'exist' only as long as they are perceived, their 'esse' is 'percipi', while world-objects are *dvaya-kāla*, i.e., they exist during and after perception, they continue to exist even after the perceiver has ceased to perceive them. *Chitta-kāla* is *pratibhāsa* and *dvayakāla* is *vyavahāra*. Again, objects in dream and illusion are projection of the individual self (*jīva-sṛṣṭa*) and are therefore dim and short-lived, while world-objects are projection of God, the Universal self (*Īshvara-sṛṣṭa*) and are therefore clear and more lasting.

Gauḍapāda emphasises that the non-dual foundational Self is the only reality and that it appears through *māyā* as this world of plurality. The supreme Self imagines itself as many through its

1. *Ibid.*, II, 6-7 mithyaiva khalu te smṛtāḥ
2. svapnamāye yathā dṛṣte gandharvanagaram yathā I tathā vishvamidam dṛṣtam Vedānteṣu vichakṣaṇaiḥ II- Ibid, II, 31.
3. In later Vedānta these are called pratibhāsa-mātra-sharīra.

own *Māyā,* and it is this Self which knows all the objects—this is the established truth in Vedānta.[1] The individual selves are non-different from the pure non-dual Self. Gauḍapāda explains the non-duality and the infinitude of the Self by means of the analogy of space. The pure Self is like universal space (*mahākāsha*), while an individual self is like space limited in a jar (*ghatākāsha*). The limitations of production, change, destruction, size, shape, colour, impurity, clearness etc. which appear to belong to 'space limited in a jar' really belong to the jar and do not at all affect the space inside it which is non-different from the universal space. Similarly, the individual self is really the pure Self and its finitude, plurality etc. are due to the adjuncts of *māyā* and do not affect it.[2] Hence, neither any object nor any self originates. There is no origination, no change, no annihilation, no birth, no death, no bondage, no aspirant and no liberation. These are appearances projected by *māyā.* This is the fearless goal, the *ajāti* beyond birth, decay and death. This is the supreme truth.[3]

The doctrine of *ajāti,* says Gauḍapāda, is established in the shruti, the Upaniṣads. The Upaniṣadic texts clearly, unmistakably, repeatedly and emphatically declare that ultimate reality is the foundational Self which is non-dual, self-luminous, self-proved, eternal and pure consciousness and bliss, and denounce difference, duality, plurality and origination as mere appearance projected by *māyā.* By proclaiming non-difference between *jīva* and pure *ātmā,* the shruti praises the non-dual reality and condemns difference and duality as illusory; the statements of the shruti agree in teaching the reality of *advaita.*[4] "There is no second to *ātmā* or Brahma.'[5] Fear originates from an 'other' "[6] 'Brahma is one without a second.'[7] 'Thou art That.'[8] 'This self is Brahma.'[9] 'How can delusion and suffering touch him who sees the non-dual

1. sa eva buddhyate bhedān iti Vedānta-nishchayaḥ *Ibid.*, II. 12.
2. *Ibid.*, III, 3-9.
3. *Ibid.*, II, 32 na nirodho na chotpattir na baddho na cha sādhakaḥ I
   na mumukṣur na vai mukta ityeṣā paramarthatā II
   and IV, 71 etat taduttamam satyam yatra kiñchin na jāyate I
4. *Ibid.*, III, 13.
5. na tu tad dvitīyam asti. Bṛh. IV, 3, 23.
6. dvitīyād vai bhayam bhavati. Bṛh. I, 4, 2.
7. ekamevādvitiyam. Chhāndogya VI, 2, 2.
8. tat tvam asi. *Ibid.*, VI, 8, 16.
9. ayam ātmā brahma. Bṛh. II, 5, 19.

Self everywhere.'[1] 'The knower of Self goes beyond sorrow'.[2] 'O Janaka! you have realised the fearless goal.'[3] 'The knower of Brahma becomes Brahma'.[4] 'There is no difference and plurality here.'[5] 'He who sees as if there is plurality here revolves in the cycle of birth and death.'[6] 'Those who are attached to creation are in utter darkness (of ignorance)'.[7] These sayings of the shruti clearly declare non-duality and denounce difference, says the Āchārya. When the shruti says that the cause alone is real and the effects are merely a verbal expression, an unreal change, a mere name, by giving the examples of clay and pots etc. made out of it, of gold and ornaments etc., made out of it, these examples should not be taken as pointing to the reality of the effects because these are merely examples and the shruti has categorically declared in this context that the cause alone is real and the effects are mere words and names.[8] By declaring that 'Those who are attached to creation are in utter darkness' (Īsha, 12), the shruti denies creation and by declaring that 'Who, indeed, can create it' (Bṛh., III, 9, 28) the shruti denies the cause of creation.[9] The creation-texts of the Upaniṣads which speak of difference (*bheda-vākya*) should be interpreted in a figurative sense (*gauṇa*) as their primary sense goes against the main teaching. The creation-texts become meaningful only as a means (*upāya*) of introducing the final teaching of non-difference which is the end (*paramārtha*)[10]

Not only by scripture, but also by independent reasoning, says the Āchārya, *ajāti* can be proved. We have seen that he has considered various theories of creation and has rejected them. He has shown that creation can be treated as neither expansion (*vibhūti*) of God, nor as the will (*ichchā*) of God, nor for the

---

1. tatra ko mohaḥ kaḥ shokaḥ ekatvam anupashyataḥ. Īsha, 7.
2. tarati shokam ātmavit. Chhāndogya, VIII, 1, 3.
3. abhayam vai Janaka! prāptó'si. Bṛh. IV, 2, 4.
4. Brahma veda Brahmaiva bhavati. Muṇḍaka, III, 2, 9.
5. neha nānāsti kiñchana. Kaṭha, II, 1, II.
6. mṛtyoḥ sa mṛtyum āpnoti ya iha nāneva pashyati. *Ibid.*, II, 1, 10.
7. andham tamaḥ pravishanti ye sambhūtim upāsate. Īsha, 12.
8. vāchārambhaṇam vikāro nāmadheyam, mṛttiketyeva satyam. Chhāndogya, VI, 1, 4. *Gauḍapāda-Kārikā*, III, 15.
9. *Ibid.*, III, 25.
10. *Ibid.*, III, 14-15. upāyaḥ so'vatārāya nāsti bhedaḥ kathañchana.

enjoyment (*bhoga*) nor as the sport (*krīḍā* or *līlā*) of God.[1] Now, to prove *ajāti* by further independent reasoning, the Āchārya enters into a dialectical critique of causality. Four alternatives (*kotyash-chatasraḥ*) are possible on the problem of causation.[2] The relation between cause and effect may be regarded as that of identity or of difference or of both or of neither. The first view maintains that causation is continuous; the cause continues in and is identical with the effect which is its real transformation. The effect is implicitly contained in its cause (*satkāryavāda*). This view of identity is advocated by Sāṅkhya and also by some older Vedāntins. The second view treats causation as emergent and advocates difference between cause and effect. The effect is a new creation and is not implied in its cause (*asatkāryavāda*). This view of difference is advocated by Nyāya-Vaisheṣika. The third view is a combination of the first and the second and believes that the effect is identical as well as different from its cause (*sadasatkārya-vāda*). This view is advocated by Jainism. The fourth view which says that things are produced by sheer chance denies causation itself. It is the view of Chārvāka. Gauḍapāda rejects all the four views. A thing, says he, can be produced neither out of itself (*svataḥ*) nor out of something else (*parataḥ*) nor out of both nor out of neither.[3] If the effect is contained in its cause, it is already an existent fact and its further production would be non-sense. There is no logic in unnecessary reduplication.[4] And if the effect is not implied in the cause, it is non-existent like a hare's horn and cannot be produced. The son of a barren woman can be born neither in illusion nor in fact.[5] The third view suffers from the difficulties of both the first and the second views. And the fourth view is the denial of causation and is obviously absurd. If as the first view says causation consists in the manifestation of the permanent cause as the changing effects, how can the permanent cause be identical with the changing effects and still be permanent?[6] If as the second view says the effect is a new creation and is not contained in the cause, it is non-existent and cannot be

1. *Ibid.*, I, 7-9; see *supra* pp. 127–8.
2. *Ibid.*, IV, 84.
3. *Ibid.*, IV, 22.
4. *Ibid.*, III, 27; IV, 13.
5. *Ibid.*, III, 28
6. *Ibid.*, IV, 11-12.

produced.[1] Again, cause and effect cannot be simultaneous, for then the two horns of a bull will be causally related.[2] Again, those who maintain that cause and effect precede each other maintain the absurd position that a son also begets his father.[3] The Āchārya says that the dualists believe in real causation and quarrel among themselves. Some (the Sāṅkhyas) say that it is the existent which is born, while others (the Nyāya-Vaisheṣikas) say that it is the non-existent which is born. These disputing dualists destroy each other's position. Satkāryavāda cancels asatkāryavāda and *vice versa.* Thus in either alternative there is no-origination.[4] We do not quarrel with these dualists because these, taken together, unknowingly proclaim the truth of No-origination. Also, there are some non-dualists (the Mādhyamikas) who openly proclaim the doctrine of No-origination and we agree with them in this.[5] We find, says the Āchārya, that there is no energy (*ashakti*) in the cause to produce the effect whether the cause is taken to be existent or non-existent or both or neither. Again, the effect which is not known (*aparijñāna*) to exist either in the beginning or in the end cannot be supposed to exist in the middle. Also, there is no order of succession (*krama-kopa*) between cause and effect; we cannot say which of these is prior and therefore is the cause. Thus have the learned clarified the truth of *ajāti.*[6] Hence it is proved that causation or origination cannot be real; it is an appearance. The Real alone may be said to appear through *māyā.*[7]

V. ĀTMAVĀDA

According to Āchārya Gauḍapāda, the Real is Brahma or *Ātmā,* the absolute and the foundational Self. It is eternal and pure consciousness, which is at once infinite and uninterrupted bliss. It is beyond senses, intellect and speech. As the foundation of all knowledge and experience, it is self-proved and self-shining. Due to its own power *māyā,* it appears as individual souls and as the

1. *Ibid.*, III, 28.
2. *Ibid.*, IV, 16.
3. *Ibid.*, IV, 15.
4. *Ibid.*, IV, 3-4.
5. *Ibid.*, IV, 5.
6. *Ibid.*, IV, 19.
7. *Ibid.*, III, 27. sato hi māyayā janma ujyate na tu tatvataḥ.

external world. These appearances are merely projections of *māyā* and are not real creation (*jāti* or *utpatti*). These are not different from their ground reality, the *Ātmā.* This Self can be realised only through immediate spiritual experience which shines in the highest samādhi called 'Asparshayoga'. Gauḍapāda's Vijñānavāda is 'nitya-ātma-vāda' for which the pure vijñāna is the eternal Self. His idealism is transcendental only, as he believes in empirical realism. Advaita or absolute non-dualism is the ultimate reality (*paramārtha*); in empirical life (*vyavahāra*), however, dvaita or dualism is accepted.[1] Though ultimately, the learned declare, the world objects too are as unreal as the dream-objects[2], yet, from the empirical standpoint, the difference between the two is obvious and should be accepted.[3] Those who believe in idealism both transcendentally and empirically (*ubhayathā*), like the Buddhist Vijñānavādins, as well as those who advocate the truth of realism without accepting this distinction, like the realists, are wrong. The Self, through *māyā,* appears as the conscious individual *jīvas* and as the unconscious world-objects, though ultimately there is no difference between the Self and these *jīvas* and material objects. *Ātmā* is like universal space (*mahākāsha*) and the individual *jīvas* are like spaces in jars (*ghatākāsha*). The attributes of production, destruction, limitation, purity, impurity, size, shape, etc. which appear to belong to the different 'spaces' in jars really belong to the jars and the space in a jar is always the universal space itself. It is neither a transformation nor a modification nor a part of universal space. Similarly a *jīva* is neither a transformation nor a modification nor a part of *Ātmā.* The differences in birth, death, name, form, function, etc. which appear to belong to the *jīvas* are adjuncts of *māyā* and do not really belong to them. *Jīvas* are non-different from *Ātmā* or Brahma, as space is non-different from spaces-in-jars.[4] The same transcendent Self is also immanent in *jīvas* and objects of Nature, in microcosm as well as in macrocosm.

This Absolute manifests itself in three forms as *Vishva, Taijasa*

1. *Ibid.*, III, 18; advaitam paramārtho hi dvaitam tad bheda uchyate.
2. svapna-jāgarita-sthāne hyekam āhurmanīṣiṇaḥ | *Ibid.*, II, 5 and 31.
3. See *supra,* p. 131.
4. *Ibid.*, III, 3-9; ākāshasya na bhedo'sti tadvajjīveṣu nirṇayaḥ | III, 6.

and *Prājña*. It is called *Vishva* (All) when it has the consciousness of outside; *Taijas* (Luminous) when it has the consciousness of inside; and *Prājña* (Intelligent) when it is concentrated consciousness.[1] These correspond to the waking (*jāgrat*), dream (*svapna*) and deep sleep (*suṣupti*) states respectively. But the Absolute in itself transcends these three states, forms, phases or poises and is called the *Turīya* or the Fourth. It is the Amātra or the Measureless. *Praṇava* or *Oṁkāra* is its symbol. But there is no difference between the symbol and the symbolised. *Praṇava* itself is Brahma, lower and higher, *saguṇa* and *nirguṇa*. *Vishva* enjoys the gross; *Taijasa* enjoys the subtle; *Prājña* enjoys the bliss. *Vishva* and *Taijasa* are both causes and effects; *Prājña* is only the cause. *Turīya* is neither cause nor effect. It is all-pervading (*vibhu*), capable of removing all suffering (*īshāna*), lord of all (*prabhu*), changeless (*avyaya*), non-dual real, immanent in all things (*advaitaḥ sarvabhāvānām*), self-luminous (*deva*) and the transcendent Fourth (*turīya*).[2] In sleep we know nothing as there is no object, neither real nor imagined, to be known; it is the state of ignorance or absence of knowledge (*ajñāna, agrahaṇa, āvaraṇa* or *laya*). In dream we know the dream-objects which are our own projections (realised as false on waking); it is the state of wrong knowledge (*mithyā jñāna, anyathā-grahaṇa* or *vikṣepa*). In waking life we know the world-objects, but their knowledge is found to be false when the Self is realised; so this too is a state of wrong knowledge or *māyā*. In sleep we do not know the truth; in dream we know otherwise; and the so-called waking life is also a cosmic dream. *Vishva* and *Taijasa* are connected with sleep (absence of knowledge) and with dream (wrong knowledge). *Prājña* is connected with sleep only. In sleep there are no objects (real or imaginary) to be known and so *Prājña* knows no objects and therefore cannot be called even the subject. It knows nothing, neither itself nor others, neither truth nor falsehood. But *Turīya* being pure self-luminous consciousness is All-seeing (*sarva-dṛk*).[3] Though duality is absent both in *Prājña* and in *Turīya*, yet *Prājña* is connected with deep sleep where the seed of ignorance is present, while *Turīya* is untouched by it.[4] When the negative absence of knowledge

1. *Ibid.*, I, 1; eka eva tridhā smṛtaḥ.
2. *Ibid.*, I, 10.
3. *Ibid.*, I, 12.
4. *Ibid.*, I, 13.

which is sleep, and the positive wrong knowledge which is dream and waking, are transcended, the Fourth, the goal is reached.[1] When the individual self (*jīva*), slumbering in beginningless Ignorance, is awakened, then the Unborn (eternal), the Sleepless, the Dreamless, the Non-dual *Ātmā,* the self-shining Absolute is realised.[2] This world of plurality appears due to *māyā;* there is no real removal of it, for it never existed; it is the projection of *avidyā* and mind and it disappears when *avidyā* and mind are transcended. Non-duality is the ultimate truth.[3] The eternal self-shining Self, transcendent as well as immanent, is called *Amātra* (measureless, infinite), *Turiya* (fourth, the transcendent) and *Oṁkāra.* He who realises this pure Self, immanent in all the three stages and yet transcendent and always the same, is a great sage (*mahā-muni*) worthy of utmost respect and veneration of all beings.[4] This Self is beyond thought-determinations and plurality. It is non-dual and is realised by the sages who have known the essence of the Vedas and who are free from attachment, fear and anger.[5] He alone and none else is a sage (*muni*) who has embraced this infinite, measureless and all-pervading *Oṁkāra* which is the cessation of all fear, suffering and duality and which is all bliss.[6] The pure Self is beyond thought and language and so it can be described negatively (*neti neti*). But these negations negate only the descriptions of the Self and not the Self to which these negations point as the ineffable and self-shining Reality.[7] To deny the Self is impossible, for the denier is himself the Self and the Self, as the foundation of knowledge, is beyond proof and disproof. To prove or affirm it is unnecessary, for it is self-shining; the attempt is laughable like revealing the sun at noon by means of a candle-light. The Āchārya says that it is the dualists, who in order to prove their respective theories, quarrel with one another; Advaita quarrels with none.[8]

1. *Ibid.*, I, 15.
2. anādimāyayā supto yadā jīvaḥ prabuddhyate I ajam anidram asvapnam advaitam buddhyate tadā II *Ibid.*, I, 16.
3. māyāmātram idam dvaitam advaitam paramārthataḥ II *Ibid.*, I, 17.
4. sa pūjyaḥ sarvabhūtānām vandyashchaiva mahāmuniḥ II *Ibid.*, I, 22.
5. vītarāgabhayakrodhair munibhir vedapāragaiḥ I nirvikalpo hyayam dṛṣṭaḥ prapañchopashamo'dvayaḥ II *Ibid.*, II, 35; cf. Gītā, II, 56.
6. amātro'nantamātrashcha dvaitasyopashamaḥ shivaḥ I oṁkāro vidito yena sa munir netaro janaḥ II *Ibid.*, I, 29.
7. *Ibid.*, III, 26.
8. *Ibid.*, III, 17; tairayam na viruddyate.

VI. ASPARSHAYOGA

The doctrine of Asparshayoga, also known as amanībhāva (cessation of mind) or *vaishāradya* (absolute purity), is based on the Upaniṣads, is described in detail in the Bhagavad-gītā (as yoga or Brahmayoga) and is developed by Gauḍapāda. Asparshayoga is *nirvikalpa samādhi* or super-conscious meditation, where the trinity of the meditator, the object of meditation and the process of meditation is completely fused into one and transcended so that even the consciousness of the object of meditation glides away and the mind along with its mother *māyā* is transcended and completely dissolved without residue and where the Pure *Ātmā* or Brahma shining with its eternal light of pure consciousness and ineffable bliss is directly realised. *Nirvikalpa samādhi* is described in the Upaniṣads, in the Bhagavadgītā, in the Buddhist works and in the Yoga-sūtra of Patañjali, and the word *sparsha* is often used in the sense of sense-object contact and subject-object duality in the Gītā and the Buddhist works, yet the word 'Asparshayoga' is perhaps for the first time used by Gauḍapāda for *nirvikalpa samādhi* and may be treated as his contribution. In the Buddhist works, both in Pāli and in Sanskrit, the words used for *nirvikalpa-samādhi* are *saṁjñā-vedayita-nirodha* and *nirodha-samāpatti.* Buddhist texts tell us that Buddha taught nine *dhyānas* or meditations called *anupūrvavihāra.* The first four *rūpa dhyānas* are : (1) meditation in which relational thought (*vitarka, vichāra*) and intellectual discernment (*viveka*) give rise to attachment with the object of meditation (*prīti*) and joy (*sukha*); (2) meditation in which discursive intellect ceases and concentration of the mind gives rise to attachment with the object of meditation and joy (*samadhija prīti-sukha*); (3) meditation in which there is indifference (*upekṣā*) to both attachment (*prīti*) and detachment (*virāga*) and there is continuous concentration (*smṛti*) on the object of meditation; and (4) meditation in which there is bliss beyond pleasure (*sukha*) and pain (*duḥkha*). The next four *arūpa dhyānas* are: (5) meditation on the infinity of space (*ākāshānantyāyatana*); (6) meditation on the infinity of consciousness (*vijñānānantyāyatana*); (7) meditation on 'nothingness' (*ākiñchanāyatana*); and (8) meditation in which there is neither relational consciousness nor unconsciousness (*naivasaṁjñā-nā'saṁjñāyatana*). And the ninth, the highest dhyāna is *saṁjñā-vedayita-nirodha* in which there is complete cessation of relational thought and sensation; this is *nirvikalpa samādhi* in which sensation and thought-determinations (including mind or *chitta* and mentals or *chaitasika-dharmas*) are transcended and the highest bliss is experienced.[1] It is nirvāna itself. Bhagavadgītā calls it samādhi, yoga or Brahmayoga (V, 21). In Pātañjala Yoga-sūtra it is called *nirvikalpa, nirbīja* or *asamprajñāta samādhi.* It is only Gauḍapāda, as far as we know, who uses the word *Asparshayoga* for it.

The word *sparsha* is frequently used in the Gītā for sense-object contact. Sense-object contact produces pleasure and pain which are momentary.[2] Pleasures arising through sense-object contact ultimately lead to suffering; these arise and vanish and the wise do not enjoy these.[3] A *yogī* does not indulge in worldly pleasures which arise due to the contact between sense-organs and external objects, leaving these outside he enjoys through yoga the eternal bliss of the *Ātmā.*[4] In Buddhist works also sparsha is used for sense-object contact. It is the sixth link in the twelve-linked wheel of causation. It gives rise to *vedanā* or sensation which may be pleasant, painful or indifferent and which, in turn, leads to *tṛṣṇā* or thirst for sensuous enjoyment and makes one rotate in the cycle of birth and death. Hence in order to remove suffering *sparsha* must be stopped.

Āchārya Gauḍapāda also uses the word *sparsha* in the sense of contact, i.e., contact between sense-organ and external object, between mind and sense-organ and between mind and mental object which generate all empirical experience, sensuous and mental. These contacts presuppose the basic contact between the self and mind, the subject and the object. But the Self really is eternal and pure and does not come into real contact with mind. So this contact is apparent and is due to *avidyā* or *māyā.* Gauḍapāda uses the words *jīva, chitta* and *manas* as synonyms; *manas* is used by him in the sense of *chitta* which includes *buddhi* and *ahaṅkāra* also. Due to the apparent contact between the subject and the object, between Brahma and *māyā,* between Ātmā and *avidyā,* the *jīva* appears to be fouled by finitude, limitation, duality, contamina-

1. Samyutta-Nikāya, XXXIV, 19-20 (PTS, London); XXXVI, 19-20 (Nalanda ed.).
2. Bhagavadgītā, II, 14.
3. *Ibid.*, V, 22.
4. *Ibid.*, V, 21 and 27.

tion and impurity. *Sparsha*, therefore, indicates these various contacts which generate all worldly experiences of sense, thought and language having their ultimate source in *avidyā* which works through subject-object duality and thought-determinations which appear to contaminate and distort the Real. And the word '*asparsha*' which is the negation of *sparsha*, therefore, means the negation of these contacts producing all worldly experience; and as mind is the moving power, the *elan vital*, of these contacts, *asparsha* implies cessation of mind called *amanībhāva* or *amanstā*. And as mind itself is rooted in and derives its power from *avidyā* or *māyā* which makes the non-dual Real appear in the form of subject-object duality, the cessation of mind implies the cessation of *avidyā* or *māyā*. And 'Asparshayoga' is the contactless and uncontaminated *nirvikalpa samādhi* or meditation in which *avidyā* and its entire creation, mind, subject-object duality, sense-experience, relational thought with its categories and the plurality of this entire universe are transcended and the pure non-dual *Ātmā* or Brahma shining with eternal consciousness and bliss is directly realised. The Real is non-dual (advaita), absolutely pure (*vishārada*), the unborn eternal (*aja*), beyond relational thought (*nirvikalpa*) and is always the same (*sāmya*).

Avidyā, says Gauḍapāda, works with *bheda* or difference or duality between the subject and the object. The trinity of knower, known and knowledge is the projection of relational thought. In fact, the 'knower' is not the individual self or *jīva*, but the pure eternal Self, *Ātmā* or Brahma; the 'known' is not the external object or the mental state, but Brahma itself which appears as such through *avidyā*; and the 'knowledge' is not the relational knowledge produced by thought-determinations, but pure eternal consciousness. There is no difference between subject, object and knowledge. It is comparatively less difficult to realise the identity of subject and knowledge because both are consciousness than to realise the identity of conscious subject and unconscious object. What appears to be the unconscious external world is neither unconscious nor external, but the pure eternal Brahma itself. Gauḍapāda stresses that Brahma alone is 'the knowable' or the *jñeya* because it alone deserves to be known and because it is the ground-reality of the apparent object. *Jñāna* or knowledge is really indeterminate (*akalpakam*) and unborn or eternal (*ajam*) and is non-different from the *jñeya* or the knowable object (*jñeyābhinnam*) because the knowable (*jñeyam*) is the unborn (*ajam*) and the eternal (*nityam*) Brahma itself. Hence the eternal Brahma is realised as, at once, eternal subject, eternal object and eternal knowledge.[1] Duality is merely a projection of *māyā*; the Real is non-dual.[2] The entire universe of duality and plurality is a projection of the mind; when the mind is transcended (*amanī-bhāva*) duality and plurality disappear.[3] When the reality of the pure *Ātmā* is realised, mind stops its function of projection and in the absence of the projected object mind also, as the perceiving ego, ceases to exist (*amanastā*)[4]; this is *nirvikalpa samādhi* in which the mind is completely controlled, is stopped from functioning and is totally annihilated along with its source *avidyā*.

This *samādhi*, says the Āchārya, must be known as different from *suṣupti* (deep sleep) where too the subject-object duality is absent; but in *suṣupti* the mind rests and sleeps (*līyate*) in the lap of its mother *avidyā* and after sleep comes out of it and distracted again resumes its function of projection (*vikṣepa*), while in samādhi the mind is completely annihilated (*niruddha*) along with *avidyā*. It merges in the fearless Brahma shining with its all-pervading eternal light of pure consciousness.[5] When both *laya* and *vikṣepa* are transcended, when the mind does not fall into sleep nor is it distracted again, when it becomes unshakable and free from its function of illusory projection, it becomes Brahma.[6] Verily, the absence of fear, the end of suffering, the perpetual wakefulness and enlightenment, the ever-lasting peace and the eternal bliss of all yogīs depend on the control of mind.[7] When Brahma is realised in this *nirvikalpa samādhi*, the yogī becomes one with the non-dual Self which is the eternal light of Omniscience in which the unborn subject becomes one with the unborn object, and which is eternal

1. akalpakamajam jñānam jñeyābhinnam prachakṣate I Brahma jñeyamajam nityamajenājam vibudhyate II *Gauḍapāda-Kārikā*, III, 33.
2. māyāmātramidam dvaitam advaitam paramārthataḥ II *Ibid.*, I, 17.
3. manaso hyamanībhāve dvaitam naivopalabhyate II *Ibid.*, III, 31.
4. *Ibid.*, III, 32.
5. *Ibid.*, III, 34-35. tadeva nirbhayam Brahma jñānālokam samantataḥ II cf. Gītā, II, 72 and VI, 20.
6. *Ibid.*, III, 46. niṣpannam Brahma tat tadā II cf. Gītā, V, 24; VI, 27.
7. *Ibid.*, III, 40. cf. Gītā, II, 71; VI, 14-15 and 20-23.

peace and indescribable supreme bliss, the *Brahma-nirvāṇa.*[1] This *nirvikalpa samādhi,* says Gauḍapāda, is called '*Asparshayoga*'. It is difficult to be realised by all *yogīs.* Even the great *yogīs* are afraid of it, imagining fear where there is no fear at all. Mistaking the annihilation of the ego as the destruction of the Self (*ātma-nāsha*), they imagine fear even in the fearless goal which is eternal consciousness and bliss.[2] It is unborn, it has neither sleep nor dream; nor has it any name or form; it is eternally self-shining and all-knowing; and it is beyond the approach of sense or thought.[3] It is the fearless and unshaken *samādhi* which is beyond all the determinations of thought and language; it is undisturbed peace and eternally self-shining light.[4] There is no category of thought here; nor is here any acceptance or rejection (of anything); here consciousness has become one with the pure non-dual *Ātmā,* unborn (eternal) and always the same.[5] This *Asparshayoga,* being beyond determinations, is free from the conflicts (*avivāda*) and contradictions (*aviruddha*) of relational thought; it is for the happiness of all beings (*sarvasattvasukhaḥ*) and is also good for all (*hitaḥ*).[6] It is non-dual self-shining consciousness, transcendental purity (*vaishāradya*) and eternal bliss. He who has realised Omniscience, the non-dual Brahma, this goal which befits a true Brāhmaṇa and is free from beginning, middle and end, what else can he desire?[7] He who realises this truth bids good-bye to all sorrow and desire and reaches the fearless goal of *mokṣa.* It is not a new acquisition. It is the eternal and ineffable nature of the Self.

VII. GAUḌAPĀDA AND MAHĀYĀNA

Gauḍapāda's Kārikā bears many doctrinal and terminological similarities with *Nāgārjuna's Kārikā* and with the works of Asaṅga and

---

1. *Ibid.*, III, 47. akathyam sukhamuttamam. cf. Gītā, V, 21, 24, 26 and VI, 28.
2. asparshayogo vai nāma durdarshaḥ sarvayogibhiḥ I yogino bibhyati hyasmād abhaye bhayadarshinaḥ II *Ibid.*, III, 39.
3. *Ibid.*, III, 36.
4. sarvābhilāpavigataḥ sarvachintāsamutthitaḥ I suprashāntaḥ sakṛjjyotiḥ samādhirachalo'bhayaḥ II *Ibid.*, III, 37. cf. Gītā, V, 24.
5. *Ibid.*, III, 38. ātmasamstham tadā jñānam ajātisamatāṁ gatam II cf. Gītā, V, 19; II, 45, 48.
6. *Ibid.*, IV, 2, cf. Gītā, II, 45; VI, 25.
7. *Ibid.*, IV, 85. Brāhmaṇyam padamadvayam; kim ataḥ paramīhate?

Vasubandhu. Besides, there is the methodological similarity in the employment of the dialectic between Gauḍapāda and the Mādhyamika Buddhists. The fourth chapter of the Kārikā, known as the Alātashāntiprakaraṇa, exhibits a strikingly Buddhist tenor and has been "a problem child" of Gauḍapāda for the interpreters. The theistic Vedāntins have condemned Advaita Vedānta as 'māyā-vāda' which is false teaching (*asat-shāstra*) and is Buddhism in disguise (*prachchhanna-Bauddha*). Some modern scholars, Indian and Western have also favoured this view. Professor Vidhushekhara Bhattacharya's work *The Āgamashāstra of Gauḍapāda* is an outstandingly searching and valuable work on Gauḍapāda. But some of the conclusions drawn by the learned Professor are unacceptable. In his view Gauḍapāda has accepted and advocated the Buddhist doctrines throughout the fourth chapter, the tenor of which is Buddhistic[1] and nothing Vedāntic will be found therein.[2] Dr. S.N. Dasgupta opines that Gauḍapāda was possibly himself a Buddhist or had, at least, "assimilated all the Buddhist Shūnyavāda and Vijñānavāda teachings and thought that these held good of the ultimate truth preached by the Upaniṣads'"[3] On the other hand, some interpreters like Dr. T.M.P. Mahadevan believe that Gauḍapāda does not agree with the Buddhist views and has simply pressed into service the procedure or methodology of the Buddhist and has used the arguments of the Buddhist idealists to refute realism.[4] Prof. Bhattacharya rightly observes that the Upaniṣadic seed of idealism developed by Buddhist teachers who flourished before Gauḍapāda has influenced him, though "it must be accepted that it did not first originate with the Buddhists."[5] But the learned Professor is wrong in emphasising that Gauḍapāda has largely borrowed from Mahāyāna Buddhism not only the technique but also the tenets and doctrines.

The different conclusions drawn by different scholars regarding the relation between Gauḍapāda and Mahāyāna may be stated as follows:

---

1. *Āgama-shāstra,* Introduction, pp. LIV-LVII.
2. *Ibid.*, p. CXLIV.
3. *A History of Indian Philosophy*, Vol. I, pp. 423 and 429.
4. *Gauḍapāda: A Study in Early Vedānta,* pp. 196 ff.
5. *Āgamashāstra,* Introduction, p. CXXXII.

1. The fourth chapter of the Kārikā is an independent work written by some Buddhist, and later on, by some one and some how, appended to the Kārikā.
2. Gauḍapāda accepts the terms, tenets and technique of Mahāyāna Buddhism and is, therefore, a crypto-Buddhist.
3. There is no influence of Buddhism on Gauḍapāda who belongs to the Vedānta tradition which is opposed to the Buddhist tradition.
4. Gauḍapāda is clearly influenced by Buddhism and has assimilated the Māhāyāna tenets into Vedānta, thinking these to be in accordance with the Upaniṣadic teachings.
5. Gauḍapāda is a Vedāntin who discards the tenets of Buddhism but uses its terms and technique.

We believe that though some scholars have hinted at the truth, it has not been fully grasped nor elaborated by them. According to us the truth appears to be as follows:

Gauḍapāda is a highly respected teacher of Vedānta and to mistake him to be a hidden or open Buddhist is absurd. He is fully conversant with Mahāyāna which he calls Agrayāna (a synonym of Mahāyāna in Buddhist literature) which flourished before him. Gauḍapāda, in the first three chapters of his Kārikā, has given a systematic exposition of Advaita Vedānta on the basis of scripture (shruti) as well as reasoning, and has composed the last fourth chapter of the Kārikā in order to elucidate his Advaita Vedānta by *comparing* it with Mahāyāna Buddhism. He shows the similarities and also differences between the two by referring to and sometimes by *reproducing* from the Mahāyāna works. He discovered that these similarities were due to the fact that Buddha himself had partly assimilated the Upaniṣadic teachings, which were, later on, developed in the Mahāyāna schools of Mādhyamika and Vijñānavāda. He approves of some Mahāyāna doctrines which are in agreement with Vedānta, because these have been borrowed from the Upaniṣads and cannot be said to be the original contribution of Buddha or the Buddhists. He also points out the vital differences between the two and brings out the philosophical soundness of Vedānta over Mahāyāna. Thus, approving of the Mādhyamika doctrine of No-origination and the dialectical critique of causation, he points out that the Absolute must be equated with the pure non-dual Self; and approving of the arguments of Buddhist Vijñānavāda in criticism of realism, he indicates that Buddhist idealism degenerates into subjectivism and pluralism, while Vedānta idealism has the merit of accommodating epistemic realism and is spiritual non-dualism.

As this view is put forward by us it needs to be explained in some detail by an exposition of the fourth chapter of the Kārikā which we now undertake.

The first two Kārikās of the fourth chapter are benedictory verses. In the *first verse* Āchārya Gauḍapāda pays his homage to that Enlightened sage (*sambuddhaḥ*) who, among men, has reached the peak of excellence (*dvipadām varam*) by realising the pure non-dual consciousness in which knowledge, known and knower become one. According to the commentator Shaṅkarāchārya, this Enlightened sage is Lord Nārāyaṇa who is Puruṣottama and who, according to tradition, is the first teacher of the Advaita Vedānta sampradāya. It is natural for Gauḍapāda to pay homage to him. In the Buddhist literature Buddha is frequently referred to as Enlightened (*sambuddha*) and as the most excellent of men (*dvipadām vara*). As Gauḍapāda in this chapter compares his Vedānta with Mahāyāna Buddhism, this benedictory verse may also imply his salutation to Buddha. And this verse also implies his salutation to any sage who has or to all those sages, who have transcended the trinity of knowledge, knower and known. He clearly tells us that he alone is a *muni* (sage) who has realised the measureless Fourth (*amātra, turīya*), the *Oṁkāra,* the pure and non-dual Self (*Ātmā*) or Brahma, where knowledge, knower and known are one and such a great sage (*mahā-muni*) is worthy of utmost respect and veneration (*pūjya* and *vandya*) of all beings.[1] In the *second verse,* he salutes *Asparshayoga* in which the non-dual *Ātma* with its eternal consciousness and ineffable bliss is realised, which is free from conflicts and contradictions of thought and which is conducive to the happiness and welfare of all beings.[2]

Gauḍapāda begins this chapter with a detailed exposition of No-origination (*ajāti*) by means of a dialectical critique of causa-

1. *Gauḍapāda-Kārikā,* I, 22 and 29; II, 35. Also, see *supra,* p. 138.
2. sarvasattvasukho hitaḥ avivādo' viruddhashcha.

tion and points out the similarities between Vedānta and Mādhyamika Buddhism. In the second chapter the Āchārya has established *ajātivāda* by proving the falsity of the world through independent reasoning and by showing that it is an appearance of the non-dual eternal *Brahma*; and in the third chapter he has proved it on the basis of shruti or scripture.[1] The main arguments used by him in the fourth chapter are also found in the preceding two chapters, but in the fourth chapter he gives a detailed exposition of his views and points out the similarities and differences between his Vedānta and Mahāyāna Buddhism and establishes the soundness of Vedānta over Buddhism. It should be noted that the similarities of tenets, terms and technique between Gauḍapāda on the one hand and the Mādhyamika and Vijñānāvādī Buddhists on the other should not be taken to mean that Gauḍapāda has borrowed these from the Buddhists. Gauḍapāda flourished at that time when Mahāyāna was prevalent and he was fully conversant with the Mahāyāna philosophy. Terms are the heritage of language and like current coins can be used by anyone who writes in that language. The dialectical method though developed in the Mādhyamika school did not originate with it or even with Buddha. Its origin is found in the Upaniṣads and its first exponent is the sage Yājñavalkya.[2] The doctrinal similarities, as pointed out by Gauḍapada himself,are due to the fact that Buddha himself took these doctrines from the Upaniṣads and these were developed in the Mahāyāna schools.

The Āchārya begins his exposition of *ajāti* from the *third verse* by saying: Some (the Sāṅkhyas) say that it is the existent which is born, while others (the Nyāya-Vaisheṣikas) say that it is the non-existent which is born, and thus they dispute each other's view. In the *fourth verse* he says: These disputing dualists (*dvayāḥ*) cancel each other's position and, taken together, unknowingly proclaim the truth of No-origination, as neither the existent nor the non-existent can be produced. Also, there are some non-dualists (advayāḥ, i.e., the Mādhyamikas) who openly proclaim the doctrine of No-origination (*ajati*) by saying that neither the real nor

1. See *supra*, pp. 129-35. See II, 31-35 and III, 17-23 and 27-31.
2. See *supra*, pp. 122-23.

the unreal can be produced. In the *fifth verse* the Āchārya clearly says: We approve the doctrine of *ajāti* proclaimed by these (Mādhyamikas). We do not dispute with them. It should be clearly understood that there can be no dispute with them (because they agree with us).[1] Then, in Kārikās 6 to 23 Gauḍapāda enters into a dialectical critique of causality with which the Mādhyamikas also agree. Kārikās 6, 7 and 8 are repetition, with a little variation, of Kārikās 20, 21 and 22 of the third chapter. Kārikās 29, 30, 38 and 40 also deal with critique of causation. As we have already explained Gauḍapāda's critique of causality above[2], we need not repeat it here. In the *nineteenth verse,* the Ācharya observes that the Buddhas (Buddha and the Mādhyamika Buddhists) have elucidated *ajāti* by giving the following three arguments: (1) absence of energy in the cause to produce the effect (*ashakti*), (2) absence of knowledge of any relation between cause and effect (*aparijñāna*), and (3) incompatibility of the order of succession (*kramakopa*).[3] And in the *twenty-second verse* the Āchārya concludes like Nāgārjuna, that nothing can originate either from itself or from other than itself; neither the real nor the unreal nor both real and unreal can be produced.[4] The real is unborn and eternal and so cannot be produced; the unreal is like a barren woman's son and it too cannot be produced. The real and unreal cannot be combined like light and darkness and hence that which is both real and unreal is impossible and cannot be produced. That which is real never changes its nature and causation is not possible without change.[5] The world is not a real creation, but a mere

1. khyāpyamānāmajātim tairanumodāmahe vayam I vivadāmo na taiḥ sārdham avivādam nibodhata II IV, 5.
2. See *supra,* pp. 133-35.
3. ashaktiraparijñānam kramakopo' thavā punaḥ I evam hi sarvathā Buddhairajātiḥ paridīpitā II IV, 19. see *supra,* p. 135. We know that the Mādhyamikas have actually used these arguments. See *Mādhyamika-Kārikā,* I, 6; XI, 1, 2, and 8.
4. svato vā parato vāpi na kiñchid vastu jāyate I sad asat sadasad vāpi na kiñchid vastu jāyate II GK, IV, 22 (For *Gauḍapāda-Kārikā* we use the abbreviation 'GK' and for Nāgārjuna's *Mādhyamika-Kārikā* 'MK'.) Compare, na svato nāpi parato na dvābhyām nāpyahetutaḥ I utpannā jātu vidyante bhāvāḥ kvachana kechana II MK, I, 1; and, na svato jāyate bhāvaḥ parato naive jāyate I MK, XXI, 13 and XXIII, 20.
5. prakṛteranyathābhāvo na kathañchid bhaviṣyati I GK, IV, 7, compare, prakṛteranyathābhavo nahi jātūpapadyate I MK, XV, 8.

appearance. It has no beginning, for it is due to beginningless Ignorance. It has no end, for had it really existed then the question of its destruction could have arisen. And that which exists neither in the beginning nor in the end cannot exist even in the middle.[1] Gauḍapāda and Nāgārjuna agree on these points.[2] The Āchārya, like the Mādhyamika, believes that nothing can originate, neither the *jiva* or *chitta* or vijñāna nor the object (*dharma*).[3] All *jivas* and objects are really unborn and they appear to be born through *māya* and *māyā* too is ultimately false.[4] As real causation is impossible, all objects of thought (including individual selves, mental states and external physical objects) are unthinkable (and indescribable) either as real or as unreal and are therefore false.[5] The Mādhyamika also says that causation is relative (*pratitya-samutpāda*) and not real and, therefore, that which arises relatively does not in reality arise.[6] The Āchārya clearly says that as long as (due to *māyā*) there is a strong attachment to cause and effect, to origination and annihilation, to birth and death, so long this world, this cycle of birth and death is expanded; when this clinging to cause and effect is dispelled, there is no cycle of birth and death (*saṁsāra*)[7]. Nagārjuna also says: that which due to clinging (*upādāya*) and relativity (*pratītya*) appears as this empirical world or the cycle of birth and death, the same, free from clinging and relativity, is called *Nirvāṇa*.[8] There is not the slightest difference between *saṁsāra* and *Nirvāṇa*.[9] Gauḍapāda has said: There is no annihilation nor origination; no one is bound and no one works

1. ādāvante cha yan nāsti vartamāne' pitattathā I GK, IV, 31. Compare, naivāgram nāvaram yasya tasya madhyam kuto bhavet I MK, XI, 2.
2. Compare, GK, IV, 8 with MK, XIV, 1, 2; GK IV, 10 with MK XI, 3-4; GK IV, 16 with MK XI, 2; GK IV, 17 with MK X, 10-11; GK IV, 18 with MK X, 8; GK IV, 19 with MK XI, 2 and 6; GK IV, 22 with MK I, 1, XXI, 13, XXIII, 20; GK IV, 40 with MK XXI, 12, VIII, 1 and 10.
3. evam na jāyate chittam evam dharmā ajāḥ smṛtāḥ I GK, IV, 46. na kashchid jāyate jīvaḥ sambhavo'sya na vidyate I GK, IV, 71
4. janma māyopamam teṣām sā cha māyā na vidyate II GK, IV, 58.
5. kāryakāraṇatābhāvād yato' chintyāḥ sadaiva te I GK, IV. 52.
6. pratītya yat samutpannam notpannam paramārthatah.
7. yāvaddhetuphalāveshaḥ saṁsārastāvadāyataḥ I kṣīṇe hetuphalāveshe saṁsāro nopapadyate II GK, IV, 56.
8. ya ājavañjavībhāva upādāya pratītya vā I so'pratītyānupādāya nirvāṇamupadishyate II MK, XXV, 9.
9. na tayorantaraṁ kiñchit susūkṣmamapi vidyate I MK, XXV, 20.

for liberation; no one desires freedom and no one attains freedom—this is the highest truth, the absolute reality.[1] Nāgārjuna also says: There is no annihilation, no origination, no momentariness, no eternity, no unity, no plurality, no coming in and no going out.[2] The Āchārya, like the Mādhyamika, believes that Reality is beyond the four categories of thought (*chatuṣkoṭi-vinirmukta*). He says: Only an unintelligent person covers the Real with existence, non-existence, both and neither. These are the four categories of thought with which the Real appears to be covered, but, in fact, it is untouched by them; he who realises this Lord (Bhagavān) himself becomes the omniscient Real.[3] The merciful Veda talks of creation only from the empirical standpoint which is a means to realise the goal of *ajāti* or advaita and preaches *karma* (action) and *upāsanā* (devotion, meditation) for the common people to lead them slowly to transcendent knowledge (*jñāna*).[4] So has Buddha preached relative creation (*jāti*) and prescribed good actions and meditation, from the standpoint of samvṛti or empirical truth for those ordinary followers who cling to this world taking it to be real due to empirical perception (*upalambha*) and pragmatic utility (*samāchāra*) and who tremble with fear at the very name of *ajāti*, so that they may not give up good actions and spiritual discipline and fall from the right path.[5]

Thus Āchārya Gauḍapāda has approved of the similarities between his Advaita Vedānta and the Mādhyamika absolutism. But there are some important differences also between them which should be noted. Though the Mādhyamika believes that the Absolute is both immanent and transcendent, yet, following Buddha, he has emphasised the transcendent nature of the Absolute and

---

1. na nirodho na chotpattir na baddho na cha sādhakāḥ I na mumukṣur na vai mukta ityeṣā paramārthatā II GK, II, 32.
2. anirodham anutpādam anuchchhedam ashāshvatam I anekārtham anānārtham anāgamam anirgamam II MK, the first benedictory verse.
3. GK, IV, 83-84.
4. GK, III, 15-16 upāyaḥ so'vatārāya nāsti bhedaḥ kathañchana I and, upāsanopadiṣṭeyam tadartham anukampayā II
5. upalambhāt samāchārād astivastutva-vādinām I jātistu deshitā Buddhair-ajātestrasatām sadā II GK, IV, 42.
There are many references in the Buddhist scripture about Buddha's 'upāya-kaushalya', i.e. his preaching according to the ability of his disciples. See MK, XVIII, 6. See *supra*, pp. 33 and 65.

has used the negative method. The Absolute, being transcendent, cannot be known through thought nor can it be expressed in language. The Mādhyamika, remaining true to the spirit of Buddha and its negative logic has given only negative description of the Absolute and has not indulged in its positive description. Emphasis is laid only on its direct realisation through immediate experience by rising above the thought-categories which falsify it. Gauḍapāda agrees with all this, but following his Upaniṣadic tradition, feels the necessity of making explicit the positive ontological nature of the Absolute by using positive characters also in order to help the aspirants and in order to avoid possible philosophical misconception of the Absolute. Thus admitting that *'neti neti'* or *via negativa* is the best method to describe the indescribable, he admits the necessity of positive description too and uses the positive terms like Brahma, Bhagavān, Īshvara, Deva, *vibhu, nitya jñāna, akṣaya* and *akathya sukha,* Oṁkāra, etc., for the Absolute. Another vital difference between Gauḍapāda and the Mādhyamika is that Gauḍapāda, following his Upaniṣadic tradition, identifies the Absolute with the foundational Self or *Ātmā.* The self-contradiction inherent in the thought-categories and the consequent nothingness of the phenomena brought out by the sharp negative dialectic can be realised only by the witnessing Self (sākṣī). Self-contradiction is neither self-revealing nor self-comprehending. It can be understood only in the light of a universal criterion of non-contradiction and by the foundational Self, which is at once eternal self-shining consciousness (*nitya svaprakāsha ātma-chaitanya*) and self-proved existence (*svataḥsiddha*) and non-dual ineffable bliss (*advaita akhaṇḍa ānanda*).

Āchārya Gauḍapāda has proved (in the 2nd and the 3rd chapters) by reasoning and on the basis of scripture that *ajāti*vāda is māyāvāda based on Brahmavāda, that it is spiritual non-dualism which is the central teaching of the Upaniṣads.[1] Buddha himself took it from the Upaniṣads and the Mādhyamika school developed it in the light of the teaching of Buddha. Gauḍapāda takes it directly from the Upaniṣads and develops it in the light of his Vedāntic tradition. This accounts for the similarities as well as differences between Gauḍapāda and the Mādhyamika and this

1. See *supra*, pp. 132-35.

also establishes the philosophical soundness of Advaita Vedānta over Mādhyamika Buddhism.

Āchārya Gauḍapāda also points out the similarities and differences between his Advaita Vedānta and the Vijñānavāda school of Buddhism. He is fully conversant with the views of Maitreyanātha, Asaṅga and Vasubandhu who were his predecessors. In order to understand and estimate Gauḍapāda's exposition of Buddhist Vijñānavāda, we should first clarify the points of agreement and of difference between them. The points of agreement are as follows:

1. Gauḍapāda agrees with and accepts the arguments of Vijñānavāda to refute realism. He also places the world-objects on a par with objects perceived in dream and illusion because of their ultimate unreality.
2. Gauḍapāda and Vijñānavāda both believe that the individual subjects, the mental states and the external objects are appearances of pure Vijñāna due to beginningless *avidyā* which projects the illusion of subject-object duality. Objects in dream and in illusion are projections of individual Vijñāna (*jīva* in Gauḍapāda and *kliṣṭa* manovijñāna in Vijñānavāda), while world-objects are projections of universal vijñāna (Īshvara in Gauḍapāda and Ālayavijñāna in Vijñanavāda). All these are vibrations (*spandana*) of Vijñāna.
3. Gauḍapāda and Vijñānavāda both maintain that the Real is the Absolute Vijñāna which is non-dual, eternal, self-shining and pure transcendental Consciousness and bliss which is beyond sense-perception, thought-determinations and expressions of language and which can be realised in immediate spiritual experience in which subject, object and knowledge become one.

Let us now note the vital differences between Gauḍapāda and Vijñānavāda which are as follows:

1. Gauḍapāda is a teacher of Advaita Vedānta and advocates ontological idealism only, while Vijñānavāda is idealism *par excellence*—both ontologically as well as epistemologically.[1] Gauḍāpāda rejects epistemic idealism as illogical and unwarranted.

1. For the exposition and criticism of Vijñānavada see *supre*, pp. 113-16.

2. Though Gauḍapāda places the world-objects on a par with dream-objects and illusory objects due to their ultimate unreality, yet he does assert the empirical difference between these; even though the difference is only of degree yet it is very important in our empirical life.[1] Vijñānavāda, on the other hand, places all objects, whether world-objects or dream-objects or illusory objects, on the same level and pronounces them as utterly unreal like a sky-flower or a barren woman's son.
3. Vijñānavāda separates the 'form' from the 'content' of consciousness, rejecting the objective 'content' as utterly unreal (*parikalpita*) and retaining the 'form' as relatively real (*paratantra*). Gauḍapāda rejects the distinction between *parikalpita* and *paratantra* which unnecessarily disturbs our empirical life and puts these both under samvṛti or vyavahāra. For him the 'content' and the 'form' of consciousness are inseparable and enjoy the same status as both arise together and vanish together.
4. Vijñānavāda rejects the objective world as utterly unreal because it does not exist outside of consciousness. Gauḍapāda, like the Madhyāmika, treats the world as ultimately unreal or false (*mithyā*), because it is indeterminate (*achintya*) either as real or as unreal or as both and so is a self-contradictory appearance due to *māyā* or *avidyā.* The world of dream and illusion and the empirical world are perceived by us. Each works on its own sphere and is set aside only when sublating consciousness dawns.
5. Gauḍapāda identifies the Absolute with the foundational Self (*Ātmā*) or Brahma, while Vijñānavada calls it Vijñaptimātra (pure eternal non-dual consciousness), Parinispanna or Dharmadhātu.
6. Vijñānavāda believes that the Parinispanna Vijñāna-mātra due to beginningless and transcendental *Vāsanā* of objectivity becomes paratantra or conditioned by the wheel of causation generating the world-cycle of origination and annihilation in which momentary vijñānas and *vāsanās* go on producing each other until *paratantra* is

1. see *supra*, p. 131.

> freed from the transcendental *Vāsanā* or *Avidyā* by rooting out 'objectivity' from the stream of consciousness and regains its original purity as Parinișpanna. Āchārya Gauḍapāda does not accept all this. He rejects epistemic idealism and the pluralism, momentariness and creativity of vijñānas and the theory of real causation. The Real itself appears as individual subjects and also as the world of objects. The subject-object duality is to be removed by the elimination of difference (*bheda*); by the realisation that *jīva* is Brahma and the world also is Brahma, because Brahma is the ground-reality of both. This realisation dawns in *nirvikalpa samādhi* in which knower, known and knowledge are immediately realised as non-different in transcendental non-dual consciousness.

In the light of the above-mentioned points of agreement and of difference between Gauḍapāda and Buddhist Vijñānavāda, we will understand and appreciate Gauḍapāda's exposition of Vijñanavāda presented in the fourth chapter of his Kārikā which we now explain.

Āchārya Gauḍapāda in the second chapter and in the fourth chapter (K.33-44)[1] places the world-objects perceived in waking on a par with the objects perceived in dream and illusion on the ground that both are found to be ultimately unreal. He agrees with Vijñānavāda in maintaining against realism that perception (*upalambha*), practical utility (*samāchāra*) and spatio-temporal determination cannot prove the objective reality of the empirical world, for these conditions are found even in the objects in dream and illusion.[2] We know that such arguments are used by Vasubandhu to refute realism.[3] Even Shaṅkarāchārya in his commentary on the Kārikā admits that the Āchārya approves of the arguments of Vijñānavādī Buddhist to refute realism.[4] Gauḍapāda says that though the difference between world-objects and dream-objects is one of degree only, yet it is important for empirical life. Dream-objects are mental (*antaḥ-sthāna*), are perceived without

1. Kārikās IV. 31, 32, 33, 34 are repetition of K. II, 6, 7, 1, 2.
2. See *supra*, pp. 129-31.
3. Vimshatikā, K. 2-10 with Vṛtti.
4. Vijñānavādino Bauddhasya vachanam bāhyārthavādi-pakṣa-pratiṣedhaparam Āchāryeṇānumoditam. *Bhāṣya* K. IV, 28.

sense-organs (*indriya*) and appear to exist only during perception (*chitta-kāla*), while world-objects are external (*bahiḥ-sthāna*) are perceived with sense-organs (*indriya*) and appear to exist even after perception (*dvaya-kāla*). So they stand on a higher level of phenomenal experience.[1] Hence, in comparison with dream-objects the world-objects are admitted as empirically real.[2] As they cannot be sublated by empirical experience, they enjoy a higher status.[3] Ultimately however world-objects too are false, because they are appearances due to *māyā* and are found to be neither real nor unreal nor both (*achintya, mṛṣā, vitatha, mithyā*).[4] The individual subjects and the external objects cannot be condemned as utterly unreal (*parikalpita*) like a barren woman's son, for a barren woman's son cannot be really born nor can he even appear in illusion.[5] Nor can they be illogically reduced to their 'forms' in consciousness, because 'the form of the object' cannot be separated from the 'object'. If vijñāna never comes into contact with the object because the object is utterly unreal it cannot assume the 'form' of the object as the 'form' cannot be separated from the 'object'.[6] If vijñāna never touches the object (*nimitta*) in all the three times, past, present and future, because the object is non-existent, then in the absence of the object, how can there be the illusory idea of objectivity (which compels vijñāna to undergo modification)?[7] Hence, the Āchārya concludes: Neither the subject nor the object (nor its 'form' in consciousness) can be produced. Causation is due to *avidyā* and is therefore an appearance. Vijñāna (*chitta*) does not undergo real modification and cannot assume the 'form' of the object; nor are the objects produced. Those who want to discover causation (origination) in the subjective or the objective realm try to find out the footprints of birds in the sky![8] It is the unborn absolute Self or Vijñāna which, due

1. See *supra*, p. 131.
2. GK, IV, 37.
3. GK IV, 39.
4. vitathaiḥ sadṛshāḥ santo'vitathā iva lakṣitāḥ I GK IV, 31. mithyaiva khalu te smṛtāḥ I GK IV, 32.
5. bandhyāputro na tattvena māyayā vāpi jāyate I GK III, 28.
6. chittam na saṁspṛshatyartham nārthābhāsam tathaiva cha I abhūto hi yatashachārtho nārthābhāsastataḥ pṛthak II GK IV, 26.
7. animitto viparyāsaḥ katham tasya bhaviṣyati I GK IV, 27.
8. tasmān na jāyate chittam chittadṛsyam na jāyate I tasya pashyanti ye jātim khe vai pashyanti te padam II GK IV, 28.

to its own power *avidyā*, appears as the individual subjects and the objects; its nature, therefore, is *ajāti* (No-origination or eternal sameness) and ultimate nature can in no way change.[1] However, the phenomenal reality of this world of subject-object duality cannot be denied. Buddha himself has preached the empirical reality of creation on account of perception (*upalambha*) and practical utility (*samāchāra*) to those who cling to the world taking it to be real and who tremble with fear at the very name of *ajāti* (so that they may not give up good actions and meditation).[2] These realists due to their attachment to dualism have swerved from the truth (but if they continue following spiritual discipline they may realise it and in that case) the defects in realism will not obstruct their vision and will be far fewer (than in epistemic idealism of Vijñānavāda which unnecessarily disturbs the common life).[3]

The Āchārya observes (K.47-52) that the non-dual absolute Vijñāna, stirred by *avidyā*, appears as the empirical world of subject-object duality. He gives the illustration of a lighted fire-brand (*alāta*) from which the name of this fourth chapter, alāta-shānti, is derived. Just as an unmoving fire-brand burns unflickeringly and produces no illusion, but the same, when moved in different ways, gives rise to the illusion of fire-lines which may be straight or curved or circular, similarly the Absolute Vijñāna is eternal and non-dual, but the same, when stirred by *avidyā*, appears to vibrate (*spandana*) in the form of this world of subject-object duality.[4] And just as the appearances of a moving fire-brand are neither identical with nor different from it and they neither go out of it nor enter into it, similarly the phenomenal world of individual subjects and external objects is neither identical with nor different from the Absolute Vijñāna and it neither goes out of it nor enters into it. Vijñānavāda is right in maintaining all this. But it should remember that this entire show is an appearance. Neither vijñānas nor objects are conditioned by causation. Causation is relative

1. GK IV, 29 ajātiḥ prakṛtistataḥ.
2. upalambhāt samāchārad astivastutvavādinām | jātistu deshitā Budhai-rajātestrasatām sadā || GK IV, 42.
3. ajātestrasatām teṣāmupalambhād viyanti ye | jātidoṣā na setsyanti doṣo' pyalpo bhaviṣyati || GK IV, 43.
4. GK IV, 47-48.

and therefore apparent. Hence they are indeterminate and false.[1] Vijñāna really is unborn (*aja*), unchanging (*achala*), unobjectifiable (*avastu*), non-dual (*advaya*) and undisturbed (*shānta*); the conditioning of vijñanas by causation (*jāti*), their creativity and plurality, their momentariness (*chala*) and objectification (*vastu*) are appearances (*ābhāsa*).[2] The Āchārya has made it clear that it is the self-shining Self (and not the momentary vijñāna) which through its own power *māyā* projects itself (as the manifold world of subject-object duality) and it is this (witness) Self which perceives and knows the different individual subjects and objects—this is the established truth in Vedānta.[3] The objects which appear to be born originate only empirically (*samvṛtyā*) and not in reality (*na tattvataḥ*); they appear to arise due to *māyā* and that māya too is ultimately unreal.[4] Similarly no individual subject (*jīva*) is ever born. No-origination is the highest truth.[5] The Āchārya concludes: Empirically the subject and the object enjoy equal status and neither can be reduced to the other, and ultimately both are appearances of the Absolute. Hence, neither the objects are projected by vijñānas (as epistemic idealism wrongly imagines) nor are the vijñānas generated by the objects (as materialism wrongly believes). Thus the wise see the self-contradictory nature of causation and realise the truth of No-origination.[6] As long as there is *avidyā* the cycle of causation will revolve and this world of suffering will stretch itself; when *avidyā* is dispelled, the cycle of causation will collapse and this world of suffering will vanish.[7] From the phenomenal standpoint or *saṁvṛti* (the Buddha has declared that) this world is neither real or eternal nor unreal or momentary (and so self-contradictory and false). Ultimately the world is non-different from the Absolute which is beyond all categories of thought and all words of language.[8]

---

1. GK IV, 49-52; kāryakāraṇatābhāvād yato'chintyāḥ sadaiva te I K. 52.
2. jātyābhāsam chalābhāsam vastvābhāsam tathaiva cha I ajāchalam avastutvam vijñānam shāntam advayam II GK IV, 45.
3. kalpayatyātmanātmānam ātmā devaḥ svamāyayā I sa eva budhyate bhedān iti vedāntanishchayaḥ II II, 12.
4. janma māyopamam teṣām sā cha māyā na vidyate II IV, 58.
5. etat tad uttamam satyam yatra kiñchin na jāyate II GK IV. 711.
6. evam na chittajā dharmāsh chittam vāpi na dharmajam I evam hetuphalājātim pravishanti manīṣiṇaḥ II GK, IV. 54.
7. GK IV, 55-56. kṣīṇe hetuphalāveshe samsāro nopapadyate.
8. nājeṣu sarvadharmeṣu shāshvatāshāshvatābhidhā I yatra varṇā na vartante vivekastatra nochyate II GK IV, 60.

Then (in Kārikā 72-100) the Āchārya by reproducing at length the views of Vijñānavāda shows that the world of subject-object duality is due to the vibration of chitta (vijñāna), but this *chitta* or Vijñāna is not really disturbed by the illusory idea of objecivity (nirviṣayam) and it is declared to be always *asaṅga,* i.e., unrelated to subject-object duality and unconditioned by causation; its vibration (*spandana*) is due to *avidyā* or transcendental beginningless Illusion which itself is ultimately unreal.[1] As the 'form of the object' (*arthābhāsa*) cannot be separated from the object itself (*na tataḥ pṛthak*), Vijñāna is neither related to the object nor does it really assume the form of the object. So the distinction between *parikalpita* and *paratantra* is not logical.[2] The *parikalpita* (i.e., the subject and the object) is not utterly unreal like a barren woman's son (as Vijñānavāda imagines) because it is perceived in the empirical world. The individual subjects and objects as well as their 'forms' in consciousness which are inseparable from them fall under samvṛti and enjoy empirical reality, though they are ultimately unreal as they are imaginary projections of *avidyā.* That which exists empirically (*samvṛti*) does not exist in reality (*paramārtha*). And *paratantra* too (which is supposed to undergo modification and assume 'forms' of objects) falls under samvṛti or empirical reality and is not ultimately real, because the *pariniṣpanna* only appears as *paratantra* and does not in fact become conditioned by causation (*paratantra*).[3] The *pariniṣpanna* or the Absolute Vijñāna, due to *avidyā* which works through thought-determinations (*abhiniṣpatti-samvṛti* or *loka-samvṛti*) appears as paratantra (relative, conditioned by causation), though in fact it is never conditioned. Even to call it *aja* (unborn, unconditioned or absolute) is a way of *samvṛti* (vyavahara or empirical truth); in reality it is beyond all thought-determinations and words.[4] The subject-object duality does not really exist; it is a projection of *avidyā* or transcendental Illusion which generates the attachment

1. chittam nirviṣayam nityam asangam tena kīrtitam GK IV, 72.
2. GK, IV, 26; see *supra,* p. 155.
3. yo'sti kalpitasamvṛtyā paramārthena nāstyasau I paratantro'bhisamvṛtyā syān nāsti paramārthataḥ II GK, IV, 73; the correct reading is 'paratantro'bhi' and not 'paratantrābhi' as found in some editions.
4. ajaḥ kalpitasamvṛtyā paramārthena nāpyajaḥ I paratantro' bhiniṣpattyā samvṛtyā jāyate tu saḥ II IV, 74.

to this unreal duality (*abhūtābhinivesha*), and this *avidyā* itself is ultimately false.[1] When the unreality of duality is realised there is no cause for origination. There is in reality no illusory idea of objectivity to defile vijñāna and subject it to the cycle of causation in which momentary vāsanās and vijñānas go on determining each other. When there is no real cause, good, bad or indifferent, to compel vijñāna to undergo modification, vijñāna never really falls from its pristine purity.[2] Vijñānavāda is right in maintaining that the Absolute Vijñana is eternally free from suffering, desire and fear;[3] that it is eternally peaceful, undisturbed, unmoving, ever-the-same, unborn, unconditioned, non-dual, untouched by sleep (covering function of *avidyā*) and by dream (projecting function of *avidyā*); that it is Dharmadhātu or the ultimate Reality (at once transcendent to and immanent in phenomena), that this Dharmadhātu, by its very nature, is self-shining consciousness which is eternally self-illumined once for all[4]; that it is beyond the four categories of thought where knowledge, knower and known are merged in self-shining non-dual consciousness; that it is to be realised through immediate spiritual experience by the Buddhas, and that he who realises it himself becomes Omniscient.[5]

The Āchārya, then, makes it clear that this spiritual non-dualism is the central teaching of the Upaniṣads. It is Vedānta unalloyed. It is Brahma itself, the highest non-dual blissful Reality, fully omniscient, without beginning, middle and end; its realisation is the goal befitting a true Brāhmaṇa and having realised it what else remains to be desired?[6] And for attaining this natural and blissfully peaceful Brahma is prescribed the spiritual discipline (*vinaya*) for the Brāhmaṇas (viprāṇām).[7] If Buddha and the Buddhists also

1. abhūtābhiniveshosti dvayam tatra na vidyate I IV, 75. cf abhūtaparikalpo'sti dvayam tatra na vidyate I *Madhyānta-Vibhāga*, I, 2.
2. GK, IV, 76.
3. vītashokam tadā'kāmam abhayam padam ashnute I IV, 78.
4. ajamanidramasvapnam prabhātam bhavati svayam I sakṛd vibhāto hyevaiṣa Dharmadhātuḥ svabhāvataḥ II IV, 81. The correct reading is 'Dharmadhātuḥ' and not 'dharmo dhātuḥ'.
5. viṣayaḥ sa hi Buddhānām tatsāmyam ajamadvayam I IV, 80. kotyash chatasra etāstu grahair yāsām sadāvṛtaḥ I Bhagavān ābhir aspṛṣṭo yena dṛṣṭaḥ sa sarvadṛk II II, 84.
6. prāpya sarvajñatām kṛtsnām Brāhmaṇyam padam-advayam I anapannādimadhyāntam kim ataḥ paramīhate II IV, 85.
7. viprāṇām vinayo hyeṣa shamaḥ prākṛta uchyate I IV, 86.

believe in this they are accepting Vedānta to this extent. It should be remembered here that the epithets used by Vijñānavāda for Vijñaptimātra or Dharmadhātu (correctly reproduced by Gauḍapāda) are the same which have been used in the Upaniṣads for *Ātmā* or Brahma. Gauḍapāda in the first three chapters of his Kārikā has described *Ātmā* or Brahma in the same way.[1] This non-dual *Ātmā* or Brahma, the Āchārya has said, is realised by the sages who have known the essence of the Veda, who are well-versed in Vedānta, who have realised Oṁkāra; and such a great sage (*mahāmuni*) deserves respect and veneration of all.[2]

The Āchārya further explains the Vijñānavāda position thus: The Vijñānavādī Buddhists say that Buddha has declared three svabhāvas or levels of existence, *parikalpita* (imaginary), *paratantra* (relative) and pariniṣpanna (*absolute*). Parikalpita is mere *laukika* or common sense reality where the object (*vastu*) and its perception (*upalambha*) both (though utterly unreal) are taken as real. *Paratantra* is called *shuddha laukika* or pure empirical reality where the object drops down (*avastu*) leaving the perception (*upalambha*) of only its form in consciousness and where the flow of the momentary vijñānas conditioned by causation is taken as real. *Painiṣpanna* is the *lokottara*, the trans-empirical, the absolute reality where the flow of vijñānas dries up and only the pure non-dual Vijnana shines forth in its eternal self-luminosity. Thus do these Buddhists proclaim the nature of the object (*jñeya*), the subject (*jñāna*) and the Absolute (*vijñeya*).[3] They say that the highly enlightened person who knows these three *svabhāvas* successively, becomes omniscient.[4] In Agrayāna (i.e. Mahāyana; here Vijñānavāda) four things have been explained which are called *jñeya, heya, pākya* and *āpya*. Of these four, except *jñeya* or the knowable object, the other three are perceivable. *Jñeya* or the object is purely imaginary (*parikalpita*) and so cannot be perceived. It is set aside by the mere knowledge of it *(parijñāna)*. *Heya* means that which is to be abandoned, removed. It stands for

1. For example, see GK, I, 16; III, 32, 35, 38, 46, 47.
2. munibhir Vedapāragaiḥ. II, 35; Vedānteṣu vichakṣanaiḥ. II, 31; sa muniḥ, I, 29; mahāmuniḥ, I, 22.
3. savastu sopalambham cha dvayam laukikam iṣyate I avastu sopalambham cha shuddham laukikam iṣyate II IV, 87. avastvanupalambham cha lokottaram iti smṛtam I jñeyam jñānam cha vijñeyam sadā Buddhaiḥ prakīrtitam II IV, 88.
4. GK, IV, 89.

paratantra, i.e., conditioned or defiled vijñānas the flow of which constitutes this world of suffering (*saṅklesha*). This defilement of *vijñānas* is to be removed (*prahāṇa*). *Pākya* means that which is to be matured through spiritual discipline. *Paratantra* is a mixture of *avidyā* and vijñāna. *Avidyā* or *vāsanā* which defiles it has to be removed and its own nature as pure non-dual vijñāna has to be matured or regained through spiritual discipline. *Āpya* means that which is to be attained or realised. It is pariniṣpanna Vijñāna, pure, non-dual, eternal and self-shining, which is to be realised through immediate spiritual experience (*prāpti* or *sākṣatkāra*).

The Āchārya has already criticised the distinction between *parikalpita* and *paratantra* as illogical and unwarranted as it leads to epistemic idealism and unnecessarily disturbs the empirical life. The object is not utterly unreal nor can it be set aside by merely knowing it. The *parikalpita* and the *paratantra* both are empirically real (*samvṛti*).[1] Here the Āchārya points out that *paratantra* is only empirically real and the over-emphasis on its reality by Vijñānavāda makes vijñāna subject to momentariness, plurality and real causation. Vijñana is always pure and non-dual and is not subject to real causation. Creativity belongs to *avidyā* and not to Vijñāna. The impurity and the purification of vijñāna are valid empirically. The Āchārya, therefore, observes: All phenomena, i.e., the individual subjects and objects, are, in essence, the Absolute itself. They are beginningless and by their very nature eternal and pure like the universal space. There is absolutely no plurality in them.[2] All individual subjects and objects are, by their very nature, the Absolute, the ever-enlightened. He who realises this attains immortality.[3] All individual subjects and objects are, by their very nature, eternally peaceful, unborn and ever-liberated. They are non-different from the Absolute which is eternal, ever-the-same, pure and fearless.[4] Those who maintain plurality are prone to difference and those who always move in difference (whether they

1. See *supra*, pp. 153-58.
2. GK, IV, 91; vidyate nahi nānātvam teṣām kvachana kiñchana ǀ
3. GK, IV, 92; so'mṛtatvāya kalpate.
4. ādishāntā hyanutpannāḥ prakṛtyaiva sunirvṛtāḥ ǀ sarve dharmāḥ samābhinnā ajam sāmyam vishāradam ǁ GK, IV, 93.
   Such descriptions are found in Mādhyamika and in Vijñānavāda works like *Lankāvatāra-sūtra; Mahāyāna-sūtrālankāra* and *Madhyāntavibhāga.* cf., anutpannā-niruddhādishāntāḥ prakṛtinirvṛtāḥ (MSA, XI, 51) and ādishāntā hyanutpannāḥ prakṛtyaiva cha nirvṛtāḥ (quoted in *Mādhyamika-Vṛtti*, p. 225).

are realists or epistemic idealists) cannot attain pristine purity and fearlessness. Their case is indeed pitiable.[1] Whosoever (whether Vedāntins, Buddhists or others) realise the Absolute, unborn and ever-the-same, they are the most enlightened; ordinary persons do not enter into the Absolute.[2] The Absolute is non-dual consciousness unrelated to the subject or the object (*asaṅga*). Even the slightest difference results in relativity and as long as it persists the covering of *avidyā* cannot be removed.[3] The Absolute is realised through immediate experience which transcends subject-object duality. The knowledge of the enlightened sage (Buddha) is not related to any object nor is any object related to it. And then the Āchārya concludes: This has not been said by Buddha–*naitad Buddhena bhāṣitam.*[4]

The above statement of Āchārya Gauḍapāda may be interpreted in three ways. It may mean:

(1) As the Absolute preached by Buddha is beyond thought and language, he preached through silence and not through words. The Buddhist texts mention this at many places.[5]

(2) Buddha preached spiritual Absolutism and not epistemic idealism. The momentariness and plurality of vijñānas and their subjection to real causation leading to epistemic idealism were the fabrication of Vijñānavādins and were not taught by Buddha.

(3) The spiritual Absolutism preached by Buddha has been taken by him from the Upaniṣads. It is not his original contribution. It is Vedānta.

---

1. vaishāradyam tu vai nāsti bhede vicharatām sadā | bhedanimnāḥ pṛthag-vādāstasmāt te kṛpaṇāḥ smṛtāḥ || GK, IV, 94.
2. GK, IV, 95. In Vedānta ātmā is described as nityashuddha-buddha-mukta-svabhāva.
3. GK, IV, 96-7.
4. GK, IV, 99.
5. From the time Buddha got enlightenment till the time he obtained nirvāṇa not a single word was spoken by him: Tathagatena ekamapyakṣaram nodāḥṛtam.--Tathāgataguhyakasūtra quoted in M. Vrtti on K. XX, 25. na kvachid kasyachit kashchit dharmo Buddhena deshitah. MK, XX. 25 avachanam Buddhavachanam. *Lankāvatara,* pp. 142-3.
   In Vedānta tradition also, gurostu maunam vyākhyānam shiṣyās tu chchhinnasaṁshayāḥ |

All these three interpretations are justified.

The Āchārya ends his Kārikā with a salutation to the Absolute which is unborn, eternal, non-dual, ever-the-same, free from difference, pure and fearless, very deep and difficult to be realised.[1]

We thus see that Āchārya Gauḍapāda's Kārikā is not only the first available systematic exposition of Advaita Vedānta, but also the first available work which brings out a correct relationship between Advaita Vedānta and Mahāyāna Buddhism.

1. GK, IV, 100; buddhvā padam anānātvam namaskurmo yathā balam.

CHAPTER FIVE

Shaṅkara-Vedānta

I. INTRODUCTION

Shaṅkarāchārya is undoubtedly one of the greatest philosophers of the world and a realised saint. He is gifted with extra-ordinary intelligence, a deeply penetrating mind, critical insight, logical reasoning, philosophical analysis, religious purity, sublimity of renunciation and profound spirituality. His literary excellence makes him shine as a writer of exemplary Sanskrit prose and soul-inspiring philosophico-religious verses.

He was born in the eighth century[1] at Kālaḍī in Kerala in a Nambūdrī Brāhmaṇa family and left his body in Kedāranātha in the Himālaya, at the young age of 32 years. During this short span of life he wrote his commentaries on the eleven principle Upaniṣads, on Gītā, and his epoch-making monumental work, the *Shārīraka-Bhāṣya* on *Brahma-sūtra* as well as a rich soul-inspiring stotra-literature. He travelled widely and established four famous Pīṭhas, at Badarīnātha (Joshī-maṭha) in the north, at Shṛṅgerī in the south, at Purī in the east and at Dvārakā in the west. His contribution to Indian philosophy and to Vedic religion and culture is unparalleled and almost super-human. He is treated as an incarnation of Lord Shiva. This uncompromising and staunch champion of knowledge dedicated his life to self-less service and devotion to God. His life itself is an ample proof that self-less service (*niṣkāma karma*) and devotion (*bhakti*) may go well with spiritual Enlightenment (*jñāna*).

The credit of establishing Advaita Vedānta as a sound philosophical system goes to Shaṅkarāchārya—the disciple of Govindapādāchārya and the grand-disciple of Gauḍapādāchārya.

---

1. Some modern scholars opine that his flourit may be pushed up to 7th century. See, *Pre-Shaṅkara Advaita Philosophy* by Dr. S.L. Pandey, chapter VII.

"His philosophy", says Dr. S. Radhakrishnan, "stands forth complete, needing neither a before nor an after... whether we agree or differ, the penetrating light of his mind never leaves us where we were."[1]

Advaita Vedānta, associated with the name of the great Shaṅkarāchārya is rightly regarded as logically the most consistent and spiritually the most advanced philosophy of India. All schools of Vedānta claim to be based on the Upaniṣads, but the claim is fully justified only in the case of Advaita Vedānta. Though the Upaniṣads are not logico-philosophical treatises in the strict sense of the term, yet undoubtedly they have been acclaimed as predominantly philosophical and as such they do have a central philosophy of their own. Shaṅkara has very clearly and logically proved that this central philosophy is Advaita. The teachers of other schools of Vedānta, mainly theistic, have fathered their respective views on the Upaniṣads to claim the sanction of the Revealed Text. One may or may not agree with Advaita; one may freely choose any other school of Vedānta or any other system of philosophy as more satisfactory; but one cannot logically deny that Shaṅkara's interpretation is the correct interpretation and that Advaita is *the* central teaching of the Upaniṣadic philosophy.

The Advaita Vedānta taught by Shaṅkara is very old, though its final form is the result of his contribution. The advaita philosophy which originates in the Upaniṣads was developed, before Shaṅkara, both within and outside the Vedic fold. References are found to the teachers of Vedānta who interpreted the Upaniṣads in the light of advaita, though their works are lost, and though the Kārikā of Gauḍapāda, the grand-teacher of Shaṅkara, is the earliest available work on Advaita Vedānta. Outside the Vedic fold, Buddha himself had assimilated the absolutism of the Upaniṣads and his teaching was considerably elaborated in the Mādhyamika and the Vijñānavāda schools of Mahāyāna Buddhism.

In order to establish his Advaita system of Vedānta, Shaṅkara had to accomplish the following objectives among others:

(1) He had to show that the systems of pluralistic realism, like Vaishesika, Nyāya and Sāṅkhya, do not represent the philosophy of the Veda at all, though they pay homage to the authority of the Veda. Earlier Sāṅkhya, which was perhaps theistic, claimed to

1. *Indian Philosophy,* Vol. II, pp. 446-7.

be based on the Upaniṣads and is often criticised by Bādarāyaṇa, the author of the *Brahma-sūtra*, and Shaṅkara takes it as the main opponent (*pradhāna malla*) of Vedānta and rejects its claim to represent the philosophy of Upaniṣads, though much of its philosophy, with or without modification, is absorbed by Vedānta.

(2) He had to reject the Mīmāmsā interpretation of the Veda. According to Mīmāmsā the import of the Vedic texts lies in the enjoining of action and therefore those texts which are not primarily concerned with action are said to be of secondary value and are to be interpreted as indirectly leading to action. Shaṅkara reverses this interpretation and points out, against Mīmāmsā, that the main aim of the Veda is to reveal the Real and therefore those texts (mainly the Upaniṣads) which deal with knowledge of Reality are primary, while the texts dealing with action are secondary as they are prescribed for the sole purpose of purification of the soul.

(3) He had also to reject the interpretation of the Upaniṣads and of the *Brahma-sūtra* by certain commentators like Bhartṛprapañcha who preceded him and who upheld the view of Brahma-pariṇāma-vāda according to which Brahma is really transformed into this world. As against this view, Shaṅkara established Brahma-vivarta-vāda or Māyāvāda as the correct interpretation of the Vedānta philosophy. Any non-advaitic view, which accepts, ultimate difference in any way, is not only inconsistent with the Vedānta texts, but is also illogical.

(4) He had to show that the conception of *Nirguṇa* Brahma, the indeterminate Real leads to spiritual absolutism and not to nihilism, because it negates only the determinations of Brahma and not *Brahma* itself.

(5) He had also to distinguish his transcendental idealism from the epistemic idealism of the Buddhist school of Vijñānavāda and the subjective idealism of momentary ideas of its later formulation which we call Svatantra-Vijñānavāda.

II. MĀYĀ, AVIDYĀ OR ADHYĀSA

Advaita Vedānta of Shaṅkara is also called Māyāvāda. It is the contention of some that the doctrine of *Māyā* or *avidyā* is not found in the Upaniṣads and that it is borrowed by Shaṅkara from Buddhism. Some have even gone to the extent of dubbing Shaṅkara as a crypto-Buddhist (*prachchhanna-bauddha*) and Māyāvāda as false teaching (*asat-shāstra*). We have shown before that this doctrine can be traced to the Ṛg-veda and that the Upaniṣads refer to it in clear and unmistakable terms and at many places[1]. We have also shown that it was considerably developed in Mahāyāna Buddhism. Its first systematic exposition in Vedānta is found in Gauḍapāda's Kārikā.[2] Shaṅkara has developed it to its fullness and his followers have amplified its implications in their logical and scholastic subtleties.

Philosophy, for Shaṅkara, is not an intellectual game but a spiritual discipline culminating in the realisation of Reality. The relative importance of thought is admitted as a help to spiritual enlightenment. The list of four-fold qualification which Shaṅkara prescribes for a serious student of Vedānta runs as follows:

(1) ability to discriminate between the eternal and the ephemeral (*nityānitya-vastu-viveka*); (2) a spirit of detachment from the enjoyment of the fruits of this world and the other world (*ihāmutrārtha-phala-bhoga-virāga*); (3) moral and spiritual discipline (*sādhana-sampat*); and (4) an intense longing for liberation (*mumukṣutva*).

Shaṅkara begins his celebrated Introduction to his commentary on the *Brahma-sūtra* with the posing of the basic philosophical problem and with an analysis of the nature of illusion empirical as well as transcendental. He says that the entire empirical life is based on a blending of two factors which are mutually incompatible. All empirical experience involves two elements—the subjective and the objective. The subjective element is the spirit, the transcendent 'I' which is pure consciousness and the objective element is the 'this,' the 'non-I', which is given as an 'other' and is known as an object by the subject. It is self-evident, says Shaṅkara[3], that these two terms, the subject and the object, are absolutely opposed to each other like light and darkness. The basic problem for philosophy is to find out as to how these two incompatibles can be united in empirical experience. Logically, it is impossible to unite two absolute contradictories. There can be no union of light and darkness.[4] But unless these two factors are somehow

1. see *supra*, pp. 123-4.
2. see *supra*, pp. 126 ff.
3. *Shārīraka-Bhāṣya,* Introduction.
4. *Ibid*: viṣaya-viṣayiṇostamaḥ-prakāshavad viruddha-svabhāvayoritaretarabhāvānupapattiḥ.

related there can be no empirical experience. Now, that power which appears to perform this logically impossible feat is *Māyā* or *Avidyā*, the transcendental Illusion. As there can be no real relation between the subject and the object, all relations must be traced to the categorising function of thought which is *a priori* and is due to this transcendental Illusion or *avidyā*. The true Subject and the Object both evade our grasp. *Avidyā* is the mother of this phenomenal world. We, as individuals, are the products of this Cosmic illusion and therefore we have no conscious control over it. It is quite natural for us, worldly people, to indulge unconsciously in this basic Illusion and to confuse between the subject and the object and between their respective attributes. All empirical life which is natural for us is based on this comingling of truth and error, this coupling of the Real and the unreal.[1] On account of this basic Illusion, a person forgets his own real nature as the Pure Self and identifies himself with external objects, with his wife, his children and friends, with his own body, with his senses, with his life, and with his mental states including thoughts, feelings and desires. This natural and beginningless confusion between the Self and the not-self, consisting in the false superimposition of the one on the other and giving rise to the notion of the 'I' and the 'mine' and the consequent notion of the agent and the enjoyer is a matter of direct experience for every one. This confusion goes on endlessly, giving rise to the cycle of birth and death, unless it is rooted out by the realisation of the true nature of the Self. It is for the removal of this transcendental Illusion, the root-cause of all suffering, and for the attainment of the immediate knowledge of the spiritual unity of the Self that the study of the Vedānta texts is undertaken.[2]

The nature of this transcendental Illusion can be explained with reference to the nature of empirical illusion, for the fact of being an illusion is common to both. Illusion is wrong knowledge. Its essence consists in super-imposition (*adhyāsa*). Shaṅkara gives *three definitions of adhyāsa* or super-imposition, which are essentially the same. The first definition is: adhyāsa is the *appearance* of

1. *Ibid*: mithyājñānanimittaḥ satyānṛte mithunīkṛtya 'ahamidam, mamedam' iti naisargiko'yam loka-vyavahāraḥ.
2. *Ibid*: asyā'nartthahetoḥ prahāṇāya ātmaikatvavidyā-pratipattaye sarve Vedāntā ārabhyante.

something, previously observed and now revived like a memory-image, in something else given now.[1] The definition demands that there must be three things in error: (i) 'something given now' is the ground, present before us and real, on which some other thing is super-imposed; (ii) 'something previously observed' which in itself may or may not be real, but now is not before us and is therefore unreal in the sense of not-given, is the object superimposed due to its impression being unconsciously revived like a memory-image; and (iii) the fact of appearance itself which is terminated by subsequent right cognition of the ground. The second definition runs thus: *adhyāsa* is the *appearance* of the attributes of something in something else.[2] It means that error is an 'illegitimate transference' of the 'what' of something to the 'that' of something else. The third definition is: *adhyāsa* is the (apparent) cognition of a thing in something else where infact it does not exist.[3] This shows that error is wrong cognition or misapprehension due to super-imposition of something on something else. These three definitions are different ways of expressing the same thing and all imply the three factors mentioned above. Error is essentially the super-imposition of the unreal (not-given) on the real (given). It consists in the false relation in a judgement between two terms which belong to two different levels of being. Whatever views of error we may take, whatever definition of error we may offer, it will have to be admitted, says Shaṅkara, that the essence of error lies in the misapprehension of something as something else, which misapprehension is due to the super-imposition of the unreal on the real.[4]

Shaṅkara is not interested in the psycho-physical factors which may help in bringing about illusion. His enquiry is neither physical nor psychological. It is metaphysical. Shaṅkara's aim is to explain illusion in terms of experience and to point out its cognitive value and status.

Illusions may be perceptual or non-perceptual. Perceptual illusions, again, may be conditioned by some media (*sopādhika*) or may not be so conditioned (*nirupādhika*). The former include the

1. *Ibid*: smṛtirūpaḥ paratra pūrvadṛṣṭāvabhāsaḥ.
2. *Ibid*: anyasya anyadharmāvabhāsaḥ.
3. *Ibid*: atasmin tadbuddhiḥ.
4. *Ibid*: sarvathāpi anyasya anyadharmāvabhāsatām na vyabhicharati.

optical illusions of reflection, like the reflected image in a mirror or water, and of refraction, like a straight stick appearing bent in water; colour-illusion; and illusion of size, distance, etc. These illusions are called 'normal', as they are shared by many percipients and continue to persist even after their falsity is known and lead to what is called 'veridical perception'. The world-illusion is more like these. But a subjective factor is definitely involved in these and a person who knows their falsity is no more under illusion even though he may continue to see them in the same way. The latter type of illusions which are not conditioned by media are like the illusions of rope-snake, shell-silver, etc., and also include dream-objects and hallucinations. These vanish for good when their ground is known. The non-perceptual illusions include wrong opinions, beliefs, dogmas etc. which pretend to be true, but on critical enquiry are found to be false. These are more dangerous and include what Bacon has called *Idola Tribus, Idola Theatri, Idola Specus* and *Idola Fori.*[1] An illusion, therefore, is wrong knowledge or belief which is due to the super-imposition of the unreal on the real and is set aside subsequently by knowledge of the real.

For realism the fact of illusion has always been a hard nut to crack. No form of realism whether Indian or Western has been able to satisfactorily explain illusion. Realism believes that the perceived content is entirely independent of the act of perception. Knowledge merely represents; it does not construct. It cannot make or unmake things. The object is in no way affected by its knowledge; it gains or loses nothing by being known. Knowledge merely represents the given without affecting its nature. Now the problem is this: If knowledge never misrepresents its object, how can error at all arise? The Indian realists have made bold, but unconvincing, attempts to explain away illusion. Prabhākara whose view of error is known as *akhyātivāda* denies the logical possibility of error by explaining it away as partial truth. According to him error is non-apprehension, and not misapprehension. Error is not a unitary cognition; it consists of two distinct cognitions having two distinct objective counterparts. Error lies in non-apprehension of the distinction (*bhedāgraha*) between these two cognitions and their respective objects. In the illusion of a rope-

1. These respectively mean dogmas of the tribe, of the religious sects, of the individual, and of the market-place arising due to language.

snake, the rope is perceived as the 'this' *minus* its ropeness, and the 'snake', perceived in the past and now revived in memory, is perceived *without* its 'thatness', and the distinction between the two is not apprehended. This view of error is entirely unconvincing. Error is not mere non-apprehension but mis-apprehension. A subjective element is necessarily involved in error and cannot be brushed aside. The rope is misperceived as the snake. The 'snake' is actually presented to consciousness as an 'object and not as a memory-image.' Moreover, if the two cognitions appear in the mind, then their distinction too must be cognized. Another bold attempt to explain error away is made by the Naiyāyika in his theory known as *anyathā-khyāti.* He goes to the length of saying that the 'snake' is perceived as an objective entity through an extra-ordinary perception called by him *jñāna-lakṣaṇa-pratyakṣa.* This is, evidently, an arbitrary assumption to save the face of realism. When pressed, he has to admit that error is mis-apprehension and involves a subjective element, though its application is restricted by him only to a false relation. The rope and the snake are distinct reals; only their relation in a single judgement is false and this wrong relation between two unrelated reals constitutes error. The presented object (rope) is perceived elsewise (*anyathā*) and the represented object (snake) exists elsewhere (*anyathā* in the sense of *anyatra*). But the difficulty is not solved by this view of error. If the rope as such is presented to consciousness, its misperception as snake would be impossible; and if the 'snake' is a memory-image, it could not have been presented as an 'object.' Further, if knowledge does not distort or construct, what accounts for the wrong relation between the presented and the represented objects? Realising this difficulty, Kumarila, in his theory known as *viparīta-khyāti,* has given up his realism to this extent and has openly admitted the subjective element in error. Error is misapprehension and is due to a wrong synthesis of two imperfect cognitions, which though really unrelated, are welded together into a unitary cognition in error (*viparita-graha*). Kumarila's theory is a link between realism and idealism. He is an eminent predecessor of Shaṅkara.

Shaṅkara refers to these realistic theories of illusion and says that even these realistic accounts of error in order to be consistent have to accept willingly or unwillingly that error consists in super-imposition (*adhyāsa*). Super-imposition, Shaṅkara explains, is the *identification* (*tādātmya*) of the unreal with the real (*satyānṛte mithunīkṛtya*). The illusory can confront us only by appearing *as* the real. This identification, again, is *mutual* (*itaretara*). Both the terms are involved in error. There can be no relation without involving both the terms. But though this identification is mutual, there is a vital difference between the identification of the unreal with the real and the identification of the real with the unreal. The unreal is by its very nature false (*svarūpataḥ mithyā*). It cannot exist except as super-imposed on the real. And even here, it does not really exist, but merely *appears* to exist. When the illusion is set aside, we realise that the illusory object did not really exist even where it appeared to do so. As contrasted with the unreal in the case of the real only its relation with the unreal is false (*samsargataḥ mithyā*). And, it is important to remember this identification itself is also *false* (*mithyā*). The fact of illusion itself, ultimately, turns out to be illusory. There can be no real relation between the unreal and the real. The two terms in illusion belong to two different levels of being and therefore no relation can subsist between them. It cannot be identity, for terms of different orders of existence cannot be identified. It cannot be difference, for, then the terms would not appear as related in the same judgement. It cannot be identity and difference, for, this conception is self-contradictory and leads to the added difficulties of both the views of identity and of difference. The only and the unique relation, therefore, which can *appear* to subsist between the unreal and the real is called identification or *tādātmya,* which is no real relation at all and suggests the impossibility of relating the unreal and the real. Relation cannot be more real than the terms related and if one of the terms is unreal their relation must also be unreal, like multiplication of any number by zero. Identification means that the unreal cannot appear *without* the real and that it can present itself only by appearing *as* the real. The unreal is that which is contradicted, cancelled, sublated in experience (*bādhita*); the real is that which can never be so contradicted (*abādhita*).

In Vedānta the illusory object, as Professor K.C. Bhattacharya rightly points out, is successively taken as real, then negated, and finally contemplated as unreal. He explains the *nature of illusion* as follows: In the first state, which is the state of illusion, the illusory object is taken as real for all practical purposes. In a 'rope-snake' illusion, the judgement 'This is a snake' is one indivisible cognition of the same content. The identification of the 'this' and the 'snake' is so complete that no doubt can be raised about their separate existence. The second state is that of negation expressed in the judgement 'This is not a snake' or 'This is but a rope'. The 'this' is the link between the 'snake' and the rope because in both the judgements 'This is a snake' and 'This is but a rope', the 'this' refers to the same subject. The latter judgement negates the identity of the 'snake' with the rope and consequently the super-imposition of the unreal on the real is cancelled. Though the passage from the state of illusion to the state of cancellation involves temporal sequence, time is not a constitutive element in the content of illusion or its cancellation. Cancellation shows that the super-imposed object is false at all time—past, present and future. The unreal does not exist even in its ground and even during illusion where and when it appeared to do so.[1] In the third and the final state, the illusory object is contemplated as false. It is realised as the indefinite and the indefinable. We can neither own nor disown it. It cannot be a subject or a predicate in any judgement. It is not possible to find any place for it among the world-objects. Its existence exactly coincides with its perception. Its being is entirely exhausted in its appearance (*pratibhāsamātra-sharīra*). It cannot be called real, as it is contradicted afterwards; it cannot be called unreal, for it appears during illusion. It is this character of being 'neither real nor unreal' that constitutes its indefiniteness and its indefinability (*sadasad-anirvachanīya*). The Advaita theory of illusion is called *anirvachanīya-khyāti* or the view that the illusory object can be characterised neither as real nor as unreal and is, therefore, false (*mithyā*).

The analysis of an empirical illusion reveals *three factors.* The first is the illusory object which is super-imposed (*adhyasta*), the 'snake' in the case of a rope-snake illusion. The second is the 'thisness' (*idantā*) of the rope, which appears as identified with the 'snake' and supports (*ādhāra*) the illusion. It is in this sense that the identification is mutual. The relation (*samsarga* or *tādātmya*) of the 'this' with the 'snake' is false. The third is the 'rope', which is the unrelated real, the ground (*adhiṣṭhāna*) of illusion, which indirectly allows itself to be super-imposed upon, but which is not

1. pratipannopādhau traikālikaniṣedhapratiyogitvam mithyātvam, Advaitasiddhiḥ.

at all involved in illusion. Ignorance of it gives rise to illusion and its knowledge cancels illusion.

This analysis also shows that the cause which gives rise to and sustains illusion is nothing but ignorance of the real. Ignorance is the stuff illusions are made of. Ignorance (*avidyā* or *ajñāna*) is not merely absence of knowledge, but also positive wrong knowledge (*bhāva rūpa*). And it is this positive aspect of ignorance which contains the sting of illusion. Ignorance, in its negative aspect, acts as a screen (*āvaraṇa*) and covers the real which remains unperceived; and in its positive aspect, it projects (*vikṣepa*) the unreal on the real so that the real is misperceived. Ignorance, therefore, is non-apprehension as well as mis-apprehension. As ignorance is usually taken to be mere absence of knowledge, Vedānta emphasises its positive aspect (*bhāva-rūpa*) in order to show that the essence of ignorance consists in super-imposition resulting in mis-apprehension. Ignorance as positive is considered as power (*shakti-rūpa*), because it produces and sustains illusion. This power is treated as beginningless (*anādi*), for the supposition that one ignorance is due to another ignorance would lead to infinite regress. As it confronts consciousness as an 'other', it is essentially unconscious (*jaḍa*). Again, ignorance cannot be defined either as real or as unreal (*sadasadanirvachanīya*). It is not real, for it is cancelled by right knowledge; it is not unreal, for it gives rise to and sustains appearance. Though it is beginningless and indefinite, it can be totally cancelled by knowledge of the real, its ground. It is removable by right knowledge (*jñāna-nirasya*).[1] Its locus (*āshraya*) and object (*viṣaya*) is Brahma which really is untouched by it.

Like knowledge, ignorance too implies a reference to the subject and the object. The subject in whom ignorance resides (*āshraya*) is the person in illusion, and the object (*visaya*) to which it refers is the object misapprehended. It is the nature of ignorance to conceal its object; it is the nature of knowledge to reveal the object.

As illusions cannot be treated as real effects, there cannot be real causation. Hence, ignorance, the material cause of illusion is at once identical with its effects. The distinction between cause and effect is apparent and ignorance and illusion are one and the

1. anādi bhāvarūpam yad vijñānena vilīyate.

same. *Māyā, avidyā, ajñāna, adhyāsa* and *bhrama* are used as interchangeable terms in Vedānta. As ignorance (*avidyā*) is beginningless, indefinite and indefinable, it necessarily presupposes a beginningless and indefinable non-empirical consciousness (*sākṣī*) as its basis, to which this ignorance is 'given' immediately without any empirical psychosis (*vṛtti*). As the illusory object cannot be perceived through any empirical psychosis, it must be directly presented to and illumined by this non-empirical consciousness. This consciousness (*sākṣī*), though appearing as associated with an individual is really the transcendental Self, the pure spiritual awareness, which is supra-relational and which illumines and reveals anything that is presented to it, real or unreal, known or unknown.[1] Being above relations, it does not even know itself as a self-conscious subject, and as it does not accept or reject or relate anything, it is indifferent to ignorance. It is the empirical ego (*jīva* or *pramātā*) which relates and which, therefore, is hostile to ignorance. That this ignorance is positive and is illumined by the *sākṣī* is also proved by the experience in deep sleep, when a person, after waking, says 'I slept happily and knew nothing'; and also by such expressions as 'I do not know what you mean', 'I do not know myself', etc.

This analysis of illusion also throws light on the nature and significance of *negation*. Negation, truly, is always a cancellation of illusion. Only the unreal can be negated and that which is negated must be unreal. The real can never be negated. Negation cannot be absolute and unqualified; it is significant. But empirically it stands on a higher level than affirmation. For, affirmation is just the position of a thing which may be real or apparent, while negation is a conscious denial of the apparent reality of a thing mistaken as real. Affirmation of the truth of the content to be negated is not a necessary condition of negation, otherwise every negation would be self-contradictory and, then, the illusory object would not be negated. What is necessary is that the object to be negated should not be a blank. Ultimately, negation itself is negated and this negation of negation does not re-instate the object negated, but the ground on which negation rests. Negation is rooted in the real which is the negation of that negation and in itself is positive. Thus the rope-snake is negated, because it is an ascribed

1. sarvam vastu jñātatayā ajñātatayā vā sākṣi-chaitanyasya viṣaya eva.

character, a super-imposition which does not belong to the real, the rope. And the negation of this negation does not re-instate the 'snake', but only the rope which is the ground of that negation. The real can be realised only by negation of its imposed character.

Shaṅkara accepts the view that all empirical knowledge implies a subject and points to an object. If there is no object there can be no knowledge. Shaṅkara, in fact, adheres to this realistic principle more thoroughly than any realist. The realists, as we have shown above, try to modify or compromise with this principle in the case of illusion. For Shaṅkara to accept the object in the case of true knowledge and to deny it, directly or indirectly, in the case of illusory knowledge is self-contradictory. He accepts that there is an object even in illusion. The illusory 'snake' is *seen* out there. It is not a mere idea masquerading as an object. Shaṅkara is vehemently opposed to epistemic or subjective idealism. For him, *to be perceived is to be*, which is an inversion of the doctrine of *esse est percipi*. The distinction between illusory and empirical knowledge is explained by him to be due to the difference in the character of the objects cognised in them, and not due to the absence or the presence of the objects in them. The illusory and the empirical are different *types* of objects and belong to different orders of being, but objectivity is common to both. Shaṅkara asserts that to be an object is not to be 'real' (this is against realism) nor is it to be 'nothing' (this is against epistemic idealism). Shaṅkara's theory of illusion has the merit of being true to experience and of explaining illusion as it occurs, instead of explaining it away as is done by other theories.

Shaṅkara shows that the fact of an empirical illusion necessarily points to the transcendental Illusion. It is not merely an analogical extension of the empirical illusion. The empirical illusion reveals the transcendental Illusion as its very basis which it logically presupposes and of which it is a part and parcel. Hence, all the characteristics and implications of an empirical illusion shown above equally apply to transcendental Illusion also. The only difference between the two is that they belong to two different spheres of which the higher includes and also cancels the lower, but the lower merely points to the higher. An empirical illusion is an ordinary illusion experienced by an individual in this empirical life and also by others at different times and in different ways so that its occasional occurrence is taken as almost 'normal' (in the sense that a person who mistakes a rope for a snake or who dreams something strange is not treated as abnormal) and which is cancelled, later on, by empirical knowledge of facts. Those empirical illusions which are conditioned by some stable media and lead to verdical perception are called 'normal' as they are shared by many percipients and continue to persist even after their falsity is known. These too are *cancelled* by knowledge in the sense that the percipients who have realised their truth are not deluded by them, inspite of their occurrence in the same way. The Cosmic or Transcendental Illusion, on the other hand, does not occur *within* our empirical experience, but lies at the very root of it. It is not individual and empirical. It is neither realised as an illusion nor cancelled within empirical experience. It belongs to a higher order and operates on a higher level as it is cosmic or transcendental. Just as an empirical illusion can be cancelled by empirical knowledge, similarly it is quite logical to suppose that the transcendental Illusion can be cancelled only by transcendental Knowledge.

The main work of *Māyā* or *Avidyā* is to give rise to the *categorising function* of the mind and consequently to the falsification of the Real. All our empirical knowledge, based on the subject-object duality, is, infact, *avidyā* or Ignorance. Thought cannot reveal Reality; it necessarily distorts it. The sole Reality is Brahma or *Ātmā*, the Pure Self which is immediate non-dual Experience, where the subject and the object are one, where being and knowing completely coincide. The ground of the subject and the object is identical. The same Brahma appears as the individual self as well as the objective world. The true Subject and the true Object evade our grasp; what we know is the false subject and the false object, as presented to us by the *a priori* categorising function of thought. They are our thought-constructs. Brahma itself is the transcendental Subject and the transcendental Object; it is the reality underlying both. *Avidyā* may be called transcendental subjectivity as well as transcendental objectivity. As the *a priori* categorising function of thought, it is transcendental subjectivity; as the primary notion of 'objectivity' confronting the Subject as the 'other', as well as the stuff of which the categorised content is made, it is transcendental objectivity. Transcendental subjectivity implies subject-object duality. It works with both analysis and synthesis. It takes up reality and cuts it up, as it were, into subject and object, then it tries to restore the original unity in self-consciousness but gives only a false unity for the gulf between subject and object remains unbridged in thought.

Vedānta distinguishes *three levels of being*. Pure Being or the ultimate Reality is Brahma. It is beyond our empirical experience, beyond senses, thought and language, as the foundational reality of all. It is *paramārtha*, the absolutely Real. Next comes our empirical world, valid for senses, thought and language, valid for all empirical experience, but not real in itself. It is the sphere of 'becoming' or 'appearance', of space-time-causation, ruled by thought. This phenomenal world is *vyavahāra*. It can neither be justified nor questioned by thought. Being appears in it in various degrees and that constitutes its reality. 'Being' is not only transcendent to 'appearance', but also immanent in it in varying degrees. Brahma is the *reality* of this world; its phenomenal character is a superimposition on Brahma and is therefore false. On the third level, stand empirical illusion, dreams, etc., which are taken as 'real' as long as they last and then rejected as 'unreal' when their ground-reality is realised. This is the level of the illusory called *pratibhāsa*. The illusory and the empirical both are indefinite and are, infact, 'unreal' mistaken as 'real'. The illusory cannot be set aside as a mere 'nothing' for it confronts us as an object of knowledge during illusion and is mistaken by us as such. It is taken as real as long as it appears. The illusory and the empirical are different *types* of objects and belong to different orders of being, but objectivity is common to both. Both are indefinite and indefinable either as real or unreal. They cannot be labelled under any category of thought. They are not 'real', for they are contradicted later on when their ground-reality is known. They are not 'unreal', for they do appear in knowledge as 'real' and are taken as such during illusion. They are not 'both real and unreal', for this conception is self-contradictory. The indefiniteness or the character of being neither real nor unreal nor both is common to both the illusory and the empirical and reveals their falsity (*mithyātva*). Each is taken as real within its sphere and turns out to be unreal from a higher order. The rope-snake is real during illusion and is set aside when the rope is known. The dream-snake is real during dream and is set aside when the dreamer awakes. Similarly, this world is real as long as we view it through senses and thought and is realised as unreal when Brahma is known. In contrast to these three levels of being, the 'non-being' stands as the 'utterly unreal', the *tuchchha,* as a pseudo-concept like a barren woman's son or a sky-flower, which cannot even appear as an object in knowledge at any time. Even the indefinite (*anirvachanīya*), i.e., the illusory and the empirical, treated as false (*mithyā*) has, like the utterly unreal (tuchchha), no 'being' at any time. Yet, the significant distinction between the indefinite and the utterly unreal is that while the former appears in our knowledge as 'real' (*sattvena pratīyamānatvam*) and is mistaken by us to be 'real' until it is set aside as unreal by the sublating knowledge of its ground, the latter has no power even to appear as 'real' (*sattvena pratītyanarhatvam*). The indefinite confronts us by appearing in the garb of the real, though its pretension to reality is later on discovered and discarded, the utterly unreal lacks this power of appearance and has no pretension to reality. It is due to this important distinction that the indefinite is accorded a place under 'degrees of reality,'while the pseudo-concept is relegated to the sphere of 'non-being'. The illusory is a projection of Ignorance. It is taken as 'real' as long as it appears; it is rejected as 'unreal' when its ground is known; and it is realised as 'indefinable either as real or as unreal or as both' when the question of determining its metaphysical status is taken up. Similarly, this empirical world is taken as real (*vāstavī*) for all practical purposes when experienced through sense-organs and thought-forms; when philosophically analysed it turns out to be indefinable either as real or as unreal or as both (*anirvachanīyā*) and is, therefore, treated as false; and when Brahma, its ground-reality, is realised through immediate spiritual experience (generated by the mahāvākya of the shruti), it is realised as totally unreal (*tuchchhā*)[1].

Brahma is *anirvachanīya* in the sense of being beyond thought and language, being trans-empirical. The indefinite, the illusory as well as the empirical, is *anirvachanīya* in the sense that it cannot be logically defined by any category of thought. Even the utterly unreal may be called 'anirvachanīya' in the sense that as a pseudo-concept it is below definition and description. Vedānta, thus, is truly a philosophy of indefinability, *anirvachanīyatā-darshana.* The

1. tuchchhā'nirvachanīyā cha vāstavī chetyasau tridhā | jñeyā māyā tribhir bodhaiḥ shrauta-yauktika-laukikaiḥ || Pañchadashī.

indefinability of Brahma proves its reality; the indefinability of the world proves its falsity; and the indefinability of the pseudo-concept proves its utter unreality.

The questions like: Why should *avidyā* at all arise? How does it condition *Brahma*? How does it project this world? are questions which thought necessarily raises, but which it cannot solve. These questions are insoluble by thought, because thought itself is a product of *avidyā*. The nature of *avidyā* can be known only when its ground-reality Brahma is realised and then there would be no *avidyā* demanding any explanation.

Some critics have often failed to understand the significance of *avidyā* or *mayā* and have, therefore, charged Shaṅkara with explaining the world away. Shaṅkara himself has raised such objections as *pūrvapakṣa* and has answered them. It is surprising that most of the critics have not considered his answers. They say: If the world is unreal, unreal means like Vedānta texts cannot lead unreal personalities to attain real liberation; if the world is real, it cannot be *māyā*.[1] A philosophy which has nothing better to say than that unreal personalities are unreally striving in an unreal world through unreal means to attain an unreal end, is itself unreal. Verily, one bitten by a rope-snake does not die nor can one use mirage-water for drinking or bathing.[2] The Āchārya replies that such objections are based on a confusion between the empirical (*vyavahāra*) and the transcendental (*paramārtha*). The opponent is hopelessly confusing the empirical with the transcendental, even as he is confusing the illusory with the empirical. The falsity of the illusory can be realised only when empirical knowledge is attained. The 'rope-snake' generates fear and an attempt to avoid or kill it and is realised as illusory only when the rope is known. The dream-water quenches dream-thrist. The roaring of a dream-tiger generates fear. Dream-objects can be discarded as false only when the dreamer gets awake. Similarly, the unreality of this empirical world can be realised only when the Absolute is attained. The Āchārya says: We have repeatedly asserted (*asakṛdavochāma*) that as long as the transcendental unity of the

1. *Shāṅkara-Bhāṣya*, II-1-14, katham tvasatyena Vedāntavākyena satyasya Brahmātmatvasya pratipattir upapadyeta?
2. *Ibid.*, na hi rajjusarpeṇa daṣṭo mriyate, nāpi mṛgatṛṣṇikāmbhasā pānāvagāhanādiprayojanam kriyate.

self with Brahma is not realised, the entire world must be taken to be true.[1] As long as this knowledge of unity does not dawn, all secular and religious practices stand as real.[2] Before Brahma-realisation, the world cannot be condemned as unreal. Thought reigns supreme in the empirical realm and its authority cannot be questioned here, otherwise the entire empirical life would be exploded[3]. It is only when the unity with Brahma is attained, the Vedānta declares the world to be unreal. This transcendental knowledge cannot be dismissed as subjective or imaginary, for it is directly experienced as unity with the Real, and it results in the total cancellation of *avidyā* along with its products, and itself cannot be contradicted by any other knowledge[4].

From the above it is clear that Shaṅkara is emphatic on preserving the empirical validity of the world. Far from taking away the reality of this world, Shaṅkara grants some reality, during appearance, even to the illusory objects which according to his opponents are unreal. The words 'real' and 'unreal' are used in Vedānta in their absolute sense. 'Real' means *real for all time* and Brahma alone is real in this sense. Similarly, 'unreal' means utterly unreal like a sky-flower, which this world is not. The world is 'neither real nor unreal' and this brings out the indefinable and self-contradictory nature of the world. It has empirical validity, but not ultimate reality. When the '*reality*' which is denied to this world means '*reality for all time,*' the '*unreality*' which is attributed to it means '*non-eternality*'. Who can say that the world is not 'unreal' if 'unreal' means 'temporal'? It is true for all practical purposes. It will be sublated only when knowledge dawns and not before. This should make us humbly strive after true knowledge rather than engage ourselves in futile quarrels. Āchārya Shaṅkara's intention is perfectly clear—none can condemn this world as *unreal;* he who does it is not qualified to do so and he who is qualified to do so, will not do so, for he would have risen above language and finite thought. Nobody can make the unreal real or transform the real into unreal. The world is what it is, neither more nor less.

1. sarvavyavahārāṇāmeva prāg Brahmātmatāvijñānāt satyatvopapatteḥ svapnavyavahārasyeva prāk prabodhāt. *Ibid.*
2. prāg Brahmātmatāpratibodhāt upapannaḥ sarvo laukiko vaidikashcha vyavahāraḥ. *Ibid.*
3. *Ibid.* II-1-11.
4. *Ibid.* II-1-14 avidyānivṛttiphaladarshanāt bhādhaka-jñānāntarābhāvāt cha.

Its reality is Brahma which is its underlying ground; its unreality consists in its ascribed characters which are superimposed on Brahma. When Brahma is realised superimposition is rejected and the ground is reinstated. The Real is ever what it is. It is only *avidyā* that appears and *avidyā* that vanishes.

We have given a detailed exposition of *avidyā* as it is the root-cause of all suffering and its annihilation results in the realisation of eternal and ineffable bliss.

III. VIVARTAVĀDA

Shaṅkara's view of causation is known as vartavāda, the view that the effect is an appearance of the cause. It is opposed to the view of *asat*-kāryavāda or ārambhavāda (upheld by Nyāya-Vaisheṣika) according to which the effect is a new creation and is not contained in its cause and the relation between cause and effect is that of difference. It is also opposed to the view of *parināmāvāda* (upheld by Sāṅkhya and later on by Rāmānuja and treated as a form of satkāryavāda) according to which the effect is a real modification or transformation of its cause which continues into the effect and the relation between the two is that of substantial identity. Shaṅkara criticises both these views and shows that the relation between cause and effect can be neither that of identity nor that of difference. Causation is a category of thought and therefore an appearance, not reality. As change, difference, objectivity are due to transcendental illusion or *avidyā,* the cause cannot undergo real modification and the effect can be treated as its appearance only. There can be no real creation. Vivartavāda is a denial of real causation and, at the same time, an affirmation of its empirical validity. Shaṅkara emphasises the fact that the creation-texts (sṛṭi-shruti) of the Upaniṣads do not preach the ultimate reality of creation, for there are many other texts which clearly deny the reality of creation and censure all duality and plurality in unmistakable terms tracing it to transcendental Illusion, and propound the essential unity of the self with Brahma or pure eternal *Ātmā.*[1] Creation is valid only for empirical life[2]. The texts declare the reality of the cause alone and treat all effects as ap-

1. na cheyam paramārthaviṣayā sṛṭi-shrutiḥ—S.B., II-1-33. For advaita-shruti, see *supra,* pp. 132-3.
2. lokavyavahāra-dṛṣṭyā bhavatu—S.B., II-1-33.

pearance of the cause which are ultimately false. The effect is declared to be a mere name (*nāmadheyam*), a mere verbal expression (*vāchārambhaṇam*), only an appearance (*vikāra*)which is dismissed as finally false, and the cause alone, which is the ground of appearance, is admitted as real.[1]

It is important to note here that the philosophical terms, *pariṇāma, vikāra* and *vivarta*, acquired their present connotation only in the post-Shaṅkara period. Henceforth, *pariṇāma* and *vikāra* are used as synonyms in the sense of real change or real modification (*satattvato'nyathā prathā*) and *vivarta* is used in the sense of unreal change or appearance (*atattvato'nyathā prathā*) and pariṇāmavāda and vivartavāda are used to signify two distinct theories of causation. In pre-Shaṅkara Advaita Vedānta and even by Shaṅkara himself the term '*vivarta*' is not specifically used for the appearance theory. Gauḍapāda uses the terms *māyā, avidyā* and *ajāti* and Shaṅkara himself uses the terms *māyā, avidyā, ajñāna* and *adhyāsa* for appearance.

It must be remembered that in the pre-Shaṅkara period and by Shaṅkara himself, the terms *vikāra, pariṇāma* and *vivarta* are treated as synonyms and are used in the general sense of 'change' (*anyathābhāva*). Similarly, the verbs vikriyate, *pariṇamate* and *vivartate* are used as inter-changeable to mean 'causal change'. It has to be found out from the context and from the intention of the writer or the spirit of the system whether this change is meant to be real modification or mere appearance. For example, Vasubandhu (5th century) uses the term *pariṇāma* in the sense of *vivarta* and gives the simile of water and waves (*Trimshika,* K.l & 15) Shāntarakṣita (8th century)uses *pariṇāma* and *vivarta* as synonyms (*Tattva-saṅgraha,* K. 328-9). Even Shaṅkarāchārya uses the verb 'vivartate' alongwith the term '*vikāra*' for the real modification undergone by Sāṅkhya Prakṛti.[2] So, if the Upaniṣad texts use the word '*vikāra*' (for example, the Chhāndogya text, VI-1-4, cited above) it does not mean that they preach real modification.

1. vāchārambhaṇam vikāro nāmadheyam mṛttikā ityeva satyam—Chhāndogya Up., VI-1-4
vachārambhaṇashabdena vikārajātasya anṛtattvābhidhānāt—S.B., II-1-14
mṛttiketyeva satyam iti prakṛtimātrasya satyatvāvadhāranāt.—*Ibid.*
The word 'vikāra' is used here in the sense of vivarta or appearance.
2. Pradhānam mṛd vad... vikārātmanā vivartate—S.B., II-2-1.

IV. ĀTMĀ OR BRAHMA

Ultimate Reality, according to Shaṅkara, is *Ātmā* or Brahma. It is pure Consciousness (*jñāna-svarūpa*) or Consciousness of the pure Self (*svarūpa-jñāna*). *Ātmā* here does not mean the individual self (*jīvātmā*), which is an appearance generated by *māyā*, though ultimately the *jīva* shorn of its limitation is Brahma itself. It stands for the Absolute, the foundational Self which is eternally self-shining and self-proved. Brahma means the Infinite, the innermost being of the individual selves as well as of the objective world. The Real is as certain as the self and as infinite as universal nature. It manifests itself as the subject as well as the object and transcends them both. *Ātmā* and Brahma are one and the same. 'This Self is really the Absolute' (*ayam ātmā brahma*); 'That thou art' (*tat tvam asi*); 'I am Brahma' (*aham brahmāsmi*); and 'All this is verily Brahma' (*sarvam khalu idam brahma*) are the great sayings (*mahā-vākya*) of the Upaniṣads.

Brahma manifests itself in two forms which infact are its two poises; in itself it is unqualified (*nirvisheṣa*), indeterminate (*nirguṇa*), transcendent or acosmic (*niṣprapañcha*) and indefinable (*anirvachanīya*), but associated with its own power *Māyā* it appears as qualified (*savisheṣa*), determinate (*saguṇa*), immanent or cosmic (*saprapañcha*) and Lord (Īshvara) of this universe, its creator, preserver and destroyer and its inner controller. It should be remembered that the acosmic view neither denies nor opposes the cosmic view; on the other hand it includes and transcends it. This distinction is at the root of the celebrated distinction made by Shaṅkara between God and the Absolute. God, the creative self-Consciousness or Knowledge-Will, the causal principle manifesting Himself as the creator, protector and destroyer of this universe as well as the immanent self (*antaryāmī*) running through and controlling the universe from within is the lower Brahma (*apạra Brahma*), while the Absolute, the transcendent in itself, independent of and unrelated to creation is the Supreme Real (*para Brahma*). These are the two phases or poises of the same Real. They appear two to our mental view; infact they are one. This has been explained by the Upaniṣadic sage Yājñavalkya, who shines forth as the first exponent of Absolutism in the world, in his answers to the questions of Uddālaka Āruṇi and of the learned lady Gārgī at the court of King Janaka, and in another context in his teaching to his wife Maitreyī.[1]

Shaṅkara makes a distinction between 'description' (*taṭastha lakṣaṇa*) and 'definition' (*svarūpa lakṣaṇa*) of a thing. The former gives only the accidental qualities or modes of a thing, while the latter reveals its essential nature. *Brahma-sūtra* (I-1-2) says that Brahma is the cause of the creation, preservation and dissolution of this universe. Shaṅkara explains that this is merely a description of Brahma and is not its definition proper. Being the cause of this universe consisting of individual selves and external objects is an accidental quality of Brahma and not its essential nature. Causality is a category of thought which has empirical validity but not final reality. It cannot be really attributed to Brahma. Creation is apparant, not real. The Āchārya points out that as the *Brahma-sūtras* are based on the Upaniṣads, the above sūtra refers to the text of the Taittirīya Upaniṣad[2] which says that Brahma is the cause from which the entire universe arises, by which it is sustained and into which it merges again. The Āchārya explains this text as follows: This text gives a description (*taṭastha-lakṣaṇa*) of conditioned (*apara*) Brahma or Īshwara who is the creator, preserver and destroyer and the inner controller of this universe. He is the material cause (*upādāna kāraṇa*) as well as the efficient cause (*nimitta kāraṇa*) of this universe. There can be no other cause except *apara*-Brahma or Īshvara who is the omnipotent, omnipresent and omniscient Lord. Para-Brahma, the unconditioned and impersonal Absolute, through its power *Māyā*, appears as conditioned and personal and it is to this personal God that causal agency is attributed. And this causal agency is treated as an accidental quality of the Lord. The Taittiriya Upaniṣad further gives the essential definition (*svarūpa lakṣaṇa*) of *Brahma* that 'Brahma is Bliss or *ānanda*' and clearly says that it is certainly from *Ānanda* itself that this entire universe arises, by which it is sustained and into which it merges again.[3] Brahma is called the cause of the world because without Brahma the world would not even appear. It is the cause in the sense of being the ground-reality (*adhiṣṭhāna*) on which this world-appearance is super-imposed. The cosmic Brahma or Īshvara is also the immanent inner controller (*antaryāmī*) of this universe of individual selves and

1. Bṛhadāraṇyaka Upaniṣad; III, 7, III, 8, IV, 3, IV, 5. See *supra*, pp. 122-3.
2. III-1, yato vā imāni bhūtāni jāyante, etc.
3. III-6, ānandāt hi eva khalu imāni bhūtāni jāyante, etc.

objective world. The acosmic Brahma is the non-dual eternal Absolute, the transcendental Self, self-luminous and self-proved which is beyond space, time and causation. It must be remembered that the distinction between the lower and the higher Brahma is the distinction in thought and not in reality; in fact they are one.

Brahma is defined in the Upaniṣads as pure Being (sat), the eternal unchanging reality, pure Consciousness (*Chit*), the undeniable Self and pure Bliss (*ānanda*), which is eternal and unmixed and beyond empirical pleasure and pain, all in one. These are not three, but one. And these are not qualities, nor essential attributes, nor even aspects or phases of Brahma, but the very nature of Brahma or rather Brahma itself. 'Brahma is Being, Consciousness and Infinitude' (*satyam jñānam anantam Brahma*)[1] Here 'Infinitude' (*anantam*) means 'Bliss' (*ānandam*) because, as the Upaniṣads say, 'the Infinite alone is Bliss, for there is no joy in the finite'.[2] 'Brahma is pure Consciousness and Bliss' (*vijñānam ānandam Brahma*)[3]. Or simply, 'Brahma is Bliss' (*ānandam Brahma*)[4] because Bliss includes Consciousness and Being, as only a conscious being can enjoy bliss. It should, however, be remembered that Brahma is not a self-conscious person enjoying its own bliss, but Bliss itself. The self is not a synthesis of the subject and the object, for such synthesis is logically impossible. The unity of the self is not abstract identity or the empirical category of unity. It is transcendental and real, but not synthetic as is supposed by Kant and Hegal in order to made it 'concrete'. Vedānta admits that the notion of the self as the unity of the subject and the object is necessary for empirical life and may be taken as the highest synthesis available in thought, yet, inspite of all this, it is not real in itself. The identification of the subject and the object is a result of *avidyā*, though it is the presupposition of all empirical life. The transcendental unity of the self is beyond thought and can be realised only in immediate spiritual experience.

But even the definition of Brahma as pure Being-Consciousness-Bliss (*sat-chit-ānanda*), though the best positive definition, is not

1. Taittirīya, II-1.
2. Chhāndogya, VII-23-1.
3. Bṛhadāraṇyaka, III-11-28.
4. Taittirīya, III-6.

final, for Brahma is really indefinable as it is transcendent to senses, thought and language. Hence, the best definition of Brahma is *via negativa,* 'not this, not this' (*neti neti*) which reveals Brahma as indefinable. But in fact it is no definition, for 'negative definition' is nothing but 'negation of definition'. It is the awareness of thought of its inability to define Brahma through its concepts and categories. '*Neti neti*' does not negate Brahma; it negates only the characteristics ascribed by thought to Brahma. By negating all descriptions of Brahma, it reveals Brahma as the underlying reality beyond senses, thought and language. There can be no better way of describing the indescribable than this negative method.[1] As negation points to the positive reality as its background, the Absolute is not negated or reduced to a blank. Brahma is not 'unknowable' nor 'as good as zero' simply because it cannot be presented and known as an 'object' of thought, because as the foundation of all knowledge it is always present as the undeniable and self-shining Self which can be realised through immediate spiritual experience. 'This is the Imperishable which the knowers of Brahma describe negatively through 'neti neti'.[2] And lest this negative description be misunderstood as the denial of reality, Yājñavalkya hastens to add: 'Verily, the Imperishable, O Gārgī, is unseen but is the seer . . . is unknown but is the knower.[3] In another context, Yājñavalkya says: 'How can the knower by whom all this is known himself be known?. . .[4] The Self is 'not this, not this'. The realisation (of the foundational Self), verily, is immortality.' Shaṅkarāchārya says that Brahma is 'unknowable' only for those who are ignorant of the Vedānta tradition. Brahma is realised through immediate spiritual experience. The knowledge of Brahma culminates in immediate experience. The Self, ultimately, is Silence (*upashānto' -yamātmā*). This silence is neither the silence of the fool nor of the dead; it is the silence of the wisest of the wise, the realised saint. It is said for Shaṅkarāchārya (and also for Buddha) that he taught finally through silence and the doubts of the disciples were automatically resolved.

1. *Shāṅkara-Bhāṣya,* III, 2, 22
2. Bṛhadāraṇyaka, III-8-8.
3. *Ibid.*, III-8-11.
4. *Ibid.*, II-4-13.

V. ĪSHVARA, JĪVA AND SĀKṢĪ

The ultimate reality for Vedānta is the non-dual, unconditioned, indeterminate and highest Brahma which is transcendent to senses, thought and language and is the non-dual eternal Self which is self-shining as Immediate Experience-Bliss and self-proved as the undeniable foundation of all knowledge, of all assertions, denials and doubts. This pure, non-dual, eternal and unconditioned Consciousness (*shuddha chaitanya*) called Brahma or *Ātmā*, through its own power *Māyā* or *Avidyā*, appears as conditioned and determinate and is then 'called lower Brahma or Īshvara. The same pure Consciousness appearing as limited by the internal organ (*antaḥkaraṇa*), which is objective and physical and is a product of *avidyā* is called individual self or *jīva*. The *jīva* is a subject-object complex. It is *jñatā* or *pramātā*. It knows, feels and wills and is an object of self-consciousness. It is also an agent (*kartā*) and enjoyer (*bhoktā*). Its subject-element is pure consciousness and is called *sākṣī*, while its object-element is the *antaḥkarana*, the internal organ. *Sākṣī* is, like Brahma, pure Consciousness, self-luminous and self-proved, unqualified, indeterminate and unknowable as an object, but, unlike Brahma, it appears in association with the *upādhi* (*upahita*) of *avidyā* or *antaḥkārana* as a witness or a disinterested looker-on illuminating itself and everything presented to it as an object.

Brahma is the transcendent ground-reality (*adhiṣṭhāna*) on which, through *māyā* or *avidyā* which is the transcendental Illusion, Īshvara, *jīva* and *jagat* (objective world) are super-imposed, and when this *avidyā* is dispelled by non-dual experience of the Self, all these vanish leaving only the non-dual Brahma. God, individual selves and the objective world are appearances of Brahma. These are non-different from Brahma. They appear when *avidyā* arises and vanish when *avidyā* is dispelled.

Īshvara or God is the personal aspect of impersonal Brahma. As *saguṇa* Brahma, He is the abode of all good qualities (*asheṣakalyāṇa-guṇa-sampanna*). He is the Perfect Personality. He is the material (*upādāna*) as well as the efficient (*nimitta*) cause of this universe, consisting of individual selves and the objective world. He is the creator, preserver and destroyer of this universe. He is immanent in the entire universe which He controls from within. He is the soul (*ātmā*) of souls (*jīvas*) as well as the soul of this objective world. As the immanent inner ruler of this universe, He is called *Antaryāmī.* He is also transcendental, for in His own nature, He transcends this universe. He is in the universe and the universe is in Him, yet He is not limited by the universe. He is Will-Consciousness, the self-conscious Supreme Individual or the Concrete Universal. He is the Giver and the Governor of the moral order. He is the inspirer of moral and spiritual life. He is the object of devotion. He helps the devotees in their spiritual realisation by showering His Grace (*anugraha*) on them. He sustains the bondage of the souls through withdrawal (*nigraha*) of His Grace. He is the Lord of *Māyā* and the 'covering power' (*āvaraṇa shakti*) of *Māyā* cannot operate on Him and does not conceal His nature; He controls the 'projecting power' (*vikṣepa shakti*) of *Māyā* through which He appears as the individual selves and the objective world. He never misses His essential identity with Brahma. He is Being-Consciousness-Bliss all in one (*sat-chit-ānanda*). God is God only for the individual selves and for them He is all in all. Finite thought can never grasp the indeterminate Brahma and therefore all talks about Brahma really refer to Īshvara. It is utterly incorrect to say that in Vedānta God is treated as insignificant and unreal. God is, for Vedānta, the highest appearance which we have, but this highest appearance is the highest workable reality for us. The phenomenal character of God is realised when Brahma is directly experienced and then there is neither God nor soul nor world. As Īshvara is essentially identical with Brahma, Brahma-realisation is also the realisation of the essential nature of Īshvara. In fact, *jīva* also is essentially identical with Brahma (*jīvo Brahmaiva nāparaḥ*), for its objective component comes from *avidyā.* The subject-element in *jīva* is *sākṣī* which is pure Consciousness and is identical with Brahma. Hence Īshvara, *sākṣī* and *jīva* are in fact non-different from Brahma; their difference is due to their association with *Māyā* or *Avidyā* in different degrees and this association, too, is finally unreal as the fact of illusion is also illusory. So, if a person in phenomenal life demands a reality higher than God that person does not know what he or she is seeking.

Āchārya Shaṅkara makes it clear that Īshvara is proved only by shruti or scripture and not by finite thought or inference (*anumāna*)[1]. In Western philosophy, Kant has rejected the proofs

1. *Shārīraka-Bhāṣya,* I-1-2.

for the existence of God offered by Descartes. Shaṅkara has criticised the proofs given by Nyāya for the existence of God. The cosmological proof can give only a finite creator, who is no creator at all. The teleological proof can only point to the fact that a conscious principle is working at the root of creation. The ontological proof can give only an *idea* of God and not a real God. The Āchārya has also made it clear that creation is apparent, not real and that God is not a real creator.

Jīva or the individual self or the empirical ego is Brahma or pure eternal consciousness itself appearing as limited by the internal organ (*antaḥkaraṇāvachchhinna chaitanya*), which is a physical product of *avidyā* and is associated with a psycho-physical organism constituted by senses (*indriya*), life-organs (*prāṇa*) and organic body (*deha* or *sharīra*). It is a subject-object complex. Its subject-element is the pure eternal consciousness appearing in association with the *upādhi* of internal organ (*antaḥkaraṇopahita chaitanya*) called the *sākṣī*, while its object-element is the *antaḥkaraṇa* which is a product of *avidyā*. The *antaḥkaraṇa* is the physical receptacle of thinking (*buddhi*), feeling (*manas*) and willing (ahaṅkāra) and in association with the *sākṣī* which illuminates it, this complex is the *jīva* who thinks, feels and wills. *Jīva* is the empirical knower (*pramātā*), the doer of all actions (*kartā*), the enjoyer of the fruits (*bhoktā*), endowed with the notion of the 'I' (*ahaṅkāra*) and the 'mine' (*mamakāra*) and is the object of self-consciousness (*ahampratyaya-viṣaya*). It is the *jīva* who suffers the miseries of life and who transmigrates and is subject to the cycle of birth and death. Slumbering in Ignorance, when he is awakened by shruti which says, '*tatvam asi*' (That thou art), then he realises that he is not the body, senses or internal organ, but is the non-dual internal Self or Brahma and attains liberation.

Jīva, in contrast to Īshvara, is subject to the cycle of birth and death, while Īshvara is ever-free. *Jīva* is the slave of *Māyā* or *Avidyā* (*Māyā-dāsa*) and is subject to its power of *āvaraṇa,* which conceals his true nature and of *vikṣepa* which makes him appear as limited and bound, while Īshvara is the Lord of *Māyā* (*Māyāpati*) on whom the *āvaraṇa shakti* or the covering power of *Māyā* does not operate and the *vikṣepa shakti* or projecting power functions under His control. *Jīva* is subject to all the three *guṇas* of *avidyā,* while in Īshvara there is only pure *sattva guṇa*. *Jīva* is limited by *antaḥkaraṇa,* senses and body, while Īshvara is not limited by physical body, senses and internal organ, He is Will-Consciousness and His body is not physical, but divine and conscious (*chinmaya*). *Jīva* is limited, finite and bound and cannot be the cause of this universe, while Īshvara is the creator, preserver and destroyer of this world and showers His Grace on the *jīva*s or withdraws it from them. *Jīva* is a mixture of being and non-being, knowledge and ignorance, pleasure and pain, while Īshvara is Being-Consciousness-Bliss. *Jīva,* due to his subjection to *avidyā,* performs actions (*kartā*) and reaps their fruits (*bhoktā*), while the creativity in Īshvara is due to His control over *Māyā* and as agency really belongs to *Māyā,* Īshvara does not imagine Himself as the doer and so the question of His enjoying the fruits of activity (*bhoktṛtva*) does not arise. *Jīva* is subject to the false notion of the 'I' and the 'mine' (*ahaṅkāra* and *mamakāra*), while Īshvara is Perfect Personality (*shuddha ahantā*) free from egoity and attachment. *Jīva,* as a finite ego has limited existence, knowledge and power, while Īshvara, as Concrete Universal, is omnipresent, omniscient and omnipotent. The Āchārya emphasises that as Īshvara is, in His essential nature, Brahma itself for His association with *Māyā* is only apparent, similarly the *jīva* too is essentially Brahma itself because, his finitude or bondage is due to his association with psycho-physical organism generated by *avidyā,* which vanishes when *avidyā* is dispelled by immediate realisation of the real Self. Shaṅkara says that he who maintains a real difference between *jīva* and Brahma and thus wants to preserve the reality of finitude and bondage, is indeed lowest among the learned (*paṇḍitā-pasada*). (Gītā-Bhāṣya, 13, 2).

Sākṣī, like Brahma, is pure eternal consciousness, self-luminous and self-proved being the presupposition of all knowledge and experience, unqualified (*nirguṇa*) and indeterminate and is the pure subject unknowable as an object. But while Brahma is unconditioned (*nirupādhika*), *sākṣī,* unlike it, is *sopādhika* as it appears in association with the *upādhi* of *māyā* or *avidyā* or *antaḥkaraṇa,* though it is not involved in or limited by this *upādhi.* It appears to be associated with *upādhi* (*upahita*) and is not limited by it (*anavachchhinna*). It is called the witness Self, a disinterested looker-on illuminating itself and everything presented to it as an object. Īshvara is full of qualities and is immanent in *māyā* as its controller, but *sākṣī,* unlike Him, is the pure self devoid of qualities and uninvolved in *upādhi. Jīva* is the subject-object complex;

jīva is consciousness limited by *antaḥkaraṇa* which is objective and is a product of *avidyā* (*antaḥkaraṇāvachchhinna chaitanya*). *Jīva* is empirical ego (*pramātā*) who is a doer of actions (*kartā*) and enjoyer of their fruits (*bhoktā*). *Sākṣī*, unlike *Jīva*, is the pure subject (*shuddha jñatā*), a disinterested looker-on, associated with but uninvolved in *upādhi* (*antaḥkaraṇopahita chaitanya*). *Sākṣī* is the pure eternal consciousness appearing in Īshvara as associated with *māyā* and in *jīvas* as associated with *antaḥkaraṇa*. The former is called Īshvara-*sākṣī* and the latter *Jīva-sākṣī*. Though the witnessing consciousness arises with the experience of object, it is not the result but the presupposition of this experience. *Sākṣī* is self-luminous and illuminates all objects presented to it. Everything, known or unknown, is an object for *sākṣī*. (*sarvam vastu jñatatayā ajñātatayā vā sākṣi-chaitanyasya viṣeyaḥ*). Svāmī Vidyāraṇya compares *sākṣī* with the lamp burning on the stage which illuminates equally the stage-manager, the actress and the audience and shines even in their absence.[1] *Ahaṅkāra* is the *sūtradhāra* or the stage-manager, *buddhi* is the dancing actress (*nartakī*) and objects (*viṣaya*) are the audience.[2] *Sākṣī* illuminates the modifications (*vṛtti*) of *chitta* or *antaḥkaraṇa* in the waking state and the mental states in dream, and it continues to shine even in deep sleep when there is no object and is responsible for the unity of the pre-sleep and post-sleep experience of the *jīva*.

VI. MOKṢA

Mokṣa, for Āchārya Shaṅkara, is the immediate experience of the real nature of the self. It is absolute and eternal freedom (*svātantrya*). It is not freedom *from* something to be given up (*heya*) (e.g., this world), nor it is freedom *to* gain something worth achieving (*upādeya*) (e.g., liberation), nor it is freedom *for* someone (e.g., the empirical self); it is freedom *itself*, pure and eternal. There is no 'becoming' in *mokṣa*; the individual self does not really 'become' Brahma for it always is Brahma itself. There is nothing to be left or acquired here.[3] As Buddha identifies *nirvāṇa* with the Absolute, so Shaṅkara identifies *mokṣa* with Brahma. 'He who knows Brahma becomes Brahma'[4] means that Brahma can-

1. *Pañchadashī*, X-11
2. *Ibid.*, X-14.
3. heyopādeyashūnyatvam.
4. Brahma veda Brahmaiva bhavati.

not be known by finite thought as an object, but is to be experienced directly by realising one's unity with it. The Shruti declares: 'This self is Brahma' (*ayam ātmā Brahma*) and 'That thou art' (*tat tvam asi*). Shaṅkara gives the following three definitions of *mokṣa* which really mean the same thing: (1) *Mokṣa* is the realisation of Brahma (*Brahma-bhāva*), (2) *Mokṣa* is the cancellation of *avidyā* (*avidyā-nivṛtti*), and (3) *Mokṣa* is eternal unembodiedness (*nityam asharīratvam*). Realisation of Brahma and cancellation of *avidyā* are the same for both reveal the Absolute as eternal consciousness and bliss. Unembodiedness means the utter unrelatedness of the self with the three types of bodies, gross (*sthūla*), subtle (*sūkṣma*) and causal (*kāraṇa*). It is not the absence of the body, but the absence of the relationship with the body. Hence *Jīvan-mukti* is admitted.

The self is really never bound and so the question of its real release does not arise. The self, through *avidyā*, is imagined to be finite, to be an agent and enjoyer, to be subject to the cycle of birth-and-death, and this constitutes its bondage. When this *avidyā* is cancelled by immediate spiritual experience, the self is realised as infinite, ever-pure and ever-free, and this is said to be its release from bondage. But in fact the self is neither bound nor released; it is only *avidyā* which appears and *avidyā* which vanishes. The self is always pure, eternal and transcendental reality. *Ātmā* and Brahma are one. In the rope-snake illusion, the rope does not become a snake even during illusion when it is so mistaken, and does not shed off snakehood and regain its ropehood when this illusion is removed by knowledge of the rope. *Mokṣa* is the cancellation of transcendental Illusion by the immediate experience of the Real (*avidyā-nivṛtti*). Though the passage from the state of illusion to the state of knowledge involves temporal sequence, yet time is not a constituent element or an intervening factor in illusion and its cancellation, because the illusory object is unreal at all time. Knowledge of the ground-reality and cancellation of illusion happen simultaneously. Removal of *avidyā*, immediate experience of Brahma and realisation of *mokṣa* are one and the same. Immediate experience of the absolute Self does not produce *mokṣa* as its effect; it simply removes *avidyā* which acts as an obstacle to *mokṣa*.[1] *Mokṣa* is the realisation of the eternal nature

1. mokṣapratibandha-nivṛtttimātram eva ātmajñānasya phalam. S.B., I-1-4.

of the Self as pure being and bliss.

Shaṅkara brings out the nature of *mokṣa* in the following passage: This is the ultimate reality, the changeless eternal, all-pervading like space (but beyond it), free from all causal modification, ever-contented pure bliss, indivisible, self-luminous by nature, untouched by actions in the form of virtue and vice along with their effects (in the form of pleasure and pain), and beyond time in its three tenses of past, present and future; this unembodied reality is called *mokṣa* or absolute freedom.[1] The following points, mentioned in this passage, about the nature of *mokṣa* may be noted. *Mokṣa* is the ultimate reality, the Absolute (*pāramārthika sat*) which is Pure Being. It is not eternal in the sense of 'enduring through change' (*pariṇāmi-nitya*), for any change in *mokṣa* would disturb its purity; it is absolutely eternal (*kuṭasthanitya*) in the sense of being totally free from change. It is infinite and all-pervading. It is an established reality (*bhūtavastu*) present everywhere and always. Though it is said to be all-pervading like space, it is beyond space as it is the universal spirit (*sarvavyāpi*). It is beyond causation and causal modifications (*sarvavikriyā-rahita*). It is ever-contented eternal bliss (*nityatṛpta*). It is not self-conscious and blissful in the sense of consciously enjoying its own bliss; it is bliss itself, not parted by subject-object-duality. It is transcendental unity, indivisible and unique (*niravayava*). It is self-proved (*svataḥsiddha*) and self-shining (*svayamjyotiḥ*) non-dual spiritual experience which is the undeniable foundation of all our empirical knowledge and experience. It is the timeless eternal (*kālātīta*). It is the cancellation of *avidyā* and the phenomenal world projected by it (*avidyā-nivṛtti*). *Karma* and its results do not touch it. It is beyond virtue and vice (*dharmādharmarahita*), beyond empirical pleasure and pain (*sukha-duhkhātīta*). It is the unembodied Self (*asharīra*). The Self has no real association with body (*sharīra*), gross (*sthūla*), subtle (*sukṣma*) or causal (*kāraṇa*). It is absolute freedom (*svātantrya*) and spiritual independence (*svārājya*) which is the own nature of the Self. It is the fearless goal (*abhaya-pada*). It is the highest end in human life (*parama-puruṣārtha*).

1. idam tu pāramārthikam, kūṭasthanityam, vyomavat sarvavyāpi, sarvavikriyārahitam, nityatṛptam, niravayavam, svayamjyotiḥsvabhāvam, yatra dharmādharmau saha kāryeṇa, kālatrayam cha, nopāvartete tadetat asharīratvam mokṣākhyam. *Ibid.*

Mokṣa is not an *effect* (*kārya*) of anything. It is eternal reality and therefore cannot be produced by anything. It cannot be the result (*phala*) of action (*karma*) or meditation (*upāsanā*). If it were something to be achieved by action or meditation, then it would be certainly perishable (*anitya*). And '*perishable mokṣa*' is a contradiction in terms. All those who believe in *mokṣa* take it to be eternal.[1] *Mokṣa* is eternal bliss which is different from and beyond empirical happiness, worldly and heavenly. The shruti declares, and reason confirms, that pleasures are produced by the efficacy of good actions (*dharma*) and last as long as that efficacy lasts and perish along with it. Even (the promised) pleasures in heaven, however great and comparatively more lasting these may be, are perishable by nature as they are generated by the energy of *Karma.*[2] No empirical pleasure can be eternal, for it is an effect produced by *Karma* and no effect can be eternal. Also, no empirical pleasure can be unmixed as it is always accompanied by pain, for virtue is necessarily related to vice. Moreover, empirical pleasure can be enjoyed only by embodied beings. Hence, if *mokṣa* be regarded as the effect produced by action or meditation, it is bound to be perishable, mixed with pain and enjoyable only in an embodied state. In that case it may, at best, be treated as the highest empirical pleasure, even higher than heavenly pleasure in the heirarchy of empirical pleasures produced by the efficacy of *Karma.* But this would not be unmixed eternal bliss of the unembodied Self which *mokṣa* is unanimously acknowledged to be. Hence *mokṣa* cannot be produced by action or meditation. Nor can *mokṣa* be treated as an effect produced by knowledge of Brahma. Immediate realisation of Brahma does not generate *mokṣa* ; it simply removes *avidyā* which obstructs the revelation of *mokṣa.* Cancellation of *avidyā,* realisation of Brahma and achievement of *mokṣa* happen simultaneously and are one and the same. Time is not an intervening factor between immediate knowledge of Brahma and cancellation of world-illusion, which obstructs *mokṣa.*[3] Brahma is the pure Self and cannot be known as an object. It cannot be presented as an object of the knowing act. Knowledge of Brahma is not a mental act (*mānasī kriyā*) like meditation. Transcendental

---

1. nityashcha mokṣaḥ sarvamokṣavādibhirupagamyate. *Ibid.*
2. Yāvat sampātam uṣitvā; kṣīṇe puṇye martyalokam vishanti.
3. shrutayo brahmavidyānantaram mokṣam darshayantyo madhye kāryāntaram vārayanti. S.B., I-1-4.

knowledge is beyond subject-object duality. It is pure experience or pure revelation. The Vedānta Shāstra does not present Brahma as an object; its purpose is to declare Brahma as the pure Self, the transcendental subject, which is to be realised through immediate experience by removing difference of known, knower and knowledge falsely imposed by *avidyā*.[1] Hence immediate experience of Brahma removes *avidyā* which acts as an obstacle to *mokṣa*, but does not produce *mokṣa* as an effect.[2]

If *mokṣa* cannot be treated as an effect (*kārya*) produced (*utpādya*) by anything, it cannot also be regarded as a result of causal modification (*vikārya*) for in both cases it would be perishable. Nor can it be taken to be a result of some purification (*samskārya*). Purification is possible either by addition of some excellence (*guṇādhāna*) or by removal of some defect (*doṣāpanayana*). Neither is possible here, for *mokṣa* is eternally pure (*nityashuddha*). Nor can it be regarded as something to be attained (*āpya*). It is the eternal nature of the Self. It is not a new acquisition (*aprāptasya prāptiḥ*), but the realisation of one's own nature (*prāptasya prāptiḥ*). *Mokṣa* is eternally there and the consciousness of its achievement is an appearance.

For Shaṅkara *jīvanmukti* is real liberation. *Mokṣa* is not reserved for the dead. *Mokṣa* is to be obtained here and now.[3] We must enjoy it in this very life. *Mokṣa* is the unembodied nature of the Self and it can be realised even in this life. The Self is really 'unembodied' even when housed in a body (*asharīram sharīreṣu*). *Mokṣa* is the cancellation of transcendental Illusion by immediate experience of the Self. And it is possible to have this experience in our life and cancel *avidyā in toto*. When a person realises Brahma *avidyā* along with its effects is completely destroyed and the world-illusion vanishes for good never to appear again. The Self is an unembodied eternal reality. Unembodiedness is not a state of the self. A state is a phase which is passed over and the self cannot pass over its own nature. Moreover, a state cannot be eternal, while unembodiedness is eternal. The self due to *avidyā* appears to undergo the various states of embodied existence. This happens

1. nahi shāstram idamtayā viṣayabhūtam Brahma pratipipādayiṣyati ki taṛhi? pratyagātmatvena aviṣayatayā pratipādayad avidyākalpitam vedya-veditṛ-vedanādibhedam apanayati. *Ibid.*
2. mokṣapratibandha-nivṛttimātram evātmajñānasya phalam. *Ibid.*
3. atra Brahma samashnute; ihaiva tadāpnoti; abhayam prāpto'si etc.

due to the superimposition of body, senses, life and mind on the self. This super-imposition makes the transcendental self appear as finite ego (*pramātā*) who is a knower, an agent and an enjoyer of the fruits of action and who undergoes transmigration. No real relation between the self and the body can be established, for the self is really beyond *avidyā* and *karma.*[1] The apparent relation between the self and the body can be due only to super-imposition, and not due to *karma.*[2] The self passes through embodied states due to its false identification with the body (*dehādhyāsa*). So when the attachment to the body due to superimposition is destroyed through the realisation of the absolute Self, *mokṣa* is attained even during life. The identification of the self with the body is false (*mithyā*) and not secondary or figurative (*gauṇa* or *upachāra*). Figurative identification of two terms is possible only where the difference between the two is known (*bhedagraha*). It cannot be due to non-apprehension of their difference (*bhedāgraha*) as Prabhākara wrongly holds. For example, in the sentence 'Devadatta is a lion,' the figurative identification of Devadatta with lion is possible for one who understands the difference between the two as well as the qualities like courage, strength and bravery shared in common by both. But in those cases where identification of two terms is due to super-imposition of the one on the other, neither the identity nor the difference between the two is cognised. For example, in the shell-silver illusion, where silver is identified with shell, such identification can be due only to superimposition of silver on shell and is false, not figurative, and is completely cancelled by the knowledge of shell. Similarly, the identification of the self with the body which is due to non-discrimination between the two is possible only as an error and cannot be figurative. As the embodied state of the self is solely due to false knowledge, it is conclusively proved that the saint who has realised the Self through immediate spiritual experience is unembodied even though alive.[3] The shruti declares : 'Him, who has lost attachment to his body and has become unembodied, empirical pleasures and pains do not touch'.[4] 'He who has realised the unity of the Self

1. ātmanaḥ sharīra-sambandhasyāsiddhatvāt. S.B., I-1-4.
2. sasharīratvasya mithyājñānanimittatvāt. *Ibid.*
3. tasmāt mithyā-pratyayanimittatvāt sasharīratvasya, siddham jīvato'pi viduṣo'sharīratvam. *Ibid.*
4. asharīram vāva santam na priyāpriye spṛshataḥ—Chh. Up., VIII-12-1.

experiences no delusion and no sorrow.'[1] 'He who enjoys the bliss of Brahma knows no fear from any quarter.[2] 'O Janaka! you have reached the fearless goal'.[3] 'When the Supreme is realised, the knot of the heart is loosened, all doubts are set at rest, and all *karmas* are destroyed.'[4] 'As the slough of a snake lies dead and cast off on an ant-hill in the very same way lies this body (of him) who has realised the Real; and he is the unembodied immortal Brahma itself'.[5] In the Gītā also the realised saint is described as completely detached from the body etc.: 'Pains do not trouble him, pleasures do not attract him; he is free from attachment, fear and anger, and his knowledge is firmly rooted in the self.'[6] In the Bhāgavata we find: 'As a person heavily intoxicated with wine does not know and is not troubled by the fact whether his garment per chance remains on his body or drifts away. Similarly a saint who has realised the self does not know and is not troubled by the fact whether his mortal body stands or falls'.[7] After the death of the body, *videhamukti* is achieved.

Realisation of Brahma takes place when the knowledge generated by the Vedānta texts culminates in immediate experience, when the '*upadesha-vākya*,' 'Thou art that' (*Tat tvam asi*), becomes '*anubhava-vākya*,' 'I am Brahma' (*aham Brahmāsmi*). An example of how verbal knowledge culminates in immediate experience is given in the 'Parable of Ten Fools'. In this story ten fools crossed a stream hand-in-hand lest some one of them may be swept away by the swift current. When they arrived at the other bank, they started counting themselves, and each of them who

1. tatra ko mohaḥ kaḥ shokaḥ ekatvam anupashyataḥ—Īsha, 7.
2. ānandam Brahmaṇo vidvān na bibheti kutashchana—Taittiriya, II-9.
3. abhayam vai Janaka prāptosi—Bṛh., IV-2-4.
4. bhidyate hṛdayagranthish chhidyante sarvasamshayāḥ I kṣīyante chāsya karmāṇi tasmin dṛṣṭe parāvare II—Muṇḍaka, II-2-8.
   The jīvanmukta's body may continue for sometime due to *prārabdha* karma, but no new actions are accumulated, just as the wheel of a potter continues to revolve for sometime due to previous force even after the push of potter's hand is withdrawn.
5. yathā ahinirlvayanī valmīke mṛtā pratyastā shayīta evam evedam sharīraṁ shete, atha'yam asharīro'mṛtaḥ Brahmaiva—Bṛh., IV-4-7.
6. Gītā, II-56: duḥkheṣvanudvignamanāḥ sukheṣu vigataspṛhaḥ I vītarāgabhayakrodhaḥ sthitadhīr munir uchyate II
7. deham cha nashvaram avasthitam utthitam vā siddho na pashyati yato' dhyagamat svarūpam.—Bhāgavata, XI-13-36.

counted left out himself and counted only nine. Thus they started bemoaning that one of them was swept away by the current. A wise man who came there told them that they were ten and that they need not lament the imagined loss of one of them. But this verbal knowledge did not convince or console them. So the wise man himself started counting and when he came to the tenth, he petted him and said: 'You *are* the tenth.' And then the person immediately realised that he was the tenth and that he forgot to count himself. Similarly, the verbal knowledge of '*tat tvam asi*' should culminate in immediate experience of the unity of the self with Brahma. Shaṅkara explains this text as advocating pure identity and not identity-in-difference 'Tat' signifies the unconditioned Brahma or Ātmā, the ground-reality, while *tvam* signifies the individual self (*jīva*), who is a subject-object complex of *sākṣī* and *antaḥkaraṇa.* The text asserts total and absolute identity between the two. The reality of the individual ego is the transcendental Self or Brahma on which its egohood is superimposed by transcendental *avidyā.* This imposed egohood is false (*mithyā*) and not figurative (*gauṇa*). The text negates the super-imposed false egohood and reaffirms the true nature of the ego as pure *Ātmā* or Brahma. For this, Vedānta prescribes the triple discipline: (1) *shravaṇa* which means a serious and sustained study of Vedānta texts through hearing or reading; (2) *manana* which means critical exposition of the pretensions of thought to know the Real and strengthening of the faith in the shruti; and (3) *nididhyāsana* which means actual realisation of the Real through moral, yogic and spiritual discipline.

VII. JÑĀNA, KARMA AND UPĀSANĀ

All these three may be used in the relative or the absolute sense. Jñāna, relatively, means determinate and mediate knowledge which is generated by the categories of finite thought and involves subject-object duality. Ultimately, Jñāna means pure immediate experience (*aparokṣānubhūti*) beyond the subject-object duality. The Āchārya makes it clear that knowledge ultimately culminates in immediate experience (*anubhavāvasāna*) and knowledge of Brahma is the direct spiritual realisation of Brahma or *Ātmā* and is identical with it.[1] It shines in the highest indeterminate *samādhi* and

1. anubhavāvasānatvād Brahmajñānasya. S.B., I-1-2.

at once removes *avidyā* which obstructs the nature of the Real. *Karma*, relatively, means an action performed with a motive by a conscious person who has freedom to choose and which action is subject to moral judgement and gives rise to its result which is to be enjoyed by the doer in the form of pleasure or pain. Ultimately, *karma* culminates in *niṣkāma karma* or absolutely disinterested action which does not bind (and is therefore not an action in the ordinary sense) and which can be performed only by a realised saint who has risen above subject-object duality. And *upāsanā*, relatively, means *dhyāna* or concentration or meditation involving the trinity of the person who meditates, the object meditated upon and the act of meditation. Ultimately, *upāsanā* culminates in the highest indeterminate *samādhi* which transcends this trinity. It is clear from the above that *karma* and *upāsanā* (which is mental activity) are possible only within the trinity of the subject, object and their relation which is the sphere of *avidyā* and finally both have to cease and yield place to indeterminate knowledge. It is true that empirical knowledge too is within the sphere of *avidyā*; yet, as consciousness, it is ultimately one with pure consciousness which alone can remove *avidyā* which obstructs the nature of the *Ātmā*. Hence the superiority of knowledge over action and meditation is self-evident.

Āchārya Shaṅkara repeatedly asserts that the Absolute can be realised through knowledge and knowledge alone; action and meditation are subsidiary. Good actions (*karma*) purify our mind (*chitta-shuddhi*) and meditation (*upāsanā*) leads to the concentration of the mind (*chittaikāgratā*). Thus, *karma* and *upāsanā* may indirectly prepare our mind to receive the light of pure knowledge (*jñāna*) when it dawns. Knowledge of Brahma which leads to eternal bliss is immediate spiritual experience and does not depend on the performance of any act. Knowledge is not an act, not even a mental act. It is revelatory and it merely removes *avidyā* and does nothing else, and then the Real shines in itself. There is no succession in knowledge. Once it dawns, it dawns for ever and at once removes all Ignorance and consequently all bondage. *Brahma-jñāna, avidyā-nivṛtti* and *mokṣa* are one and the same.

The Āchārya says that knowledge and action are opposed like light and darkness. Action results in its performance (*kāraka*), while knowledge merely instructs (*jñāpaka*). The object of action is merit or demerit which is to be acquired in future (bhavya) through the performance of that action, while the object of knowledge is already an established fact (*bhūta-vastu*). Again, action is subjective and depends on the sweet will of the agent (*puruṣa-tantra*) and it may be done, misdone or left undone (*kartum akartum anyathākartum shakyam*), while knowledge is objective (*vastu-tantra*) and depends on the object itself; it is not given to us to know a thing or to know it otherwise or not to know it at our sweet will, if the conditions generating valid knowledge are there. Again, action binds a person in the cycle of birth and death, while knowledge enlightens and frees him from this cycle. Further, the fruit of moral actions is happiness or prosperity (*abhyudaya*) here and hereafter, which is perishable (*anitya*), because it is produced by the efficacy of actions and lasts as long as that efficacy lasts, while the fruit of knowledge of Brahma is absolute freedom which is eternal (*nitya*) Bliss (*mokṣa* or *niḥshreyas*).

The Āchārya *refutes the Mīmāmsā interpretation* that action is the import of the Veda. The Mīmāmsaka says: 'The purpose of the Veda lies in enjoining action and therefore those portions of the Veda which do not directly or indirectly fulfil that purpose will be of no use.'[1] Thus *karma-kāṇḍa* is the principal portion of the Veda because it clearly and directly deals with action enjoining religious and secular duties in the form of injunctions (*vidhi*) and prohibitions (*niṣedha*). *Upāsanā* (meditation) is evidently a mental activity. The Vedānta texts, therefore, in order to be purposeful, should be regarded either as directly enjoining action in the form of meditation (*upāsanā-karma-paraka*) or as subsidiary portion of injunctions enjoining action (*kriyā-vidhi-sheṣa*) in the sense that they indirectly lead us to action. For example, such texts[2] as: 'The Self should the seen (realised)', 'The Self should be meditated upon', etc., directly enjoin action in the form of realisation and meditation. And such texts[3] as: 'Brahma is Bliss', 'Brahma is Being, Knowledge and Infinitude' have the purpose of indirectly leading us to action. Their implied meaning is: Because Brahma is Being, Knowledge, Bliss, etc., therefore meditate on it and realise it so that you may also enjoy its Being, Bliss, etc. Moreover, liberation can be obtained only by the act of meditation on Brahma, as

1. āmnāyasya kriyārthatvād ānarthakyam atad-arthānām. *Mīmāmsā-sūtra*, Ī-2-1.
2. ātmā draṣṭavyaḥ,. . . nididhyāsitavyaḥ.
3. ānandam Brahma. Satyam jñānam anantam Brahma.

bondage cannot be removed by mere knowledge of statements about the nature of Brahma.

Shaṅkarāchārya refutes this view and shows that knowledge alone, not action or meditation, is the import of the Veda. *Karma* and *upāsanā* are subsidiary and lead respectively to purification and concentration of the mind so that it may receive the light of knowledge when it dawns. Action, meditation and empirical knowledge are all based on subject-object duality and presuppose *avidyā*. Realisation of Brahma cancels *avidyā* and all duality for ever. It is therefore clear that the Vedānta texts which teach the unity of the self with Brahma can, in no way, be connected with action or meditation, either directly or indirectly; nor can they be treated as subsidiary to texts enjoining action or meditation.[1] When the Vedānta texts unanimously and repeatedly reveal the nature of Brahma as pure Being, the statement of the Mīmāmsaka that there is no portion of the Veda dealing with eternal reality is a great venture indeed![2] Also his statement that knowledge cannot cancel *avidyā* is most surprising because *avidyā* can be cancelled only by knowledge and by nothing else. Of course, this knowledge is not empirical but transcendental, for this *avidyā* or Ignorance is also transcendental. Again, his statement that knowledge of Brahma has no reference to any human end as there is nothing to accept or reject here is illogical and absurd, because realisation of Brahma is the highest end in life as it completely cancels Ignorance and all suffering for ever and is eternal Bliss in itself.[3]

VIII. SHRUTI, TARKA AND ANUBHAVA

Shaṅkara says that shruti or the Vedānta-texts alone can reveal Brahma. The scripture is the only means to Brahma-realisation; for Brahma cannot be grasped by tarka or finite thought or intellect. Brahma is not an object of sense-perception for it is super-sensible (*atīndriya*); it is also not an object of thought for it, being indeterminate (*nirvikalpa*), cannot be grasped by the

1. ato na kartavyasheṣatvena Brahmopadesho yuktah. S.B., Ī-1-4.
2. ato bhutavastuparo Vedabhāgo nāstīti vachanam sāhasamātram. *Ibid.*
3. heyopādeyashūnya-brahmātmatāvāgamādeva sarvakleshapraṇāshāt puruṣārtha-siddeḥ. *Ibid.*

categories of thought nor can it be inferred; it cannot be expressed in language for it is indescribable (*anirvachanīya*). Shruti or the Vedānta-texts are the verbal expression of the spiritual experience of the sages who have realised Brahma and are, therefore, helpful in Brahma-realisation. Tarka or logical thought is helpful in interpreting shruti and in supporting it with rational arguments, but its place is secondary to scripture. Sutarka or valid reasoning is accepted; only kutarka or logical quibbling or 'reason run amock' is condemned. Shaṅkara admits that the authority of thought cannot be questioned in the empirical world. Here, 'you obey while you rebel'. Even the statement 'thought stands condemned' can be made only by thought.[1] Only a rational being can understand the meaning of shruti. Shaṅkara never asks us to accept shruti blindly. The apparent contradictions in shruti can be resolved by reason in the light of its central teaching. If shruti contradicts reason, reason must be our guide for it is nearer our experience.[2] Even if hundred shrutis declare that fire is cool and without light we cannot accept them.[3]

The ultimate criterion of truth in Shaṅkara is immediate Experience or svānubhava. Shruti and reason both point to it. The teaching of shruti (*upadeshavākya*) should be converted into immediate experience (*anubhva-vākya*) in order to realise Brahma. And self-conscious reason knows its limitation and points to immediate experience to realise the Real.

IX. CRITICISM OF OTHER SCHOOLS

Shaṅkara dismisses extreme scepticism and agnosticism as self-condemned. The materialistic school which maintains the reality of the object only and reduces the subject to the object is also rejected by him as below criticism. The pluralistic schools of realism, like Vaisheṣika, Nyāya, Sāṅkhya, Mīmāṁsā, Jainism and also the theistic schools of Vedānta (which though developed after Shaṅkara had their fundamental ideas prevalent before his time) are criticised by him. He points out that identity and difference both cannot be real. Pure identity is different from

1. tarkāṇām apratiṣṭhitattvam tarkeṇaiva pratiṣṭhāpyate. *S.B.*, II-1-11.
2. S.B., II-1-4. yuktir anubhavasya sannikṛṣyate.
3. *Gīta-Bhāṣya*, XVIII, 66; *Bṛh-Bhāṣya*, II-1-20.

abstract identity of thought because it is the transcendental unity of the self which is the only reality. Difference belongs to *avidyā* and cannot be real nor can it be combined with spiritual identity, though it has empirical validity. The subject-object duality is empirically real and transcendentally ideal. Early Buddhism, representing the philosophy of pure difference, reduces the subject and the object to momentary particulars and thus contradicts all empirical life. Vijñānavāda denies the object even its empirical reality and degenerates into subjective idealism, throwing overboard all empirical life. He is also opposed to Brahma-pariṇāma-vāda for, according to him, creation is only an appearance and cannot be treated as real.

We have already explained Shaṅkara's criticism of Mīmāmsā[1] and his criticism of causation.[2] We shall explain his criticism of Vaisheṣika and Nyāya in brief and shall present his criticism of Sāṅkhya, of Sarvāstivāda Buddhism in some detail with special reference to its theory of momentariness and of Vijñānavāda Buddhism as his criticism of these schools has become classical.

X. CRITICISM OF VAISHEṢIKA AND NYĀYA

Vaisheṣika and Nyāya are allied systems. The former is older and develops metaphysics while the latter develops logic and epistemology. Nyāya accepts mostly the metaphysics of Vaisheṣika with some difference. Shaṅkara criticises the atomic theory of Nyāya-Vaisheṣika and shows that atoms cannot be the cause of the material world. Are the atoms essentially active or inactive or both or neither? If active, then creation would be permanent; if inactive, then there would be no creation; if both, the conception would be self-contradictory; and if neither, then their activity must come from outside and this outside agency must be either seen or unseen; if seen, then it should not exist before creation, and if unseen, then it being always present near the atoms, creation would be permanent and if the proximity of the unseen to the atoms is denied, then creation would be impossible. In all cases, therefore, there can be no creation from atoms.[3]

1. see *supra*, pp. 202-3.
2. see *supra*, pp. 183-4.
3. S.B., II-2-11 to 14.

Against the seven categories of the Vaisheṣika (included by Nyāya under Prameya), Shaṅkara points out that these categories cannot be taken as metaphysical realities. All these can be reduced to the primary category of 'substance' which alone is independent. And this 'substance' on philosophical analysis would give place to the transcendental 'subject' as the only reality. These categories turn out to be mere assumptions and then, instead of seven, we may assume as many categories as we like.[1]

The Nyāya-Vaisheṣika view of the self and of its liberation is highly defective. The self is deprived of consciousness and bliss and is reduced to a material object like a stone-slab. Again, if God is only the efficient cause of this universe He would be a mere supervisor and not a creator, nor would He have any inner and necessary relationship with atoms or souls.[2] Also, the arguments given by Nyāya to prove the existence of God are not conclusive proofs, because God cannot be proved through inference or thought, but only by shruti or scripture.[3]

Relation, too, is neither internal nor external. If it inheres in one of the two terms, it would not relate it with the other term; the same relation cannot inhere in both the terms as it is indivisible; and if it falls outside both the terms, it becomes a third term which requires another relation to relate it with the first two terms and so on *ad infinitum*.[4] And without a real relation there is no causation and hence no creation.

XI. CRITICISM OF SĀṄKHYA

Shaṅkara takes Sāṅkhya as the main opponent (*pradhāna-malla*)[5] of Vedānta. First, he rejects the claim of Sāṅkhya to be based on the shruti. He makes it clear that Sāṅkhya philosophy is based on inference (*anumāna*), not on the shruti. The shruti does not teach dualism, nor does it say that an unconscious principle, the ab-

1. S.B., II-2-17.
2. *Ibid*, II-2-37.
3. *Ibid*, I-1-2.
4. S.B., II-2-13.
5. S.B., I-4-28.

stract object, is the cause of the world.[1] On the other hand, the shruti clearly declares at many places that the Omniscient, Omnipresent and Omnipotent Self or Brahma is the only cause of this universe.[2] The shruti attributes will and desire to the world-cause in the texts like 'He willed to create the world,' 'He willed: 'I should be many, I should create'; 'He desired to become many, to create', etc.; and evidently only the Self can have will or desire.[3] The will to create cannot be attributed to unconscious Prakṛti even figuratively.[4]

Also, Sāṅkhya philosophy cannot be rationally defended.[5] The unity in the cosmos can come only from the spiritual source; unconscious Prakṛti cannot introduce unity in this world. Even the design and form of a pot is the result of a potter's thinking. Houses, etc., are built with a design and a plan introduced by intelligent workmen. Hence unconscious Prakṛti cannot create this cosmos.[6] Further, there is a purpose in this creation and purpose can be due only to a conscious source; unconscious Prakṛti can have no purpose of its own nor can it consciously serve the purpose of a conscious being. The evolution of Prakṛti would be mechanical not teleological. Again, Prakṛti cannot account for the original impetus, the first push, which is supposed to disturb the equilibrium of the three *guṇas.*[7] If motion is inherent in Prakṛti (in the form of *rajas*), then there should be no dissolution. If motion is imparted to Prakṛti by something external, then Prakṛti would not be independent. Even the distinction between homogeneous and heterogeneous change which Sāṅkhya has introduced to explain evolution is not of much avail. Sāṅkhya says that Prakṛti is eternal in the sense of 'enduring through change.' (*pariṇāmi-nitya*) and that homogeneous change (*sarūpa-pariṇāma*) which means change of each *guṇa* into its own forms, is always going on in Prakṛti. But as there is no clash among the *guṇas* in this change, it does not lead to evolution. When this homogen1eous

1. S.B., I-1-10.
2. S.B., I-1-11.
3. S.B., I-1-5 and I-1-18.
4. S.B., I-1-6.
5. S.B., II-2-1.
6. *Ibid.*
7. S.B., II-2-2.

change transforms itself into heterogeneous change (*virūpa-pariṇāma*), in which each *guṇa* clashes with and tries to dominate the other two *guṇas,* the process of evolution begins. But the important question: What is the cause which leads to the sudden transformation of homogeneous change into heterogeneous change? is not satisfactorily answered by Sāṅkhya. The unconscious Prakṛti is not responsible for this sudden change which ushers in evolution. Puruṣa has to be brought in as the final cause of evolution.[1] Again, even if we grant activity to Prakṛti, the immanent teleology cannot be explained. The argument of Sāṅkhya that just as unintelligent milk flows for the nourishment of the calf, similarly unintelligent Prakṛti works for the emancipation of the Puruṣa is illogical, because the flow of milk is accounted for by the presence of a living cow and a living calf and the motherly love in the cow for the calf.[2] Nor can the modification of Prakṛti be compared to that of grass turning into milk, as grass turns into milk only when eaten by a milch cow, not when it lies uneaten or is eaten by a bull.[3] Further, unconscious Prakṛti can have no purpose; indifferent Puruṣa too can have no purpose.[4] The attempt of Sāṅkhya to solve this difficulty by pointing out that Prakṛti and Puruṣa combine like the blind and the lame in which case the lame person sits on the shoulders of the blind person and shows the way and the blind person moves and thus both reach their goal, is untenable, for the blind and the lame persons are intelligent and active beings and have a common goal, while Prakṛti is unconscious and Puruṣa is indifferent.[5] Again, if the mere presence of the Puruṣa (*puruṣasannidhi-mātra*) is sufficient to disturb the equilibrium of the *guṇas,* then Puruṣa being always co-present, evolution would be perpetual and the liberation of Puruṣa would be impossible. Further, Prakṛti and Puruṣa can never be related. Prakṛti is unconscious; Puruṣa is indifferent; and there is no third principle, no *tertium quid,* to relate them.[6] The chasm which Sāṅkhya has created between the subject and the object by

1. S.B., II-2-9.
2. S.B., II-2-3.
3. S.B., II-2-5.
4. S.B., II-2-6.
5. S.B., II-2-7.
6. S.B., II-2-7.

treating them as two independent and eternal entities can never be bridged by it. It must recognise a higher spiritual principle which transcends and yet preserves the empirical validity of the subject-object duality.

Again there are many contradictions in the Sāṅkhya system.[1] By treating Prakṛti as agent and Puruṣa as enjoyer, Sāṅkhya opens itself to the charge of vicarious suffering and violates the law of moral responsibility. Why should Puruṣa suffer for the actions of Prakṛti? And if Prakṛti acts purposefully why can it not enjoy the fruits of its acts? Sāṅkhya also confuses between the empirical and the transcendental nature of Puruṣa which makes it believe in the plurality of Puruṣas. The arguments given by Sāṅkhya to prove the plurality of Puruṣas are in fact arguments which prove the plurality of empirical selves and these arguments clearly contradict some of those arguments offered by Sāṅkhya to prove the transcendental nature of Puruṣa as pure Consciousness. If all the Puruṣas are essentially the same (as Sāṅkhya says they are), there is no sense in proclaiming their numerical plurality which makes no difference. Again, the confusion between empirical happiness and eternal spiritual bliss is responsible for the negative view which Sāṅkhya takes of liberation. Liberation is said to be without pleasure and pain, a state where all the three kinds of pain are absent, but where there is no positive experience of joy as joy is related to pain. Sāṅkhya forgets that spiritual bliss is beyond empirical pleasure and pain, and that it is not empirical pleasure produced by sattva-guṇa. Again, if Sāṅkhya can reduce all objects to one Prakṛti, it should also reduce all empirical souls to one Puruṣa by the same logic. Puruṣa and Prakṛti should be treated as aspects of the Transcendental Puruṣa, the Absolute. Creation should be taken not as real, but as appearance of this Absolute.

XII. CRITICISM OF SARVĀSTIVĀDA BUDDHISM

Shaṅkara says that the Sarvāstivāda school of Buddhism believes in the reality of the momentary atoms and the momentary ideas. These atoms and ideas are also supposed to form two kinds of aggregates (*sanghāta*). Shaṅkara points out that belief in the theory of momentariness goes against the formation of such aggregates

1. S.B., II-2-10.

and renders all empirical life useless. The momentary atoms cannot combine by themselves. The momentary ideas too cannot unite themselves into the aggregate of five skandhas. And no self, individual or universal, is admitted in Buddhism which may be responsible for the unity of the aggregates. Moreover, when difference alone is taken as real and unity is discarded as illusion, how can the Buddhists logically talk of aggregates as no aggregate can be formed without unity? Even in the wheel of relative causation, the preceeding link may be taken as the immediate efficient cause of the succeeding link only, not of the whole series.[1] But on logical analysis, the antecedent link in the causal series cannot be regarded as the efficient cause even of the subsequent link, because the antecedent link ceases to exist when the subsequent link arises. If it is urged that the antecedent moment when fully developed (*Parinispannāvasthaḥ*) becomes the cause of the subsequent moment, it is untenable, because the assertion that a fully developed moment has a causal efficiency necessarily presupposes its connection with the second moment and this repudiates the theory of momentariness.[2] Again, if it is said that the mere existence of the preceeding moment means its causal efficiency (*bhāva evāsya vyāpāraḥ*), this too is untenable, because no effect can arise without imbibing the nature of the cause and to admit this is to admit the continuity of the cause in the effect which would overthrow the theory of momentariness.[2] Again if the preceeding moment is admitted to last till the arising of the succeeding moment, cause and effect will become simultaneous; and if the preceeding moment perishes before the arising of the succeeding moment, then the effect would arise without a cause. Hence, either momentariness or causation is to be given up.[3]

Again, these Buddhists believe in three uncaused (*asamskṛta*) reals (dharmas) which are evidently not momentary for they are uncaused. These are space (*akāsna*), the revolution of the wheel of causation or *pratītyasamutpāda* in which the destruction of each momentary link after its arising is eternally going on (*apratisaṅkhyā-nirodha*) and *nirvāṇa* where the process of the causal wheel is stopped for ever through pure knowledge (*pratisaṅkhyā-nirodha*).

1. S.B., II-2-18, 19.
2. S.B., II-2-20.
3. S.B., II-2-21.

If these three are admitted as uncaused eternal realities, then the theory of universal momentariness is given up. And if, to save the theory of momentariness, these three are declared not as 'reals', but as 'negation' (*abhāva-mātra*) further contradictions would arise. It would be illogical to regard space as merely 'negation of covering' or emptiness (*āvaraṇābhāva*), for space provides room for extension of things.[1] Again, to say that the causal wheel is merely 'negation of permanence' would be untenable, for this 'negation of permanence' (*nityatvābhāva*) applies only to a momentary link, and not to the wheel itself which is eternally going on, even though the liberated may escape from it. Even to say that the process or the flow of the series is 'eternal' only in the sense of 'enduring' (*santati-nitya*) is to give up momentariness. Moreover, there must be some unchanging eternal conscious being to perceive this flow, as consciousness of change necessarily presupposes an unchanging consciousness. Again, if each unit flashes only for a moment, then even the talk of the flow is ruled out, for there is nothing to flow. This would lead to complete annihilation of all empirical life.[2] Further, to treat *nirvāṇa* as mere 'negation of suffering' (*duḥkhābhāva*) would be to give up *nirvāṇa* as Buddha taught and to give up *nirvāṇa* would be to blow up Buddhism. If *nirvāṇa* is complete annihilation, none will try to attain it. Again, if Ignorance is destroyed by Pure Knowledge then the theory of universal destruction without any cause is given up; and if it is destroyed by itself, then the path of spiritual discipline prescribed by Buddha becomes futile.[3]

Again, the facts of knowledge, memory and recognition give a death-blow to the theory of momentariness. Knowledge necessarily presupposes the eternal transcendental Self as its foundation. Everything else may be momentary, but not the undeniable Self which is self-shining. Memory also presupposes the self. Memory and recognition imply consciousness of at least three moments —the first moment in which something is experienced, the second moment in which its past impression is revived or it is again experienced and the third moment in which the first and the second moments are compared and the thing remembered

1. S.B., II-2-24.
2. S.B., II-2-22.
3. S.B., II-2-23.

or recognised as the same. Even if identity is rejected and similarity substituted in its place, a subject who persists for at least three moments is necessary to compare and recognise two things as similar.[1] Again, if the self is a stream of momentary ideas, the law of *Karma* and the moral life and bondage and liberation will all be overthrown. One momentary idea will perform an act and another will reap its fruit. One idea will be bound, another will try to obtain liberation, and still another will be liberated. It is thus clear that the theory of momentariness destroys all empirical and moral life and renders the teachings of Buddha about bondage and liberation useless.[2]

XIII. CRITICISM OF VIJÑĀNAVĀDA BUDDHISM

Shaṅkara says that the Vijñānavādī Buddhists maintain that Buddha taught the reality of the objects to his inferior disciples who cling to this world, while his real teaching is that Vijñāna alone is real. If external objects exist, they should be either substances having qualities or wholes made up of parts. We know only qualities which are mental; we do not perceive any substance over and above qualities. Again, if atoms are regarded as the units and the objects are said to be their aggregates, this view is unsound. Neither the atoms can be proved to be indivisible units nor can their aggregates be possible, as these aggregates can be neither identical with nor different from the atoms. It is the ideas themselves which appear as external objects, as a pillar, a wall, a pot, a cloth, etc. The fact that the idea is identical with the object is proved also by the rule that both are always experienced together (*sahopalambha-niyama*), the object and its perception are one, *esse est percipi.* If it is urged that this rule is negative in character and that 'the ego-centric predicament' is common to both realism and idealism, Vijñānavāda supplies the positive proof for the identity of idea and object by an analysis of illusory and dream objects. Just as in illusion or dream there are no external objects but the ideas themselves appear as objects, so in the waking state too ideas themselves appear as objects. To the objection that illusion or dream should not be universalised, Vijñānavāda replies that the

1. S.B., II-2-25.
2. *Ibid.* kṣaṇabhaṅgavādī vaināshikaḥ.

dreaming and the waking states are on a par, because the fact of experience, *qua* experience, is the same in both, and because in both the states the creativity of consciousness is clearly manifested. Again, the plurality of ideas need not be attributed to the plurality of the so-called external objects. It can be satisfactorily and logically explained as being due to the difference of impressions (*vāsanā*), which are the seeds of ideas. In this beginningless world, impressions and ideas, like seeds and sprouts, go on conditioning each other. It is far more logical to believe that an idea is generated by a mental impression rather than by the so-called material object. Hence there are no external objects; consciousness itself assumes the 'form' of the object and projects and perceives it as objective.

After giving this correct exposition of Vijñānavāda,[1] Shaṅkara proceeds to criticise it. Shaṅkara believes in epistemic realism and ontological idealism. He is equally opposed to subjective idealism and ontological realism. For him, the empirical reality of this world of subject-object duality cannot be denied nor can its ultimate reality be upheld. The world is empirically real and transcendentally unreal. It would be absurd to suppose that Shaṅkara, while criticising Buddhist idealism, compromises with his own idealism or becomes a realist or uses the arguments of realism in which he himself does not believe. Shaṅkara accepts and defends only epistemic realism as it is not incompatible with his absolute idealism. His criticism is directed mainly against subjective idealism. He also carefully distinguishes his Vedāntic idealism from the Buddhist idealism which he criticises. Vijñānavāda condemns the subject and the object as totally unreal; they do not enjoy even empirical reality. They are purely imaginary (*parikalpita*). Only their 'forms' which appear in knowledge are empirically real; they are superimpositions on the modification of consciousness (vijñāna-pariṇāma). Consciousness, infected with transcendental Illusion of Objectivity, appears in the form of subject and object. Consciousness assuming these forms is empirically real, for it is conditioned by *avidyā* (*paratantra*). Pure Consciousness which is totally free from this *avidyā* and the subject-object duality projected by it is the ultimate reality (*pariniṣpanna*). Shaṅkara's main objection is that the denial of even empirical reality to the

1. S.B., II-2-28.

individual subject and the external object is extremely illogical and contrary to our experience. From the empirical standpoint, it is illogical to separate the 'form' of consciousness form its 'content' and retain empirical reality for this 'form' and reject the 'content' as totally unreal. When both the form and the content appear in knowledge together and both vanish together, what is the sense in making this uncalled for and impossible separation between the two? And when even this 'form' is discarded as ultimately unreal, why this needless partiality in favour of the 'form' and the prejudice against the 'content'? You cannot cut a hen into two to cook one half and reserve another half for laying eggs, says Shaṅkara.[1] The individual subject and the external object enjoy equal status. Both are empirically real, though transcendentally both are superimpositions on pure consciousness. But their empirical reality cannot be questioned and they cannot be rejected as purely imaginary (*parikalpita*). To do so is to disturb our empirical life without any compensatory gain.

Hence Shaṅkara declares: The object cannot be rejected as utterly unreal because we experience it. It does appear in knowledge as an object and is perceived by us as such. The fact that the idea and the object are always experienced together (*sahopalambha-niyama*) does not prove that the *esse* of an object is *percipi.* Their simultaneous presentation in a knowledge-situation does not establish their identity. This argument is merely negative; it can neither prove idealism nor disprove realism. 'The egocentric predicament' is common to both realism and idealism. It merely asserts that we cannot know without knowing. To be perceived by the mind is not to be a portion of the mind. If objects depend epistemologically on the mind, it does not mean that they cannot exist ontologically apart from the mind. The proposition 'Objects cannot be known without mind' is certainly not equivalent to the proposition 'Objects cannot exist without mind'. Nobody normally takes his perception as identical with the perceived object. The arguments of the Vijñānavādī in denying the external world, though he is himself experiencing it, are like the words of a person who while he is eating and feeling satisfied says he is not eating or feeling satisfied.[2]

1. *Māṇḍūkya-Kārikā-Bhāṣya,* IV-12.
2. S.B., II-2-28.

Again, if there is no object, how can its 'form'appear in knowledge? A form, unrelated to a content, is an impossibility. Even the 'objects' which appear in illusion or dream presuppose our experience of world-objects. A person who has never seen or heard of a snake can never mistake a rope for a snake nor can he dream of a snake. The contention of Vijñānavāda that the idea of objectivity is a transcendental Idea and not an empirical one, and therefore, even though there are no real objects, the Idea of objectivity does the trick is untenable, because the transcendental Illusion of objectivity can work only by projecting objects which are empirically 'given' to us and are experienced by us as real and objective. When the transcendental Illusion is set aside, the subject-object duality may be realised as unreal, but as long as we are engrossed in this phenomenal world we have no option but to take the subject and the object as equally real. The form and the content of knowledge cannot be separated here. So if there be no object given to us, even its form cannot appear in knowledge. Even the Buddhist while explicitly denying the external object implicitly accepts it. Diṅnāga[1] says that 'the internal idea itself appears *as if* it were something external'[2]. Now, if there is no external world, how can he say that the 'form' in consciousness appears *as if* it were external? Indeed, no sane person says that Viṣṇumitra appears like the son of a barren woman. There can be no hypothetical without a categorical basis. Possibility always implies actuality. The possibility or impossibility of things can be determined only through means of right knowledge. That is possible which can be proved by valid means of cognition; and that is impossible which can be so disproved. Now, the external objects are apprehended by all valid means of cognition. How can their existence be then legitimately denied? It is therefore established that ideas and objects are distinct.[3]

It cannot be argued that just as in illusion or dream consciousness assumes the form of the object and projects it as objective, without there being any real object, similarly in waking state too consciousness itself appears in the form of objects, for the simple

1. In first half of the sixth verse of his Ālambana-parīkṣā.
2. yadantarjñeyarūpam tad bahir vad avabhāsate (*Ālambana-parīkṣā*,6) quoted in S.B., II-2-28.
3. tasmād arthajñānayorbhedaḥ. S.B., II-2-28.

reason that dream and waking states cannot be placed on a par. Things seen in a dream are sublated in waking state. Their falsity is realised when the dreamer awakes. But world-objects are never contradicted in empirical life. Moreover, the projection of the object in illusion or dream is possible because of our experience of the real object in waking life. Without the object being 'given' to us in waking state, even its form cannot appear in illusion or dream. Again, illusion and dreams are private, while waking life is public. Even if this world is an illusion, it is a transcendental illusion, and even if it be a dream, it is a cosmic dream. It is wrong to treat dream and waking states on the same level on the pretext that both are experienced through consciousness. Even the Vijñānavādī Buddhist realises the difference between the two and what is directly experienced cannot be refuted by intellectual jugglery.[1]

Again, the difference in ideas is due to the difference in objects. The idea of a jar is different from the idea of a cloth, because a jar is different from a cloth. This means that an idea is different from an object.[2] The Buddhist assertion that the plurality of ideas is due to the plurality of impressions and not due to the plurality of objects is wrong, because if objects do not exist then impressions themselves cannot arise. Moreover, impressions are mental modifications and they need a self to inhere. But in Vijñānavāda there is no substratum where impressions may inhere.[3] Ālaya-vijñāna too which is held to be momentary cannot be, like individual cognitions (pravṛtti-vijñāna), the substratum of impressions.[4]

Those Vijñānavādins (*Svatantra-Vijñānavādins*) who uphold the reality of the momentary vijñānas only make the position worse by degenerating into solipcism. Shaṅkara says that his criticism of the theory of momentariness also applies to Vijñānavāda.[5] Momentary ideas cannot ideate themselves. They can neither apprehend nor be apprehended by themselves. There must be a permanent self to synthesise the fleeting ideas and give them unity and meaning.[6] If the Vijñānavādī Buddhist replies that the idea

1. S.B., II-2-29 ubhayor antaram svayam anubhavatā.
2. S.B., II-2-28.
3. S.B., II-2-30.
4. S.B., II-2-31.
5. S.B., II-2-31.
6. S.B., II-2-28.

is self-conscious and is self-shining like a luminous lamp, he is wrong, for to say that the momentary idea illuminates itself is as absurd as to say that fire burns itself. Infact, it is only the eternal Self which is self-luminous and self-proved as the undeniable foundation of all our knowledge.[1] A momentary idea which arises and falls cannot be treated as self-shining. An idea is apprehended by the self. An idea is just like an object in relation to the knowing self, who is the subject. If the Vijñānavādī Buddhist says that by idea he means pure consciousness and that we Vedāntins too who accept the ultimate reality of pure consciousness accept his view, he is utterly mistaken because for us an idea is only like an object to be illumined and known by the self (*vijñānasyāpi avabhāsyatvāt*). It is the self, not a momentary idea, which is pure consciousness. Again, if the Vijñānavādī rejoins that our transcendental Self which is self-shining and self-proved is only his idea in disguise, he is wrong, because whereas his ideas are many and momentary and are no better than scattered objects originating and dying away and depending on the self for being illumined and known, our Self, on the other hand, is non-dual and eternal and is the transcendental Subject, the foundation of all knowledge and experience, which synthesises these scattered ideas into a unity and illuminates them and makes them known.[2] If the momentary vijñāna were the only reality and there is no self, then there would be no experience at all. And all empirical life, morality, spiritual discipline, bondage and liberation, etc., will crumble down.[3]

For Shaṅkara the correct way to prove the ultimate unreality of this world of subject-oject duality is not to reject the subject-object duality even empirically, but to show the essentially self-contradictory character of this world as indescribable either as real or as unreal or as both, and thus prove its falsity from the ultimate standpoint, by treating it as a projection of *avidyā* on the ground reality of pure Consciousness.

As Vijñānavāda as well as Svatantra-Vijñānavāda both accept idealism *par excellence,* both epistemologically and ontologically, Shaṅkara's classic criticism of epistemic idealism applies to both these schools. But as Vijñānavāda believes in absolute idealism

1. S.B., II-2-28. svayam-siddhasya sākṣiṇo'pratyākhyeyatvāt.
2. S.B., II-2-28 vijñānasya utpatti-pradhvamsā'nekatvādi visheṣavatvābhyupagamāt.
3. *Ibid.*

and its Absolute called the Vijñānamātra is pure, non-dual and eternal consciousness which is beyond *avidyā* and its subject-object duality and which can be realised only by immediate spiritual experience, it is partly saved from Shaṅkarāchārya's criticism to this extent. His criticism applies with full force to Svatantra-Vijñānavāda which has degenerated into subjective idealism and has vigorously revived the theory of universal momentariness.

XIV. CRITICISM OF SHŪNYAVĀDA BUDDHISM

Āchārya Shaṅkara summarily dismisses Shūnyavāda by taking it to be self-condemned nihilism. He says that Shūnyavāda is contradicted by all valid means of cognition and is below criticism, for this phenomenal world, the empirical reality of which is established by all valid means of cognition, cannot be negated without reference to and realisation of transcendental Reality which must be admitted as its ground.[1] It is now well known that Shūnyavāda is not nihilism; it is absolutism which believes in transcendental reality and negates the world only with reference to it. Nāgārjuna himself defines '*tattva*' or ultimate reality thus: 'That which is realised in immediate experience, that which is calm and blissful, that where all plurality ceases, that which transcends the categories of thought and is super-sensuous, that non-dual experience is Reality; this is its definition.'[2] Shaṅkara takes Shūnyavāda in its popular sense of nihilism, but his above criticism may imply that if Shūnyavāda believes in transcendental Reality then it is absolutism.

Shaṅkarāchārya makes it clear that he has criticised other views not for any interest in discussion for its own sake, but for the sole purpose of helping the aspirants for liberation to enable them to reject false views hindering the true path leading to pure Bliss.[3] The self-awareness of thought of its own limitation should lead to a firm conviction in the truth of the Vedānta teachings and finally to its realisation through spiritual discipline.

1. S.B., II-2-31. shūnyavādipakṣastu sarvapramāṇa-vipratiṣiddhaḥ iti tannirākaraṇāya nādaraḥ kriyate, na hi ayam sarvapramāṇaprasiddho lokavyavahāraḥ anyat-tattvam anadhigamya shakyate apanhotum.
2. *Mādhyamika Kārikā,* XVIII-9; see *supra,* p.67.
3. samyag-darshana-pratipakṣabhūtāni darshanāni nirākaraṇīyāni. S.B., II-2-1; Also, tatrāvichārya yat kiñchitpratipadyamāno niḥshreyasāt pratihanyeta anartham cheyāt. S.B., I-1-1.

CHAPTER SIX

Post-Shaṅkara Vedānta

I. MAṆḌANA-SURESHVARA-EQUATION

According to tradition, the household name of saṁnyāsī Sureshvara, the famous disciple of Shaṅkara, is Vishvarūpa Mishra popularly known as Maṇḍana Mishra. Prof. M. Hiriyanna and Prof. S. Kuppuswami Shastri have challenged this traditional identification by pointing out important doctrinal divergences between Maṇḍana and Sureshvara. Some other scholars have tried to defend the traditional view. We are not in a position to decide this issue with certainty. We know that the author of the famous work *Brahmasiddhi* is Maṇḍana Mishra (8th cen.) who is a contemporary of Shaṅkarāchārya (and who may have been older in age and may have survived Shaṅkara). He is a self-confident teacher of Advaita Vedānta and does not refer to Shaṅkara as his teacher. He is one of those earlier teachers of Advaita Vedānta, who treat Mīmāmsā and Vedānta as two parts of the same shāstra and who pass on from Mīmāmsā to Vedānta. But we do not know whether his *Brahmasiddhi* was written before Shaṅkara's *Brahmasūtra-Bhāṣya* or almost at the same time. And we cannot say with certainty whether he is identical with or different from Sureshvara. It is on account of this uncertainty that we have included Maṇḍana Mishra under this chapter. We want to make it clear that by including him under this chapter, we do not mean to say that he is definitely a Post-Shaṅkarite teacher of Advaita or that he, later on, became a follower of Shaṅkara or that he is the same as Sureshvara.

Prof. Hiriyanna and Prof. Kuppuswami Shastri have pointed out the following doctrinal differences between Maṇḍana and Sureshvara:

1. Maṇḍana advocates dṛṣṭi-sṛṭi-vāda, later on championed

by Prākāshānanda by maintaining that the seat, support or locus (*āshraya*) of *avidyā* is the *jīva,* while Brahma is only the object (*viṣaya*) of *avidyā.* Brahma neither by itself nor as conditioned by or reflected in *māyā* is the cause of this world. It is only the individual *jīvas,* who on account of their inherent ignorance (*naisargikī avidyā*) create the world-appearance which is destroyed by adventitious knowledge (*āgantukī vidyā*). Individual experiences agree due to similarity and not due to identity. The world-appearance has no objective basis. Sureshvara, following Shaṅkara, maintains that Brahma itself is both the locus and the object of *avidyā.* The controversy led, later on, to the two important schools of Advaita Vedānta, the Bhāmatī School of Vāchaspati Mishra, who followed Maṇḍana, and the Vivaraṇa School of Prakāshātmā who followed Sureshvara and Padmapāda.

2. Maṇḍana maintains prasaṅkyāna-vāda. The knowledge arising out of the Upaniṣad-mahāvākya (*tat tvam asi*) is only mediate, indirect and relational. Its mediacy is to be removed by meditation (*upāsanā*) before it may lead to liberation. Sureshvara upholds the view that knowledge of the *mahāvākya* as taught by the Guru flashes as immediate knowledge on the disciple.
3. Maṇḍana supports bhāvādvaita or ens-monism which excludes another positive entity. Dissolution of Ignorance (*avidyā-dhvaṁsa* or *prapañcha-vilaya*) is a negative reality which does not violate monism. Sureshvara, like Shaṅkara, maintains that negation as a separate entity cannot exist. Dissolution of Ignorance is not a negative entity but positive Brahma-hood.
4. Maṇḍana favours *jñāna-karma-samuchchaya* or combination of knowledge and action for liberation. Sureshvara, like Shaṅkara, believes that *karma* is possible only in *avidyā* and that knowledge alone leads to liberation.
5. For Maṇḍana real liberation is *videha-mukti*; a *jīvan-mukta* is a highly advanced *sādhaka.* For Sureshvara, *jīvan-mukti* is real *mukti.*
6. Maṇḍana accepts viparīta-khyāti while Sureshvara accepts *anirvachanīya-khyāti.*
7. Maṇḍana does not refer to Shaṅkara or his *Bhāṣya* and

his *Brahma-siddhi* is based on the *prasthāna-traya* of Vedānta, while Sureshvara admits that he is a direct devoted disciple of Shaṅkara.

II. MĀYĀ OR AVIDYĀ

Among the most eminent Post-Shaṅkara teachers of Advaita Vedānta are Padmapāda and Sureshvara, the two direct disciples of Shaṅkarāchārya, Vāchaspati Mishra, Sarvajñātma-Muni, Vimuktātmā, Ānandabodha, Shrīharṣa, Prakāshātma-Yati, Chitsukhāchārya, Vidyāraṇya-Svāmī, Ānandagiri, Prakāshānanda, Madhusūdana Sarasvatī and Nṛsimhāshrama Sarasvatī. Padmapāda (8th-9th cen.) is the author of Pañcha-pādikā which is a commentary on the first four sūtras of Shaṅkara's *Brahmasūtra-Bhāṣya*. Sureshvara (8th-9th cen.) has written his famous commentaries known as *Vārtika* on Shaṅkara's *Bṛhadāraṇyaka-Bhāṣya* and *Taittirīya-Bhāṣya* and is therefore called *Vārtika-kāra*. He is also the author of *Naiṣkarmya-siddhi*. Vāchaspati Mishra (9th cen.) is the author of the celebrated commentary called *Bhāmatī* on *Shāṅkara-Bhāṣya* from which the Bhāmatī School derives its name. It has been commented on by Amalānanda (13th cen.) in his *Kalpataru* which has been further commented on by Appaya Dīkṣita (16th cen.) in his *Parimala*. Sarvajñātma Muni (9th cen.) is the disciple of Sureshvara and is probably a younger contemporary of Vāchaspati Mishra. Prakāshātmā (12th cen.) is the author of the commentary called *Vivaraṇa* on the *Pañcha-pādikā* of Padmapāda from which the Vivaraṇa School derives its name. Maṇḍana, Vāchaspati and Prakāshānanda (16th cen.) believe that the individual *jīva* is the locus, seat or support (*āshraya*) of *avidyā* and thus advocate dṛṣṭi-sṛṣṭi-vāda. It should, however, be remembered that this doctrine in Maṇḍana and Vāchaspati does not mean *esse est percipi* for they do believe that the object (*viṣaya*) of *avidyā* is Brahma itself and that *avidyā* is also the positive stuff of which appearances are made and that the external objects exist outside of the individual percipients. Prakāshānanda perhaps is the only Advaitin who advocates dṛṣṭi-sṛṣṭi-vāda in the sense of *esse est percipi* denying the objective basis of the world and claiming that the *jīva* creates the objects during perception. However, he too believes not in subjective idealism but in absolute idealism, because the *jīva* is an appearance and the non-dual Brahma is the only reality. Except these three, almost all other Post-Shaṅkara Advaitins believe that

Brahma itself is both the support (*āshraya*) and the object (*viṣaya*) of *avidyā*, as explained by Sureshvara and Padmapāda.

With this background, let us now proceed to note the views of some of these eminent Advaitins regarding *māyā* or *avidyā*. *Māyā*, *avidyā*, *adhyāsa* and *vivarta* are often used as synonymous in Vedānta. The two schools in post-Shaṅkara advaita are divided on the question whether *māya* and *avidyā* are identical or different. The general trend of the advaitins including Shaṅkara himself has been to treat these two terms as synonymous and to distinguish between the two aspects of *māya* or *avidyā*, which are called *āvaraṇa* and *vikṣepa*, the former being the negative aspect of concealment and the latter the positive aspect of projection. The advocates of the other school bring out the following differences between *māya* and *avidyā*. *Māyā* is the indefinable, inseparable and positive power of Brahma which projects this world of appearances, while *avidyā* is negative in character being pure ignorance or absence of knowledge. Secondly, *māyā*, the cosmic power of projection, conditions Īshvara who is not affected by *avidyā*; while *avidyā*, the individual ignorance, conditions the *jīva*. Brahma reflected in *māyā* is Īshvara and Brahma reflected in *avidyā* or *antaḥkaraṇa* is *jīva*. Thirdly, *māyā* is made mostly of *sattva guṇa*, while *avidyā* is made of all the three *guṇas*. But really speaking, the two schools are not opposed. Both the schools agree that Īshvara is ever free from ignorance and that in Him *sattva* predominates. Hence, whether concealment and projection are treated as two aspects of the same power or the former is called *avidyā* and the latter *māyā*, the difference is only in words.

Again, the Advaitins mostly agree in treating *māyā* or *avidyā* as an inseparable power (*shakti*) of Brahma, as beginningless (*anādi*), as something positive (*bhāva-rūpa*), the objective stuff the appearances are made of, as Illusion or superimposition (*bhrānti* or *adhyāsa*), which conceals (*āvaraṇa*) the nature of Brahma and projects (*vikṣepa*) the world of plurality on it, as indescribable and indefinable for it can be described neither as real nor unreal nor both (*sadasadanirvachanīyā*), as removable by right knowledge (*vijñāna-nirasyā*)[1] and as essentially self-contradictory and inconsistent (*durghaṭa*) in nature which defies all logic (*pramāṇāsahiṣṇu*)

1. anādi bhavarūpam yad vijñānena vilīyate |
tad ajñānam.... *Tattvapradīpikā*, p. 57.

and is ultimately cancelled as illusory when the ground reality is realised; and as such its relation with Brahma is in-explicable for it is neither identity nor difference nor both; it is called tādātmya' or false identification which reveals the impossibility of real relation.

Avidyā, says Maṇḍana, is illusion or false appearance (*mithyābhāsa*), because it is neither the characteristic nature (*svabhāva*) of Brahma nor an entity different from Brahma (*arthāntaram*). It is indescribable either as real or as unreal (*anirvachanīya*). It is not real for it is cancelled afterwards; it is not unreal like a sky-flower for it does appear as real and serves our practical purpose. All philosophers, says Maṇḍana, in order to be consistent must necessarily accept it as such.[1]

Maṇḍana and Vāchaspati both believe that the locus (*āshraya*) of *avidyā* is the individual *jīva* and not Brahma, for Brahma is pure consciousness which *avidyā* cannot even touch. It is true that *jīvas* themselves are the product of *avidyā* and so *avidyā* should not depend on them. But this, says Maṇḍana, should not shock us because *avidyā* itself is an inconsistent category and so its relation with the *jīvas* is also inconsistent.[2] Maṇḍana agrees with Avidyopādānabhedavādins who say that *avidyā* and *jīvas*, like seed and sprout, depend on each other in a beginningless cycle.[3] Through inherent *avidyā* the *jīvas* become entangled in the cycle of birth and death and through adventitious *vidyā* they become liberated.[4] Vāchaspati says that Brahma is associated with two kinds of *avidyā* (*avidyā-dvitaya-sachiva*).[5] One is psychological ignorance which is, as explained by the commentator Amalānanda, 'the preceding series of beginningless false impressions (*pūrvāpūrvabhrama-samskāra*). The other is an objective entity forming the material cause of the mind as well as of the material world outside. It is the material stuff the appearances are made of. The *jīva* arises due to a false illusion which itself is due to another previous false illusion and so on *ad infinitum*. Vāchaspati makes it clear that though the locus of *avidyā* is the *jīva*, the object of *avidyā* is Brahma itself, which it hides and through which it

1. sarvapravādibhishcha ittham iyam āstheyā. –*Brahmasiddhi*, p. 9.
2. anupapadyamānārthaiva hi māya. *Ibid.*, p. 10.
3. *Ibid.*, p. 10.
4. *Ibid.*, p. 12.
5. *Bhāmatī*, opening verse.

makes its appearances appear. An appearance, in order to appear, must be confused with Brahma. An appearance is an appearance because it is wrongly identified with the self-revealing consciousness and is thus given a semblance of reality. It is afterwards sublated by right knowledge.

Except Maṇḍana, Vāchaspati and Prakāshānanda, all other eminent advaitins maintain that Brahma itself is both the locus and the object of *avidyā*. All of them also maintain that *avidyā* is the beginningless positive wrong knowledge which is indefinable either as real or as unreal or as both and which is removable by right knowledge. Sureshvara says that *avidyā* is a beginningless error, the root-cause of *samsāra,* is indescribable either as real or as unreal, is an inconsistent and self-contradictory category which can be annuled by right knowledge.[1] It is based on Brahma and yet it is a baseless illusion (for Brahma is not touched by it) opposed to all reason and cannot stand a logical scrutiny even as darkness cannot stand the sun.[2]

Padmapāda distinguishes between two meanings of falsehood (*mithyā*). It may mean, firstly, simple negation (*apahnava-vachana*), and secondly, something indescribable (*anirvachanīyatā-vachana*).[3] *Avidyā* is indescribable either as real or as unreal and is an inconsistent category. It is an expert in making even the impossible appear as possible.[4] Brahma associated with *māya* or *avidyā* is the cause of this world-appearance. Prakāshātmā, in his Vivaraṇa, explains three possible alternatives: (1) Both Brahma and *māya,* like two twisted threads of a rope, are the joint cause of this world; (2) Brahma having *māyā* as its power is the cause; and (3) Brahma having *māyā* supported on it is the cause. But in all these alternatives, it is the Brahma which is the cause since *māyā* is treated as dependent on it.

Sarvajñātma-Muni says that *avidyā,* resting on Brahma and obscuring its real nature, gives rise to threefold appearances; God, soul and nature. All the three arise together and vanish together. When Brahma is associated with *avidyā,* there are two false entities, (1) *avidyā,* and (2) Brahma associated with *avidyā.* The Real

1. *Naiṣkarmyasiddhi,* II, 103; III, 111.
2. seyam bhrāntir nirālambā sarvanyāyavirodhinī I sahate na vichāram sā tamo yad vad divākaram II *Ibid.,* III, 66.
3. *Pañchapādikā,* p. 4.
4. asambhāvanīyāvabhāsachaturā hi sā. *Ibid.,* p. 23.

is the Pure Brahma, the true ground *(adhiṣṭhāna)* underlying all appearances. Brahma associated with *avidyā* is only a false support (*ādhāra*). Sarvajñātmā clarifies the distinction between *adhiṣṭhāna* and *ādhāra* and maintains that *avidyā* resides neither in the *jīva* nor in Pure Brahma, but in Brahma which appears to support the threefold appearances by revealing itself as *jīvas* and *jagat* (*pratyak-chit*).[1]

Post-Shaṅkara Vedāntins make it clear that indescribability in Vedānta does not mean 'absolute indescribability' or *avāchyatā*, but only indescribability either as real or as unreal or as both, i.e., *sadasadanirvachanīyatā*, and that this indefinability which brings out the self-contradictory nature of *avidyā* is not its defect, but its merit.

Vimuktātmā (11th-12th cen.) says that *avidyā* is indescribable in the sense that it cannot be described either as real or as unreal, and not in the sense that nothing whatsoever can be said about it.[2] This indefinability or inconsistency of *avidyā* is not its defect, but its merit.[3] Shriharṣa (12th cen.), Chitsukha (13th cen.) and Ānandajñāna (13th cen.) refute Udayana's criticism that 'indefinability' means the inability to define or describe (*nirukti-viraha*) by explaining that indefinability means that all possible ways in which the opponent wants to describe a thing are proved to be self-contradictory and so untenable. Shriharṣa says that indefinability is the very nature of all objects of thought, for all that can be grasped by thought cannot be described either as real or as unreal and is, therefore, found to be self-contradictory and false.[4] Chitsukha remarks that the knowers of Vedānta declare that to be 'indescribable' which cannot be grasped by any category of thought and described either as real or as unreal.[5] Ānandajñāna also says that the essence of indescribability lies in proving that all possible ways in which the opponent wants to describe a thing are untenable.[6] It is exactly this character of being indefinable

1. *Saṅkṣepa-Shārīraka*, II, 211.
2. sadasattvābhyām anirvachanīyā, na punar avāchyā. Iṣṭa-siddhi, p. 35.
3. durghaṭatvam avidyāyā bhūṣaṇam na tu dūṣaṇam. —*Ibid.*, I, 140.
4. meyasvabhāvānugāminīyam anirvachanīyatā. —*Khaṇḍana-khaṇḍa-khādya*, p. 32
5. pratyekam sadasattvābhyām vichārapadavīm na yat | gāhate tad anirvāchyam āhur vedāntavedinaḥ || —*Tattvapradīpikā*, p. 79.
6. yena yena prakāreṇa paro nirvaktum ichchati | tena tenātmanāyogas tad-anirvāchyatā matā || *Tarka-saṁgraha*, p. 136.

either as real or as unreal that constitutes the falsity of all world-objects. Vidyāraṇya Svāmī (14th cen.) explains that this empirical world of *māyā* is known in three ways by three kinds of knowledge: When it is experienced by empirical knowledge (*laukika-bodha*) through sense-organs and thought-forms it is taken as real (*vāstavī*) for all practical purposes; when it is critically analysed through reason (*yauktika-bodha*), it turns out to be indefinable either as real or as unreal or as both (*anirvachanīyā*) and is therefore treated as philosophically false; and when Brahma, its ground-reality is realised through immediate experience generated by the *mahāvākyas* of the shruti (*shrauta-bodha*), it is at once realised as totally unreal (*tuchchhā*).[1] When Brahma is realised *avidyā* or *māyā* with all its appearances is realised as something which never was, never is and never shall be.[2]

III. ĀTMĀ OR BRAHMA

In the previous chapter we have explained the nature of *Ātmā* or Brahma according to Shaṅkarāchārya.[3] All post-Shaṅkara advaitins accept it. All of them maintain that the eternal non-dual Self which underlies the world-appearance is self-shining and self-proved ultimate reality which is at once self-revealing consciousness and ineffable bliss. As the self-revealing foundation of all knowledge and experience it is beyond proof, disproof, doubt and denial. It is beyond origination, annihilation, change and momentariness because all these notions presuppose it. This eternal self-luminous consciousness is not subject to rising and setting.[4] All means of cognition (*pramāṇa*) presuppose the Self and cannot prove or disprove it.[5] The Self is the judge presupposing whose existence and to whom addressing their case, philosophers, like lawyers, propelled by heated and headaching arguments, feverishly fight and delude each other.[6]

Chitsukhāchārya defines self-revelation (svaprakāsha) as that

1. tuchchhā'nirvachanīyā cha vāstavī chetyasau tridhā I jñeyā māyā tribhir bodhaiḥ shrauta-yauktika-laukikaiḥ II *Pañchadashī*
2. Vivaraṇaprameyasamgraha, p. 175.
3. see *supra*, pp. 185-8.
4. nodeti nāstametyekā samvid eṣā svayamprabhā. –*Pañchadashī*, I, 7.
5. yato rāddhiḥ pramāṇānām sa katham taiḥ prasiddhyati?
6. imam prāshnikam uddishya tarkajvara-bhṛshāturāḥ I tvāchchhiraska-vachojālair mohayantītaretaram II *Naiṣkarmya-siddhi*, II, 59.

which is immediate (*aparokṣa*) even though it cannot be known as an object of thought (*avedya*).[1] This definition, says Chitsukha, has the merit of distinguishing self-revealing consciousness (*svaprakāshā chit*) from the external objects like pot, cloth, etc., and the mental objects like pleasure, pain, etc., on the one hand, and dream-objects and erroneous objects like rope-snake, shell-silver, etc., on the other hand. The external objects like pot, cloth, etc., and the mental objects like pleasure, pain, etc., are directly perceived and in this sense may be called 'immediate', but they are known as objects of thought and are perceived through the *vṛtti* of the internal organ (*vṛtti-bhāsya*). On the other hand, 'objects' in dream and error are not perceived through the vṛtti of the internal organ but are directly illumined by the *sākṣī* (*sākṣi-bhāsya*) and in this sense they are not perceived like real objects, yet, being illusory superimpositions, they cannot be called immediate. Hence, self-revealing consciousness alone can be called immediate even though it cannot be known as an object of thought.[2]

Moreover, says Chitsukha, besides being immediate, self-revelation can also be inferred. The inference is as follows:

> Immediate Experience (*anubhūtiḥ*) is self-revealing (*svayam-prakāshā*), because it is immediate; That which is not immediate cannot be self-revealing, as for example, a pot.[3]

Chitsuka says that our empirical experience itself points to the immediate self-revealing consciousness as its undeniable foundation. This self-revealing consciousness transcends the trinity of knowledge, knower and known, and should not be mistaken as self-consciousness which presupposes subject-object duality. It is Immediate Experience which is at once eternal bliss.

IV. ĪSHVARA, JĪVA AND SĀKṢĪ

In the previous chapter we have explained the nature of these three[4] and its repetition here is not required. We will deal here

1. na tāvat svaprakāshe lakṣaṇāsambhavaḥ avedyatve sati aparokṣa-vyavahārayogatāyāstallakṣaṇatvāt. —*Tattvapradīpikā*, p. 9.
2. *Ibid.*, pp. 9-11.
3. anubhūtiḥ svayamprakāshā, anubhūtitvāt, yannaivam tannaivam yathā ghataḥ, ityanumānam. —*Ibid.*, p. 11.
4. see *supra*, pp. 189-93.

with the theories regarding Īshvara and *jīva,* which the post-Shaṅkara advaitins have woven. According to some, Īshvara is the reflection of Brahma in *māyā,* while *jīva* is the reflection of Brahma in *avidyā* (*antaḥkaraṇa*). Some regard *jīva* as the reflection of Īshvara. According to others, Brahma, limited or conditioned by *māyā* is Īshvara, while Brahma limited or conditioned by *avidyā* or *antaḥkaraṇa* (which is a product of *avidyā*) is *jīva.* The former view is called Reflection Theory (pratibimba-vāda) and the latter Limitation Theory (avachchheda-vāda). The defect in Reflection Theory is that Brahma and *māyā* both being formless, how can a formless original be reflected in a formless receptacle? To avoid this difficulty, some have suggested the identity of the original and the reflected image (bimba-pratibimbābhedavāda). But this too cannot be accepted. The defect in Limitation Theory is as to how can *māyā* limit the limitless Brahma? Those who do not agree with either of these theories have suggested a third, called Appearance Theory (ābhāsa-vāda) according to which Īshvara and *jīvas* are inexplicable appearances of Brahma. Shaṅkara himself favours Appearance Theory. Shaṅkara uses the similes of the reflection of Sun or Moon in the waves or in different vessels of water and the simile of the reflection of red colour of the japā-flower in the white crystal, as well as the simile of the limitation of the universal space (*mahākāsha*) as the different 'spaces in the jars' (*ghaṭakāsha*), and of course, the similes of water and waves, of rope-snake, of shell-silver and of mirage which clearly show the illusory nature of change. The similes of reflection and limitation are used to show that reflection and limitation are not real, but mere appearances. Gauḍapāda also uses the simile of universal space and 'spaces in the jars' in order to show the unreality of limitation; the Self only appears as the *jīvas.*[1] He also uses the simile of the rope-snake.[2] The similes of reflection and limitation are used only as metaphors for their suggestive value and should not be taken literally and woven into theories. Īshvara and *jīvas* are the inexplicable appearances of Brahma due to *māyā* or *avidyā.*

Regarding *sākṣī,* some advaitins make a distinction between Īshvāra-*sākṣī* and *jīva-sākṣī.* Some believe that there is only one sākṣī in all the *jivas,* while others believe that each *jīva* has a *sākṣī*

1. *Kārikā,* III, 3-8.
2. *Ibid.,* II, 17-18.

of his own. Really speaking, the distinction among Īshvara, *jīva* and *sākṣī* is valid only in empirical life; ultimately all the three are Brahma itself. Īshvara, *jīva* and *jagat* are appearances projected by *māyā*; they arise together and they vanish together when *māyā* is cancelled.

V. OBJECTIONS AGAINST MĀYĀ AND ADVAITA ANSWERED

The post-Shaṅkara non-advaita Vedāntins have been criticising the doctrine of *māyā* or *avidyā* and have been rejecting advaita. The advaitins have not only answered these objections, but have also attacked and refuted the views of these Vedāntins. Most of the objections against *māyā* or *avidyā* are based on the famous seven charges (*anupapatti*) levelled against it by Rāmānujāchārya (1017-1137). These are as follows:

(1) *Āshrayānupapatti:* There is no locus or support (*āshraya*) of *māyā* or *avidyā*. It cannot reside in Brahma for then the non-dualism of Brahma would break down; moreover, Brahma is pure consciousness, then how can *avidyā* or ignorance exist in it? Again, *avidyā*, cannot reside in the *jīva* or the individual self, for the *jīva* himself is said to be a creation of *avidyā*; then how can the cause depend for its existence on its own effect? Hence, *avidyā* cannot exist anywhere. If it resides anywhere, it resides only in the mind of the advaitin who has imagined this wonderful pseudo-concept, this logical myth.

(2) *Tirodhānānupapatti:* How can *avidyā* act as a veil and conceal (*tirodhāna*) the nature of Brahma? Brahma is said to be self-luminous consciousness, then how can Ignorance cover or conceal it? It is as absurd as to say that darkness can hide light or that night can act as a veil on day.

(3) *Svarūpānupapatti: Avidyā* has no nature (*svarūpa*) of its own. Is it positive or negative or both or neither? If it is positive, how can it be absence of knowledge? And how can it be removable by right knowledge as no positive entity can be removed by knowledge? And then the non-dualism of Brahma will be thrown overboard. And if *avidyā* is negative, then how can it project this world-illusion on Brahma? To say that *avidyā* is both positive

and negative is to embrace self-contradiction. And to admit that it is neither is to give up all logic.

(4) *Anirvachanīyānupapatti: Avidyā* is defined as indefinable; it is described as indescribable (*anirvachanīya*). To avoid this self-contradiction, the advaitin says that 'indescribable' means that which cannot be described either as real or as unreal. But this is absurd because reality and unreality are exhaustive and exclusive. They are contradictories not contraries. A thing must be either real or unreal. To maintain a third alternative is to violate the Law of Contradiction and the Law of Excluded *Middle.*

(5) *Pramāṇānupapatti:* There is no *pramāṇa* or means of valid cognition to prove *avidyā.* It cannot be perceived, for perception can give us an entity or a non-entity. It cannot be inferred, for it lacks a middle term or a valid reason. Nor can it be proved by scripture, for it declares *māyā* as God's real power of creation.

(6) *Nivartakānupapatti:* There is no remover (*nivartaka*) of *avidyā*. The advaitin believes that indeterminate knowledge of unqualified Brahma removes *avidyā.* Now knowledge is essentially determinate and there can be no indeterminate knowledge. Also, reality is always an identity-in-difference and Brahma, the highest reality, can never be an undifferentiated and unqualified Being. Hence the supposed indeterminate knowledge of unqualified Brahma being impossible, there can be no remover of *avidyā.*

(7) *Nivṛtyanupapatti:* There is no removal (*nivṛtti*) of *avidyā,* for *avidyā* is said to be positive and a positive entity cannot be removed by knowledge.

All these charges of Rāmānuja are based on the misunderstanding of the meaning of *avidyā* or *māya.* The advaitin admits that it is a self-contradictory category which defies all logic. *Avidyā* is transcendental Ignorance which is the source of all empirical thought and logic and so cannot be explained by it. Rāmānuja mistakes it as a 'real entity' and demands a seat and a *pramāṇa* for it. The advaitin says that Brahma is the support of *avidyā* and as *avidyā* is not real, Brahma remains the only reality and non-dualism is not destroyed. Some advaitins maintain that *jīva* may be taken as the support of *avidyā* in the sense that they go on determining each other in a beginningless cycle. Rāmānuja himself, when he fails to explain the cause of bondage of the pure soul, falls back upon the notion that the relation of *karma* and *avidyā* with the individual soul which is treated as intrinsically pure is beginningless. *Avidyā* does not really affect Brahma even as a rope-snake does not affect the rope. *Avidyā* does not really conceal Brahma even as a cloud does not conceal the sun, though it may hide it from our vision. Again, *avidyā* is called positive to emphasise the fact that it is not merely negative. In fact, it is neither positive nor negative. There is no point in saying that indescribability of *avidyā* either as real or as unreal is self-contradictory, when the advaitin himself admits it. But its self-contradictory nature is realised only when one rises above it by realising Brahma and not before, just as the unreality of a dream or of an illusion is realised only on waking or on knowing the ground on which the illusory object is superimposed.

Again, 'real' and 'unreal' in advaitā are used in the absolute sense. Real means 'absolutely real', eternal and unchanging, always and everywhere, and Brahma alone is real in this sense; unreal means 'absolutely unreal' in all the three tenses like a 'sky-flower' or a 'barren woman's son' which no worldly object is. And in this sense, these two terms are neither contradictories nor exhaustive. Hence the Law of Contradiction and the Law of Excluded Middle are not overthrown. The Law of Contradiction is maintained since all that can be contradicted is declared to be false. The Law of Excluded Middle is not violated because, 'absolutely real' and 'absolutely unreal' are not exhaustive and admit of the third alternative, the 'relatively real' to which belong all world-objects. Again, since *avidyā* is only a superimposition it vanishes when the ground-reality, the Brahma, is immediately realised, just as the rope-snake vanishes for good, when the rope is known. *Avidyā* can be removed only by the immediate intuitive knowledge of Reality, which is the cause of liberation. Removal of *avidyā*, Brahma-realisation and attainment of *mokṣa* or liberation are one and the same, the self-luminous Real. Rāmānuja himself admits that immediate intuitive realisation of the Real is the only cause of liberation, though he calls it highest (*parā*) *bhakti* which dawns by the grace of God.

Veṅkaṭanātha, also known as Vedānta-deshika, a great follower of Rāmānuja has made a vigorous attack on advaita in his work *Shatadūṣaṇī* ('Century of Defects').[1] Most of these charges are either repetitions with minor variations or deal with minor points of detail or are of theological and sectarian interest carrying little philosophic or truly religious value. These objections have been successfully answered by the advaitins. Even in our times, Mahāmahopādhyāya Pt. Anantakriṣṇa Shāstrī has written his *Shatabhūṣaṇī* ('Century of Merits') in refutation of *Shatadūṣaṇī.* We present here some of the most important charges of Veṅkatanātha and their replies by the advaitins:

(1) If Brahma is qualityless and indeterminate then there can be no inquiry into its nature, for all inquiries are possible about qualified objects only. No knowledge, whether general or specific, is possible about an unqualified Brahma. Again, if Brahma is beyond thought and language, the Vedānta-texts would not reveal it and this knowledge of Brahma would be false and would not lead to liberation.

The advaitin replies that the opponent is confusing between the relative and the absolute standpoints. The Vedānta-texts do not say that Brahma can be known as an 'object' of thought; they reveal Brahma as transcendent to thought and language and teach that Brahma being the self-luminous Self is realised through immediate experience. Thought, language and the Vedānta-texts are transcended only on Brahma-realisation, not before. They work efficiently on the empirical level and point to immediate experience as the ultimate goal.

(2) Liberation can be obtained by devotion and action and not by mere knowledge. Even all illusions do not vanish by a mere knowledge of them. A jaundiced person continues to see white things 'yellow' even after knowing the truth and can be cured only by taking medicine. If mere knowledge of unity-texts leads to liberation then all those scholars who know their meaning should have obtained liberation.

The advaitin replies that illusions can be removed only by knowledge and by nothing else. Let there be no illusion about this. If a person knows that he is suffering from jaundice and the

1. In this work 66 charges are found. So either this work as available now is incomplete or the word 'shata' (hundred) is used here in the general sense of 'many'. For a summary of these charges the interested reader is referred to Dr. S.N. Dasgupta's *History of Indian Philosophy,* Vol. III, pp. 304-46.

'yellowness' belongs to the bile and not to perceived objects, then certainly he is not labouring under an illusion, though suffering he might be from a disease. Again, Brahma-knowledge is not verbal knowledge but knowledge which has culminated in immediate experience through removal of *avidyā*.

(3) If the world is false because it is knowable, then Brahma too, being knowable, would be equally false. Again, if the world is false there is no sense in saying that it is negated by right knowledge.

The reply is that the world is false because it is indescribable either as real or as unreal. Everything which is knowable as 'object' of thought is false in this sense. But Brahma is the transcendental ground of all empirical knowledge and stands self-luminous and self-proved. It is not 'knowable' as an object of thought. Again, it is only the false that can be negated.

(4) If the world is false because it is indescribable either as real or as unreal, then Brahma too should be false because it also is indescribable either as real or as unreal.

The reply is that Brahma is 'indescribable' in the sense that being transcendent to thought and language, it cannot be grasped by any category of thought. But as the ground of all experience it shines as the only self-proved Real.

(5) Differences cannot be denied. The so-called 'absence of difference' is itself *different* from 'difference' and therefore establishes the reality of difference. Moreover, without difference there can be no identity also for the two terms are relative and inseparable.

The advaitin replies that difference cannot be real for as a category of thought it is a projection of *avidyā* on the transcendental unity. So 'absence of difference' does not establish difference but only the transcendental unity. The advaitin admits that identity and difference are categories of thought and are empirically relative terms and so bare identity and bare difference are mere abstractions. He also admits that identity-in-difference is the highest category for thought, but it is not the highest reality, for the Real is beyond all categories of thought. 'Advaita' does not mean formal identity; it means, on the other hand, 'transcendental unity', which is beyond all categories of thought including the category of unity and shines as their ground-reality.

(6) The falsity of the world is proved by logical proofs which

are themselves false. The distinction between the empirical and the absolute standpoints is a distinction within thought itself and therefore by its own logic false. So the falsity of the falsity of the world establishes the reality of the world.

The advaitin replies that the world is false because it is superimposed on the ground-reality of Brahma. And so the falsity of the falsity of the world does not reinstate the reality of the imposed world but the reality of the ground. Again, the distinction between the two standpoints is ultimately transcended, yet on the phenomenal sphere it reigns supreme.

VI. DIFFERENCE REFUTED AND ADVAITA ESTABLISHED

Maṇḍana refutes difference by means of dialectical arguments. We do not perceive any 'difference'. Three alternatives are possible regarding perception: (1) perception may manifest a positive object; (2) it may distinguish an object from other objects; and (3) it may manifest a positive object and may also distinguish it from other objects. In the third alternative again there are three possibilities: (a) manifestation of a positive object and its distinction from other objects may be simultaneous; (b) first there may be positive manifestation and then negative distinction; and (c) first there may be negative distinction and then positive manifestation.[1]

Now, in the first alternative where only a positive object is manifested, no 'difference' is perceived. The second alternative is untenable because, pure negation is an impossibility. Perception always manifests some positive object; it does not negate anything. Hence perception cannot reveal mere difference.[2] Possibilities (a) and (c) of the third alternative are untenable, for positive manifestation and negative distinction can be neither simultaneous nor can there be first negative distinction without positive manifestation. Negation is necessarily rooted in affirmation. Difference or distinction is a relation between two positive objects which it presupposes. Even the negation of a non-entity like the sky-flower is only a denial of the false relation between two positive entities, the sky and the flower. Possibility (b) of the third alternative is

1. *Brahmasiddhi,* p. 44.
2. *Ibid.,* p. 39.

also untenable, for perception is one unique process and there cannot be two or more moments in it.[1]

Further, Maṇḍana points out that unity and difference cannot be combined like light and darkness. And, to say, like the Buddhist, that difference alone is real and unity an appearance, is highly absurd, for if difference be the very nature of things, then there would be no difference among them at all. Again, difference being 'formless', the objects themselves would be 'formless'. Again, difference being of the nature of negation, objects themselves would be of the nature of negation. Again, difference being dual or plural, no object would be the same single object for the same thing cannot be both one and many.[2]

Hence, it has to be admitted that unity alone is real and difference is only an appearance. Difference in qualities does not imply difference in reality. Just as the same fire has diverse activities of burning, cooking and illuminating, similarly it is the extraordinary potency of the one supreme Brahma that enables it to appear as this diverse phenomenal world.[3]

Vimuktātmā in his *Iṣṭa-siddhi*, Shrīharṣa in his *Khaṇḍana-khaṇḍa-khādya*, Chitsukha in his *Tattva-pradīpikā*, Madhusūdana in his *Advaita-siddhi* and Nṛsimhāshrama in his *Bheda-dhikkāra* have entered into a trenchent dialectical refutation of difference and have established advaita. The essence of their arguments is as follows: Brahma is non-dual transcendental unity which is beyond all thought-categories. The manifold world is an appearance of Brahma and there can be no relation between them, neither that of unity nor that of difference nor that of both. The world therefore is false and with it all its 'difference' is also false. Neither perception nor inference nor any other means of cognition can prove 'difference' nor contradict non-duality of Brahma because Brahma or the pure Self is the foundation of all means of cognition and all proof, disproof, doubt and denial. Difference is due to *avidyā* and its empirical validity is not questioned; only its ultimate reality is denied. To contradict advaita, therefore, is impossible.

1. *Ibid.*, pp. 39-45.
2. *Ibid.*, pp. 47-48.
3. *Ibid.*, pp. 54-55.

VII. FURTHER DIALECTICAL EXPOSITION OF THE ULTIMATE UNREALITY OF THE WORLD

Shrīharṣa and Chitsukha undertake a thorough inquiry into the nature of the categories and concepts of thought and point out their utter dialectical hollowness. Their main polemic is against Nyāya. Nyāya and Mīmāṁsā have given various definitions of right knowledge (*pramā*), of the means of right knowledge (*pramāṇa*), of the various categories of experience (*padārtha*) and of the concepts involved in these categories. Shrīharṣa and Chitsukha take all these definitions one by one and with their irresistable dialectic tear them into pieces pointing out that they are all 'baseless fabrics of a vision that leaves nothing behind.'

Chitsukha has commented on the Khaṇḍana of Shrīharṣa and has also written an independent work *Tattvapradīpikā,* popularly known after him as *Chitsukhī.* The criticisms offered by Shrīharṣa and Chitsukha are mostly destructive. Shrīharṣa's work is mainly polemical. Like the Mādhyamika, he has no thesis of his own to prove and no definitions to offer. He mainly refutes the definitions of Nyāya writers. He often criticises the language of the definitions rather than their thought. Dr. S.N. Dasgupta is right in remarking: 'If these criticisms had mainly been directed towards the defects of Nyāya thought, later writers would not have been forced to take the course of developing verbal expressions (in order to avoid the criticisms of Shrīharṣa) at the expense of philosophical profundity and acuteness. Shrīharṣa may therefore be said to be the first great writer who is responsible indirectly for the growth of verbalism in later Nyāya thought'.[1] Shrīharṣa has written a long introduction (*Bhūmikā*) to his *Khaṇḍana,* which is an excellent piece of literary and philosophical merit and is free from formal verbalism often found in the main body of the work and gives us a good summary of his philosophy. Chitsukha in addition to refuting Nyāya definitions also refutes other definitions. He also gives us an accurate analysis and an elaborate interpretation of the main concepts of advaita. Thus he fulfils the work left unaccomplished by Shrīharṣa.

All that is known (*prameya*) has a defined real existence, says the Naiyāyika. All that is known is indefinable and therefore unreal, rejoin Shrīharṣa and Chitsukha. Thought which works with its

1. *History of Indian Philosophy,* Vol. II, p. 146.

concepts and categories and presupposes the subject-object duality is necessarily relational. All objects of thought are relational and therefore indefinable either as real or as unreal or as both. Hence they are false.

The opponent objects: If you are unable to describe and define the world-objects, you should go to some learned teachers and learn how to describe and define the objects of thought. Shrīharṣa replies: This contemptuous outburst of the opponent would have been valid only if we had said that some particular person or persons was or were unable to define world-objects due to his or their lack of learning. Our contention, which the opponent has hopelessly missed, is that indefinability is the very nature of all world-experiences. All that can be known as an object of thought necessarily turns out to be indefinable either as real or as unreal or as both and therefore self-contradictory and false. Our opponent seems to be proud of his ability to define the world, but we shatter his false pride by pointing out to him that his definitions, by his own logic, are found to be self-contradictory and false.[1]

The opponent here strongly objects by saying that Shrīharṣa is indulging in logical quibbling. The advaitin says that he has no thesis of his own to prove, no definitions to offer and he even goes to the extent of saying that he has no logic of his own because all arguments are self-contradictory. The advaitin is indulging in manifest self-contradiction. Even to say that the world is indefinable is to *define* it as indefinable; even to say that reality is indescribable is to *describe* it as indescribable. The advaitin is applying all the categories to reality and yet shamelessly says that reality is beyond all the four categories of thought.[2] If all arguments are self-contradictory, then this argument of the advaitin, by his own logic is also self-contradictory. Hence, the advaitin has no right to enter into a fruitful philosophical discussion or even to utter a word.

Shrīharṣa, like Nāgārjuna and Chandrakīrti, faces these objections boldly. He replies: It is not necessary that each participant

1. yadapi nirvaktum asāmarthye gurava upāsyantām yebhyo niruktayaḥ shikṣyante iti upālambhavachanam tat tadā shobheta yadi meya-svabhāvānugāminīyam anirvachanīyateti na brūyuḥ vaktṛdoṣāt iti cha vadeyuḥ. *Khaṇḍana*, pp. 31-2.
2. tattve dvi-tri-chatuṣkoṭi-vyudāsena yathāyatham I niruchyamāne nirlajjair anirvāchyatvam uchyate II —*Nyāyasiddhāñjana*, p. 93.

in a discussion must have a view of his own or must accept the reality of logic. What is necessary for a fruitful discussion is that both the participants must accept, during discussion, the common rules of logic. The advaitin, during discussion, accepts provisionally the rules of logic which the opponent accepts as true and shows to the opponent that his (opponent's) view, by his own logic, is self-contradictory and therefore false. Rejection of all views is itself not a view. Shrīharṣa frankly admits that he is not denying the empirical validity of logic or thought. In the empirical world thought undoubtedly reigns supreme and its authority cannot be questioned here. But thought itself points to its own limitations and finally merges in non-dual immediate experience. The highest philosophy is the philosophy of transcendent Silence. Reality is the eternal non-dual Self which is pure consciousness, self-shining and self-proved, being the foundation of all thought-categories, all affirmation, denial, doubt and discussion. Reality is indefinable or indescribable because it is beyond thought as its undeniable self-shining foundation. The world of plurality is indefinable or indescribable either as real or as unreal or as both and is therefore self-contradictory and false. Even the distinction between the empirical and the ultimate is a distinction made by thought and is within thought. Reality is advaita or non-dual consciousness which is transcendent to sense, thought and language and is to be realised in immediate experience. Hence, says Shrīharṣa, the advaitin is not interested in weaving views about Reality, which cannot grasp it. He has no thesis to prove, no argument to offer, no contention to support. He is only interested in showing to the opponent that his (opponent's) position, from his own logic, is found to be self-contradictory and false.[1] If the opponent accepts this, he is giving up his position and embracing advaita. If, on the other hand, the opponent challenges this, he is challenging the validity of his own logic and is thereby accepting advaita. In either case, therefore, advaita becomes established. Hence, it is proved that the entire world is indefinable either as real or as unreal or as both and is therefore, self-con-

1. na sādhvīyam bhavatām vichāra-vyavasthā bhavatkalpita-vyavasthayaiva vyāhatatvāt. Khaṇḍana, p. 33.

tradictory and false, as it is only a super-imposition on the ground-reality of Brahma.[1]

Chitsukha also observes that the world of plurality, when dialectically examined, is found to be indefinable either as real or as unreal. It can be proved neither by itself nor by anything else; it turns out to be a superimposition on the pure Self. Thus the falsity of the world is a proved fact.[2]

Again, there can be no relation between the self-revealing consciousness which is the ultimate knower (*dṛk*) and the object known (*dṛshya*). An object of knowledge turns out to be neither real nor unreal, like an illusory object. The subject-object relation is due to *avidyā* and the object can be explained only as superimposed on the subject. Hence, the self-revealing subject alone is real and it transcends the subject-object duality. The subject can never be related to the object. Chitsukha stresses that though the world is false, it is not absolutely unreal like the hare's horn. The world is false only when the Absolute is realised. Till then, it is true for all practical purposes. Chitsukha admits the similarity of the Buddhist *samvṛti-satya* with the Vedāntic *vyavahāra-satya* and defends the former against the attacks of Kumārila Bhaṭṭa. Kumārila criticises the distinction between the empirical and the ultimate truth. He says that samvṛti or empirical truth is no truth at all. If samvṛti is true, how can it be later set aside? And if it is false, how can it be treated as truth? Chitsukha's reply is that samvṛti is falsity which on account of ignorance is mistaken as truth. But as long as we are on the empirical plane, the workable truth of samvṛti cannot be questioned.[3]

We have seen above that Shrīharṣa employs negative dialectic which very much resembles the Mādhyamika dialectic of Nāgārjuna

---

1. vyāvahārikīm pramāṇādisattām ādāya vichārārambhah. *Khaṇḍana*, p. 10.
   yo hi sarvam anirvachanīyasadasattvam brūte sa katham anirvachanīyatāsattva-vyavasthitau paryanuyujyeta. *Ibid.*, pp. 32–3.
   tataḥ parakīyarītyedam uchyate anirvachaniyatvam vishvasya paryavasyatīti. vastutastu vayam..... svataḥsiddhe chidātmani Brahmatattve kevale.... sukham āsmahe. *Ibid.*, pp. 33-34.
   Compare with the arguments of Chandrakīrti on pp. supra. 60-61.
2. dṛshyaprapañchasya svataḥ parataḥ chāsiddher dṛgātmanyadhyastatayaiva siddhir iti siddham mithyātvam. *Tattvapradīpikā*, p. 32.
3. idamapyapāstam yadāhur Bhaṭṭāchāryāḥ 'Samvṛter natu satyatvam satyabhedaḥ kutonvayam l satyā chet samvṛtiḥ keyam mṛṣā chet satyatā katham ll' iti. vastuto'-satyasyaiva yāvad bādham.... satyatvena svīkārāt. *Ibid.*, pp. 42-3.

and Chandrakīrti. Shrīharṣa himself admits the similarity between the two. He frankly says that the Mādhyamika 'shūnya' is not pure negation, but it means 'relative', because it is indescribable either as real or unreal or both. Shūnyavāda condemns thought as relational and its categories as fraught with inherent contradictions. This Mādhyamika view, says Shrīharṣa, cannot be refuted because so far as the world is concerned, it is the same as that of the Advaitin himself.[1] Shrīharṣa openly declares that as both Shūnyavāda and Advaita Vedānta take all objects of thought as indefinable either as real or as unreal or as both and believe that the categories of thought are relational and fraught with inherent contradictions, the criticisms directed by both against all world-objects are valid against all views of all systems without any hindrance.[2] Shrīharṣa then points out the fundamental difference between Buddhist Shūnyavāda and Advaita Vedānta. Shūnyavāda, he says, regards everything including even consciousness to be indefinable either as real or as unreal and therefore relational and false; as Buddha has declared in the *Laṅkāvatāra* (II, 175): All things which can be known as objects by thought have no reality of their own. They are therefore said to be indescribable (either as real or unreal or both) and so relational and false. But Vedānta makes an exception in favour of consciousness and the Brahmavādins declare everything except pure consciousness as indescribable and false.[3] For Vedānta, says Shrīharṣa, consciousness is pure, eternal, non-dual, self-shining and self-proved and is the undeniable foundational Reality.[4] He also says that the momentary vijñāna (of the Vijñānavādī Buddhist) cannot be treated as self-luminous because it is known as an object by the pure Self which alone is the self-luminous Reality. Advaita Vedānta alone, says Shrīharṣa, can be called Svaprakāsha-Vijñānavāda which up-

1. Mādhyamikādivāgvyavahārāṇam svarūpāpalāpo na shakyate. *Khaṇḍana*, p. 21.
2. yadi shūnyavādānirvachaniyapakṣayor āshrayaṇam tadā tāvad amūṣām khaṇḍanayuktīnām nirbādhaiva sārvapathīnatā. *Ibid.*, p. 61.
3. Saugata-Brahmavādinor ayam visheṣaḥ yad ādimaḥ sarvamevānirvachanīyam varṇayati, taduktam Bhagavatā Laṅkāvatāre: buddhyā vivichyamānānām svabhāvo nāvadhāryate | ato nirabhilapyāste niḥsvabhāvāshcha deshitāḥ || iti; vijñānavyatiriktam punaridam vishvam sadasadbhyām vilakṣaṇam Brahmavādinaḥ saṅgirante. *Ibid.*, p. 31.
4. vijñānam tāvat svaprakāsham svata eva siddhasvarūpam. *Ibid.*, p. 21.
We know Shūnyavāda accepts Prajñā-pāramitā as the ultimate Reality. See, *supra* pp.67-8.

holds the reality of the self-shining and self-proved consciousness.

Madhva, the champion of the dvaita school of Vedānta and his follower Jaya-tīrtha have vigorously attacked the Advaitins and have been replied to by the latter with redoubled vigour. Vyāsatīrtha in his *Nyāyāmṛta* and Rāmāchārya in his *Taraṅgiṇī* commentary on it undertake a detailed refutation of advaita and try to prove the reality of the world of difference by criticising Vāchaspati, Prakāshātmā, Shrīharṣa and Chitsukha. Madhusūdana Sarasvatī in his *Advaita-siddhi* has refuted the charges of Vyāsatīrtha and the controversy between these two great dialecticians has become classic.

Madhusūdana takes up the five principal definitions of falsity (*mithyātva*) given by the Advaitins which are selected by Vyāsatīrtha for his attack and defends these by refuting the charges of Vyāsatīrtha against them:

(1) The first definition of falsity is given by Padmapāda in his *Pañchapādikā* and runs thus: 'Falsity is the indescribability either as being or as non-being.'[1] Vyāsatīrtha, like Rāmānuja against *avidyā*, says that as being and non-being are contradictories, which are exclusive and exhaustive, there can be no third alternative and therefore both cannot be denied. Everything must necessarily be either being or non-being. The denial of both is against the Law of Excluded Middle and also against the Law of Contradiction.[2] Again, 'different from being' means 'non-being' and 'different from non-being' means 'being'; so 'different from being and non-being' means 'both being and non-being' which is admitted to be self-contradictory by the Advaitin himself.

Madhusūdana replies that being and non-being are not exhaustive as these are used by us in their absolute sense and between the two is the third alternative, 'the relative being' to which belong the entire world-objects. So the Law of Excluded Middle is not violated. Again, as being and non-being belong to different orders of reality, there is no contradiction in their simultaneous affirmation or simultaneous denial. Moreover, non-contradiction is admitted as the test of truth and that which is contradicted is said to be false, so the Law of Contradiction is maintained in tact.

---

1. mithyāshabdo'nirvachanīyatāvachanaḥ. sadasadvilakṣaṇatvam anirvachanīyatvam. sattvānyattvābhyām anirvachanīyatvam mithyātvam.
2. For Rāmānuja's similar objections and their reply, see *supra*, pp. 229-31.

(2) The second definition of falsity is given by Prakāshātmā in Vivaraṇa which runs thus: 'Falsity is the counter-entity of an absolute negation with regard to the substratum in which it is cognised.'[1] This means 'falsity is that which can be denied at all times even where it appears to exist'. Vyāsatīrtha objects that if falsity is true, then non-dualism of Brahma will vanish; and if falsity is false, then the world will be true.[2] Again, appearances are said to be 'real' as long as they appear. Now, if they are denied even at the time of perception, then they are absolute non-being like the hare's horn. Again, the falsity of the world is also treated as false. Thus the falsity of the falsity of the world leads to the affirmation of the reality of the world.

Madhusūdana Sarasvatī refutes all these objections. To the objection that if falsity is true, then non-dualism of Brahma will vanish, Madhusūdana replies that falsity is not true for it is set aside by knowledge and therefore non-dualism of Brahma is not destroyed. Moreover, as the world-appearance and its falsity are simultaneously removed by the same Brahma-knowledge, non-dualism remains in tact. And as falsity is not absolute unreality but only apparent reality, its falsity does not make the world real. To the objection that the falsity of the falsity of the world does lead to the affirmation of the reality of the world, Madhusūdana replies that negation of negation in all cases does not mean reaffirmation. Negation of negation leads to affirmation only in those cases where the thing negated and the negation enjoy the same status and have identically the same scope. But when a negation negates both the thing and its negation, then negation of negation does not lead to affirmation.[3] True negation is always a cancellation of illusion. Only the apparent can be negated and that which is negated must be false, for the real can never be negated. Negation is rooted in the real which is the negation of that negation and in itself is positive. If the object negated and its negation remain in the same ground, then negation of negation does not re-instate the object negated but only the ground

1. pratipannopādhau traikālikaniṣedhapratiyogitvam.
2. mithyātvam yadyabādhyam syāt syādadvaitamata-kṣatiḥ l mithyātvam yadi bādhyam syājjagat-satyatvam āpatet ll *Nyāyāmṛta*, p. 47.
3. yatra tu pratiyogi-niṣedhayor apyubhayor niṣedhastatra na pratiyogisattvam. *Advaitasiddhi*, pp. 105-6.

on which negation rests. Negation of world-appearance is identical with its ground Brahma, and therefore the negation of this negation does not re-instate the world, but reaffirms only Brahma, the ground-reality.[1]

To the objection that if world-appearances are denied even at the time of perception then they are absolutely unreal like the hare's horn, Madhusūdana replies that though ultimately the indescribable world-appearance (*anirvachanīya*) and the hare's horn (*tuchchha*) are equally unreal, yet, empirically these two must be distinguished. The indescribable appearance, whether *pratibhāsa* (ordinary illusion) or *vyavahāra* (world-illusion), does appear in knowledge as 'real' and is mistaken as 'real' during perception, while the hare's horn cannot even appear in knowledge and is therefore called absolutely unreal. Moreover, appearances cannot be denied during perception when they are mistaken as 'real'; these can be denied only when their ground-reality is known and then it is realised that these did not really exist even during perception.[2]

(3) The third definition of falsity is also by Prakāshātmā which runs thus: 'Falsity is that which though beginningless and positive is sublated by right knowledge.'[3] Vyāsatīrtha objects that appearance or illusion cannot be beginningless nor can it be positive nor can the world be sublated by knowledge. Illusion is due to defects in the causes of knowledge and so knowledge sublates the non-existent thing. But the world is neither non-existent nor is its knowledge due to any defects. Hence it cannot be sublated by knowledge.

Madhusūdana replies that though *avidyā* is neither positive nor negative, it is called 'positive' because it is not merely negative as it is generally mistaken to be. As Vyāsatīrtha himself admits that it is only the appearance of the non-existent 'shell-silver' as the existent 'silver' that is sublated, similarly the world-appearance, though ultimately unreal, is taken as 'real' during empirical life

1. prapañcha-niṣedhādhikaraṇībhūta-Brahmābhinnatvān.... mithyātva-mithyātve'pi prapañchasatyatvānupapattiḥ. *Ibid.*
2. traikālikaniṣedhapratiyogitvam yadyapi tuchchhānirvachanīyayoḥ sādhāraṇam, tathāpi kvachidapyupādhau sattvena pratītyanarhattvam atyantāsattvam, tachcha shuktirūpye prapañche cha bādhāt pūrvam nāstyeveti na tuchchhattvāpattiḥ. —*Advaitasiddhi*
3. anādi-bhāvarūpatve sati jñāna-nivartyatvam.

and is sublated by the immediate experience of Brahma, the ground on which it is super-imposed. The sublation of the illusory objects like 'shell-silver' and also the world-objects is possible only when the ground-reality (shell in the former case and Brahma in the latter case) is directly realised and not before. The world-appearance is beginningless because its locus, Brahma, is beginningless.

(4) The fourth definition of falsity is given by Chitsukha in *Tattvapradīpikā* which is as follows: 'Falsity is the counter-entity of its absolute negation located in its own substratum.'[1] Madhusūdana explains it thus: 'Falsity is the appearance in the locus of its absolute negation.'[2] Vyāsatīrtha objects that according to such definitions falsity becomes present as well as absent at the same time and in the same locus. This reveals utter self-contradictions in the Advaita position. This sweeps away all distinctions between existence and non-existence and as such even practical existence cannot be claimed for the world.[3]

Madhusūdana replies that falsity (*mithyātva*) or *avidyā* is not reality, but a self-contradictory appearance, so it is possible for it to be both present and absent in the same place and at the same time. Moreover, as has been shown before, only the apparent can be negated. Negation is rooted in the real, which is the negation of that negation and in itself is positive. Thus the apparent object and its negation are located in the same ground and the negation of this negation is identical with the ground.

(5) The fifth definition is taken from Ānandabodha's *Nyāyamakaranda* and runs as: 'Falsity is that which is different from the real.'[4] The real is defined as that which is never contradicted and Brahma alone is real in this sense.[5] The unreal is defined as absolute non-being (*tuchchha*) like the hare's horn which can never even appear in knowledge.[6] All our empirical experiences including *pratibhāsa* (illusory objects, dream-objects, etc.) and

1. svāshrayaniṣṭhātyantābhāvapratiyogitvam.
2. svātyantābhāvādhikaraṇa eva pratīyamānatvam. *Advaitasiddhi*
3. tathā sati bhāvābhāvayoruchchhinnakathā syāt iti vyāvahārikyapi vyavasthā na syāt. *Nyāyāmṛta*
4. sadviviktattvam.
5. sattvam trikālābādhyatvam, tat cha Brahmarūpatvam.
6. pratītyanarhatvam atyantāsattvam.

vyavahāra (world-objects) fall within the sphere of the indescribable either as real or as unreal (*sadasadanirvachanīya*) which is treated as false.[1] As the unreal, the absolute non-being, is below our empirical experience, it is ruled out of the above definition and the false is defined as 'different from the Real' meaning 'the apparent' including *pratibhāsa* and *vyavahāra.* This explanation rejects the objection of Vyāsatīrtha that 'different from the real' means only 'the unreal'.

Some of the other main charges levelled by the Madhvites against Advaita are the same which have been raised by Rāmānuja and Veṅkatanātha and have been replied to by the Advaitins in the same way.[2] The defence of difference and of the reality of the empirical world by the Madhvites collapses against the attacks of the Advaitins. Even Dr. S.N. Dasgupta, who is all admiration for the Madhvites and in whose opinion 'Jayatīrtha and Vyāsatīrtha present the highest dialectical skill. . . . almost unrivalled in the whole field of Indian thought'[3] has to admit that 'This defence of difference appears however, to be weak when compared with the refutations of difference by Chitsukha in his *Tattva-pradīpikā*, Nṛsimhāshrama Muni in his *Bheda-dhikkāra*, and others. . . . Vyāsatīrtha does not make any attempt squarely to meet these arguments.'[4]

1. sadasadanirvachanīyatvam.
2. see *supra*, pp. 229-34.
3. *A History of Indian Philosophy*, Vol. IV, Preface, viii.
4. *Ibid.*, pp. 179-80.

PART THREE

KĀSHMĪRA SHAIVISM

CHAPTER SEVEN

Kāshmīra Shaivism: An Exposition

I. INTRODUCTION

We have discussed above the three main systems of *advaita* or spiritual non-dualism or absolutism in India, namely, Mādhyamika, Vijñānavāda and Advaita Vedānta. We now proceed to deal with Kāshmīra Shaivism which is the fourth main system of advaita in India.

This system claims to be based on the Shaiva Āgamas, also known as Tantra, which are accorded the same authority and status as the Veda. *Shiva-sūtra* (said to have been revealed to Vasugupta by Lord Shiva himself), Vasugupta's (8th cen.) *Spanda-kārikā,* Somānanda's (9th cen.) *Shiva-dṛṣṭi,* Utpaladeva's (10th cen. 1st half) *Pratyabhijñā-kārikā,* Abhinavagupta's (10th cen. 2nd half) *Pratyabhijñāvimarshinī, Paramārtha-sāra* and *Tantrāloka,* and his disciple Kṣemarāja's (10th-11th cen.) *Shiva-sūtra-vimarshinī* and *Spanda-sandoha*—are some of the most important works of this system which has a voluminous literature.

Kāshmīra Shaivism is also known as Pratyabhijñā or Spanda or Trika system. It is also called Īshvarādvaya-vāda or Shivādvaita, as Īshvara or Shiva is the only reality in this system. Pratyabhijñā or recognition which is treated as immediate awareness and which leads to *mokṣa* and is also identical with it is a key-concept of this school from which it derives its name. Spanda, also called Kriyā, which for want of a better word may be translated into English as 'spontaneous vibration or activity' and which is treated as entirely different from Karma or action, ethical or mechanical, is another key-concept of this school from which it derives its another name. We shall explain these concepts later on. It is also called Trika because it believes in three triads, higher (*para*), combined (*parāpara*) and lower (*apara*). The higher triad is that of Shiva, Shakti and their Union. The combined is of will, knowledge and activity. And the last is of Shiva, Shakti and Nara. Shiva is the supreme Self, Shakti is His Will-Power, inherent in and non-different from Him and Nara is the manifested universe of individual souls and objective world. In the Gītā (XV, 16-18) these are called *Puruṣottama, Akṣara puruṣa* and *Kṣara puruṣa* respectively. This system also deals with the triad of *Pati* (Shiva), *Pashu* (individual soul) and Pāsha (the binding string).

This system attempts a synthesis of Vijñānavāda Buddhism and Advaita Vedānta, while accepting the realism of Sāṅkhya with some modifications and fusing it with the theology of the Shaiva Āgamas. Its main aim is to emphasise the transcendental unity of the Self without losing its creative and synthetic character and without compromising with the reality of the manifested universe.

II. THE UNION OF SHIVA-SHAKTI

The key-principle of this system which constitutes its unique and distinctive feature is the perfect union (*sāmarasya*) of Shiva and Shakti. Shiva is the only reality, the one without a second. He is the absolute Self or infinite pure consciousness. He is the foundation of all knowledge and all proof, disproof, doubt or denial presuppose His existence. He is indeterminate (*nirvikalpa*) and immediate (*aparokṣa* or *anya-nirapekṣa*) consciousness which is beyond sense, thought and language. As transcendental He is the Supreme (*anuttara*) and beyond the universe (*vishvottīrṇa*). He is also immanent (*vishvātmaka*) in the universe manifested by Him. He is the eternal light (*prakāsha*), the self-shining pure consciousness (*chit*). He is one with His own eternal and inherent Power called Shakti. Shakti is Shiva's own power of self-consciousness or will-consciousness (vimarsha). This system, unlike Advaita Vedānta, believes that pure consciousness (*prakāsha*) is at once self-consciousness (*chit-shakti*) or free will (*vimarsha*) in which there is complete synthesis of the subject and the object. Shiva, through His own inherent Shakti, realises Himself as the self-shining infinite self-consciousness; without *shakti*, He would not be conscious even of His own eternal consciousness.[1] *Chit* or pure con-

1. Shivaḥ Shaktyāyukto yadi bhavati shaktaḥ prabhavitum | na chedevam devo na khalu kushalaḥ spanditum api ||

sciousness or immediate awareness is always pure self-consciousness or *chit-shakti.* Shakti is Shiva's own power of self-consciousness or pure will (*vimarsha*) which is at once His own power of absolute freedom (*svātantrya*) and infinite bliss (*ānanda*). Shakti is *vimarsha* which is spontaneous vibration (*spanda*) or activity (*kriyā*). This is Shiva's perfect self-consciousness called '*pūrṇāhantā*' or absolute I-ness or '*aham-vimarsha*', the pure 'I am', which is at once Shiva's awareness of His own absolute freedom (*svātantrya*) and infinite bliss (*ānanda*) and the fullness of His glory (*aishvarya*). As Shiva and Shakti are one and the same, so *prakāsha* (self-luminosity of consciousness) and *vimarsha* (spontaneous vibration of self-consciousness) are also one and the same. Similarly, *chit-shakti* (spontaneous vibration of self-luminous self-consciousness) and *ānanda-shakti* (power of absolute freedom and bliss), though distinguished as two aspects of *Shakti*, are really one and the same, because *ānanda* or bliss is the awareness of the spontaneous inner activity of consciousness and cannot be experienced without self-consciousness. *Chit* and *ānanda* constitute the *svarūpa-shakti* of Shiva. Pūrṇāhantā (perfect I-ness) or Aham-vimarsha (the pure 'I am') is the essential nature of Shiva, the absolute Self, and is therefore eternal. As consciousness is essentially self-active, the spontaneous and free vibration (*spanda*) or throb (*sphuraṇa*) or energy (*sphurattā*) or activity (*kriyā*) or inward flow of consciousness eternally goes on as the awareness of Shiva of His infinite consciousness, absolute freedom and eternal bliss. This activity is absolutely free, natural, effortless, indeterminate and unmotivated and is for the sheer joy of it. It is the activity of the pure subject and is not related to the object or the not-self which is absorbed here in the subject. Self-consciousness here is indeterminate awareness and the will here is pure in which the desire to create the world has not yet arisen. It must be remembered that the three other aspects of Shakti (apart from *chit* and *ānanda* which constitute *svarūpa-Shakti*) known as *Ichchhā-Jñāna-Kriyā* are determinate and pertain to the creation of the world when Shiva's joy overflows outwardly as it were and may therefore be described in Vedānta-terminology as aspects of *taṭastha-Shakti.* The 'outward' flow is also within consciousness as there is nothing outside of it.

To treat pure consciousness as self-consciousness and to ascribe activity to it is in direct opposition to Advaita Vedānta which treats subject-object duality and action as due to *māyā* or *avidyā.* Kāshmīra

Shaivism says that the Absolute of Advaita Vedānta which is devoid of self-consciousness and self-activity is a static, rigid, inactive and lifeless Absolute no better than inert matter or like a physical light self-illumined but not self-conscious; and the world instead of being treated as a manifestation of Shiva's blissful self-creativity, is reduced to an illusory show of unconscious *māyā* or *avidyā*.

It is important to note that Kāshmīra Shaivism emphasises the difference between *kriyā* or spontaneous activity and *karma* or action. *Kriyā* or spanda is a key-concept of this system and is used in a special sense. *Kriyā* is the natural activity of self-consciousness out of freedom and joy. It is very much different from karma which is admitted to be an impurity (mala) leading to bondage and suffering. Action or *karma* may be physical action like locomotion, upward or downward movement, contraction or expansion, or mechanical movement or automatic action of a robot; or physiological action like heart-beats or breathing or reflex action; or voluntary ethical action in which sense alone the word *karma* is used in philosophy. *Kriyā* is different from all these actions. A voluntary ethical action involves volitional effort, is guided by some motive or purpose and suggests imperfection and leads to bondage. Kriyā, on the other hand, is spontaneous (*svataḥ-sphūrta*), natural (*svābhāvika*) and effortless (*anāyāsa*); it has no motive or purpose but flows out of sheer joy and is the awareness of perfect self-hood, absolute freedom and infinite bliss. A physical, mechanical or automatic action is unconscious and determined. *Kriyā*, on the other hand, is absolute freedom of self-consciousness. The identification of *chit* and *kriyā*, *prakāsha* and *vimarsha*, Shiva and Shakti is the unique feature of this system.

Advaita is the complete union of the two (*ekarasyam ubhayoḥ*). It means identification (*tādātmya*) or inseparability (*apṛthaktva*) of the two which appear 'two' only in thought, but in reality are one and the same like moon and moon-light. Shiva and Shakti are in complete union (*sāmarasya*); in fact they are one and the same. They are distinguishable in thought, but inseparable in reality. In art this union is represented by the image of *Ardhanārīshvara* in which the same person is presented as half-Shiva and half-Shakti, half-male and half-female. But this is only a representation in art. In reality, Shiva is fully Shakti and Shakti is fully Shiva. A better representation in art would be if the same image, viewed from one angle appears as Shiva and viewed from another angle appears as Shakti.

III. THE THIRTY-SIX TATTVAS

Kāshmīra Shaivism believes in thirty-six *tattvas* or principles of cosmic manifestation. The transcendental Self or Parama-Shiva who manifests Himself as thirty-six *tattvas* is beyond all *tattvas.* He is *tattvātītā* or *vishvottīrṇa.* Abhinavagupta calls this Absolute Reality or *Parama-tattva* as the thirty-seventh. The number of these *tattvas* is given as thirty-six on the basis of the Āgamas. The first manifestation of Parama-Shiva is Shiva-tattva or manifestation of His own nature as pure consciousness (*chit* or *samvit*), the self-shining eternal light (*prakāsha*) of the transcendental Self. The second is Shakti-tattva or manifestation of Shiva's own power of will (*vimarsha*) which is His awareness of this own infinite self-consciousness, freedom and bliss (*ānanda*). It should be noted that Shakti-tattiva, though called 'second manifestation', is manifested along with Shiva-tattva with which it is inseparably united. It should also be remembered, as explained before[1], that in Shiva-Shakti tattva, the spontaneous vibration of consciousness-force eternally goes on as the inward flow for the sheer joy of it unrelated to objectivity or to the desire to create the universe. Shiva is free to create or not to create. The desire for creation arises with the manifestation of the third tattva called the Sadāshiva-tattva. Hence, strictly speaking, the process of creation starts with the manifestation of the third Sadāshiva-tattva.[2] The reason why Shiva-Shakti tattvas are included as the first two tattvas in this list seems to be that creativity really belongs to them and they are the ground of this manifestation.

Shakti has five aspects, consciousness (*chit*), bliss (*ānanda*), will (*ichchhā*), knowledge (*jñāna*) and activity (*kriyā*). Of these the first two, *chit* and *ānanda* constitute the eternal essential nature of Shiva and are, therefore, treated as svarūpa-shakti; the other three, in their determinate sense are treated not as the essential nature of Shiva, but as dependent on His absolute freedom (*svātantrya*) and may be described in Vedānta-terminology as *taṭastha-shakti.* In this system the word *chit* or consciousness is used in the sense of indeterminate and

1. *Supra,* pp. 250-51.
2. shrimat-sadāshivodāra-prārambham vasudhāntakaṃ *Bhāskarī,* Vol. II, p. 211. sṛṣṭikramopadeshādau prathamam uchitam tatsadākhyam tattvam *I.P. Vimarshinī,* Vol. II, p. 191.

immediate spiritual experience, which is Shiva's self-conscious awareness of His own infinite Consciousness (*chit-shakti*) and this immediate awareness is at once Shiva's direct experience of His own absolute freedom (*svātantrya*) and eternal bliss (*ānanda-shakti*). The words *ichchhā* (will), *jñāna* (knowledge) and *kriyā* (activity) are generally used in their determinate and relative sense in relation to subject-object duality and creation of the universe and in this sense these depend on Shiva's absolute freedom and are not treated as his *svarūpa* or essential eternal nature. But they are also used in their absolute sense in which they are one with *chit-shakti*. *Ichchhā* as pure desireless will, *jñāna* as indeterminate awareness and *kriyā* as spontaneous and eternal vibration of self-consciousness (*aham-vimarsha*) are identical with *chit*.

It should be clearly noted that *aham-vimarsha* (the pure 'I am') of Shiva is immediate awareness of His infinite consciousness, absolute freedom and eternal bliss (*chidānanda*), is His *svarūpa* or essential nature and eternally goes on irrespective of the fact whether there is creation or no creation. This spontaneous vibration (*spanda*) or free natural activity (*kriyā*) is the eternal inward joyful flow (*antarunmeṣa*) of consciousness.

Sisṛkṣā or the will to create the universe which starts with the manifestation of the third Sadāshiva tattva is not Shiva's essential nature (*svarūpa*), because it depends on His absolute freedom. He is free to create or not to create or withdraw creation within Himself. He does not always create. When the will to create the universe arises in Shiva, Consciousness starts to flow outwardly also (*bahirunmeṣa*) in excessive joy and the process of creation begins. The outward flow is also within consciousness. When He so desires He withdraws the created universe (*nimeṣa*) within Himself. Spanda or *kriyā* flowing inwardly or outwardly is spontaneous, free, natural, effortless and unmotivated and is for the sheer joy of it. Creation is natural in the sense that it emanates from His free will (which is His essential nature) though it does not constitute His essential nature as He is not bound to create. This also explains that the performance of the five functions (*pañcha-kṛtya*) reserved for Shiva depends on His absolute freedom and does not constitute His essential nature. These five functions are (1) creation (*sṛṣṭi*), (2) sustenance (*sthiti*), (3) dissolution (*samhāra*), (4) Concealing Himself by withdrawal of His Grace (*nigraha* or *vilaya*) and (5) Revealing Himself through His Grace (*anugraha*). These are said to be 'natural' for Shiva in the sense that they proceed from His spontaneous activity (spanda or *kriyā*) out of His own free will.

Aham-vimarsha is the eternal inward joyful flow of consciousness, while creation is *Ahamidam-vimarsha* in which consciousness overflows outwardly out of sheer joy. The former is represented in art as the smile of Lord Shiva in *shāmbhavī mudrā,* while the latter as the joyful cosmic dance of Naṭarāja. Creation is "the ecstatic dance of Shiva; .... its sole absolute object is the joy of the dancing."

We now present a brief exposition of the thirty-six *tattvas* or principles of cosmic manifestation admitted in this system. The first two *tattvas* have been explained above. In *Shiva-tattva* self-luminous (*svaprakāsharūpā*) self-consciousness (*chit-shakti*) dominates and the experience is of the perfect 'I' (*aham*) or *pūrṇāhantā.* In *Shakti-tattva* absolute freedom (*svātantrya*) and bliss (*ānanda-shakti*) dominate and the experience is of the pure 'I am' (*ahamasmi*) which is the same as *pūrṇāhantā.* In the third *Sadāshiva-tattva* will to create (*ichchhā-shakti*) dominates and the experience is of 'I am this' (*aham idam*) with an emphasis on the 'I' (*aham-amsha*). Here the object remains subdued. The fourth is the *Īshvara-tattva* where determinate knowledge (*jñāna-shakti*) dominates and the experience is of '*This is* I' (*idam aham*) with an emphasis on the 'this' (*idam-amsha*). The object here is explicit and dominant (*bahirunmeṣa*). The fifth is the *Shuddha-Vidyā-tattva* where activity (*kriyā shakti*) dominates which is the power of manifestation. Here the experience is of 'I and this' (*aham cha idam cha*) where both are held in even balance. It is a state of bhedābheda because 'I' (*ahantā*) and 'this' (*idantā*) are known separately and yet both are realised as one with consciousness (*chidrūpa*). These five tattvas are called transcendental and are manifested by the five aspects of *shakti* respectively. Their manifestation is called 'pure creation' or '*shuddha sṛṣṭi* or *addhvā*' because in them the object is realised as one with the subject and the unity with Shiva is always experienced.

The manifestation of the remaining thirty-one *tattvas* from *māyā* to *pṛthvī* is called 'impure creation' (ashuddha *sṛṣṭi* or *addhvā*). The first manifestation of impure creation is *Māyā-tattva* which is sixth in the list. It is the principle of externality (*bāhyatā*) and difference (*bheda-pratīti*) because the object here is taken as different from the subject. It is the power of obscuration (*moha*) because it acts as a veil (*āvaraṇa*) on the unity of the Self. It is the root cause of all limitation (*parichchheda*). It is pervasive (*vyāpaka*) and subtle (*sūkṣma*) and is the cause of the manifestation of all sentient individual *jīvas* and insentient material objects. It is that aspect of *Shakti* which makes the infinite appear as finite. It gives rise to five 'coverings' (*kañchuka*) called power (*kalā*), knowledge (*vidyā*), attachment (*rāga*), time (*kāla*) and space (*niyati*), which obscure respectively free creativity, omniscience, desirelessness or joy, eternality and freedom or pervasiveness of the 'self' and which figure as seventh to eleventh *tattvas.* The infinite Shiva, due to these coverings, appears as the finite self or *Puruṣa* which is the twelfth *tattva.* The remaining twenty-four *tattvas* are *Prakṛti,* the thirteenth *tattva* and its twenty-three evolutes recognised in the Sāṅkhya system, which are Mahaṭ or Buddhi (14th), Ahaṅkāra (15th), Mānas (16th), five sensory organs (17th to 21st), five motor organs (22nd to 26th) five tan-mātras (27th to 31st) and five gross elements (32nd to 36th tattvas).

IV. ĀBHĀSAVĀDA

Shiva, the supreme Self is not only pure consciousness (*prakāsha*) but also free will (*vimarsha*). The Self is pure subject (*jñatā*) as well as free creator (*kartā*). In His Will (*ichchhā*), knowledge (*jñāna*) and activity (*kriyā*) stand united. His knowledge is activity and His activity is knowledge. By His free will He manifests Himself as this Universe. The changing manifestations do not in the least stain His purity and unchanging nature because He also transcends them. He is at once transcendent (*vishottīrṇa*) and immanent (*vishvātmaka*). In His immanent aspect He is called 'pure and free consciousness' (*prakāsha-vimarsha-maya*) because on the transcendental background of His pure consciousness He manifests, by His free will-power, the entire universe. The manifested universe is within Him and is one with Him. There is no other material (*upādāna*), ground (*ādhāra*) or canvas (*bhitti*) on which it is projected.[1] All manifestations are by Him, on Him and in Him. He is all-embracing, all-inclusive; nothing falls outside Him. Consciousness-Force, self-luminous and self-creative, is the essen-

1. anupādānasambhāram abhittāveva tanvate |
jagachchitram namastasmai kalānāthāya shūline || —Vasugupta

tial nature of the Self. It is described in this system as Self-consciousness (*chit-shakti*), Will-consciousness (*vimarsha*), perfect freedom (*svātantrya*), infinite bliss (*ānanda*), supreme power (*aishvarya*), perfect self-hood or I-ness (*purṇāhanta*) and vibration (*spanda*), throb (*sphuraṇa*), energy (*sphurattā*) or activity (*kriyā*) of consciousness.

To take the Self as pure consciousness or eternal light without any power of self-consciousness or will, as is done in Advaita Vedānta, says Kāshmīra Shaivism, is to reduce it to mere nothing (*shūnya*). To deny free self-creativity of consciousness is to miss the essence of it. Will-consciousness or the free creative power of the Self cannot be attributed to *avidyā* and dismissed as false (*mithyā*). Everything is a real manifestation of Shiva and therefore nothing can be said to be false. There can be no subject and no object other than Shiva, the Supreme Self. The Vedānta unity is purely formal and abstract and therefore unreal. Even the denial of duality presupposes its existence. The real unity is the complete harmony (*sāmarasya*) between the two, where the two are fused into one. Non-duality consists in a perfect union of the two (*ekarasyamubhayoḥ*). The subject and the object are held in complete synthesis in self-consciousness. Truth does not lie in the elimination of the object, but in its synthesis with the subject. Shiva and Shakti are in perfect and eternal union. Shakti is the Consciousness-force (*chit-shakti*) of Shiva and is one with Him. The entire manifested universe is non-different from the manifesting Self. This is true advaita. When the object is mistaken as outside of (*bāhya*) or external to or independent of the projecting universal consciousness, error creeps in. All difference is false as there can be nothing different from the Supreme Self who manifests everything within Himself. The manifested universe is neither a real modification (*pariṇāma*) nor a modification without change (*avikṛta-pariṇāma*) nor a false appearance (*vivarta*) of the Self. The Self cannot undergo modification for it cannot change its nature; modification without change is impossible; nor can its projections be treated as unreal show for they are due to His real self-creative power. They are called 'manifestations' (*ābhāsa*) and as projection of the Will-power of the Self are real within Him and are one with Him; the falsity lies in mistaking them to be external to and different from Him. In Advaita Vedānta, the word *ābhāsa* is frequently used in the sense of unreal appearance (*vivarta*), but in this system it is used in the sense of real manifestation. *Avidyā* or *māyā* in this system is not total absence of knowledge nor is it a baseless illusion, nor can it be something indescribable either as real or as unreal, nor can it be the stuff appearances are made of, nor can it be dismissed as false. *Avidyā* is only imperfect knowledge and *māyā* is the real power of the Supreme which makes the One appear as many and which generates the notion of difference and limitation. Hence it must be admitted that the Supreme manifests everything within Him through His own power of free will.

The essence of the Self lies in its creative self-consciousness. Even the finite self, in its limited way, feels itself a real knower, agent and enjoyer. Consciousness is creative, not neutral or indifferent (upekṣārūpa). As self-luminous, the self may be called the substance of its attributes, modes, forms and impressions. In this aspect it may be compared to a mirror which is the substratum of the images reflected in it, with this difference that a mirror being an object needs external light to reflect images in it, but the self being self-luminous needs no illumination from any external source. Besides its self-luminous (*prakāsha*) aspect in which it may be conceived as a spiritual substance, the self has another distinctive character of self-consciousness (*vimarsha*) in which it manifests itself as a synthesising subject in knowledge and as a free creative subject in erroneous and dream experience and in literature, art, morality, religion and philosophy. The self has a power to create its objects in error and dream and in imagination and to know them as objective. The powers of the self are limited due to its finitude. The *yogis*, through their yogic powers, create objects by sheer force of will. Similarly Shiva, the supreme Self, through His unlimited will power, projects on the background of His infinite consciousness, this entire universe which, like an image reflected in a mirror (*darpaṇa-pratibimba-bhāva*) is within Him but appears as though it were different from Him. Through his power of differentiation (*apohana-shakti*) and power of obscuration and limitation (*māyā-shakti*), the manifested universe appears as if it were external to and different from His consciousness. Everything which is an object of perception or conception or imagination is a 'manifestation of consciousness' (*ābhāsa*). The empirical world of individual subjects and external objects is nothing but a manifestation of Supreme Self and is within Him. The manifested object does not differ from the manifesting consciousness, nor does the manifesting consciousness differ from the manifested object; nor does a finite self differ from another; nor does an object differ from another. These apparant differences are due to *apohana-shakti* and *māyā-shakti* of the Supreme Self. In fact, every manifestation is within and is identical with Shiva. The Supreme is absolutely free to conceal Himself or to reveal Himself.

V. BANDHA, MOKṢA AND PRATYABHIJÑĀ

Ignorance (*ajñāna*) is admitted to be the cause of bondage. Ignorance is not total absence of knowledge, but only imperfect knowledge. This basic ignorance is not intellectual (*bauddha*), but innate (*pauruṣa*) and is called the 'innate impurity' (*āṇava-mala*). It is beginningless (*anādi*), though removable. It conceals the real nature of the self and leads to its supposed imperfection and limitation.[1] It is consciousness of the individual self of its supposed finitude and limitation (*apūrṇammanyatārūpam ajñānam*). The innate impurity of the finite self is twofold. Its free will-power is obscured by *māyā* and it is also ignorant of the fact that this perfect freedom, obscured for the time being, really belongs to it. This basic ignorance leads to the impurity of *Karma* (*karma-mala*) which, in turn, gives rise to the impurity of transmigration (*māyīya-mala*). These three impurities (*malas*) constitute the fetters (*pāsha*) of the individual self (*pashu*) and are responsible for its degradation (*pashutva*). This is *Bandha* or bondage of the individual self which really is Shiva Himself under self-limitation.

Mokṣa or liberation is knowledge of the union of the finite self with Shiva or the Infinite Self. This unity was missed by the self in its supposed finitude; now it is realised. The beginningless innate Ignorance (*āṇava-mala*) is destroyed in both of its aspects and consequently both the *veil* (*āvaraṇa*) of *māyā* obscuring the perfect power of will, as well as the *ignorance* of this perfect freedom as the own innate nature of the self, vanish and the imaginary distinction between the individual and the Supreme Self is removed. *Mokṣa* is the immediate knowledge (*pauruṣa-jñāna*) of the perfect purity of consciousness. It is the realisation of the true nature of the self as perfect freedom (*svātantrya*). *Mokṣa* is

1. malam ajñānam ichchhanti samsārāṅkurakāraṇam I *Tantrāloka*, I-23.

not a new acquisition and involves no change in status; it is not a thing one has to obtain or regain, nor is it a place where one has to go; *Mokṣa* is simply the realisation of the self's own nature as perfect freedom on removal of innate Ignorance (*pauruṣa-ajñāna*). The rising of *pauruṣa-jñāna* or immediate self-realisation by itself, unrelated to anything else, leads to *Mokṣa.*[1] The transcendental 'I' (*prakāsha*) is also the pure 'I am' (*vimarsha*). Pure being is pure consciousness which is self-conscious bliss and perfect freedom of will. *Mokṣa* is the realisation of this perfect I-ness (*pūrṇāhantā*). It is the realisation of the one-ness with Shiva. The Upanisadic saying 'All this is Brahma' is actually experienced in *mokṣa.* It is an all-embracing experience where everything is seen in its true nature as non-different from Shiva, the supreme-Self;[2] where absolute freedom and infinite bliss of pure self-consciousness is eternally enjoyed. Jīvanmukti is admitted and the person who has this self-realisation is liberated here and now. He realises himself as Shiva and sees everything as the projection of his own glory and as non-different from the Self.[3]

This self-realisation is called self-recognition, Pratyabhijñā,[4] a name which this system bears. Recognition is different from both memory (*smṛti*) and cognition (*pratyakṣa-jñāna*) and involves a union of both. Memory arises due to mental impressions alone (*samskāra-janya*). In perception the object may be perceived and cognised, but may not be recognised. In recognition the mental impression is invariably coupled with the direct perception of the object. The novelty of recognition consists in identifying the object, now perceived, with that seen or known before. In recognition the emphasis is on the intuitive awareness of the identity of the substance which persists through its two states (*ubhayoḥ sāmarasyam*).

---

1. pauruṣam punar jñānam uditam sat anyanirapekṣam eva mokṣa-kāraṇam. *Tantrāloka,* I-24.
2. akhilam abhedenaiva sphurati.
3. sarvo mamāyam vibhava ityevam parijānataḥ | vishvātmano vikalpānām prasare'-pi maheshatā || —*Īshvara-pratyabhijña* IV-1-12.
4. In pratyabhijñā, four things are required:

   (1) The object recognized should have been seen or known before. (2) It should be now directly perceived. (3) Its memory-image in the form of mental impressions should be revived now. And, (4) Identification of the object seen or known before with the object perceived now which leads to intuitive awareness of the identity of the object.

Intellectual knowledge (*bauddha jñāna*), which includes perceptual knowledge, may remove the veil covering the object and consequently the object may be perceived or known, yet the ignorance about the real nature of the object may continue in the form of an imaginary distinction between the object now perceived and the object which we desired to perceive. This latter ignorance in the form of an imaginary distinction between the two can be removed only by immediate spiritual awareness (*pauruṣa-jñāna*) or intuitive knowledge (*prātibha-jñāna*) which leads to *pratyabhijñā* or recognition in the form of identification of the two. This is illustrated with the example of a love-sick lady: A lady, on hearing of many good qualities of a particular man, falls in love with him without even seeing him. Unable to bear her lovesickness, she writes a love-letter requesting him to visit her and sends it through her friend. He comes to her. When she sees him she does not recognise those good qualities in him and taking him to be an ordinary man, she finds no consolation or joy. But when her friend tells her that he is the same person, she recognises him and becomes all joy. This will also apply to other cases, where, for example, a known lover or husband comes *in cognito* to his beloved or wife who perceives him but (mis)takes him as someone else, and who, later on, recognises him and becomes joyful. These examples prove that there can be no joy without recognition. Similarly, even if the finite self knows about the qualities of the Supreme Self and is always perceiving His manifestations which are really one with Him does not get liberation unless he recognises his self as Supreme by removing the ignorance responsible for the imaginary distinction and by thus identifying himself with the Supreme Self. This is also the meaning of the famous Upanisadic saying 'That thou art' (*tat tvam asi*). The individual self recognises himself as one with the Supreme Self. Recognition is immediate realisation and at once overcomes bondage. It is the same as *aparokṣānubhūti* in Vedānta. Intellectual knowledge may remove the veil on the object; in the above examples the beloved person, whether seen or known before, is now present before the lady and is perceived by her, but not recognised. This intellectual knowledge has to be transformed into immediate awareness (*pauruṣa-jñāna*) or recognition (*pratyabhijñā*) in order to remove the innate Ignorance (*pauruṣa-ajñāna* or *āṇavamala*) in the form of imaginary distinction between the two phases of the same object and bring about their identification. This immediate awareness may be generated by the spiritual instruction (*dīkṣā*) imparted by the teacher or by the word of the Sacred Text (*shāstra-vākya*), as in the former example cited above, by the word from the friend of the lady. Or, it may be generated by the vision or the intuition of the person concerned (*pauruṣa* or *prātibha-jñāna*) as in the latter example given above by the vision of the lady herself. Ultimately however, this spiritual experience dawns by the will of the Supreme, by His Grace (*anugraha* or *shaktipāta*). He reveals Himself to him whom He chooses.[1]

1. yamevaiṣa vṛṇute tena labhyaḥ. Kaṭha Up. I-2-22.

CHAPTER EIGHT

Kāshmīra Shaivism: A Critical Estimate

I. THE UNITY AND CREATIVITY OF THE ABSOLUTE

The charge of Kāshmīra Shaivism against Advaita Vedānta that its Brahma is abstract, formal and inactive and therefore is as good as 'nothing' is incorrect. On the other hand, the truth is that the Shaiva conception of unity as 'union of the two' falls short of the transcendental unity and is not the true 'advaita'. Advaita is not afraid, as this system imagines, of duality, for really there is no duality and Advaita is not troubled by illusion and hallucination. The transcendental unity in Advaita Vedānta is above the thought-forms of unity and duality. Real unity cannot be 'union of the two', for if the two are equals they are two independent reals which cannot be related; and if one of the two is primary and the other secondary, this dependent 'other' will be found to be dispensable and will glide away into the principal which alone can be called real. It is Kāshmīra Shaivism which is afraid of losing the finite self and its world and therefore wants to retain them in some form even in the Absolute. If Shiva is the Supreme Self, the pure Subject, how can He be the unity of subject and object? No trace of the object can be ultimately retained in the subject. If this supposed 'unity', this 'union of subject and object' is the subject, there can be no objectivity in it; and if it is an object, it cannot be the unity of subject and object. To describe the unity of the Self as the unity of subject and object, as the union of Shiva and Shakti, of knowledge and activity, where everything is retained and seen in a new light, where an all-embracing wonderful experience shines, where there is self-conscious experience of being and bliss may represent a grand achievement of thought, but does not point to ultimate reality; it may be good poetry, but it is not sound philosophy. It may satisfy our religious instinct, but it does not resist dialectical scrutiny. Objectivity, duality and attachment are due to transcendental Illusion. To try to retain them in the Absolute is an impossibility. It reflects our attachment to the 'I' and the 'mine' and is Ignorance *par excellence.* To pretend to give up attachment to this world, but to carry the load of the 'I' and the 'mine' into the Absolute is, as Nāgārjuna says, the greatest attachment (*mahā-graha*).[1] Even great yogis, as Gauḍapāda observes, are troubled by this basic Ignorance and tremble at the thought of losing their personality in the Absolute, imagining fear even in the fearless goal (abhaye bhayadarshinaḥ).[2]

Kāshmīra Shaivism is right in saying that the ultimate reality is the Supreme Self, the transcendental Subject, which is pure consciousness, immediate and indeterminate awareness, self-shining eternal light (*prakāsha*). But it is wrong in believing that this pure consciousness is, at the same time, self-consciousness (*vimarsha*). *Prakāsha* or pure consciousness and *vimarsha* or self-consciousness or will cannot be identified. Self-consciousness involves subject-object duality and objectivity cannot belong to the Self. It need not be argued that in self-consciousness the self itself is both the subject and the object, for the pure Self can never be an object, not even for itself. Again, to say that the object here is pure and that it is not explicitly enjoyed, but implicitly contained in the subject will not save the situation, for no object can be pure and even if it is implicit the reference to it is necessarily there. Objectivity can be traced only to transcendental Illusion. Pure consciousness, due to *avidyā,* appears as self-consciousness or will. It is not the real nature or power of the Self. This system is confusing between the empirical self and the transcendental Self. In the case of the empirical self pure consciousness remains as its transcendental background and self-consciousness appears as its essence; here the subject and the object are synthesised and every empirical experience, cognitive, emotive, or conative, is based on this synthesis and necessarily refers to an object. This system wrongly imagines that what is true in the case of the empirical

1 MK., XVI-9. 2. GK., III-39.

self should also be true in the case of the transcendental Self. Hence the supposition that if the pure Self is not united with the object, it would not be even conscious of its consciousness, would not be able to enjoy its bliss and freedom and would not be able to create anything by the force of its will. So this system treats objectivity as the inherent power of the pure Self and binds the subject eternally to the object. It puts Shiva in eternal embrace of Shakti; without his Shakti or mātrā (measure) 'Shiva' would remain a mere 'Shava'(corpse). This may be true of God and His divine Consort, but not of the Absolute. This is an illegitimate imposition of the empirical nature generated by *avidyā* on the transcendental Self. Pure consciousness is self-shining and self-proved; it needs no other consciousness for its awareness, as this would lead to infinite regress. Pure consciousness is at once pure being and pure bliss. Its unity, its being and its bliss are transcendental and beyond duality. This unity is beyond the categories of unity and difference; this being is beyond the concepts of being and non-being; this bliss is beyond empirical pleasure and pain. To identify this pure consciousness with self-consciousness so that it may know, feel and will itself, is to miss its nature as transcendental Self and to involve it in *avidyā* and thereby degrade it to the level of the empirical self. Hence pure consciousness cannot be identified with self-consciousness or will; it appears as will due to its false association with *avidya. Prakāsha* is not *vimarsha,* for *prakāsha* is self-luminous pure consciousness and *vimarsha* is will-consciousness which involves objectivity (*vedyāmsha*) due to *avidyā. Vimarsha* presupposes *prakāsha,* but not *vice versa,* because *prakāsha* is the transcendental background on which *vimarsha* appears. Pure Consciousness is the transcendental subject and may be called the 'Perfect I' (*pūrṇāhantā*) provided no 'I-ness' or egohood in the sense of self-consciousness is attributed to it. The pure Self is also 'perfect freedom' (*svātantrya*) because it is the ultimate reality; it is not freedom from want or freedom of will. It is also pure bliss (*ānanda*) itself. It cannot be a self-conscious person who enjoys his freedom and bliss. Creativity of the world (*kartṛtva*) cannot be attributed to it, because all activity is due to *avidyā.* Volition (*ichchhā*), cognition (*jñāna*) and activity (*kriyā*) these three powers must be traced to *avidyā.* The pure Self, due to *avidyā,* appears as God (Īshvara), who has perfect will, knowledge and activity and also as finite selves whose will, knowledge and action are imperfect. The distinction between *chit* (pure consciousness) and *jñāna* (determinate cognition) made in this system is not justifiable, for *jñāna* really is indeterminate and identical with *chit*; determinate knowledge (*savikalpa jñāna*) is empirical and is really *ajñāna*. Out of the five aspects of Shakti, the first two may be identified with the Real, if *chit* is taken as pure consciousness and *ānanda* is taken as pure bliss; in this sense they are not 'powers' nor are they 'two'. They are one and the same and are Shiva or the Self itself. If, however, *chit* is treated as self-consciousness and *ānanda* as self-conscious enjoyment of bliss by the Self, both of these are tinged with *avidyā* and so included in 'will' and need not be mentioned separately. The remaining three aspects are clearly due to *avidyā*.

Shiva as the Supreme Self cannot be tinged with *avidyā* and therefore there can be no activity in Him. He cannot be a real creator nor can this universe be treated as His real creation. If the Supreme is perfect (*āpta-kāma*) He cannot have any will or desire to create this world, for desire presupposes imperfection. The world cannot be treated as His play (*krīḍā* or *līlā*), for He is Himself perfect bliss and need not seek any joy in creation. And as creation is not treated in this system as His essential nature, it should be taken as appearance due to *avidyā* or *māyā*.

If creation is taken as real, it would be impossible to explain the relation between the Real and its creation. The supposed relation can be neither identity nor difference nor both. If this relation were that of identity then either the Absolute will have to be degraded to phenomenon and will suffer all the imperfections and mutilations of the world, or the world will have to be treated as eternal and pure like the Absolute. And if this relation were that of difference then the two will fall apart as two 'reals' and the Absolute will not be immanent in the world. Again, any attempt to combine identity and difference, like light and darkness, is bound to fail. Hence the only relation, if it were relation at all, between the Absolute and the world can be that of 'non-difference' or 'identification' (*tādātmya*) in the sense that the world is superimposed *(adhyasta)* on the Absolute, and would not even appear without it. This 'identification' is due to *avidyā* and is, therefore, false (*mithyā*). Hence it is no relation at all; it only reveals the impossibility of any relation between the two. It makes it clear that the Absolute is the real ground on which the world is illusorily imposed, that the world appears as 'real' only as identified with its ground apart from which it cannot exist, and that the Absolute is the *reality* of the world. Kāshmīra Shaivism is aware of the difficulty in relating the Absolute with the world, for the two can be neither identical nor different nor both. It maintains, like Advaita Vedānta, that the relation between the two is 'tādātmya' or identification. But whereas for Advaita Vedānta the superimposed world is false, for Kāshmīra Shaivism the manifested world is real. But as we have pointed above, the reality of the manifested universe cannot be logically proved.

II. KĀSHMĪRA SHAIVISM AND VIJÑĀNAVĀDA BUDDHISM

Kāshmīra Shaivism agrees with Vi*jñāna*vāda Buddhism in believing that consciousness is the only reality and that it is creative. The individual subjects and the objective world are only projection of consciousness. It is consciousness alone which projects the world on itself and perceives it as objective. Error lies in our mistaking 'the forms of the objects' assumed by consciousness as 'physical material objects' external to and independent of consciousness. As consciousness is the only reality and as everything is a projection or manifestation of consciousness within itself, there can be no material or physical (*jaḍa*) objects existing out-side of consciousness as independent reals. The differences between the two systems are as follows: Kāshmīra Shaivism identifies pure consciousness with the supreme Self, the eternal self-shining light and treats it as self-consciousness and regards the supreme Self as the self-conscious Creator of this world of manifestations; while earlier Vijñānavada though it takes pure consciousness as the eternal ultimate reality, yet it refuses to treat it as essentially will-consciousness and does not identify it with the Self as the self-conscious Creator, and the later school of Vijñānavāda does not agree even to take this pure consciousness as eternal because it takes the momentary vijñāna alone as the Real. Kāshmīra Shaivism identifies self-shining consciousness (*prakāsha*) with free will (*vimarsha*), Shiva with Shakti, and the Lord with His inherent real Power which is one with Him projects the world of manifestations on Himself and within Himself; Vijñānavāda, on the other hand, traces the will-aspect of consciousness to beginningless transcendental *avidyā* or *vāsanā* which is not treated as the essential, inseparable and eternal nature or power of Vijñāna, but as transcendental ignorance removable by immediate spiritual experience. Again, in Kāshmīra Shaivism, the subject and the object are held in eternal embrace, while in Vijñānavāda the subject-object duality is due to transcendental *avidyā* or *vāsanā* which consists in the transcendental illusion of objectivity. Again, in Kāshmīra Shaivism, the object is unreal if it is treated as external to and different from Consciousness, but as a manifestation by the Self on and within Himself it is real; while in Vijñānavāda the object is treated as utterly unreal (*parikalpita*) or purely imaginary like a hare's horn or a sky-flower and is denied even empirical validity which is granted to its 'form in consciousness' (*paratantra*) and pure formless consciousness is accepted as ultimate reality (*pariniṣpanna*) which is identified with pure being and bliss and on the realisation of which both the object and its form in consciousness along with the individual subject vanish at once.

III. EVALUATION OF ĀBHĀSAVĀDA

Kāshmīra Shaivism admits that cause and effect can be neither different nor identical nor both. It discards *ārambhavāda* for causation cannot be discontinuous or emergent as cause and effect would then fall apart. It does not accept *pariṇāmavāda* for the Real cannot undergo any real change. The concept of *avikṛta-pariṇāma* or transformation without change does not appeal to it as the self-contradiction in it is patent. The Advaita concept of *vivartavāda* or appearance in the sense of an unreal show also does not appeal to it, for it takes away all reality from the world. Hence Kāshmīra Shaivism develops its own theory of causation known as '*ābhāsa-vāda*' or the theory that the effect is a real manifestation (*abhivyakti*) of the cause. The word *ābhāsa* means appearance and is frequently used in Advaita Vedānta in this sense. But Kāshmīra Shaivism wants to treat this appearance as real manifestation. Causally, it is an attempt to somehow combine the concepts of *pariṇāma* and *vivarta*; ontologically it is an attempt to fuse Vijñanavāda idealism with Vedāntic idealism.

Shiva, the absolute Self, for shear joy (*ānanda*) and sport (*līlā*), manifests the entire universe by His free will on Himself and within Himself. The projected world is His *ābhāsa* or manifestation and is real, because it is within Him and one with Him. It has been shown above that pure consciousness appears as creative will due to its apparent association with *avidyā* and when *avidyā* is removed by immediate experience, the world of manifestations disappears with it. Kāshmīra Shaivism is wrong in holding that immediate experience dispels only the false notion through which the manifested world appears as external to and different from the manifesting consciousness. This amounts to an impossible attempt to separate the form from the content of consciousness and retain the form and reject the content. Vijñānavāda also makes such an attempt but it confines it to empirical consciousness alone and treats transcendental consciousness as utterly and eternally free from subject-object duality. Kāshmīra Shaivism admits that the world appears as objective and external to consciousness to a finite self labouring under innate Ignorance, but this very world on removal of this Ignorance would continue to exist, eternally and really, within the supreme Self as one with Him. This is highly illogical, for it separates the content from the form of consciousness and rejects the content and retains the form even at the level of transcendental consciousness of the supreme Self.

The distinction between the content and the form of consciousness is made in thought, when the nature of an illusory or dream object is analysed; in fact its content and form are inseparable, so inseparable that they always appear or disappear together and are never perceived as two. Hence the attempt of Kāshmīra Shaivism to reject the world as *external* (*bāhya*) to and *different* (*bhinna*) from the pure Self, and to retain it as a real manifestation (*ābhāsa*) within the Supreme is impossible. It may be argued by the Kāshmīra Shaiva that he is not trying to make the impossible separation between the content and form of consciousness, that he also admits that to project anything is to project it as objective, and that he is not opposed to the *objectivity* of the projected, but to its *externality* to the projecting Consciousness. He may say that the projected idea or image is necessarily perceived as objective, but it need not always be perceived as something material, as something external to and different from Consciousness. Due to our innate Ignorance *(ajñāna* or *āṇava-mala)* we (mis)take the world as material (*jaḍa*), as finite (*parichchhinna*), as external (*bāhya*) to and different (*bhinna*) from the manifesting Consciousness (*chit-shakti*), but when this Ignorance is removed, this very world will be perceived in its true nature as one with Consciousness. The liberated self will realise his essential unity with the Supreme Self as well as with the manifested world. In the pure Self, there is a complete union of subject and object. The pure Self is both the subject and the object, the manifestor as well as the manifested, the perceiver and the perceived; there is nothing else except Him. As the subject-object duality is transformed into a wonderful unity in the Supreme Self, the world of diverse manifestations will be perceived as *objective,* but as one with the *Supreme.* The whole universe will be realised as manifestation by, on and within the Supreme and as non-different from Him. But all this is untenable. The Kāshmīra Shaiva is trying to make another impossible distinction between 'objectivity' and 'externality'. Externality, he too admits includes materiality (*jaḍatva*), finitude (*parichchhinnatva*) and difference (*bheda*). But he forgets that objectivity necessarily means otherness. The object is that which is different from or other than the subject. Thus objectivity means 'difference' or 'otherness' from the subject or consciousness. This difference of the object from consciousness is the fundamental difference to which all other differences among the objects may be traced. The subject or pure consciousness can never be presented as an object, not even to itself. Its indubitable certitude is implied in its self-luminosity and its being the foundation of all our experience. It is self-shining and self-proved, though never an object. The notion of objectivity is due to transcendental Illusion or *avidyā.* That which can be presented as an object is, for that very reason, something different from or other to or external to the subject, and therefore something non-consciousness or material, finite, and super-imposed on the subject; it is mere appearance and so ultimately false. To try to retain subject-object duality in any form in the pure Self is to give up its reality as foundational Consciousness.

Kāshmīra Shaivism says that *ābhāsa* is like an image reflected in a mirror. The mirror has a capacity to receive reflection and the reflected image is identical with the reflecting mirror (*darpaṇa-pratibimba-bhāva*). The self-luminous Self, unlike a mirror which is an object and therefore needs external light for reflecting images in it, reflects everything by its own light. The Supreme Self by His power of *vimarsha* projects the world on His transcendental aspect of prakāsha and the world reflected therein is one with the Self, though appearing as external through innate Ignorance. Creation is without any material cause (*upādāna*). The pure Self is perfect freedom and creates the world by the sheer force of His will without any material (*nirupādāna sṛṣṭi*). The Lord paints the multi-coloured world-picture without any canvas, brush or colour simply by His perfect will.[1] There is no original (*bimba*) to be reflected, no object to be pictured, no arche-type to be copied, nothing to be mirrored, except the Lord Himself. This means that the Lord Himself, through the force of His perfect will, projects Himself as the world of diverse manifestations on His pure Consciousness, wherein these manifestations shine as identical with Him and are perceived by Him as brought forth by His Power revealing His absolute freedom, His glory and grandeur.[2] Now, the least that can be said against this ābhāsavāda is that if there is nothing except Him, He need not indulge in this futile act of projecting Himself on Himself and perceiving His reflections as identical with Him and thereby realising His freedom and greatness. As He is pure consciousness, which is at once pure being and bliss, He does not stand in need of creation to realise His being and bliss. If He does, He would be imperfect. Hence, self-consciousness, will, creativity, etc., cannot be really attributed to the pure Self; these must be traced to *avidyā.* The pure Self, due to *avidyā,* appears as this world of plurality. As its reality, the Self is immanent in it; as its background on which it is super-imposed, the Self is transcendent to it. Hence *ābhāsa* can mean only appearance, not a real manifestation. The *ābhāsa* in Kāshmīra Shaivism, when philosophically analysed, turns out to be nothing but *adhyāsa* in disguise. If there is no other reality except the Supreme Self and if all difference is due to innate and beginningless Ignorance as Kāshmīra Shaivism itself is keen to emphasise, then the reality of the manifestations cannot be admitted. When the pure Self is realised by the removal of this innate Ignorance, the whole world of subject-object duality will vanish. It cannot be said that only the false notion of difference due to which we mistake the world as different from the Supreme on which it is projected will vanish, while the world will continue to exist within the Supreme as His real manifestation and will be perceived as non-different from Him. For, if all difference is due to Ignorance, the basic difference between the subject and the object cannot be retained in the Absolute and the manifestations cannot be perceived as objective within the Absolute. The removal of innate Ignorance will not

1. See footnote on p. 256 *supra.*
2. sarvo mamāyam vibhavaḥ.

only destroy the difference between the Absolute and the world, but also the difference among the manifestations and among the liberated selves. Hence in the Absolute, there would be no individual self to perceive and no manifested world to be perceived. The removal of innate Ignorance will at once remove all the difference and along with the externality, materiality and finitude of the world, its objectivity, its character of being manifested and the plurality of manifestations within the Absolute would vanish. The manifestated Universe (even within consciousness) is superimposed on the ground-reality of the Supreme Self as pure consciousness and its rejection leads to the reaffirmation only of its ground, i.e., pure consciousness of the Supreme Self. The individual selves and the manifested objects can be retained only as one with the pure Self. This means that the pure Self is the reality of the individual selves and of the manifested objects which are superimposed on it due to avidyā. When avidyā is destroyed, the superimposed vanish as unreal, leaving only their ground as real. Creation, projection or manifestation cannot be taken as ultimately real. Only the ground of this manifestation can be ultimately real.

Kāshmīra Shaivism is opposed to māyāvāda of Advaita Vedānta, but its '*ābhāsa*' turns out in the end as 'adhyāsa' in disguise. It says that *māyā* or *avidyā* cannot be taken as transcendental Illusion which hides the Real and projects the unreal on it. Nor can *māyā* be defined as 'indefinable either as real or as unreal or as both', for this is self-contradictory. It rejects 'anirvachanīya-khyāti' or the Vedāntic view of error as indescribable either as real or as unreal. Its theory of error is called 'apūrṇa-khyāti' which is a form of 'akhyāti', according to which error is treated as imperfect knowledge or as 'non-apprehension' and not misapprehension. But it has to admit that during illusion even the false appears in knowledge and should be treated as non-different from the projecting consciousness. Now, if the 'rope-snake' which appears in knowledge is said to be due to imperfect knowledge and is accepted as 'real' in the sense of being non-different from the projecting consciousness and as 'unreal' in the sense of being an object out there, then even the so-called real snake, by the same logic, is due to imperfect knowledge and must be rejected as unreal in the sense of being different from the universal consciousness which projects it. From this it follows that everything, whether real or imaginary by our empirical standard, is equally 'real' as a manifestation of consciousness (*prakāshamānatayā sattvam*) and equally 'unreal' as an object different from consciousness (*bāhya-rupeṇa asattvam*). This removes the logical distinction between error and knowledge, between empirical error (*pratibhāsa*) and transcendental error (*vyavahāra*), and also between empirical reality (*vyavahāra*) and transcendental reality (*paramārtha*). Vijñānavāda Buddhism also places empirical and transcendental error on an equal footing (*parikalpita*), but it does maintain the logical distinction between error and truth and also the distinction between empirical consciousness (*paratantra*) and transcendental consciousness (*pariniṣpanna*). And Kāshmīra Shaivism has not gained anything by obliterating the aforesaid distinction, for in the end by its own logic everything, real or imaginary, turns out to be *unreal* as experienced by us in our empirical life. Advaita Vedānta says that everything as experienced by us in our empirical life turns out to be ultimately false because it is a superimposition by *māyā*, but it has the advantage of safeguarding its empirical reality. In 'ābhāsavāda' the world ultimately turns out to be false and there is no emphasis on its empirical reality. In its zeal to preserve the reality of the world, Kāshmīra Shaivism wants to take the whole world into the Absolute and after shedding off its materiality, externality, finitude, etc., clings to its reality as the manifestation of the Absolute within and non-different from itself. But the reality of the world even as manifested within Consciousness as we have seen above cannot be upheld. Thus *ābhāsa* turns out to be *adhyāsa, vivarta* or *māyā* minus its advantage of preserving empirical reality.

Again, inspite of its opposition to *māyā* or *avidyā,* Kāshmīra Shaivism has to accept all the characteristics of *māyā* in some form or the other. In Advaita Vedānta, *māyā* is transcendental Illusion which hides (*āvaraṇa*) the Real and projects (*vikṣepa*) the unreal on the ground-reality. It is the principle of objectivity, externality, difference, limitation, finitude. All the characteristics of *māyā* are accepted in Kāshmīra Shaivism in some form or the other. This system frankly admits *māyā-tattva* as the sixth in its list of thirty-six *tattvas.* To distinguish it from the Vedāntic *māyā,* it is called a *tattva* or reality. It is said to be an aspect of Shakti. It is the first manifestation of impure creation. It is the principle of externality (*bāhyatā*) and difference (*bheda-pratīti*). It is the power of obscuration (*moha*), because it acts as a veil (*āvaraṇa*)[1] on the unity of the Self. It is the root-cause of all limitation and finitude (*parichchheda*). In it the objectivity (*viṣayatā*) is fully manifest. Shakti is treated as pure transcendental objectivity which remains in eternal union with the transcendental subject, so that the pure Self is at once self-consciousness or will, who enjoys his own bliss and creates the world through his free will-power. This Shakti called *svātantrya, vimarsha, ānanda* etc. is responsible for projecting the world. That aspect of knowledge-power (*jñātṛtva-shakti*) which is responsible for exclusion and differentiation through thought-forms is called Apohana-Shakti. That aspect of the will-power (*ichchhā-shakti*) through which the Supreme conceals His own nature is known as *svarūpa-gopana-shakti* and is called *māyā.*[2] And, above all, basic innate beginningless Ignorance or *pauruṣa-ajñāna* is also admitted and called '*āṇava-mala*' (the innate impurity of the Self). Though beginningless, it is removable by right knowledge. It conceals the real nature of the self and leads to the consciousness of its supposed imperfection and limitation (*Apūrṇam-manyatā*). It obscures the free will of the self and makes it ignorant of the fact that this freedom belongs to it. It sprouts into *samsāra.*[3] In addition to these Prakrti *tattva* is admitted as the principle of materiality (*jaḍatva*). Thus we see that though openly avoiding the Vedāntic concept of *māyā*, Kāshmīra Shaivism has to accept it in so many forms.

IV. EVALUATION OF PRATYABHIJÑĀ

In this system self-recognition or *pratyabhijñā* is accepted as leading to *mokṣa.* This seems to be due to two basic dogmas of this system, first, that reality is the union of the two, and second, that knowledge always has an objective reference and generates and receives impressions (*samskāra*). In recognition there is an intuitive awareness of the identity underlying the two states of the same substance (*ubhayoḥ sāmarasyam*), and in it the mental impression is invariably coupled with the direct perception of the object. Both these dogmas can be challenged. Reality is pure transcen-

1. bhedāvabhāsane māyā-shaktiḥ. tirodhāna-kāriṇī māyā.
2. māyā svarūpa-gopanātmikā ichchhā-shaktiḥ.
3. samsārāṅkura-kāraṇam.

dental unity and it cannot be taken as the union of the two. We have explained this above.[1] Again, pure consciousness is pure knowledge and has no objective reference at all and so the question of its being the substance of mental impressions does not arise. This system makes a distinction between pure consciousness (*chit*) and knowledge (*jñāna*), by using the word 'consciousness' in the sense of pure indeterminate awareness and by taking the word 'knowledge' in the sense of determinate intellectual knowledge. But this distinction is not justifiable. Pure knowledge is indeterminate awareness, immediate experience and is identical with pure consciousness.

Kāshmīra Shaivism feels the necessity of self-recognition (*pratyabhijñā*) for the removal of innate Ignorance (*pauruṣa-ajñāna* or *āṇavamala*) and the consequent realisation of the Real. As the innate Ignorance is not empirical it cannot be removed by intellectual knowledge (*bauddha-jñāna*). It can be removed by immediate spiritual awareness (*pauruṣa-jñāna*) or intuitive knowledge (*prātibha-jñāna*) which at once generates self-recognition or intuitive awareness of the identity underlying the two states (images) of the same substance. Intellectual knowledge (including perceptual knowledge) may remove the veil covering the object and consequently the object may be perceived or known. Yet, the ignorance of the real nature of the object may continue in the form of an imaginary distinction between the object now perceived and the object which we desire to perceive. In the example of a love-sick lady given above,[2] she fails to get any joy even though her lover was present before her because she was mistaking him as some one else, but when she *recognises* him she becomes all joy. Similarly, the finite self who has heard about the qualities of the Supreme Self and who is always perceiving His manifestations which are really one with Him, does not obtain liberation unless he *recognises* his own self as one with the Supreme Self. When we analyse this self-recognition we find that it glides away in self-realisation or immediate spiritual experience. It is not recognition, but pure cognition or immediate realisation of the pure Self. The lady who fails to recognise her lover who is present before her has no right cognition of her lover, because she is

1. *Supra*, pp. 263-5.
2. *Supra*, p. 261.

mistaking him as some one else. She is in illusion. When she gets rid of her illusion, his ascribed character which she was perceiving vanishes and his reality is directly perceived. The important point here is *not the identification* of the image of the lover formed and retained in the mind due to hearing about his qualities or his previous perception with the image generated by his present perception, but the *direct perception of the identity* of the person inspite of the difference in his states due to time, place, etc. Hence, it is right cognition, not recognition, which plays the crucial part here: the person must be perceived as what he really is and not as what he appears to be.

By the use of the word 'recognition', this system wants to emphasise the fact that in *mokṣa,* the Self is not known for the first time. The Self is self-shining and eternal and is always intuitively perceived. It is the transcendental foundation of all knowledge and therefore its presence is never missed. As this system accepts the theory of '*apūrṇa-khyāti*' (a form of *akhyāti*) it takes error as 'imperfect knowledge'. Hence, according to it, the Self which has been formerly perceived imperfectly is now fully perceived. *Mokṣa* is not knowledge of the unknown, but knowledge of the known (*jñātasya jñānam*). In Vedānta too *mokṣa* is not a new acquisition; it is the realisation of the realised (*prāptasya prāptiḥ*). Kāshmīra Shaivism calls it recognition because in it that which was formerly cognised, though imperfectly, is again cognised in full. But error is not imperfect knowledge; it is wrong knowledge or misperception. Hence there is no recognition, but correct cognition; that which was formerly mis-perceived is now correctly perceived. It is not identification of the two; but removal of error by knowledge of the ground-reality on which the erroneous character was superimposed.

The Upanisadic saying 'That thou art' (*tat tvam asi*) emphasises the unity of the individual self with the Supreme Self, inspite of their imposed difference. The possibility of recognition is ruled out here, because the individual self has not seen the Supreme Self before and retains no mental impressions of it. Moreover, the Supreme Self can never be seen as an object and therefore the question of retaining its impressions in the mind is absurd. If it is said that by reading about its nature in the Sacred Texts or by hearing about it from the teacher, its image may be formed in the mind, this too is impossible, because, first, the Sacred Texts of the different schools may describe it in different ways; second, in the Sacred Texts of the Vedānta and also in the Shaiva Āgamas it is said to be beyond thought and language and therefore to be directly realised; third, even if it is taken as the abode of all good qualities, it is impossible to form its image in the mind. It would be evidently a mistake to extend empirical analogy to the Transcendental. Moreover, it is not recognition, but correct cognition, which is needed here. It need not be argued that the import of the saying 'That thou art' lies in the assertion of the identity of the two states of the same substance, i.e., the identity of the Supreme Self as the manifestor with the individual self as the manifested within the Supreme Self. The saying does not mean that the Supreme Self is both the manifestor and the manifested. It asserts, on the other hand, the identity of the subject inspite of imposed difference. It means that the individual self is absolutely identical with the Supreme Self. The individuality, finitude and limitations of the individual self are false because they are imaginary characters superimposed by *avidyā*. When *māyā* is dispelled by the immediate experience of the Self, it shines in its own nature as pure consciousness.

Kāshmīra Shaivism admits *jīvanmukti*, emphasises the ultimate reality of the pure Self alone, traces all difference to innate Ignorance, treats bondage and liberation as ultimately unreal, takes everything as the manifestation of the Real, regards immediate spiritual experience as leading to *mokṣa*, admits *māyā shakti* as veiling the Real and as the root-cause of all difference, finitude and limitation and emphasises the need for spiritual discipline to realise the Self. Pratyabhijñā glides away in *aparoksānubhūti* of Vedānta. There are many passages in the classical works of this system emphasising the transcendental unity of the Supreme Self and condemning all difference in unmistakable terms. Inspite of all this, this system has a bias against the inactivity of Brahma and the theory of *māyā* as advocated in Advaita Vedānta and wants to preserve the reality of everything by treating it as the manifestation of the Supreme. We have seen that it is not possible to do so. The School of Kāshmīra Shaivism appears to be a house divided against itself and its inner contradictions can be removed from the standpoint of Advaita Vedānta, which is often implicitly contained in it.

Index

Abhidhamma-piṭaka, 16,35
Ābhāsavāda, 256-9
    criticism of, 268-74
Abhinavagupta, 9, 211, 249-53
Abhūta-parikalpa, 107-8
Absolute, the 5, 47, 66-71
    as creative, 256
    its criticism, 263-7
Absolutism, 1-2, 10-2, 28-34, 47, 66-71
Adhyāsa, 167-83, *see* Avidyā,
    definition of, 169-70
    nature of, 173-74
Advaita-vāda, 1-2, 10-12, 125-43
    objections against and their answers, 232-4, 249, 252-3
Advaita Vedānta, 121-3, 184-200,
    and Mādhyamika, 146-51
    and Vijñānavāda, 152-63
    and Kāshmira Shaivism, 263-7, 268-77
Āgama-shāstra, 125-6, 144
Agra-yāṇa, 145, 160
Aham-vimarsha, 251, 254
Ajāti-vāda, 10, 51-5, 127-35
Alāta-shānti, 126, 144
Ālaya-vijñāna, 75-7, 94-9
Amātra, 122, 126, 138
Ānanda, 27, 30
Ānanda-jñāna, 225
Anirvachanīyatā-darshana, 180-1
Antinomies, 24-5
Anātma-vāda, 25-33, 63-5
Āṇava-mala, 259, 262
Āryadeva, 65
Asaṅga, 3, 34, 73
Asatkārya-vāda, 53-4, 134
Ashuddha-Adhvā, 255
Ashvaghoṣa, 37
Asparsha-yoga, 139-43, 146
Aṣṭasāhasrikā prajñāpāramitā, 40
Ātmā, 2, 121-3, 135-8, 185-8, 226-7
Atoms, 65
Avidyā, 4, 18-9, 51, 70, 80, 91, 123, 167-83, 221-6
    Objections against, and their answers, 229-31
Avyākṛta, 20-5

Bādarāyaṇa, 119, 124
Bhagavad-gītā, 119, 140
Bhakti, 231
Bhāmatī, 221
Bhattacharya, Prof. K.C., 173
Bhattacharya, Prof. Vidhushekhara, 125-6, 144
Bliss, 68, 143, 251
Bodhi, 67
Bodhisattva, 37
Bodhisattva-Bhūmis, 42
Brahma, 2, 121-2, 135-8, 185-8, 226-7
Brahma-sūtra, 119
Bṛhadāraṇyaka Upaniṣad, 124, 132-3
Buddha, philosophy of, 15-36
Buddha-pālita, 60
Buddhist Council, 16

Causation, Criticism of, 51-55, 133-5
Chandrakīrti, 3, 50, 60-9, 240
Chatuṣkoṭi, 44-50, 134-5
Chitta, 140
Chitta-kāla, 131
Chitta-mātra, 75-8
Chitsukhāchārya, 8, 225, 226-7, 235-41
Chhāndogya Upaniṣad, 124, 132-3
Consciousness-only, *see* vijñaptimātratā
Constructive consciousness, *see* Ālaya-vijñāna
Critical realism, 73-4

Dasgupta, Prof. S.N., 144, 236, 245
Davids, Mrs. Rhys, 32-3, 35
Dependent Origination, *see* pratītya-samutpāda
Dharmas, 38
    Asaṁskṛta, 66, 210-11
Dharmatā, 38
Dharma-chakra-pravartana, 15-6
Dharma-dhātu, 45, 72, 75, 106, 159
Dharma-kāya, 75, 106
Dharma-kīrti, 5, 111
Dharma-nairātmya, 34, 63
Dhyānas, 42, 139
Dialectic
    Mādhyamika, 45-57
    Vedāntic, 146-51, 236-40

Difference,
refutation of, 234-45
Dīgha-nikāya, 21, 27-31
Diṅnāga, 5, 73, 111, 215

Esse est percipi, 83, 177-214
Epistemic Idealism, 103-4
refutation of, 113-6
Error, theories of,
Akhyāti, 84, 171-2
Anyathākhyāti, 84, 172
Anirvachanīya-khyāti, 172-4
Apūrṇa-khyāti, 272-7
Viparīta-khyāti, 172

Falsity, *see* Mithyātva
Four Noble Truths, 10
Fourth, the, *see* Turīya
Fourfold qualifications for study of Vedānta, 168

Gauḍapādāchārya, 5, 125-43
and Mādhyamika, 144, 151
and Vijñānavāda, 152-63
Gauḍapādea-kārikā, 125-6
God, *see* Īshvara

Hīnayāna, 3, 21-2, 29
Hiriyanna, Prof. M., 15, 219

Illusion, empirical, 83-5
transcendental, 45, 89, 93, 177-8
Immediate Experience, 47, 49, 67, 69
128, 193, 199, 204, 227, 275
Indescribable, 44, 46, 127, 224-6
Indefinite, 174-5, 180
Īsha Upaniṣad, 124, 133
Ishvara,
in Advaita Vedānta, 98, 189-91, 228-9
in Kāshmīra Shaivism, 255

Jaimini, 124
Jayatīrtha, 241
Jīva, 191-2, 228-9
Jīvan-mukti, 197-9, 260
Jñāna, 200-2
Jñeyāvaraṇa, 64

Kamalashīla, 73
Karma, 200-2, 252

Kaṭha Upaniṣad, 123, 133
Kāshmīra Shaivism,
Shiva-Shakti Union, 250-3
Thirty-six Tattvas, 253-6
Ābhāsa-vāda, 256-9
Bandha and Mokṣa, 259-60
Pratyabhijñā, 260-2
Evaluation, 263-7, 268-77
Kāshmīra Shaivism and
Vijñānavāda, 267-8
Kena Upaniṣad, 120
Kleshas, 64, 100
Kleshāvaraṇa, 64
Kliṣṭa-manas, 99-100
Krīḍā, 127, 134
Kriyā, 252
Kṛṣṇa, Lord, 119
Kṣemarāja, 9, 249
Kumārila Bhatta, 172

Lalita-vistara-sūtra,42
Laṅkāvatāra-sūtra, 40, 75-8
Laukika, 160
Liberation, *see* mokṣa
Līlā, 134
Lokottara, 160

Madhusūdana Sarasvatī, 8, 221, 241-5
Madhva, 121, 241
Madhyamā-pratipat, 20, 43
Mādhyamika-kārikā, 43
Mādhyamika-school, 43-71
Shūnya or Shūnyatā, 43-5
Dialectic, 45-50
Critique of Causation, 51-5
Objections answered, 58-63
Nirvāṇa, 65-71
Madhyānta-vibhāga-sūtra, 78, 107-10
Mahadevan, Prof. T.M.P., 144
Mahāparinirvāṇa-sūtra, 29-30
Mahāsāṅghika, 37
Mahāvākya, 185, 199-200, 204, 276-7
Mahāyāna-schools, 37-8
Mahāyāna-sūtras, 38-42
Maitreya-Nātha, 37, 73
Majjhima-nikāya, 21, 27, 31
Manana, 200
Maṇḍana-Mishra, 219-20, 223-4, 234-5
Māṇḍūkya Upaniṣād, 125
Māṇḍūkya-kārikā, *see* Gauḍapāda-kārikā

Māyā, 40, 123, 141, 221-2, 255-6, *see* also Avidyā
Measureless, *see* Amātra
Middle Path, 20, 43
Mīmāmsā, 84, 171-2, 202
Mithyā, 6, 131, 173
Mithyātva, 241-5
Mokṣa, 193-7
Momentariness, theory of, 56-7,
Criticism of, 209-12
Muṇḍaka Upaniṣad, 123

Nāgārjuna, 3, 45-71
Nāsadīya-sūkta, 1
Negation, 1, 46-7, 108, 176-7, 242
Negation of Negation, 242-3
Nibbāna, *see* Nirvāṇa
Nimbārka, 121
Nihilism, 45, 218
Nirvāṇa, 28-31, 39, 65-71
No-soul theory, *see* Anātma-vāda or Nairātmya-vāda
No-origination, doctrine of, 52-5, 127-35
Nṛsimhāshrama-Muni, 235, 245
Nyāya-Vaisheṣika, criticism of, 205-6

Object, as 'dharma' or 'all objects of thought', 63
as 'artha' including individual subjects and external and mental objects, 103
Objectivity, Transcendental Idea of, 87-9, 94
Omniscience, 143
Omkāra, 126, 137-8, 146
Ontological Idealism, 113

Padmapāda, 221, 224
Pāli Canon, 16
Paramārtha, 40, 47, 69, 179-80
Paratantra, 4, 104-5, 160-1
Parikalpita, 4, 103-4, 160-1
Pariṇāmavāda, 52-3, 183-4, 268
Pariniṣpanna, 4, 105-6, 160-1
Pauruṣa-ajñāna, 259-60
Pauruṣa-jñāna, 259-62
Prabhakara, 171
Prajñā, 43, 49, 70, 137
Prajñā-pāramita, 40, 67
Prakāsha, 250-1, 260
Prakāshānanda, 221, 224
Prakāshātmā, 221, 242
Prakṛti, 65
criticism of, 207-9
Pramāṇas, 59-60, 236-8
Praṇava, 126, 137-8
Prashna Upaniṣad, 124
Pratibhāsa, 179-80
Pratibhāsa-mātra-sharīra, 174
Pratīyasamutpāda, 18-20, 43-5
Pratyabhijñā,
nature of, 249, 260-2
evaluation of, 274-7
Pudgala-nairātmya, 34, 63
Puruṣa, 2, 208-9, 256
Puruṣottama, 146
Puruṣa-sūkta, 2
Pūrṇāhantā, 251, 260

Rādhākrishnan, Prof. S., 166
Rāmānujāchārya,
Charges against Māyā, 229-30
their replies, 230-1
Rāmāchārya, 241
Rānade, Prof. R.D., 124
Ratnakuṭa-sūtra, 62
Ṛṣi, 120
Relativity of thought, *See* Shūnyatā
Revelation, 120

Sadāshiva, 253-4
Saddharmapuṇḍarīka-sūtra, 39
Sādhanā, 200
Sahopalambha-niyam, 83, 214
Sākṣī, 99, 151, 192-3, 228-9
Samādhi, 5, 42, 140-3
Samādhirājasūtra, 41
Samavāya, 206
Samsāra, 70
Samvṛtī, 47-9, 68-70, 106, 131, 157-8, 239
Sāmarasya, 9, 250, 252
Saṁghāta, 209
Saṁjñāvedayitanirodha, 139
Sāṅkhya, 51, 133
criticism of , 200-9
Sarvajñātma-Muni, 221, 224
Sarvāstivāda, 35, 66
Satkāryavāda, 52-3, 133

Sautrāntika, 4, 73-4
Sautrāntika-Yogāchāra, 111
Shaiva Āgamas, 9, 249
Shakti, 250-1
aspects of, 251-4
Shaṅkarāchārya, 2, 6, 121, 154, 165-218
Adhyāsa, Avidyā, Māyā, 167-184
Ātmā or Brahma, 185-8
Īshvara, Jīva, Sākṣī, 189-93
Mokṣa, Jīvanmukti, 193-200
Jñāna, Karma, Upāsanā, 200-3
criticism of
Mīmāmṣā, 201-3
Nyāya-Vaisheṣika, 205-6
Sāṅkhya, 206-9
Sarvāstivāda and
Momentariness, 209-12
Vijñānavāda, 212-18
Shūnyavada, 218
Shāṅkara-Bhāṣya on Brahmasūtra
(Shārīraka-Bhāṣya), 168 *et seq.*
Shāntarakṣita, 73, 111
Shāntideva, 68
Shatasāhasrikā-Prajñāpāramitā, 40
Shravaṇa, 200
Shrīharṣa, 8, 221, 236-40
Shruti, 132, 203-4
Shuddha-Adhvā, 255
Shuddha-Laukika, 108, 160
Shūnya, *see* Shūnyatā
Shūnyatā, 43-5, 58-63
Shūnyavāda, 43-71
Dialectic, 45-50
Critique of Causation, 51-5
Objections Answered, 58-63
Nairātmyavāda, 63-5
Nirvāṇa, 65-71
Shvetāshvatāra-Upaniṣad, 123
Skandhas, 56
Spanda, 249, 252
Sthaviravāda, 15-6
Sthiramati, 3, 73, 89-93
Sureshvara, 219-22, 224
Suttapitaka, 16
Svātantrya, 251
Svatantra-Vijñānavāda, 110-2, 115-6

Taijasa, 137
Taittirīya Upaniṣad, 186
Tantra, 9, 249
Tathāgata, 20, 31, 45, 75
Tathāgata-garbha, 75, 77-8
Tathatā, 45
Thibaut, George, 121
Thomas, Dr. E.J., 33
Tipitaka, 16
Transcendental Ignorance, *see* Avidyā and Transcendental Illusion
Transcendental Illusion, 11, 91, 94, 102, 168-70
Trika, 249-50
Trisvabhāva, 102-6
Tuchchha, 7, 180, 226, 243
Turiya, 122, 129, 137

Upaniṣads, 2, 3, 119-124
Upāsanā, 201
Upāya-kaushalya, 33
Utpaladeva, 9, 249

Vāchaspati Mishra, 221, 223-4
Vachchhagotta, 27-8
Vaibhāṣika, 35
Vaisheṣika, 205-6
Vaishāradya, 143, 162
Vallabha, 121
Vasubandhu, 3, 73, 78-89, 94-110
Vasugupta, 9, 249
Vedas, 1-2
Vedānta,
meaning of, 119
source of, 119-21
central teaching of, 121-3
Ancient teachers of, 124-5
Pre-Shaṅkara, 125-163
Shaṅkaras, 165-218
Post-Shaṅkara, 219-45
Veṅkaṭanātha, 231-4
Vidyāraṇya Svāmi, 221, 226
Vigraha-vyāvarttanī, 59-60
Vijñānavāda, 73-112
evaluation of, 113-6
Vijñāna-pariṇāma, 89-102
Vijñaptimātratā, 78-80, 105-6
Vijñaptimātratā-siddhi, 78-89
Vikalpa, 40, 71
Vikalpaka manas, 77
Vikṣepa, 128, 137
Vimarsha, 250-1
Vimuktātmā, 221, 225-6

Vinaya-pitaka, 16
Vishva, 137
Vishvottīrṇa, 250
Vishvātmaka, 250
Viṣaya-vijñapti, 100-2
Vivartavāda, 183-4

Wheel of Causation, *see* Pratītyasamutpāda
Winternitz, Prof. M., 111
World, unrelality of, 129-31, 236-42

Yājñavalkya, 2, 122-3, 147
Yajurveda, 2
Yogasūtra, 140
Yogāchāra, *see* Vijñānavāda